Communications
in Computer and Information Sc

T0238146

For further volumes:
http://www.springer.com/series/7899

Yuyu Yuan · Xu Wu · Yueming Lu (Eds.)

Trustworthy Computing and Services

International Conference, ISCTCS 2013
Beijing, China, November 2013
Revised Selected Papers

Springer

Editors
Yuyu Yuan
Xu Wu
Yueming Lu
Beijing University of Posts
   and Telecommunications
Beijing
China

ISSN 1865-0929   ISSN 1865-0937 (electronic)
ISBN 978-3-662-43907-4   ISBN 978-3-662-43908-1 (eBook)
DOI 10.1007/978-3-662-43908-1
Springer Heidelberg New York Dordrecht London

Library of Congress Control Number: 2014942251

Springer is part of Springer Science+Business Media (www.springer.com)

Preface

Trusted computing and services represent one of the most promising and challenging technologies today. It is the core technology of cloud computing, which is currently the focus of international competition, and its standardization work is the premise and guarantee of the successful application of technology and the promotion of industry. The International Standard Conference on Trustworthy Computing and Services (ISCTCS) 2013 was hosted by the Key Laboratory of Trustworthy Distributed Computing and Service (BUPT), Ministry of Education and National Software Testing Standards Working Group, China, in order to lay the foundation for the establishment of the Trusted Computing Service Standards Working Group. Scholars, experts, and corporate leaders from all around the world had chance to share ideas on technologies of trustworthy computing and services, their evolution, application, and industrialization.

The main topics of this meeting included: architecture for trusted computing systems, trusted computing platforms, building trusted systems, network and protocol security, mobile network security, network survivability and other critical theories and standard systems; credible assessment, credible measurement and metrics, trusted systems, trusted networks, trusted mobile networks, trusted routing, trusted software, trusted operating systems, trusted storage, fault-tolerant computing and other key technologies; trusted e-commerce and e-government, trusted logistics, trusted Internet of Things, trusted cloud and other trusted services and applications.

The conference began with an opening ceremony and the conference program featured a welcome speech, seven keynote speeches, and two presentations by local and international experts. During the two-day program, all paper presentations were given in four parallel sessions. The conference ended with a closing ceremony. The conference received more than 267 papers, each paper was carefully reviewed by the Program Committee members, and finally 49 papers were selected.

On behalf of the Organizing and Program Committees of ISCTCS 2013, we would like to express our appreciation to all authors and attendees for participating in the conference. We also thank the sponsors, Program Committee members, supporting organizations, and helpers for making the conference a success. Without their efforts, the conference would not have been possible.

Finally, we hope everyone who attended enjoyed the conference program and also their stay in Beijing. We look forward to the impact of ISCTCS 2013 in promoting the standardization of trusted computing and services.

February 2014

Yuyu Yuan
Xu Wu
Yueming Lu

Conference Organization

The International Standard Conference on Trustworthy Computing and Services (ISCTCS 2013) was organized by the Key Laboratory of Trustworthy Distributed Computing and Service of BUPT, the Ministry of Education, and sponsored by the National Software Testing Standards Working Group.

General Chair

Binxing Fang

Key Laboratory of Trustworthy Distributed Computing and Service (BUPT), Ministry of Education, China

TPC Chair

Yuyu Yuan

Key Laboratory of Trustworthy Distributed Computing and Service (BUPT), Ministry of Education, China

Workshop Chair

National Software Testing Standards Working Group

Publication Chair

Xu Wu

Key Laboratory of Trustworthy Distributed Computing and Service (BUPT), Ministry of Education, China

Finance Chair

Beijing University of Posts and Telecommunications, China

Registration Chair

Beijing University of Posts and Telecommunications, China

Main Organizers

Beijing University of Posts and Telecommunications, China
National Software Testing Standards Working Group, China
National University of Defense Technology, China
Fraunhofer Institute for Open Communication Systems, Germany

ISCTCS Technical Program Committee

Axel Rennoch	Fraunhofer Institute for Open Communication Systems, Germany
Tomonori Aoyama	Keio University, Japan
Jørgen Bøegh	Beijing University of Posts and Telecommunications, China
Enjie Liu	University of Bedfordshire, UK
Enrico Viola	ECLAT, Italy
Yukio Tanitsu	IBM Japan, Ltd., Japan
Ho-Won	Korea University, Korea
Alain Renault	CRP Henri Tudor, Luxembourg
Juan Garbajosa	Technical University of Madrid, Spain
Nigel Bevan	Serco Usability Services, UK
Yuji Shinoki	Hitachi, Ltd., Software Division, Japan
Mitsuhiro Takahashi	DENKEN, Japan
Juan Carlos Granja	Granada University, Spain
Krishna Ricky	University of Montana, USA
Anakpa Manawa	Université de Lomé, Togo
Miandrilala	University of Antananarivo, Madagascar
Xin Chen	Nangjing University, China
Jianwei Yin	Zhejiang University, China
Yan Jia	National University of Defense Technology, China
Li Guo	Chinese Academy of Sciences, China
Hong Li Zhang	Harbin Institute of Technology, China
Xue Qi Cheng	Institute of Computing Technology, Chinese Academy of Science, China
Cong Wang	Key Laboratory of Trustworthy Distributed Computing and Service (BUPT), Ministry of Education, China
Tie Jun Lv	Beijing University of Posts and Telecommunications, China
Yue Ming Lu	Beijing University of Posts and Telecommunications, China
Chun Lu Wang	Beijing University of Posts and Telecommunications, China
Tian Le Zhang	Key Laboratory of Trustworthy Distributed Computing and Service (BUPT), Ministry of Education, China

Chuan Yi Liu	Key Laboratory of Trustworthy Distributed Computing and Service (BUPT), Ministry of Education, China
Dong Bin Wang	Key Laboratory of Trustworthy Distributed Computing and Service (BUPT), Ministry of Education, China
Jin Cui Yang	Key Laboratory of Trustworthy Distributed Computing and Service (BUPT), Ministry of Education, China
Xi Zhang	Key Laboratory of Trustworthy Distributed Computing and Service (BUPT), Ministry of Education, China
Yang Yang Zhang	Key Laboratory of Trustworthy Distributed Computing and Service (BUPT), Ministry of Education, China

Contents

Security Memory System for Mobile Device or Computer Against Memory Attacks

Genxian Liu[1]([⊠]), Xi Zhang[2], Dongsheng Wang[1], Zhenyu Liu[1],
and Haixia Wang[1]

[1] Tsinghua National Laboratory for Information Science and Technology,
Department of Computer Science and Technology, Tsinghua University,
Beijing, China
liugx08@mails.tsinghua.edu.cn,
{wds,lzy,whx}@tsinghua.edu.cn
[2] School of Computer Science, Beijing University of Posts
and Telecommunications, Beijing, China
zhangx@bupt.edu.cn

Abstract. Security is a crucial element of information systems. Extensive research for cryptographic algorithms that provide the sound theoretical basis of security. Among them security and integrity of memory has been a longstanding issue in trusted system design. Main memory is a critical component of all computing systems. Most of those systems are vulnerable to memory attacks, in which an attacker gains physical accesses to the unattended hardware, obtains the decryption keys from memory. We propose a method for protecting memory systems against attacks with hardware authentication and full memory encryption. The method is secure against all known type of memory attack. We have tested the method with software simulator and Field Programmable Gate Array (FPGA) platform. The results show that the method can authenticate and encrypt the contents of DRAM with 2.5 % performance penalties.

Keywords: Security · Memory system · Computer · Attacks

1 Introduction

Protecting the integrity and confidentiality of sensitive information is gaining importance in modern society. Users concerned about security typically employ several protective methods to ensure the security of their data such as passwords, disk encryption. The trusted computer system need to ensure the security of data from unauthorized access.

Extensive research for cryptographic algorithms that provide the sound theoretical basis of security. And many data protection system is based on the assumption that information from the memory disappears completely after power off. But that is not the case. Data remanence has been observed in Static Random-Access Memory (SRAM), which is typically considered volatile [2] As an integral part of most modern computer systems is left largely unprotected: Dynamic Random Access Memory (DRAM) or non-volatile device based main memory. Figure 1 shows memory system

Y. Yuan et al. (Eds.): ISCTCS 2013, CCIS 426, pp. 1–8, 2014.
DOI: 10.1007/978-3-662-43908-1_1, © Springer-Verlag Berlin Heidelberg 2014

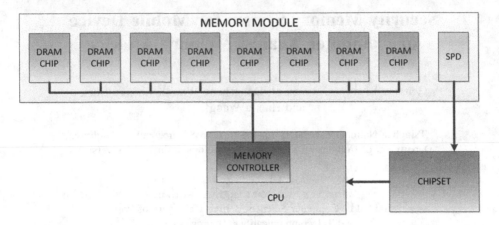

Fig. 1. Memory system of modern computer

architecture of modern computer. During runtime all of the relevant sensitive information is stored in memory. However, for an ambitious attacker with physical access to the system, these protections are generally not enough [1].

The effectiveness of our clustering scheme is validated by comprehensive experiments. The logic analyzer attacking with industry interposers has been shown to present serious troubles to the security of data that is stored in the memory modules. The attacker can dump the data from memory modules with a logic analyzer. With physical address trigger or sensitive data trigger, the attacker can gather sensitive data easily.

Increased availability of easy-to-use memory attacking tools has raised the threat to trusted computer system. The cold boot attack has been shown to present serious troubles to the security of a modern computer [1]. In short, The attacker exploits DRAM remanence by first obtaining physical access of a computer while it is powered on, then briefly turn off power, rebooting by a special operating system, and dumping the still-remnant contents of DRAM out to memory analyzer. Because of data remanence feature, the contents of the DRAM modules are largely intact and can be analysed off-line for sensitive information such as encryption keys.

Most of cold boot attacks take place off line. In those case the attacker can slow decay by chilling the DRAM modules and transplant the DRAM modules into another computer system for attacking, bypass the need to reboot the attacked system into a customized OS.

A solution to these types of attacks is to encrypt all data that is sent to DRAM and authenticate and decrypt all data that is read from DRAM. We present an secure memory system against memory attacks by hardware authentication and full memory encrypting. The method is secure against all known type of memory attack. We have verified the method with simulator and FPGA platform. The results show that the method can authenticate and encrypt the contents of DRAM with 2.5 % performance penalties.

2 Related Work

There have been various previous attempts to protect memory. Some research groups have performed intensive study of the performance impact of memory encryption and authentication. And some groups have devoted a large amount of effort to reducing the performance penalty for security.

2.1 Memory Encryption Against Cold Boot Attacks

Primarily work has addressed cold boot attacks in software, by making sure that sensitive data never send out of the processor. That is, software routines are custom coded such that it will not let a cipher key be stored in DRAM and will, instead, keep the cipher key and all intermediate computed data in registers [5].

The protections provided by these methods mostly protect small keys that are then in turn relied upon to be used to protect the contents of mass storage devices via encryption. These methods do not provide confidentiality, integrity, or authentication for arbitrary contents of DRAM.

Whereas software encryption methods have the distinct advantage of not requiring hardware modifications, they also do not provide all of the protections that hardware-based solutions provide.

Kgil et al. propose an architecture named ChipLock. It is based on AES algorithm for encryption and decryption data and the Secure Hash Algorithm (SHA) for verification of modification [3]. And Lee et al. propose a secure architecture processor which selectively encrypts and authenticates specific regions of memory space based on whether or not they are containing sensitive data [4].

2.2 Tree-Based Authentication for Memory Integrality

One of the early models for protecting information was to build a Merkle Tree over the contents of memory. Merkle tree is useful because it allows efficient and secure verification of the contents of larger data structures. A Merkle Tree uses a hash function applied to blocks of memory to generate leaf nodes and verify that the contents of these memory block have not been modified without permission [8]. Hashes of leaf nodes are then been combined into blocks and hashed again, with the process repeated until the final root hash is produced. The root hash is kept in on-chip SRAM all the time, while other levels of the tree may be sent out to DRAM and stored.

To address the problems of the Merkle Tree, the Parallelizable Authentication Tree (PAT) was introduced by Hall et al. [9]. The PAT is designed in such a way that both authentications and updates can be done on all levels of PAT in parallel.

The Tamper-Evident Counter Tree (TEC-Tree) combines both encryption and authentication into one operation [10]. The final nonce value is kept in on-chip SRAM. The TEC-Tree is also able to process authentication and updates in parallel. An added feature of the TEC-Tree is that all traffic to and rom memory by encrypting it before sending to off-chip DRAM.

3   System Architecture

We present an secure memory system architecture for sensitive data protection. The architecture could be implemented in software or hardware. It provides three features as following: the memory modules hardware authentication, full memory encrypt and memory integrity verification. The Fig. 4 shows a FPGA based test platform for the architecture. The secure memory system consists of three parts. The first part is the memory secure controller and AES encrypt engine which integrated in processor. The second part is memory modules with symmetric key-based bidirectional secure authentication and encryption device. And the last part is a dedicated hardware-accelerated SHA engine to generate SHA-256 message authentication codes (MAC) for memory verification (Fig. 2).

The memory secure controller is critical part of secure memory system. The controller implements the memory encryption and decryption with the AES engine for full memory encryption. All the data will be encrypted when it be written out to DRAM. It's an effective method to against key searching for the known cryptographic structure of the cipher and layout of the key data in memory. And these data will be decrypted automatically when it be read into processor. The memory secure controller is located between CPU core and DRAM memory controller. It cooperates with AES engine for data encryption and decryption when communication with memory controller. The secure controller can not only encrypt the data. But also it can encrypt the address bus with a bijective address mapping scheme. The AES engine implemented AES-128 algorithms which are specified in the AES document [7].

We add the authentication feature for memory modules with a enhanced Serial presence detect (SPD) device. The JEDEC standards require that DRAM module

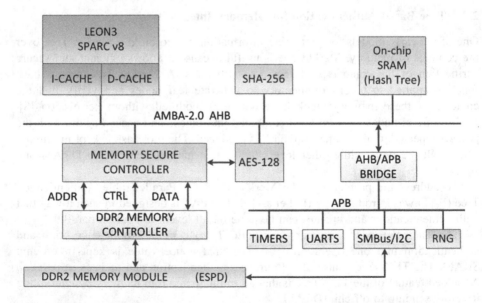

Fig. 2. Security memory system for embedded system

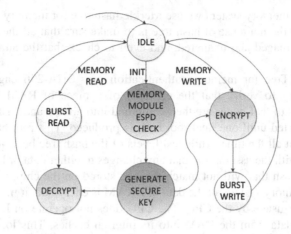

Fig. 3. Operation flow of secure memory system

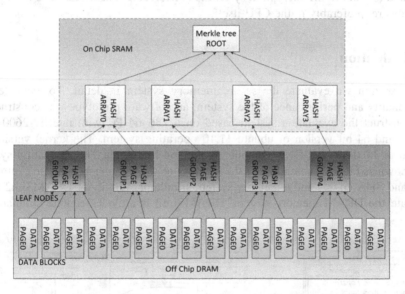

Fig. 4. Merkle hash tree for memory authentication

parameters be stored in an SPD device located on the memory module. When computer turned on, the SPD device is accessed using an I2C protocol based SMBus. The SPD chip identifies the module to the BIOS during POST so the Motherboard knows its characteristics and timings that can be used. In the secure memory system, an User-Programmable secret in stored in the SPD device protected register. And the BIOS will check the memory module with secure challenge-and-response authentication when system power on. The SPD device also facilitates encrypted read and write with BIOS using a one time pad computed by the SHA-256 engine. If memory module pass the authentication, the BIOS and SPD device will generated the key for encrypt engine through consultation.

In the secure memory system we use Merkle hash tree for memory data integrality verify. Currently the main use of hash tree is to make sure that all the data read from DRAM are undamaged and unaltered, and even to check that the attacker send fake data.

The Merkle Tree for memory authentication uses SHA-256 engine applied to pages of memory to verify that the contents of a piece of RAM have not been modified. Hashes of leaf nodes are then combined into groups and hashed again, with the process repeated until one final root hash is produced. This root hash is stored in on-chip SRAM at all the time, while last levels of the hash tree be sent out to DRAM and encrypted, with the assumption that any changes to either data or hash values will produce a root hash that will not match the one stored on the chip.

In secure memory system all the data in DRAM is encrypted, it must be decrypted automatically for usage by the CPU. The CPU does not operate on RAM directly; it loads code and data from the RAM into its internal caches. This loading/unloading process is transparent for both the applications and the operating system. This means that an automatic RAM encryption system is conceivable, but would have to be done in hardware, preferably in the CPU itself.

4   Evaluation

In the section we evaluate the secure memory system in detail. To evaluate the functionality and performance of the system, an software prototype was constructed. We construct the evaluation system based on a x86_64 PC with intel i7-2600 processor, and 64-bit version of ubuntu 11.10 operating system. The kernel version of ubuntu is 3.0.0-32, and GNU compiler is x86_64-linux-gnu. The evaluation system that shown as Fig. 3 is composite of the memory testbench, memory secure controller, AES and SHA engine and a memory system simulator. We revise DRAMSim2 as to simulate the DRAM memory system. DRAMSim2 is a cycle-accurate simulator of

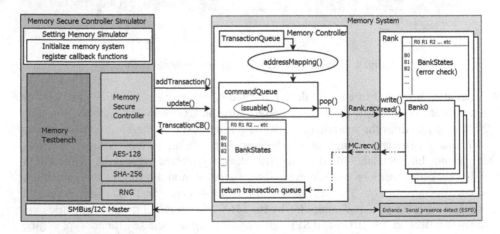

Fig. 5. Secure memory system software simulator

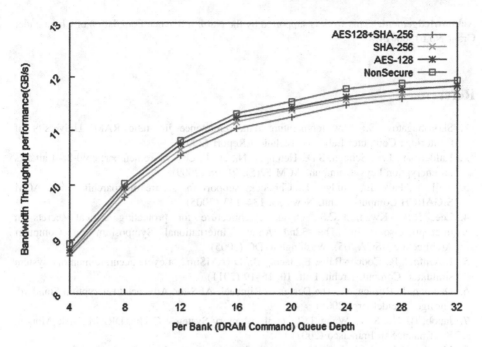

Fig. 6. Bandwidth performance of memory system

DRAM controller and memory modules [7]. It can simulate memory controller and memory modules with different DRAM chips from MICRON company.

The test model drives the DRAM memory simulator to evaluate the performance penalties of the system with memory secure controller proposed in this paper (Fig. 5).

We use a DDR3 DRAM timing model from Micron company, with 8 banks, 32768 rows, 1024 columns and 8-bit data width. The system parameter row buffer policy is set as open page policy, both transaction queue depth and command queue depth are set as 4 to 32, and the epoch length is set as 10,000 cycles. Both latency of AES engine and SHA engine are set as 8 cycles. We use DRAMSim2 to examine DRAM memory system throughput with fully saturated queues. DRAMSim2 outputs log file consist of the bandwidth, latency, and power for each simulation epoch.

In Fig. 6, the real bandwidth decrease to 11.8GB/s with AES-128 when command queue depth set as 32, and further the bandwidth is drop to 11.6GB/s when with AES-128 and SHA-256 engine.

5 Conclusions

We propose a method for protecting memory systems against attacks with hardware authentication and full memory encryption. The method is secure against all known type of memory attack. We have tested the method with software simulator and FPGA platform. The results show that the method can authenticate and encrypt the contents of DRAM with 2.5 % performance penalties.

8   G. Liu et al.

Acknowledgement. This work is supported by the Natural Science Foundation of China under Grant No.61300014.

References

1. Skorobogatov, S.: Low temperature data remanence in static RAM. University of Cambridge Computer Laborary Technical Report (2002)
2. Halderman, J.A., Schoen, S.D., Heninger, N., et al.: Lest we remember: cold-boot attacks on encryption keys. Commun. ACM **52**(5), 91–98 (2009)
3. Kgil, T., Falk, L., Mudge, T.: Chiplock: support for secure microarchitectures. ACM SIGARCH Comput. Archit. News **33**, 134–143 (2005)
4. Lee, R.B., Kwan, P.C.S., et al.: Architecture for protecting critical secrets in microprocessors. In: The 32nd Annual International Symposium on Computer Architecture (ISCA '05), Washington, DC (2005)
5. Rosenfeld, P., Cooper-Balis, E., Jacob, B.: DRAMSim2: a cycle accurate memory system simulator. Comput. Archit. Lett. **10**, 16–19 (2011)
6. Daemen, J., Rijmen, V.: The Design of Rijndael: AES-the Advanced Encryption Standard. Springer, Heidelberg (2002)
7. Jacob, B., Ng, S.W., Wang, D.T., et al.: Memory Systems: Cache, DRAM, Disk. Morgan Kaufmann, San Francisco (2007)
8. Merkle, R.C.: A digital signature based on a conventional encryption function. In: Pomerance, C. (ed.) CRYPTO 1987. LNCS, vol. 293, pp. 369–378. Springer, Heidelberg (1988)
9. Hall, W., Jutla, C.S.: Parallelizable authentication trees. In: Preneel, B., Tavares, S. (eds.) SAC 2005. LNCS, vol. 3897, pp. 95–109. Springer, Heidelberg (2006)
10. Elbaz, R., Champagne, D., Lee, R.B., Torres, L., Sassatelli, G., Guillemin, P.: TEC-Tree: a low-cost, parallelizable tree for efficient defense against memory replay attacks. In: Paillier, P., Verbauwhede, I. (eds.) CHES 2007. LNCS, vol. 4727, pp. 289–302. Springer, Heidelberg (2007)

Research on Technologies of Software Requirements Prioritization

Zhixiang Tong, Qiankun Zhuang, Qi Guo, and Peijun Ma[⊠]

School of Computer Science and Technology, Harbin Institute of Technology,
Harbin, China
{tongzhixiang,ma}@hit.edu.cn

Abstract. With the expansion of the scale of software projects and the number of users, excessive software requirements are repeating and overlapping one another. It is getting more fundamental and important to sort the requirements according to their priority using the technologies of software requirements prioritization for costs saving and demands satisfying. This paper analyzed the merits and demerits of the technologies of software requirements prioritization based on sorting and searching, summarized and discussed some important problems demanding prompt solution, related to requirements clustering and redundancy elimination, customers clustering and requirements prioritization based on customer groups, the management of the dependencies between requirements.

Keywords: Requirements prioritization · Requirements clustering · Requirements prioritization based on customer groups · Management of the dependencies

1 Introduction

With the expansion of the scale of the software systems and users, it's getting more and more difficult to accurately obtain the customers' expectations to the target system about its functions, behaviors, performance and design. According to an investigation report, carried out by an American company, Standish from 1994 to 2009, about the success rate of software projects, the proportion of projects which are completely successful remains 30 % from the year of 1996, and at least 65 % projects overran, or were insufficient, or failed. The main reasons consist of the change, incompleteness of requirements, and the lack of customers' participation [1].

This paper first summarizes the main technologies of requirements prioritization, and then analyzes some key theoretical problems demanding urgent solutions in this field. Finally some solutions aimed to solve these problems are proposed (Fig. 1).

2 The Definition of Requirement Prioritization Technology

If you want to provide better consumption experience for customers, you have to let them express their expectations to the software system adequately, which will naturally lead to the overmuch redundancy of requirements and bring challenges to the

Y. Yuan et al. (Eds.): ISCTCS 2013, CCIS 426, pp. 9–21, 2014.
DOI: 10.1007/978-3-662-43908-1_2, © Springer-Verlag Berlin Heidelberg 2014

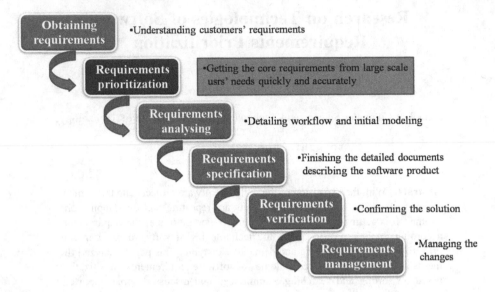

Fig. 1. Requirement engineering process [2]

requirement prioritization technologies. For example, the FBI's Virtual Case File Project, which is worth 1.7 million dollars, involved series of Joint Application Development (JAD) sessions lasting 6 months and generated 800-plus pages of requirements [3]. Patton, a security consultant of this project, said that this document is bloated because of too many details and the ignorance of essentials. What requirements the system should realize or give preference to has become an unavoidable problem during the process of software development [4]. In this situation, the Requirement Prioritization Technology arises.

The Requirement Prioritization Technology sorts the requirements by its priority using the ways of searching and sorting, to select the approximately optimal subsets from a huge set of requirements, aimed at better satisfying the demands of customers and making sure there are enough resources to realize the requirements in the meantime.

3 Analyzes on the Main Requirement Prioritization Technology

It can date back to 1970's to apply the idea of prioritization to software engineering, and one of the earliest jobs was done by Miller and Spooner in their research paper in 1976 [5], in which they applied the prioritization technologies in the field of software testing. After that, it has become an important research area of requirement engineering gradually. In 1992, Xanthakis and his partner applied heuristic searching method in software engineering for the first time [6]. Then in 2001, Harman and Jones came up with the concept of Search Based Software Engineering (SBSE), and for the first time expounded the idea of using search based prioritization technology to solve problems throughout software engineering in their paper, which was of remarkable significance to the requirement prioritization technology.

3.1 Sort Based Requirement Prioritization Technology

The essence of any prioritization problems is to determine the relative ordering between different objects in a collection by attaching a certain weight to every object. Sort based requirement prioritization technology can show the ordering of requirements clearly by allocating a weight to each of them. The easiest way to evaluate a requirement is order measurement, by which we can sort the requirements according to a certain measurement scale, so that we can know directly which of these requirements is more important. Compared with the order measurement, the relative measurement is obviously more convincing because it can describe the difference of importance between requirements quantificationally, from 0 to 100 %. Absolute Measurement is an even better way, but it requires a prerequisite that we can allocate an integer to each requirement, like the time cost and economic cost of them, which makes it possible to carry out more complex evaluation and computation. At present, the most widely-used technologies consist of The Analytic Hierarchy Process, Quality Function Deployment, Cumulative Voting, Numerical Assignment, Ranking, Top-Ten Requirements. Their advantages and disadvantages are listed as the following Table 1.

Generally speaking, sort based prioritization technology could not deal with problems which require efficient sorting method for large quantities of requirements, management of dependencies between requirements, avoidance of employers' preference, and balance of the conflicts among employers.

3.2 Search Based Requirement Prioritization Technology

During the prioritization process, it is a difficult and unavoidable problem that how to achieve the balance between the expectations of customers, and the balance between the system and customers' demands, which is hard to solve by sort based requirement prioritization technology. We need to find a decision support algorithm to handle those contradictive and conflicting constraints. Essentially, these problems are all complex optimization problem, which is a typical NP problem. In other words, no accurate solution is given yet to find the optimal answer in polynomial time. We usually adopt search based requirement prioritization technology to solve them. First we need to shape these problems into optimization problem based on search, and search for the optimal or quasi-optimal answers under fitness functions. Researchers studied requirement prioritization technology based on single-objective search and multi-objective search, explored management of interaction of dependencies between requirements, and even developed toolkits for management. Some researchers made some meaningful exploration about balancing the conflicts between customers using Web-filtering technology. We made a summary about the merits and demerits of those search based requirement prioritization technologies, as listed in Table 2.

Table 1. Technical point and weakness of sort based requirement prioritization techs.

No	Method	Technical point	Weakness
01	Analytic Hierarchy Process (AHP) [7]	(1) Decide the relative importance of factors in every hierarchy by pairwise comparison and combine the factors based on the hierarchical model, to obtain the final sequence of the decision-making factors' importance to goals (2) Make decisions by pairwise comparing requirements which are hierarchical classified and measured from level 1 to 9 [8]	(1) Too many pairs and not practicable for huge quantities of requirements (2) It could only handle requirements prioritization relationships in the same higher hierarchy and it could not deal with dependencies among requirements [9]
02	Quality Function Deployment (QFD)	(1) Investigate and analyze the requirements systematically and turn them into demand information of the features of products, components, process, quality and design program (2) Decompose and cascade the customers' requirements into the process of product designing, component configuration, process planning, and quality control, and convert original requirements into specifications of product development	(1) It can only handle about 30 requirements and is not suitable for large-scale requirements (2) It is hard to make changes to requirements. We have to re-compute to apply any alterations (3) Honesty of customers and dependencies between requirements can't be handled
03	Cumulative Voting (the 100-Dollar Test) [10]	There are 100 virtual units, time or many, for each customer to allocate to requirements. The prioritization results can be represented by the relative ratio	(1) Large-scale requirements can't be handled (2) The customers may allocate their virtual units according to their preference rather than real priorities [11]
04	Numerical Assignment	Customers arrange requirements into groups with variable sizes, such as critical, standard, optional and allocate priority to each group [12]	(1) Requirements belonging to the same group have the same priority. Each requirement does not have a unique priority, leading to the weakness of its utility (2) Customers may think all the requirements are pivotal [13]
05	Ranking	Customers allocate a sequence number to each requirement according to their importance and then we can rank the requirements by Bubble sort or Binary Search Tree [14]	(1) Two or more requirements might own the same priority and we could not determine their differences (2) It works only where there's one customer and it is hard to accord the views of all customers
06	Top-Ten Requirements	Customers pick the top 10 requirements in their views and no more sorting is needed [15]	There could be conflicts between customers, even leading to the dissatisfaction of all customers

Table 2. Technical points and weakness of search based requirement prioritization technology.

No	Method	Technical point	Weakness
01	Requirement prioritization based on single-objective search	(1) Bagnall first applied SBSE to the field of requirements analysis remove the conflicts between the expectation of customers and resources [16] (2) Ruhe regarded price and resources, implementation order and priority order respectively as a single objective in genetic algorithm and obtained the NRP's requirements set by weighting those objectives [17–19] (3) Feather and Menzies first applied Pareto Optimality to SBSE and built the iterative model for single-objective function with simulated annealing algorithm [20] (4) Baker adopted Greedy algorithm and simulated annealing algorithm to select and sort the candidate software groups, and obtained components that each version of software need to include [21] (5) Harman also saw the requirements analysis as the prioritization of character of subset and successfully applied this method to a real dataset from Motorola [22]	(1) Simply regard the requirements selection as a single-objective optimization problem and cannot satisfy expectations of multiple customers and objectives (2) Optimizing a certain objective may require the sacrifice of the optimization of another objective and there might be deviations in the final result
02	Requirement prioritization based on multi-objective search	(1) Srinivas and Deb applied the non-dominated sorting evolution algorithm to multi-objective optimization in 1995 and got satisfying results [23] (2) Finkelstein used multi-objective optimization technology to optimize fairness objectives differently defined concurrently [24, 25] (3) Zhang and Durillo considered dual goals of the minimization of the cost of supplier and the maximization of the satisfaction of the customers [26, 27] (4) Ruhe and Omolade considered the two objectives that balance the tension between user-level and system-level requirements [28] (5) Saliu and Ruhe optimized the software release planning with the consideration of satisfying the commercial needs and benefits of implementation [29] (6) Zhang first proposed the model of NRP problem based on multi-objective optimization in 2007, and in 2011 she took the satisfaction of every customer as an independent optimization goal [30]	(1) It is difficult to solve high-constrained problems or when there is a sharp increase of optimization of objectives (2) This prioritization algorithm was based on the assumption that each requirement is independent and did not take the dependencies between requirements into account, thus the result was not satisfying

(continued)

Table 2. (*continued*)

No	Method	Technical point	Weakness
03	Requirement prioritization based on social network	(1) Lim proposed to recognize and prioritize customers by social network and collaborative filtering: The demand analysis engineers provide initial customers, who recommend other customers to us. Based on the relationship of recommendation we can build the social network to search for the important customers [31] (2) Collection of customers' requirements: The demand analysis engineers provide initial demands and the customers chosen above can evaluate those demands and propose other requirements (3) Requirements prediction: By collaborative filtering algorithm we can predict congeneric customers and recommend requirements among them. In turn customers can evaluate requirements recommended (4) Requirements prioritization: Based on the results of step 1 and 3 we can compute the impact factor that customers have to projects and to requirements. With this we can calculate the priority level of each requirement and pick out proper requirements	This algorithm assumes the customers' impact factor to project is constant, but actually the factor should change as time changes. A constant factor may lead to an inaccurate prioritization result
04	Requirements dependencies analysis and management based on search	(1) Carlshamre took the requirements dependencies into the prioritization model using Linear Programing [32] (2) Ruhe and Saliu also came up with a method based on Integer Linear Programming to remove the conflicts between the computational intelligence and human judgments [33] (3) Van den Akker furthered the study of the linear programming technology and developed a toolset based on Integer Linear Programming [34, 35] (4) Bagnall considered the precedence dependencies between requirements, that is, one requirement must be realized before another one [36] (5) Greer and Ruhe regarded Precedence and dependencies as two constraints [37] (6) Frank Moisiadis used Binary Matrix or Tree Structure to describe the dependencies and developed Requirements Prioritization Tool to deal with dependencies [38]	(1) It cannot reflect weak dependencies which can't be converted into inequality constraints, such as value-related and cost-related dependencies (2) Algorithms we have implemented so far are insufficient to handle practical problems with multiple dependencies

These studies did make some breakthroughs in the aspect of multi-objective optimization, dependencies management and conflicts resolution, but there is no satisfying, general method yet to solve all of the requirement prioritization problems. There is still a long way to go, especially in the situation that there are a large number of requirements and conflicts, varied requirement dependencies management.

4 Key Problems to be Solved in the Field of Requirements Prioritization

Let's take a look at the overall situation of our research process. Ever since the concept, Search Based Software Engineering, was proposed, many researchers all over the world have realized its important practical value. With the help of the figures from Harmen's work31, we can see the number of published papers on the field of SBSE based on search and the general situation of the application of SBSE technology on various fields. It's clear that there's a remarkable growth of papers related to this field. SBSE has been adopted to handle different problems throughout the software development life cycles. But still we noticed that most of their work concentrated on software testing, accounted for 54 % in the first place, and requirement prioritization comes last, accounted for only 2 %. Therefore, with the presence of quantities of requirements and customers, it is very meaningful to apply SBSE to requirements prioritization and determine their priorities. In China, some research institutions did lots of studies about the elicitation, verification, formalization, and modeling of requirements, but research on requirements prioritization is still in the early stages. By analyzing existing questions and the research situation, we think more in-depth researches are needed to handle the problems of large-scale requirements prioritization, dependencies among requirements, and conflicts resolution.

5 Some Thoughts on the Problem of Search Based Requirements Prioritization and Its Solution

5.1 How to Eliminate Redundancies and Cluster Large-Scale Requirements?

The bottleneck of prioritization of large-scale requirements lies in, on the one hand, the lack or insufficiency of customers' participation leading to incomplete requirements, yet full expression of customers will result in excess and redundant requirements. We need an efficient way to discover and remove those redundancies. On the other hand, even if an effective way of redundancy elimination is found, masses of customers will inevitably propose large requirements, bringing high computational complexity to requirements prioritization (Fig. 2).

Our main idea is as follows. First we use Natural Language Processing Technology to eliminate redundancies of requirements. We can compute the semantic similarity between each pair of requirements, and if the similarity reaches the threshold we set, we consider the pair of requirements as one. Repeat the process and

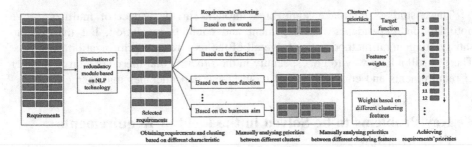

Fig. 2. Requirements clustering and prioritization based on natural language technology

we will gain a set of requirements without redundancy. Therefore, we can contract the many and diverse original requirements into a small number of groups with a certain topic using hyper-graph partitioning based clustering method. This technology brings us some conveniences. It takes the overall information into account rather than the local information, and it is highly consistent internally and inconsistent externally. Besides, the pre-set number of clusters is not needed so that the human and empirical factors are excluded. With these work done, we can compare the clusters of requirements to decrease the comparing times, increase the algorithms' efficiency and lay a solid foundation of the upcoming work.

5.2 How to Balance the Conflicts Among Customers?

For most development projects there will be many customers participation. How to carry out the requirement prioritization process to eliminate the conflicts between customers and find a solution to maximize their benefits to satisfy each of them as much as possible? In the process of requirements evaluation, some customers will exaggerate or understatement the importance of some requirements out of certain reasons and we need a way to manage the customers' honesty. If we take the satisfaction of each customer as our optimization objectives, no existing search based prioritization algorithms could handle so many objectives, so that a more efficient way is needed (Fig. 3).

Let's take a look at the general ideas. The key to the problems to deal with the high computational complexity resulted from the large number of customers, and the inaccuracy due to the customers' preference, to make as many customers as possible to get a satisfactory solution. First of all, customers make and rate requirements and we take each customer's satisfaction as an independent optimization objective. In this way, we formalize the problem into an independent multi-objective optimization problem. Secondly, we cluster customers into groups by K-means algorithm according to their similarity to reduce the algorithm complexity. Thirdly, every group of customers is considered as an independent optimization objective and we can find optimized sets of requirements to maximize their satisfaction by using non-dominated sorting genetic algorithm to find the Pareto Optimal solution under the constraints of budget or cost.

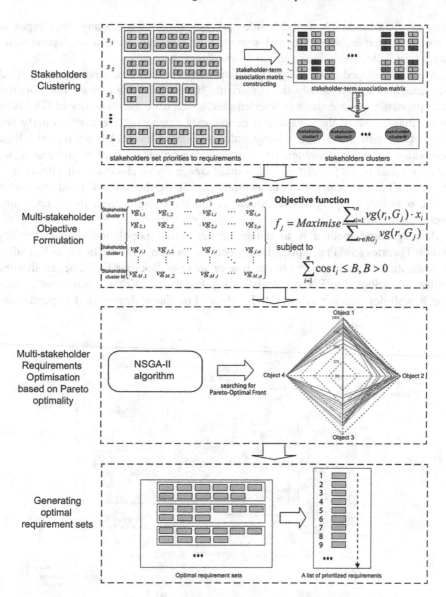

Fig. 3. Method based on the prioritization model of multi-customer-group

5.3 How to Manage the Dependencies Between Requirements?

Sometimes after computing we know that the priority of requirement A is higher than that of B, but A can only be conducted after B, that is, A relies on B. Thus the priority order generated by the prioritization technology might be improper. For example, there are two requirements, the house and bricks. According to the requirements of customers, the priority of house must be higher than bricks. But the house shall never be built without those bricks. So we cannot just simply say the house is more important than bricks. Actually, besides precedence there are many other types of interactions such as And, Or, and some deep, invisible correlative dependencies among cost, value, techniques, structure and functions.

A well-developed method to solve this problem is to use genetic algorithm (GA) and make iterations to satisfy the constraints better. But how can we find superior initial population whose size can be controlled to improve the efficiency of GA? How can we manage all of those various dependencies among requirements properly and remove the conflicts between priority order and dependencies? If we regard all the deep-seated, invisible dependencies as strong constraints to filter requirements, we will only get an initial population with a small size, even no choices at all. However, if we regard all of the weak constrains as fitness functions, the scale of initial population will be oversize, bringing lots of trouble to the searching process in the upcoming genetic algorithm.

A burgeoning method is to obtain proper initial population by Satisfiability Modulo Theories (SMT) and bring it to genetic algorithm. This method is to formalize the realization of requirements to the true or false of Boolean formulae, so that the problem is attributed to Boolean Satisfiability Problem (SAT), for which we already have a well-developed method, SMT solver. For those deep-seated dependencies

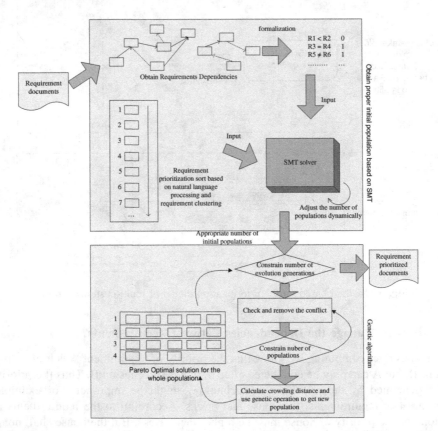

Fig. 4. Interactive requirements prioritization model based on SMT

among requirements we can select some crucial ones as strong constraints and put them into SMT solver to generate an initial population of a certain size, as the preparation for genetic algorithm. For the rest of the dependencies, we can convert them into fitness functions to guide the search process for optimal solutions. In this way we can obtain the initial population, finish genetic algorithm quickly and take all of the dependencies into account perfectly (Fig. 4).

6 Conclusion

We have analyzed and summarized sort based and search based prioritization technologies, and proposed some solutions to the problems, in the situation of large-scale requirements and customers, of the conflicts among customers, dependencies among requirements, and high time complexity resulted from the oversized number of customers and requirements. We come up with methods for redundancy elimination based on semantics similarity, requirements clustering based on hyper graph partitioning, customers clustering based on entry similarity, multi-objective optimization of customer groups using non-dominated evolutionary algorithm, obtaining superior initial population by SMT solver, and the removal of conflicts between requirements dependencies and priority based on genetic algorithm. With these methods, we can obtain the core requirement sets quickly. In the future we will further our study to discuss the standards and methods to evaluate the results of prioritization, and construct a relatively intelligent and automatic platform with these technologies, for requirement prioritization.

References

1. The Standish Group. http://standishgroup.com (Accessed on 10 September 2009)
2. Huang, G., Zhou, Y.: Software Requirement Engineering, vol. 57. Tsinghua University Press, Beijing (2008)
3. Goldstein, H.: Who killed the virtual case file? IEEE Spectr. 42(9), 24–35 (2005)
4. Peng, S.: Sample selection: an algorithm for requirements prioritization. ACM (2008)
5. Miller, W., Spooner, D.L.: Automatic generation of floating-point test data. IEEE Trans. Softw. Eng. 2(3), 223–226 (1976)
6. Xanthakis, S., Ellis, C., Skourlas, C., Le Gall, A., Katsikas, S., Karapoulios, K.: Application of genetic algorithms to software testing. In: Proceedings of the 5th International Conference on Software Engineering and Applications, Toulouse, France, pp. 625–636 (1992)
7. Saaty, T.L.: The Analytic Hierarchy Process. McGraw-Hill, New York (1980)
8. Regnell, B., Höst, M., Nattoch Dag, J., Beremark, P., Hjelm, T.: An industrial case study on distributed prioritisation in market-driven requirements engineering for packaged software. Requir. Eng. 6, 51–62 (2001)
9. Lehtola, L., Kauppinen, M.: Empirical evaluation of two requirements prioritization methods in product development projects. In: Dingsøyr, T. (ed.) EuroSPI 2004. LNCS, vol. 3281, pp. 161–170. Springer, Heidelberg (2004)

10. Leffingwell, D., Widrig, D.: Managing Software Requirements – A Unified Approach. Addison-Wesley, Boston (2000)
11. Berander, P., Wohlin, C.: Differences in views between development roles in software process improvement – a quantitative comparison. In: Proceedings of the 8th International Conference on Empirical Assessment in Software Engineering (2004)
12. Sommerville, I., Sawyer, P.: Requirements Engineering – A Good Practice Guide. Wiley, New York (1997)
13. Karlsson, J.: A systematic approach for prioritizing software requirements (1998)
14. Karlsson, J., Wohlin, C., Regnell, B.: An evaluation of methods for prioritizing software requirements. Inf. Softw. Technol. **39**, 939–947 (1998)
15. Lauesen, S.: Software Requirements – Styles and Techniques. Addison-Wesley, Boston (2002)
16. Bagnall, A.J., Rayward-Smith, V.J., Whittley, I.M.: The next release problem. Inf. Softw. Technol. **43**(14), 883–890 (2001)
17. Greer, D., Ruhe, G.: Software release planning: an evolutionary and iterative approach. Inf. Softw. Technol. **46**(4), 243–253 (2004)
18. Ruhe, G., Greer, D.: Quantitative studies in software release planning under risk and resource constraints. In: Proceedings of the International Symposium on Empirical Software Engineering (ISESE'03), pp. 262–270. IEEE (2003)
19. Ruhe, G., Ngo-The, A.: Hybrid intelligence in software release planning. Int. J. Hybrid Intell. Syst. **1**(1–2), 99–110 (2004)
20. Feather, M.S., Menzies, T.: Converging on the optimal attainment of requirements. In: Proceedings of the 10th IEEE International Conference on Requirements Engineering (RE '02), Essen, Germany, pp. 263–270. IEEE (2002)
21. Baker, P., Harman, M., Steinhofel, K., Skaliotis, A.: Search based approaches to component selection and prioritization for the next release problem. In: Proceedings of the 22nd IEEE International Conference on Software Maintenance (ICSM'06), pp. 176–185. IEEE (2006)
22. Harman, M., Skaliotis, A., Steinhfel, K,: Search-based approaches to the component selection and prioritization problem. In: Proceedings of the 8th Annual Conference on Genetic and Evolutionary Computation (GECCO '06), Seattle, Washington, USA, pp. 1951–1952. ACM (2006)
23. Srinivas, N., Deb, K.: Muiltiobjective optimization using nondominated sorting in genetic algorithms. Evol. Comput. **2**(3), 221–248 (1994)
24. Finkelstein, A., Harman, M., Mansouri, S.A., Ren, J., Zhang, Y.: "Fairness analysis" in requirements assignments. In: Proceedings of the 16th IEEE International Requirements Engineering Conference (RE'08). pp. 115–124. IEEE (2008)
25. Finkelstein, A., Harman, M., Mansouri, S.A., Ren, J., Zhang, Y.: A search based approach to fairness analysis in requirement assignments to aid negotiation, mediation and decision making. Requir. Eng. **14**(4), 231–245 (2009)
26. Zhang, Y., Harman, M., Mansouri, S.A.: The multi-objective next release problem. In: Proceedings of the 9th Annual Conference on Genetic and Evolutionary Computation (GECCO'07), pp. 1129–1137. ACM Press, New York (2007b)
27. Durillo, J.J., Zhang, Y., Alba, E., Harman, M., Nebro, A.J.: A study of the bi-objective next release problem. Empirical Softw. Eng. **16**(1), 29–60 (2011)
28. Saliu, M.O., Ruhe, G.: Bi-objective release planning for evolving software systems. In: Proceedings of ESEC/SIGSOFT FSE 2007 (2007)
29. Saliu, M.O., Ruhe, G.: Bi-Objective release planning for evolving software systems. In: Proceedings of the 6th Joint Meeting of the European Software Engineering Conference and the ACM SIGSOFT Symposium on the Foundations of Software Engineering, pp. 105–114. ACM Press, New York (2007)

30. Zhang, Y., Harman, M., Finkelstein, A., Afshin Mansouri, S.: Comparing the performance of metaheuristics for the analysis of multi-stakeholder tradeoffs in requirements optimisation. Inf. Softw. Technol. **53**, 761–773 (2011)
31. Harman, M., Afshin Mansouri, S., Zhang, Y.: Search based software engineering trends, techniques and applications. ACM Comput. Surv. **45**(1) (2012)
32. Carlshamre, P.: Release planning in market-driven software product development: provoking an understanding. Requir. Eng. **7**(3), 139–151 (2002)
33. Ruhe, G., Saliu, M.O.: The art and science of software release planning. IEEE Softw. **22**(6), 47–53 (2005)
34. Li, C., van den Akker, J.M., Brinkkemper, S., Diepen, G.: Integrated requirement selection and scheduling for the release planning of a software product. In: Sawyer, P., Heymans, P. (eds.) REFSQ 2007. LNCS, vol. 4542, pp. 93–108. Springer, Heidelberg (2007)
35. Van Den Akker, M., Brinkkemper, S., Dieplen, G., Versendaal, J.: Flexible release planning using integer linear programming. In Proceedings of the 11th International Workshop on Requirements Engineering for Software Quality (RefsQ'05), pp. 247–262 (2005)
36. Bagnall, A.J., Rayward-Smith, V.J., Whittley, I.M.: The next release problem. Inf. Softw. Technol. **43**(14), 883–890 (2001)
37. Greer, D., Ruhe, G.: Software release planning: an evolutionary and iterative approach. Inf. Softw. Technol. **46**(4), 243–253 (2004)
38. Moisiadis, F.: The fundamentals of prioritising requirements, in systems engineering. In: Test & Evaluation Conference (2002)

MD5 Calculation and Decryption Using CUDA on GPU

Yanjun Jiang and Mingshan Lei[✉]

School of Computer, Beijing University of Posts
and Telecommunications, Beijing, China
jiangyanjun0718@163.com, leimingshan116@gmail.com

Abstract. It is difficult to get the original information from a MD5 hash since MD5 is an irreversible hash algorithm. MD5 decryption is based on MD5 calculation for brute force attack, which requires great computing resources. This paper presents an approach for MD5 calculation and decryption on GPU, which has high concurrency. The CUDA program performed on a PC with NVIDIA GTX 560TI graphics card. The experimental result has shown that the calculating speed is 150 million words per second, increasing from 10 to 20 times compared to program run on CPU (Core i7-950 @3.07 GHz). GPU has great potential in future general-purpose computing and concurrent computing.

Keywords: MD5 · Calculation · GPU · CUDA · Multithreading · Parallel

1 Introduction

The MD5 message-digest algorithm is a widely used cryptographic hash function that produces a 128-bit (16-byte) hash value. MD5 has been utilized in a wide variety of security applications, and is also commonly used to check data integrity. MD5 digests have been widely used across the world for security applications [1]. For example, MD5 can provide some assurance that a transferred file has arrived intact.

The 128-bit MD5 hashes are typically represented as a sequence of 32 hexadecimal digits. The following phase demonstrates a 10-byte ASCII input and the corresponding MD5 hash:

MD5 ("Hello MD5") = E5DADF6524624F79C3127E247F04B548

The hash is totally different if we change only one character:

MD5 ("Hello Md5") = F940261A5B6321092532EA909D3973C0

Algorithm: MD5 Algorithm

Step 1: Padding. The input message is padded so that its length is divisible by 512.

Step 2: Initialization. The main MD5 algorithm operates on a 128-bit state, divided into four 32-bit words, denoted A, B, C and D. These are initialized to certain fixed constants.

Step 3: Calculation. MD5 consists of 64 basic operations, grouped in four rounds of 16 operations based on a non-linear function F. There are four possible functions F, which is shown in Fig. 1; a different one is used in each round [2].

Y. Yuan et al. (Eds.): ISCTCS 2013, CCIS 426, pp. 22–28, 2014.
DOI: 10.1007/978-3-662-43908-1_3, © Springer-Verlag Berlin Heidelberg 2014

$$F(B,C,D) = (B \wedge C) \vee (\neg B \wedge D)$$
$$G(B,C,D) = (B \wedge D) \vee (C \wedge \neg D)$$
$$H(B,C,D) = B \oplus C \oplus D$$
$$I(B,C,D) = C \oplus (B \vee \neg D)$$

$\oplus$, $\wedge$, $\vee$, $\neg$ denote the XOR, AND, OR and NOT operations respectively.

Fig. 1. Non-linear function F

This step includes most of the calculations in MD5 algorithm. We will focus on this step for parallelism and multithreading.

Step 4: Finalization. End an MD5 message-digest operation, and the message digest is stored in A, B, C and D.

End of MD5 algorithm. Talking about MD5 security, MD5 hash function is severely compromised. It has since been shown that MD5 is not collision resistant; as such, MD5 is not suitable for applications like SSL certificates or digital signatures that rely on this property. And most U.S. government applications now require the SHA-2 family of hash functions to replace MD5 [3].

MD5 hash is a one-way function and nowadays it is impossible to decrypt MD5 using an algorithm directly. Brute force decryption is used in most of MD5 decryption situations. This method consumes large amounts of computing resources for large password space and it's not practical for common computer [4]. General-purpose computing on graphics processing units (GPGPU) is the utilization of a graphics processing unit (GPU), and it has provided us a way to parallelize original programs based on the multi-core architecture of GPU. The dominant proprietary framework is NVIDIA's CUDA.

In this paper, we perform parallelism for MD5 calculation on CPU and GPU. CUDA is used to develop a program running on GPU. The experimental evaluations have shown us strong ability of parallel computing of GPUs and their potentials in future general-purpose computing.

2 MD5 Calculation on CPU Using OpenMP Multithreading

Classic MD5 Algorithm's sample code is shown in RFC2312. In this chapter we perform multithreading MD5 calculation on CPU. We choose OpenMP to accomplish the task.

OpenMP (Open Multi-Processing) is an API that supports multi-platform shared memory multiprocessing programming in C, C++ and FORTRAN on most processor architectures and operating systems.

The pragma omp parallel is used to fork additional threads to carry out the work enclosed in the construct in parallel. The program used a recursive function to generate words based on the given character set and the word length. After that each word is given to one thread to calculate its MD5 hash and parallelism is implemented.

The key parallel pseudo code is shown below:

```
Calc(word, index)
{
  if (index == 0) {
    MD5calculate(word)
  } else {
#pragma omp parallel for num_threads(4)
    for (i = 0 to char_set length) {
      word[index - 1] = char_set[i];
      Calc(word, index - 1);
    }
  }
}
```

[Pseudo code of parallel MD5 hash calculation]

The performance test on CPU is shown in Fig. 2.

We have designed two functions for performance test. One is a recursive function shown before and the other is to generate a word based on values. We set OpenMP for 2 threads, 4 threads and 8 threads for test. The performance will slow down if race

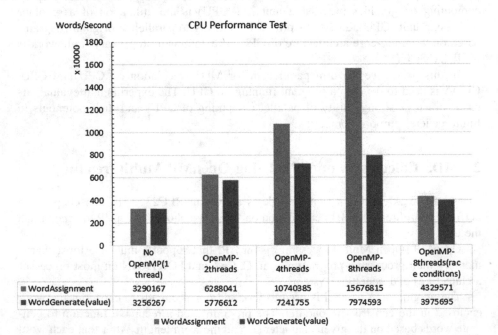

Fig. 2. Performance test on CPU

condition happens. With the highest concurrency, the testing CPU was able to calculate about 10 million words per second.

3 MD5 Decryption Using CUDA on GPU

3.1 GPU and CUDA

In recent years, driven by the insatiable market demand for real-time, high-definition 3D graphics, the programmable Graphic Processor Unit (GPU) has evolved into a highly parallel, multithreaded, multi-core processor with tremendous computational power and high memory bandwidth [5]. The new generation of NVIDIA's flagship graphics card - GeForce GTX Titan has reached 4500 theoretical GFLOP per second, almost 10 times over Intel's Sandy Bridge CPU, which is about 480 GFLOPS per second [5]. CPU and GPU emphasize on different usage: CPU is good at data caching and flow control while GPU is specialized for compute-intensive, highly parallel computation - exactly what graphics rendering is about.

GPU is especially well-suited to solve problems that can be expressed as data-parallel computations, such as calculating MD5 hashes. The same program of MD5 calculating runs in parallel on many data elements (words) - with high arithmetic intensity. It turns out performance of parallel computations of CPU is higher than that of CPU.

CUDA is a general-purpose parallel computing platform and programming model that leverages the parallel compute engine in NVIDIA GPUs. CUDA is designed to support various languages and application programming interfaces [5].

With the key features of GPU and CUDA, GPU is an appropriate solution to solve MD5 calculating and decryption problems, where each CUDA thread is able to calculate MD5 for one word and GPU is able to get thousands of thread run in parallel at the same time.

3.2 Algorithms in CUDA on GPU

A. Definitions
According to thread hierarchy of CUDA, thread running on GPU are organized into blocks. A kernel function can be executed by multiple equally-shaped thread blocks, so that the total number of threads, denoted as P, is equal to the number of threads per block (up to 1024 threads) multiple the number of blocks [5]. Assuming that there are totally N passwords, the kernel should run N/P times to finish the task [6].

For MD5 decryption, we are given the passwords' maximum length and a character set which includes all possible characters that could be shown in one password. A MD5 hash is given for us to find out the original password [7].

First we should check out the password space. The password space is defined as follows:

- The character set is denoted as C_S. Here is one example C_S = {a-z, A-z, 0-9}.
- The length of one C_S, denoted as N, is the number of element of the C_S. For C_S = {a-z, A-z, 0-9}, N = 62.
- The maximum length of password is denoted as M_L.
- M_L subsets will be generated and S_i is the set of passwords having the length of i which i is no more than M_L.

For example, assuming that

$$C\_S = \{a\text{-}z, A\text{-}z, 0\text{-}9\} \quad N = 62 \quad M\_L = 4 \quad P = 1024$$

Information about this C_S is shown in Table 1:

Table 1. C_S information

i	Si (Word quantity)	Processing times
1	62	1
2	3844	4
3	238328	233
4	14776336	14431

B. Algorithm in CUDA

Algorithm 1: The following code shows us how the passwords in a certain password space is divided and calculated in parallel on GPU. First we get a subset of passwords of length i. Each time P threads could run in parallel on GPU, so we get values of 0 to P-1, P to 2P-1, 2P to 3P-1, etc. Each value represent a password. Second we generate the password based on the value. Finally we calculate the MD5 hash in one thread on GPU and compare it to the target to get the result.

```
for (i = 1 to M_L) {
  num = length(Si); // the total number of passwords in Si
(length of i)
  count = num / P + 1;
  for (j = 0 to (count - 1)) {
    base_num = j * P; // the set's first password's value
    for (index = 0 to (P-1) execution in parallel on GPU) {
      password = GeneratePassword(base_num + index, i); //
generate a password according to the value and word length
      md5 = md5_calculate(device, password); // launch the
kernel of the CUDA device
      compare(md5, target_md5); // compare the md5 to the
target we find
    }
  }
}
```

Algorithm 2: Calculate the word based on value. The following code shows how it works. Assume the password's length is n:

$$Password = GeneratePassword(value, n) = C_0C_1C_2\ldots\ldots C_{n-2}C_{n-1}$$

$$C_{n-1} = C\_S[value \bmod N] \; C_{n-2} = C\_S[(value \bdiv N) \bmod N]\ldots$$

$$C_1 = C\_S[(value \bdiv N^{n-2}) \bmod N] \; C_0 = C\_S[(value \bdiv N^{n-1}) \bmod N]$$

For example, assuming that C_S = {abcd0123}   N = 8, we get:
Value = 0, n = 5, word = aaaaa
Value = 1, n = 5, word = aaaab
Value = 5934 = $1*8^4 + 3*8^3 + 4*8^2 + 5*8^1 + 6*8^0$, n = 5, word = bd012

4 Performance Test and Evaluations

The program implemented algorithms in CUDA and was deployed on test PC with one NVIDIA graphics card GTX560Ti and CUDA 5.5 SDK installed.

The Performance test for GPU used the following parameters: C_S = {a-z, A-Z, 0-9}, N = 62, maximum password length is 5, number of threads per block is 512, and the number of blocks is 384. The GPU on GTX560Ti has 8 multiprocessors and each multiprocessor has 48 CUDA Cores, and 384 CUDA Cores could be used in CUDA program in total.

The program written in CUDA C ran in parallel on the above testing environment. The calculating speed was highly increased compared to CPU-OpenMP versions. GPU could calculate 155 million words per second, about 10 times of CPU when CPU runs in 8 threads in parallel, which is 15 million hashes per second.

Table 2 shows time for calculating in password space on GPU for C_S = {ABCDEFGHIJKLMNOPQRSTUVWXYZabcdefghijklmnopqrstuvwxyz0123456789}.

Table 2. Time for calculating in password space

Max word length	Password number	GPU time	CPU time
1	62	1.268 ms	0.234 ms
2	3,906	2.281 ms	2.510 ms
3	242,234	4.631 ms	32.19 ms
4	15,018,570	0.1066 s	0.9890 s
5	931,151,402	6.049 s	68.33 s
6	57,731,386,986	5 m 12 s	1 h 18 m
7	3,579,345,993,195	5 h 26 m	3 d 8 h
8	221,919,451,578,091	13 d 8 h	187 d

5 Conclusion

In this paper, we implemented MD5 calculation and decryption algorithm in parallel on CPU and GPU and compared the experimental results between them. The result showed that GPU has greatly increased the speed of calculating MD5 hashes and showed higher concurrency and higher performance than CPU.

Further work could be done to improve the performance of program in CUDA. We plan to do some optimizations to maximize GPU instruction throughput and utilization to get a higher speed to calculate MD5.

References

1. MD5 Wiki. http://en.wikipedia.org/wiki/MD5
2. RFC 1321, section 3.4, Step 4. Process Message in 16-Word Blocks, p. 5
3. NIST.gov: Computer Security Division, Computer Security Resource Center. http://csrc.nist.gov (2010). Accessed 9 Aug 2010
4. Wang, F., Yang, C., Wu, Q., Shi, Z.: Constant memory optimizations in MD5 Crypt cracking algorithm on GPU-accelerated supercomputer using CUDA. In: 2012 7th International Conference on Computer Science & Education (ICCSE), pp. 638–642 (2012)
5. CUDA C Programming Guide. http://docs.nvidia.com/cuda/index.html
6. Nguyen, D.H., Nguyen, T.T., Duong, T.N., et al.: Cryptanalysis of MD5 on GPU Cluster. In: 2010 international conference on information security and artificial intelligence. 2, 910–914 (2010)
7. Wu, H., Liu, X., Tang, W.: A Fast GPU-based implementation for MD5 hash reverse. In: 2011 IEEE International Conference on Anti-Counterfeiting Security and Identification, pp. 13–16 (2011)

Transparency and Semantics Coexist: When Malware Analysis Meets the Hardware Assisted Virtualization

Guofeng Wang[1,3]([⊠]), Chuanyi Liu[2,3], and Jie Lin[1,3]

[1] School of Computer Science,
Beijing University of Posts and Telecommunications, Beijing, China
{cutebupt, jie_lin}@bupt.edu.cn
[2] School of Software Engineering,
Beijing University of Posts and Telecommunications, Beijing, China
cy-liu04@mails.tsinghua.edu.cn
[3] Key Laboratory of Trustworthy Distributed Computing and Service (BUPT),
Ministry of Education, Beijing, China

Abstract. Modern malware attacks are designed intricately, transport data encrypted, so monitoring network traffic can't solve such attacks completely. Therefore, network monitoring and analysis need to be combined with system behavior monitoring and memory analysis, and the latter is more important. In this article we propose a hardware-based virtualization prototype system, combined with memory analysis tools to monitor and counterwork malicious attacks actively. The system is based on Xen virtualization platform, which monitoring virtual machine behavior by capturing specific events. The events are triggered by some specific behaviors associated with malicious software monitoring, such as executing privileged instruction, system calls, memory writing, etc. When necessary, we can dump the memory of the virtual machine, use memory analysis tools for detailed analysis, so as to achieve the purpose of monitoring and counterworking.

Keywords: Hardware assisted virtualization · Malware attacks detecting · Memory analysis

1 Introduction

Modern malware attacks are well designed, usually use some 0 day vulnerabilities, which is difficult to counterwork. Before the malware attacks, the target is determined by some means, which can be in a network, in LAN, even without networking.

Monitoring network traffic can't solve such attacks completely, because malicious software can use encrypted transmission. So just monitoring network traffic can't know plaintext contents, using a common protocol (http, https, etc.) can't filter a particular session. Therefore, network monitoring and analysis need to be combined with system behavior analysis and memory analysis, and the latter is more important.

Some modern security monitoring programs can't be widely applied to various operating systems, because some of which have high false negative rate and false

Y. Yuan et al. (Eds.): ISCTCS 2013, CCIS 426, pp. 29–37, 2014.
DOI: 10.1007/978-3-662-43908-1_4, © Springer-Verlag Berlin Heidelberg 2014

alarm rate, as well as some are implemented costly and time-consuming. With the development of the "cloud computing", virtualization technology has been used more and more widely. Typical virtualization systems consist of Xen [1], HyperV [2], VMWare [3], and so on.

In this article we propose a hardware-based virtualization prototype system, which monitoring and counterworking malicious attacks actively.

This article has three main contributions:

- Based on hardware virtualization technology and event trigger mechanisms, proactively capturing abnormal behavior of the virtual machine, which modifies the VMM (Virtual Machine Manager) codes very little, bringing small performance overhead. With real time monitoring, we can capture a specific moment to dump memory and process detailed analysis.
- Our system has transparency to malware, ensuring the safety of the monitoring program.
- Our system has good portability. We can monitor and counterwork the malicious program whether it is running in Window, Linux or MacOS..

2 Related Work

There are three main ways to detect malicious programs in virtualization environment:

The first way embeds the monitoring program inside the virtual machine, this method has the advantage that monitoring software and malicious software are in the same system environment, the monitoring software can understand the semantic information of the virtual machine well, but obvious shortcomings of this approach is that, exposure to malicious programs, monitoring software is vulnerable to attack.

The second way is modifying the VMM codes, so as to detect malware program inside a virtual machine. This method locates monitoring software in a higher privilege mode, and thus well protected from attacks of malicious software. But modifying VMM codes needs to be familiar with the system architecture, often for a specific version, and it is easy to bring performance penalty and poor portability.

The third way is based on specific virtual machine platform, making use of platform interfaces to detect processes, kernel modules, and other important system information in a virtual machine, without changing the VMM codes. This method can be divided into active ways and passive ways. Obvious disadvantage of passive detection is that it needs to perform regular testing, easy to miss an important time, such as the execution time of malicious programs, thus can't report system intrusion information timely. Active detection through the event trigger mechanism can capture system events, process events, analyze suspicious behavior timely.

Some related works of detecting and counterworking malware programs are as follows:

Frankie Li [4] described the specific behaviors and characteristics of APT (Advanced Persistent Threat) malicious attack, which has more offensive attack modes that wherever pointed wherever attacked, completely changes the traditional attack modes. Ying Cao [5] et al. proposed Osiris system, but based on the host it is vulnerable to malware attacks. Bryan D. Payne et al. proposed Lares [6] system, but it needs to embed probes in the virtual machine, thus has poor portability. Artem Dinaburg [7] designed the Ether system, monitoring virtual machine system calls, memory writing operation proactively without modifying the virtual machine, but it is vulnerable to bypass attack and difficult to be transplanted to the modern high version system.

3 Hardware Assisted Virtualization

Our system is based on Xen open source virtualization platform, using hardware virtualization technology to achieve system security. Here we introduce hardware virtualization technology from the following aspects: system privilege management, memory mapping management, system debugging etc.

3.1 System Privilege Management

Hardware virtualization technology brings a new privilege layer for system privilege management. With hardware assistance, VMM can be in a higher privilege layer, perform some privileged instructions that the virtual machine can't perform. In x86 platforms, VMM catches and emulates a number of protected privileged instructions for virtual machine to achieve virtualization capabilities.

There are two privilege modes in Intel VT hardware virtualization technology. One is VMX root mode, which is the root mode with higher privileges, VMM runs in this mode. The other one is VMX non-root mode, which executes privilege instructions will be caught to switch to the root mode. The virtual machine is running in non-root mode.

The two modes switch using VMExit or VMEntry operation. VMExit switches from VMX non-root mode to VMX root mode, and VMEntry switch from VMX root mode to VMX non-root mode. In VMX non-root mode, virtual machine executes privilege instructions (including specific exceptions, CR3 register changes, page faults, etc.) will lead to VMExit operation, the virtual machine enters a dormant state, on this time we can pause the virtual machine, analyzes information about the virtual machine system. When necessary, we can copy the memory of the virtual machine using memory analysis tool for a more detailed analysis. After the end of the analysis, we can restore the virtual machine, and the operation we do is completely transparent to the virtual machine (Fig. 1).

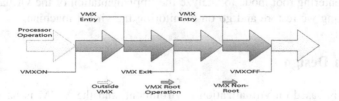

Fig. 1. VMX operation

3.2   Memory Mapping Management

Memory mapping management of modern Xen system replaces the software simulation techniques with hardware assisted virtualization techniques such as Intel EPT page table. EPT page table is only effective in non-root mode, when the virtual ma-chine is running. The EPT page table pointer is obtained from VMCS structure by the system. EPT page table transforms the given virtual machine physical address to host machine physical address, without intervention of hypervisor. The EPT page table is not in use when VMExit occurs, and VMM can create, maintain and update the EPT page table.

Translation from 64-bit virtual machine physical address to host machine physical address goes through PML4table, PDPT, PD, and PT page table. The page table entry not exist or incorrect will cause EPT violation, causing VMExit or abnormal exception. We list each bit of the lowest level page table entry structure PTE (PT Entry) as below. PTE pointer points to real physical page, e bit represents executable, w represents writable, r represents readable. Changing the corresponding bit can modify the corresponding page permissions. Specific translation is shown below (Fig. 2):

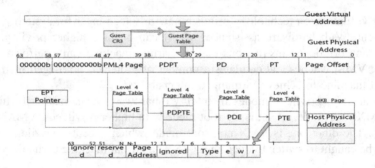

Fig. 2. Intel EPT page table

3.3   System Debugging

In order to analyze the system status of the virtual machine, we need debug the virtual machine. Here we can choose coarse-grained or fine-grained debug mode.

For coarse-grained debug mode, we can register a CPU register event or memory event, and then listen. When the system hits our registered event, VMExit is raised for debugging. In order to make fine-grained single-step debugging, we can make use of the Xen interface that setting xen MTF (Monitor Trap Flag) to achieve the target. MTF can be used as a debug flag, making the VMExit raised after stepping one instruction, entering root mode to analyze the implementation of the virtual machine. After analyzing we restore and go on monitoring the virtual machine.

4   System Design

Our system is based on virtualization environment, and the VMM is based on Xen platform. Xen has a special virtual machine system Domain0 that can access physical

I/O resources directly, and interacts with other guest virtual machine systems. Other guest virtual machine systems running in Xen are called domU that has restricted permissions. Our monitoring program is located in Domain0, using Xen management interfaces to obtain information about the virtual machine. Our monitoring program can register events to monitor system calls, execution of privilege instruction, memory writing, context switching and other information of the virtual machine. When necessary it can copy the memory of the virtual machine for forensic analysis. Our system also can obtain semantic information through binary strings, further obtain the desired information. For example through the system call number we can get the system call name, parameters, return address etc.

We use synchronization mechanism to get registered events. That is, we stop the virtual machine when registered events occur, and inform the monitoring program. When this event is done, we restore execution of the virtual machine (Fig. 3).

4.1 System Call Monitoring

We monitor system calls using the x86 fast system call mechanisms. All modern x86 processors have a special register in the system, when system calls happened, the instruction jumps to the address pointed by the register. Thus if we set an invalid value to the register, and store the original value in some place, when system call happened, the jumped address does not exist, which will lead to instruction prefetching error, resulting in a page fault. Error on this address will induce VMExit and be caught by our monitoring program, indicating a virtual machine system call happened. After analysis, we set the virtual machine instruction pointer the original value and restore the system. Our monitoring program can report semantic information of the system calls, such as the name of the system call, the parameters and the return address.

4.2 Memory Writes Monitoring

We can monitor memory writes using EPT page tables. When the virtual machine starts, we set the physical memory belong to this virtual machine not writable by modifying the EPT page table permission. When virtual machine writes something to a physical page, page faults will happen, which causes VMExit. Page faults caused by normal operation of the guest forward to the virtual machine, and we process memory write page faults triggered by our registered events. After handling the page faults, we set corresponding page writable to restore the system. Further we can make detailed analysis of the virtual machine information using single-step debugging.

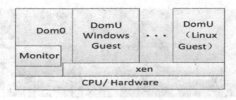

Fig. 3. System design

4.3 Memory Audit

For the dumped memory, we can use memory analysis tools to obtain process lists, the kernel modules, files and network connection information of the virtual machine. Specific data in memory can be audited by the way of string search.

Process audit can test and view suspicious or malicious programs. The operating system allocates some specific memory pools consists of kernel memory pages in advance. When we create a process, the operating system allocates the pages to the process from the specific memory pools. General process scanning tools get process lists by traversing the ActiveProcessLinks list. However, a specially designed malware such as the FU Rootkit [9] will remove certain malicious process in the list, thus the hidden process can't be scanned. Our audit method analyzes memory page allocation mechanism and the POOL_HEADER structure in the memory pools. The POOL_HEADER structure holds information relating to the allocated process, by analyzing POOL_HEADER structure we can view the running process, as well as the hidden processes.

In the same way, we analyze POOL_HEADER structures to discover the hidden modules, files, and so on.

Network connection scanning can view the network connection of the operating system. Through tcpip.sys driver we can obtain a particular linked list, which involves LAN-related information. Thus, by scanning the list we can audit its network connection information, including the process ID, the sender IP address and port, the receiver IP addresses and ports.

5 Effectiveness

Malware attacks may appear in many forms and avenues. We use two kinds of malicious attacks to analyze the effectiveness of our prototype system. For Windows Poison IVY [8] Trojan we mainly use event mechanism analysis, for Win32.Fu Rootkit [9] we mainly use memory dump analysis.

When the virtual machine begins to run Poison IVY service end, it will create the process, change the virtual machine CR3 register contents, which resulting in VMExit. At this time we can't find the EPROCESS structure corresponding to the virtual machine CR3 because the virtual machine has not created this structure. At this time we can stop the virtual machine, dump its memory, and restore the virtual machine. Similarly, when virtual machine closes a process, we can also monitor it. Than we can determine the ID of the newly created process and monitor system calls of the process, as shown below (Fig. 4):

```
wait......
get a page fault event.
vcpu 0 cr3 = 11cb800
caught a system call, RAX = 0, the system call is AcceptConnectPort
system call page: 4df6f0, Permission: rw-
wait......
get a single step event.
vcpu 0 cr3 = 11cb800
wait......
get a CR3 event.
```

Fig. 4. System call monitoring

We can also monitor memory writes of the process as shown below (Fig. 5):

```
Got event from Xen
PAGE ACCESS: -w- for GFN f015b (offset 000889) gla 00000000f7bae889 (vcpu 0)
Got event from Xen
PAGE ACCESS: -w- for GFN f015c (offset 0001e9) gla 00000000f7baf1e9 (vcpu 0)
Got event from Xen
PAGE ACCESS: -w- for GFN f015c (offset 0001e9) gla 00000000f7baf1e9 (vcpu 0)
Got event from Xen
PAGE ACCESS: -w- for GFN f015d (offset 0004a9) gla 00000000f7bb04a9 (vcpu 0)
```

Fig. 5. Memory writes monitoring

We can perform a detailed analysis of the virtual machine behavior with single-step debugging. As shown below, we choose s key to close stepping the virtual machine, the other key to start the single-step debugging (Fig. 6):

```
wait......
get a single step event.
single step vm context:
VCPU: 0, GFN: 47cf GLA: 00000000f867e164, RIP: f867e164
CR3: 39000, MSR_SYSENTER_EIP = 804df6f0, RAX: 502ad480
wait......
get a single step event.
```

Fig. 6. System debugging

For Win32.Fu Rootkit [9] we mainly use memory dump analysis. When Fu Rootkit creates process or have abnormal behavior, we dump the memory of the virtual machine actively. FU Rootkit is a kind of malicious programs that can hide processes and modules. As shown below we can detect the process FU Rootkit hides (Fig. 7).

```
0x01bf23c0 svchost.exe      1032   584 0x01ff15000 2013-09-29 09:28:14
0x01c1c558 360Tray.exe       844  1460 0x13105000 2013-09-29 09:28:31  2013-09-29 09:31:05
0x01c113e0 fu.exe           3624  3132 0x0e9a8000 2013-09-29 09:42:06  2013-09-29 09:42:07
0x01c36800 baidubrowser.ex   912  1460 0x17cd8000 2013-09-29 09:28:15
0x01c62a70 services.exe      584  540 0x9dc5c000 2013-09-29 09:28:11
0x01c686f0 ZhuDongFangYu.e  1132  584 0x103610008 2013-09-29 09:28:15
0x01c68da0 svchost.exe      1116  584 0x1029c000 2013-09-29 09:28:15
0x01c8ada0 ctfmon.exe       1044  1460 0x1332f000 2013-09-29 09:28:32
```

Fig. 7. Hidden process detecting

This article discovers the hidden modules by analyzing POOL_HEADER structures. We can detect kernel modules FU Rootkit hides as shown below (Fig. 8):

```
0x062df740 win32k.sys       0xbf800000  0x1c3000 \SystemRoot\System32\win32k.sys
0x06495530 dxg.sys          0xbf9c3000  0x12000  \SystemRoot\System32\drivers\dxg.sys
0x064b2b28 cirrus.dll       0xbff60000  0x17000  \SystemRoot\System32\cirrus.dll
0x0644e2e8 IsDrv122.sys     0xf62fc000  0x34000  \SystemRoot\System32\Drivers\IsDrv122.sys
0x06244af0 HTTP.sys         0xf5420000  0x41000  \SystemRoot\System32\Drivers\HTTP.sys
```

Fig. 8. Hidden module detecting

6 Performance Analysis

Because we basically make no change to VMM, so we do not introduce additional costs when the virtual machine starts normally. After we turn on the monitoring program, register memory events, our monitoring monitor will judge the events of the virtual machine and execute the corresponding callback function, resulting in a certain cost. However this has little effect on the performance of the virtual machine. The following figure is measured by PASSMARK Performance Test [10], which runs in the virtual machine. The first test results in normal circumstances, and the second in our system. We can see that our monitoring program has little effect on the virtual machine performance (Fig. 9):

Fig. 9. Test results in normal circumstances and in our system architecture

7 Conclusion

In our system, when we need to dump memory to use the memory analysis tool for detailed analysis, we stop the virtual machine in dumping time, which will bring additional performance costs. In the near future, we can take over synchronization mechanism. For example, we can process virtual machine memory analysis without stopping the virtual machine.

References

1. Chisnall, D.: The definition guide to the Xen hypervisor
2. http://www.microsoft.com/zh-cn/server-cloud/windows-server/hyper-v.aspx
3. http://www.vmware.com/
4. Li, F., Lai, A., Ddl, D.: Evidence of advanced persistent threat: a case study of malware for political espionage
5. Cao, Y., Liu, J., Miao, Q., Li, W.: Osiris: a malware behavior capturing system implemented at virtual machine monitor layer
6. Payne, B.D., de A. Carbone, M.D.P., Lee, W.: Secure and flexible monitoring of virtual machines

7. Dinaburg, A., Royal, P., Sharif, M., Lee, W.: Ether: malware analysis via hardware virtualization extensions. In: CCS' 2008, 27–31 October
8. http://www.poisonivy-rat.com/
9. Virus and threats descriptions. Rootkit.Win32.Fu. http://www.f-secure.com/v-descs/fu.shtml (accessed)
10. http://www.passmark.com/products/pt.htm

Imbalanced Chinese Text Classification Based on Weighted Sampling

Hu Li[✉], Peng Zou, WeiHong Han, and Rongze Xia

College of Computer, National University of Defense Technology,
Changsha, 410073 Hunan Province, People's Republic of China
lihu@nudt.edu.cn

Abstract. Traditional text classification methods assume that dataset is balanced. But, in the real world, there are plenty of imbalanced data on which traditional classification methods could not get satisfactory results. Based on comprehensive analysis of existing researches on imbalanced data classification, we propose a data rebalance method based on weighted sampling. The method assigns weights to each class by calculating the ratio between different categories. Then, each class is sampled with different ratios using weighted sampling methods. Experimental results on real Chinese text data set show that the proposed method can effectively improve the classification accuracy.

Keywords: Imbalanced data · Text classification · Weighted sampling

1 Introductions

Internet provides a lot of convenience for people's lives, but also produces too much information which cannot be dealt with by people in a certain time. Among them, text data occupies the most part. How to handle these massive text data has become an important issue. One widely adopted solution is text classification which has been used in web classification, spam filtering and etc.

Traditional text classification methods assume that the data set is balanced, which means each category contains similar number of samples. But, in the real world, imbalanced data is ubiquitous. For example, during the web page classification process, one web page can be classified into sport, economic, political and etc. But the number of web page belongs to each category is not the same. Some categories may contain only dozens of pages while some other classes may contain thousands or even more pages. In this case, traditional text classification methods could not get satisfactory results. On the one hand, the classifier is based on the overall classification accuracy which is biased to the majority class, i.e. the class contains much more samples. Assume that 99 % samples in the data set belong to the majority class, 1 % samples belong to the minority class, i.e. the class contains fewer examples. Then, the classifier can get 99 % accuracy rate by simply classifying all samples into the majority class. But none minority class samples is rightly classified, so the result is meaningless. On the other hand, traditional methods assume that majority class and minority class play the same role during the classification process. But, since minority class is usually much smaller than majority class, it is very likely to be ignored.

Y. Yuan et al. (Eds.): ISCTCS 2013, CCIS 426, pp. 38–45, 2014.
DOI: 10.1007/978-3-662-43908-1_5, © Springer-Verlag Berlin Heidelberg 2014

Based on the aforementioned analysis, it can be concluded that different classes should be assigned with different weights. Assign weights can be achieved either by designing specific classifier or resampling the data set. The first method requires a deep understanding of the classifier and the application domain, so it is difficult to implement. On the contrary, resampling the data set does not need to change the classifier, so it is easy understood and thus with wider range of applications. Therefore, we also use data resampling methods in this paper.

This paper is structured as follows. Section 2 gives a review of researches on imbalanced data classification. Section 3 describes key technologies of the proposed imbalanced text classification method based on weighted sampling. Experiments and results analysis are showed in Sect. 4. We concluded the paper and showed acknowledgement in the end.

2 Related Works

Imbalanced data classification methods can be divided into three categories [1]: Data-level approach, algorithm-level approach and the combination of the two. Data-level approach tries to change the data distribution within the data sets so as to reduce the imbalance ratio. This kind approach includes over-sampling and under-sampling, which increase the minority class or reduce the majority class respectively. Algorithm-level approach tries to modify the traditional classification algorithms or adjust the internal parameters of the algorithm according to the characteristics of the imbalanced data. The combination or integrated approach combines the data-level and the algorithm-level approach so as to take advantages of both methods and avoid disadvantages. In this paper, we focus on the data-level approach and improve it using weighted sampling strategy.

The simplest over-sampling method copy samples randomly to increase the number of minority class samples. But the problem is that simply copy is likely to cause the classifier over learning. The simplest under-sampling method deletes the majority class samples randomly to balance the class distribution and it may delete some useful samples. Against these shortcomings of the original method, many scholars have proposed their improvement strategies. Chawla [2] proposed Synthetic Minority Over-sampling TEchnique (SMOTE). SMOTE reduced the data imbalance ratio by artificial insert synthetic minority samples between minority classes samples. The method can effectively avoid over fitting problems and many follow researches are based on it. Han [3] proposed the so-called Borderline-SMOTE which only apply SMOTE on those samples on the Borderline. Sukarna [4] proposed Majority Weighted Minority Oversampling TEchnique (MWMOTE). The method first identify those hard-to-learn informative minority class samples, then assign weights to different samples according to the Euclidean distance between the corresponding sample and the majority class samples within the nearest neighbor. Finally, new minority class samples were generated by clustering. Gustavo [5] proposed to combine the over-sampling and under-sampling together and showed that the combination method can usually achieve better results. Ashish [6] first computed the distance between samples and the decision plane, then the Fisher ratio of samples in minority class respected to samples in majority class was calculated. At last, under-sampling was done based on the Fisher ratio. Chumphol [7] proposed Density-Based Synthetic Minority Over-sampling TEchnique (DBSMOTE) which generates synthetic samples along a shortest path from each minority class sample to a pseudo-centroid of a minority-class cluster. Atlántida [8] proposed Synthetic Oversampling of Instances Using Clustering, i.e. SOI-C and SOI-CJ. The methods create clusters from the minority class samples and generate synthetic samples inside those clusters. The proposed approaches avoid creating new instances in majority class regions and thus are more robust to noisy examples. Enislay [9] proposed a hybrid sampling method using SMOTE and Rough Set Theory. Luengo [10] analyzed SMOTE-based oversampling and evolutionary under-sampling using data complexity measures, in which C4.5 and PART method were used to learn and classify the data. Cardie [11] applied the imbalanced data classification techniques on text data classification. Liu [12] tackled the problem using a simple probability based term weighting scheme which directly utilizes two critical information ratios.

There are many text classification methods, but most of which are based on the Vector Space Model (VSM) proposed by G. Salton [13]. In VSM, each document is represented as a high dimensional vector and elements in the vector are called features. The similarity between two documents can be obtained by calculating the cosine angle between two vectors. VSM simplifies the text classification into the operation within the vector space, thus greatly reduces the complexity of the problem. In this paper, we also use VSM to represent text information.

3   Rebalance Strategy Based on Weighted Sampling

In this section, we focus on the rebalance strategy against imbalanced data set and propose a combination sampling method based on weighted sampling strategy. We will elaborate our approach in details next.

3.1   Weighted Sampling Strategy

Traditional SMOTE [2] algorithm generally reduce the imbalance ratio through generating new minority class samples. Based on the similarity within the feature space, SMOTE was used on each minority class samples. For sample x_i, SMOTE selects K nearest neighbor samples each time. Then, one of these K neighbors was randomly selected, denoted as x_{knn}. Finally, new sample was generated in a synthesis way, i.e. $x_{syn} = x_i + (x_{knn} - x_i) \times \alpha$, where α is a random number between 0 and 1. SMOTE avoids the over-fitting problems brought by random over-sampling method, and makes the decision boundary move to the majority class. Thus, it improves the classification accuracy of the minority class and has been widely used. However, this method still has some problems. Since the entire K samples are treated fairly, the probability of one sample being selected is the same, no matter it come from the majority class or the minority class. Therefore, it is necessary to assign different weights for different classes when generate new samples. Weights should be determined based on such assumption: the category that contains fewer samples should be given greater weight and vice versa. Therefore, we propose to calculate the weight by formula (1).

$$w_i = \left(\frac{\max_{j=1}^{K}(n_j)}{n_i} \right) \bigg/ \sum_{j=1}^{K} n_j \quad i,j = 1,\ldots,K \tag{1}$$

Among formula (1), the numerator is the ratio between the classes with the most samples and the current class. The fewer samples current class contains, the greater its value. The denominator is the sum of all categories. It is used to normalize the weight so that it would be within the range of (0, 1).

When apply SMOTE on real dataset, it is necessary to set a reasonable sampling rate, i.e. how many samples should be generated relative to the original samples. In this paper, we adopt the same idea of calculating class weights and hold that classes with fewer samples should have a greater sampling rate and vice versa. In order to adjust the sampling rate and obtain the optimal parameters, we use the following formula.

$$r_i = w_i \cdot \sigma \tag{2}$$

Where w_i is weight of class i, σ is the ratio factor which depend on the data set and should be adjusted by experiments.

3.2 Combination of Over-Sampling and Under-Sampling

In some data sets, there may be one or more categories contain much more samples than other categories. In this case, if one simply use the strategies proposed in sub Sect. 3.1, it may cause some new problems. On the one hand, the more new synthesis samples be generated, the greater the risk of over-fitting. On the other hand, resample of minority class respected to the class contains the most samples will greatly increase the size of the dataset, and thus run time of the program will increase greatly. Therefore, the class with much more samples than other classes should be treated differently. In this paper, we set threshold to avoid this situation. When the ratio between one class and another class is greater than the threshold, random under-sampling would be used to reduce the majority class until the ratio becomes less than threshold and then stop. The optimal parameters for each dataset should be adjusted during training process. The initial threshold is set by the following formula.

$$Th = 2 \cdot \left(\sum_{i=1}^{K} n_i \bigg/ K \right) \tag{3}$$

4 Experiment and Result Analysis

4.1 Experimental Environment and Preparation

All experiments were done on a PC with Intel(R) Core(TM) i5-1320 CPU @2.5 GHz, 10 G Memory, 500 G Hard Disk Capacities. We used Fudan University's Chinese

Text Classification Corpus[1] in our experiment. The corpus contains 20 categories and is of 101 MB size. The corpus contains 19637 documents, in which 9804 as training documents and 9833 as test documents. Train set and test set do not overlap each other. The class distribution within the data set is imbalanced. The biggest category contains 1601 documents while the smallest category contains only 25 documents. Among them, 11 categories contain no more than 100 documents. The statistic information of the dataset is show in Fig. 1.

We did Chinese word segmentation by Chinese lexical analysis system ICTCLAS (Java version[2]) which was developed by the Institute of Computing, Chinese Academy of Sciences. In order to validate the proposed method, open source tool Weka[3], which was developed by the University of Waikato, was used. We did programming based on Weka's API. All programs were written in Java under Eclipse Juno Service Release 1.

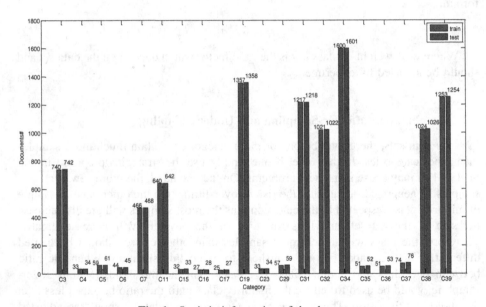

Fig. 1. Statistic information of the dataset

4.2 Evaluation Criteria

Commonly used evaluation methods for text classification include precision, recall and F value. F value combines precision and recall together and is a comprehensive assessment method. Therefore, we also adopt wildly used F1 measure as one of the evaluation criteria in this paper. In addition, we also take the running time of the program into consideration. Because even if the classification accuracy is very high,

---

[1] The corpus is available at http://www.nlpir.org/download.
[2] http://www.ictclas.org
[3] http://weka.wikispaces.com

too long run time will limit the scope it can be used. Run time was measured from reading the dataset to printing the results. Because the Chinese text segmentation was done for preparation, and simply run only once, we ignored the time for segmentation.

4.3 Results and Analysis

The dataset used in this paper contains more than one category; therefore, we cannot use the conventional imbalance method directly. For simplicity, we use the decomposition strategies named OVO (One-Versus-One) [14]. In addition, SVM (Support Vector Machine) and Naïve Bayesian are used as the basic classifiers in our experiments. We use SVM and Naïve Bayesian with parameters as default settings.

Firstly, we trained classifiers on original training set and used it to classify test set. Then, the training set was resampled based on the strategy proposed in Sect. 3 and we abbreviate it as WS (Weighted Sampling). Classifiers were trained again and be used to classify the same test set. The F1 before and after applying the proposed sampling strategy is shown in Fig. 2.

From Fig. 2, we can see that the proposed approach can effectively enhance the classification results, especially for minority class C4, C5, C6 and C7. The F1 of those majority classes, e.g. C11, C31 and C34 kept the same before and after sampling which means the proposed method has little effects on majority class. In addition, we can see that SVM performed better than Naïve Bayesian most of the time. So, it is a better choice to use SVM when classify imbalanced Chinese text.

In order to verify the effect of our proposed method in a macro way, we compared the average F1 and the overall run time before and after sampling, which is shown in Fig. 3.

As can be seen from Fig. 3(a), the proposed method can slightly improve the overall classification result when SVM be used as basic classifier while no overall improvements when Naïve Bayesian used. We can conclude that the proposed method

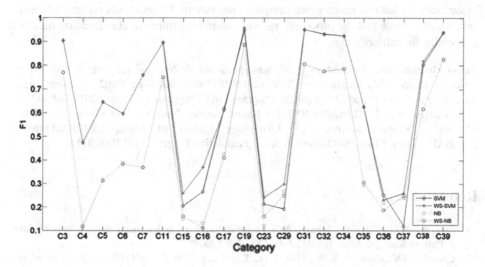

Fig. 2. Comparison of F1 under different conditions

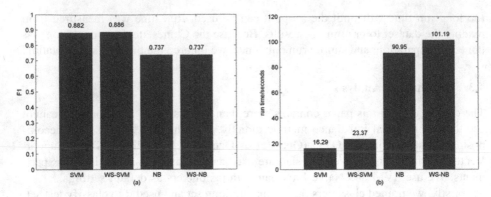

Fig. 3. Comparison of average F1 (a) and run time (b) before and after sampling

is more applicable based on SVM. In addition, Fig. 3(b) shows that run time after sampling increased in some extent, but is still acceptable. Furthermore, it can be seen that Naïve Bayesian need much more time than SVM. This can be explained by the fact that SVM just used sampling near the decision margin while Naïve Bayesian used all those samples when train classifiers.

5   Conclusions

Imbalanced text data is very common in the real world. Traditional classification methods are not applicable on imbalanced data. Therefore, it is of great practical significance to research on imbalanced data classification problem. Based on the comprehensive analysis of related researches on imbalanced data classification, we propose to improve original SMOTE method by assigning different weights to different classes, which is called Weighted Sampling. In addition, we under-sampled those classes contains much more samples than others. Experiments on real Chinese text datasets show that the proposed method can indeed improve classification results, especially for minority class.

Acknowledgements. The authors' work was sponsored by National Program on Key Basic Research Project (973 Program) of China (2013CB329601, 2013CB329602), National High Technology Research and Development Program (863 Program) of China (2011AA010702, 2012AA01A401 and 2012AA01A402), the Nature Science Foundation of China (60933005, 91124002), Support Science and Technology Project of China (2012BAH38B04, 2012BAH38B06), China Postdoctoral Science Foundation Program (2012M520114).

References

1. Sun, Y., Wong, A.K.C., Kamel, M.S.: Classification of imbalanced data: a review. Int. J. Pattern Recogn. Artif. Intell. **23**(4), 687–719 (2009)
2. Chawla, N.V., Bowyer, K.W., Hall, L.O., Kegelmeyer, W.P.: SMOTE: synthetic minority over-sampling technique. J. Artif. Intell. Res. **16**(1), 321–357 (2002)

3. Han, H., Wang, W., Mao, B.: Borderline-SMOTE: a new over-sampling method in imbalanced data sets learning. Adv. Intell. Comput. Int. Conf. Intell. Comput. **3644**, 878–887 (2005)
4. Barua, S., Islam, M.M., Yao, X., Murase, K.: MWMOTE: majority weighted minority oversampling technique for imbalanced data set learning. IEEE Trans. Knowl. Data Eng. (IEEE TKDE) **25**(1), 206–219 (2013)
5. Gustavo, E.A., Batista, P.A., Ronaldo, C.: A study of the behavior of several methods for balancing machine learning training data. SIGKDD Explor. **6**(1), 20–29 (2004)
6. Ashish, A., Ganesan, P., Fogel, G.B., Suganthan, P.N.: An approach for classification of highly imbalanced data using weighting and undersampling. Amino Acids **39**(5), 1385–1391 (2010)
7. Chumphol, B., Krung, S., Chidchanok, L.: DBSMOTE: density-based synthetic minority over-sampling technique. Appl. Intell. **36**(3), 664–684 (2012)
8. Atlántida, S., Eduardo, M., Jesus, A.G.: Synthetic oversampling of instances using clustering. Int. J. Artif. Intell. Tools **22**(2) (2013)
9. Ramentol, E., Caballero, Y., Bello, R., Herrera, F.: SMOTE-RSB*: a hybrid preprocessing approach based on oversampling and undersampling for high imbalanced data-sets using SMOTE and rough sets theory. Knowl. Inf. Syst. **22**(2), 1–21 (2012)
10. Luengo, J., Fernandez, A., Garcia, S., Herrera, F.: Addressing data complexity for imbalanced data sets: analysis of SMOTE-based oversampling and evolutionary undersampling. Soft. Comput. **15**(10), 1909–1936 (2011)
11. Cardie, C., Howe, N.: Improving minority class predication using case-specific feature weights. In: Proceedings of the 14th International Conference on Machine Learning, Nashville, TN, pp. 57–65 (1997)
12. Liu, Y., Loh, H.T., Sun, A.: Imbalanced text classification: a term weighting approach. Expert Syst. Appl. **36**(1), 690–701 (2009)
13. Furnkranz, J.: Round Robin classification. J. Mach. Learn. Res. **2**, 721–747 (2002)
14. Hastie, T., Tibshirani, R.: Classification by pairwise coupling. Ann. Stat. **26**(2), 451–471 (1998)

Hijacking Activity Technology Analysis and Research in Android System

Yunlong Ren[1,2(✉)], Yue Li[2], Fangfang Yuan[2], and Fangjiao Zhang[2,3]

[1] Beijing University of Aeronautics and Astronautics, Beijing, China
[2] Institute of Information Engineering,
Chinese Academy of Science, Beijing, China
{renyunlong,zhangfangjiao}@nelmail.iie.ac.cn,
{liyue,yuanfangfang}@iie.ac.cn
[3] Beijing University of Posts and Telecommunications, Beijing, China

Abstract. Since Android is open, as many as people begin to pay close attention to Android, such as the program developer, the users. In this paper, on the basis of an Android application program, we expound the basic characteristics of the Activity, Including the life cycle of Activity. According to the characteristics of the Activity, we focus on explaining the management mechanism and the switch bug of the Activity. At the end we describe the exploits of the Activity and finish the Activity hijack.

Keywords: The life cycle · Hijack · Switch

1 Introduction

The android [1] operating system, which is designed for custom intelligent terminal operating system, is launched by the google company based on the open source Linux operating system. Since Android is open, as many as people begin to pay close attention to Android, such as the program developer, the users. The development of Android will certainly have important influences on the development of the operating system in handheld devices [2].

The Activity [3] which is one of the four main components of the Android plays an important role in the process of interaction with users. The basic components of the Android contains Activity, Service, Broadcast Receiver and Content provider. Every display in the android application program is established by inheriting and extending the base class Activity class. The Activity which is the presentation layer of the application program Use the view to finish the application of graphical user interface. The mobile phone users directly interact with the application through the GUI which show information to the users and issue commands to the programs.

2 Activity Scheduling Mechanism

2.1 The Composition of the Android Program

In the architecture, android system is divided into four parts: the application layer, the application framework layer, android native libraries and runtime environment and

Y. Yuan et al. (Eds.): ISCTCS 2013, CCIS 426, pp. 46–53, 2014.
DOI: 10.1007/978-3-662-43908-1_6, © Springer-Verlag Berlin Heidelberg 2014

linux kernel layer. For an android application created by the android architecture, there are four basic architectures [4]:

(1) Activity: it's the most important part of the application. As the application's interface framework, it is responsible for dynamically loading various user interface views, realizing message delivery of the bottom, etc.
(2) Service: as a component as a background process in the application, it mainly has two functions. One is the performance some tasks consuming time, such as music playback and Internet downloads. The other is the interaction between the components.
(3) Broadcast Receiver: it is usually used to receive and process broadcast messages, regardless of system messages or custom message.
(4) Content Provider: it's mainly used for other applications to provide data that can be stored in the file system.

2.2 Activity Component

Activity which is to provide the interface is one of the components of a program. The users can complete some tasks through it, for example Dialing, taking pictures, sending email or looking at a map. Each activity is given a window on which program can map the user interface and the windows typically fills the screen, but can also be smaller than the screen and float on top of other Windows.

The Activity has four basic states:

1. Active/Running: after started into the stack, the Activity is on the front screen, at the top of the stack, at this moment it is visible and stay activated state which can interact with the users.
2. Paused: When the Activity is covered by another transparent or Dialog style Activity, It still keeps connection with window manager, and the system continues to maintain its internal state, So it is still visible, but it has lost its focus and not interacts with the users.
3. Stopped: When the Activity is covered by another Activity, It lost the focus and can't be visible.
4. Killed: The Activity is Killed by the system for recovering the system resources.

When an Activity instance is created, destroyed or start another Activity, It switch between the four states, the happening of this kind of transformation depends on the action of the user program. Figure 1 illustrates the Activity switch between different states under different time and conditions:

When a Activity stops by starting anther new activity, the state transition of the activity is through the activity lifecycle callback function. An activity might receive many callback function from its own change of state. Regardless the system create it, stop it, restore it, or destroy it - and each callback provides you complete for the state of the specified job opportunities, for example, When you stop your activity, the system should release any large objects, such as the network connection. When the activity recovery, you can regain the necessary resources and restore the interrupted action. These state transitions are all part of the activity lifecycle.

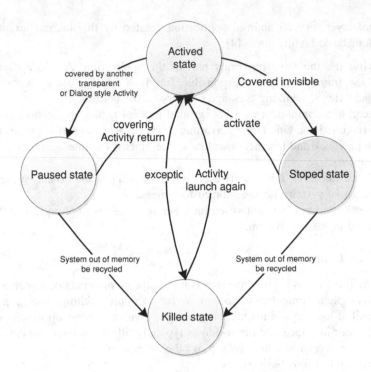

Fig. 1. Activity state switch figure

2.3 Activity Lifecycle

Android is a multitasking operating system (Multi - Task),by which the user can listen to music at the same time, also perform other multiple programs. When launching an new application program, it will cost more system memory. When executive program too much at the same time, or we do not have the right to release the memory, the system will be more and more slowly, or even instability. In order to solve this problem, Android introduces a new mechanism, Life Cycle (Life Cycle) [5]. The Android application lifecycle is managed by the Android framework, rather than directly controlled by the application. Usually, each application (entrance is generally an Activity's onCreate method), produce a Process (Process). When the system memory is insufficient, the system will be in accordance with the priority to recycling process (process) automatically. Either the user or developer, can't sure when the application is recycled [6]. So, in order to good to prevent data loss and other problems, it is very important to understand the life cycle.

In android. App. Activity class, android defines a series of methods related to the life cycle, Contains many the Activity lifecycle methods. The life cycle process of activity come from the creation to destruction, including active, pause, stop state, destroy, four kinds of condition (Fig. 2).

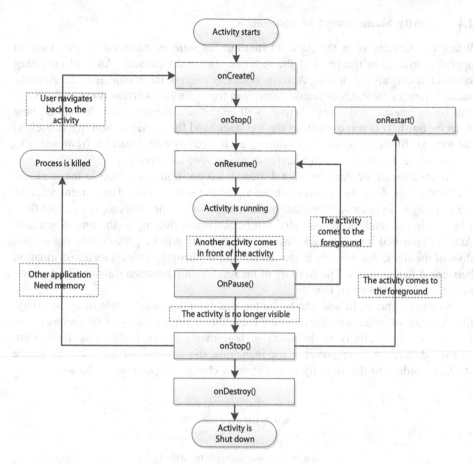

Fig. 2. Activity life cycle methods

Main life cycle methods is as follows [7]:

1. The trigger events come From creating state to the running state:
   onCreate()—>onStart—>onResume()
2. The trigger events come From running state to the stopping state:
   onPause()—>onStop()
3. The trigger events come From stopping state to the running state:
   onRestart()—>onStart()—>onResume()
4. The trigger events come From running state to the pausing state:
   onPause()
5. The trigger events come From pausing state to the running state:
   onResume()

2.4   Activity Management Mechanism

When the Activity is in the Android runtime, its state is managed by the Android operating system in the form of the Activity stack management. Android operating system tracking all the running Activity object, it will put these objects in the Activity stack. When a new Activity starts, Activity in top stack (the current running Activity) will be suspended, and a new Activity will be put into the top stack. When the new Activity finish, it is removed from the top stack, and the previous Activity is back to the top. As different applications running, each Activity could transfer from active to inactive state, is also likely to transfer from inactive to active [8].

An instance of the Activity state decided what position it will start in the stack. At the front of the Activity is always at the top of the stack. When The current stage of the Activity were destroyed because of the exception or other reasons, the second floor which is in the stack of the Activity will be activated, floating to the top. When new Activity launched into the stack, the original Activity will be pressed into the second floor of the stack. An Activity in the stack location changing reflects its transformation between different states. The Activity of the relationship between state and its position in the stack, as shown in Fig. 3:

As shown above, In addition to the top that is in the Active state of the Activity, the Activity of other are likely to be recycled in the system out of memory. An instance of the Activity is the more in bottom stack, the higher risk for system recovered. System is responsible for managing the instance of the Activity in the stack, according to the Activity of the state to change its position in the stack.

Activity1(Actived state)
Activity2(Paused/Stoped/Killed state)
Activity3(Paused/Stoped/Killed state)
Activity4(Paused/Stoped/Killed state)
....

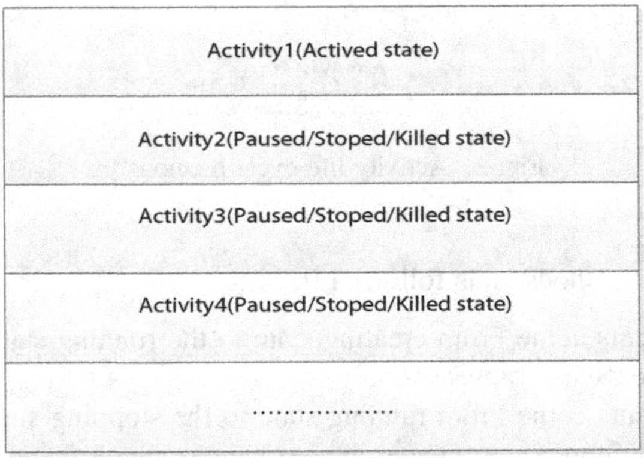

Fig. 3. The activity state in the stack

3   Activity Hijack Principle and Implementation Technology

3.1   Activity Switch Bug

In order to improve the user experience, switching between different applications in android system is basically seamless. The switching between applications is only a switching Activity, and the Activity scheduling is managed by the Android system of

AMS (Activity Manager Service) [9]. Each application which wants to start or stop a process must in the first report to AMS.

When AMS received to start or stop the Activity, it first update internal records, and then inform the corresponding process run or stop the specified Activity. When a new Activity starts, the previous Activity stopped, these activities are held an Activity history stack in the system. Whenever an Activity starts, it is pressed into the history stack, and are displayed on a mobile phone. When the user presses the back key, the top stack popup the Activity, and the top point to the current Activity. when starting an Activity, giving it a sign FLAG_ACTIVITY_NEW_TASK, it will be in the top stack and presented to the user immediately. But this design has a defect. If this Activity is used to hack your disguise the Activity, As shown in Fig. 4.

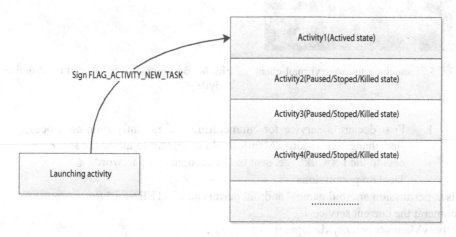

Fig. 4. The effect of the sign

3.2   Implementation of the Hijack Technology

In Android system, programs can enumerate the current running process and does not need to declare other permissions [10]. So we will be able to write a program to start a background service which constantly scanning the currently running process. If It found the target process started, It will start a Activity in disguise. If the Activity is the login interface, you can obtain user account password. We implement hijacked camouflage Activity which alternative wangyi mail client program activity (Figs. 5, 6, 7, and 8).

Fig. 5. Launching the wangyi mail client   **Fig. 6.** Background services start the disguise activity

1、 First declare a service for enumerating the currently running process. Just change the AndroidManifest file statement to allow the service access to the network （get sent to the account and password）。

Declare permissions：

```
<uses-permission android:name="android.permission.INTERNET" />
```

Enumerat the current service：

```
ActivityManager activityManager =
(ActivityManager) getSystemService(Context.ACTIVITY_SERVICE);
List<RunningAppProcessInfo> appProcessInfos =
er .getRunningAppProcesses();
```

2、 When found a target process (wangyi mail client) runs, the service immediately start a preliminary disguise Activity to deceive users.

```
Intent jackingIsComing = new Intent(getBaseContext(),
  mSadStories.get(processName));   jackingIsCom-
  ing.addFlags(Intent.FLAG_ACTIVITY_NEW_TASK);
getApplication().startActivity(jackingIsComing);
  ((HijackingApplication) getApplication())
  .addProgressHijacked(processName);
```

Below is a program run renderings:

Fig. 7. Input information

Fig. 8. Click login, to return to the interface of normal process

4 Conclusion

This paper introduces the related information of the Activity component in android system and hijack principle and implementation technology. As the company promoted the Android platform and Android smartphones, we believe that people will pay more and more attention to the Activity of relevant knowledge. Study of the Activity of safety problems also will be more and more deeply.

References

1. Developers A. What is android?, Feb. 2011. http://developer.android.com/guide/basics/what-is-android.html
2. Wang, R., Jiang, Z., Liu, Q.: Under the android binder inter-process communication mechanism analysis and research. Comput. Technol. Dev. **9**, 107–110 (2012)
3. Enck, W., Octeau, D., McDaniel, P., et al.: A study of android application security. USENIX Security Symposium (2011)
4. Brahler, S.: Analysis of the android architecture. Karlsruhe Institute for Technology (2010)
5. Alliance OH. Android overview. http://www.openhandsetalliance.com. Accessed 8 Oct 2007
6. Chen, L., Zhang, C.: Design and implement of binder extension model based on android inter-process communication. J. Xi'an Univ. Post Telecom **18**(3), 96–99 (2013)
7. Developers A. The activity lifecycle. http://developer.android.com/intl/de/reference/android/app/Activity.html. Accessed Aug 2010
8. Duan, L.: In-depth analyze android activity. The new technology and new products of China, 16: 034 (2011)
9. Ongtang, M., McLaughlin, S., Enck, W., et al.: Semantically rich application-centric security in android. Secur. Commun. Netw. **5**(6), 658–673 (2012)
10. Felt, A.P., Chin, E., Hanna, S., et al.: Android permissions demystified. In: Proceedings of the 18th ACM Conference on Computer and Communications Security, pp. 627–638. ACM (2011)

A Mobile Botnet Model Based
on Android System

Peng Wang[1]([⊠]), Chengwei Zhang[2], Xuanya Li[2], and Can Zhang[2]

[1] School of computing, Beijing University of Posts and Telecommunications,
Beijing, China
wpeng@nelmail.iie.ac.cn
[2] Institute of Information Engineering, Chinese Academy of Sciences,
Beijing, China
{zhangchengwei,lixuanya}@iie.ac.cn,
zhangcan@nelmail.iie.ac.cn

Abstract. The rapid development of mobile Internet provides conditions for traditional botnets to spread to mobile Internet. Combined with the development tendency of mobile botnet, this paper presents an Android-based mobile botnet model from the perspective of an attacker. In this model, we adopt the social engineering means as the main route of propagation of bots and build a C&C (Command and Control) Channel based on SMS-HTTP protocol and a centralized-structured topology. In addition, we design an intelligent bot model to improve the robustness of the whole botnet and implement it on Android System. In the end we discuss the corresponding defense against the botnet.

Keywords: Mobile botnet · Android · Social engineer · SMS · Intelligent bot · Defense

1 Overview

With the rapid development of the mobile communication technology, mobile terminal technology and mobile operating system, smartphones have more powerful computing ability, easier ways to access network and larger storage, which creates conditions for the emergence of mobile botnets.

So far, there have been multiple rudiments of mobile botnets, which cover current popular platforms, including Symbian [1], iOS [2] and Android [3]. Hereinto Android is gradually becoming the main attack target for its openness and large market share, and a variety of Android malware emerge endlessly [4]. Reference [5] predicts that Android will most likely become the target of large-scale mobile botnet.

Unlike traditional botnets, whose bots are mainly PCs, mobile botnets are composed of various mobile terminals, such as smartphones and tablets. Masters establish a controllable smartphones group by propagating malware and then publish commands to control them to launch a series of attacks, such as crank calls, sending spam SMS and emails, ordering high SP services etc., which poses serious threats to the privacy and property security of smartphone users.

The both sides of network attack and defense fight with each other just like a double helix. As the defense side, it's not enough to merely study the existing botnets.

Y. Yuan et al. (Eds.): ISCTCS 2013, CCIS 426, pp. 54–61, 2014.
DOI: 10.1007/978-3-662-43908-1_7, © Springer-Verlag Berlin Heidelberg 2014

We should go ahead of attackers to study the most likely technology attackers might adopt. So far there have been lots of studies on mobile botnet and most of them concentrate on how to design a C&C channel that matches the characteristics of smartphones and can be adopted by mobile botnet [6–12]. Reference [13] points out some differences on hardware and application scenarios between smartphones and PCs, which makes it difficult to establish a large and effective mobile botnet currently. (1) Considering the limited battery capacity, it's easy to cause abnormality on battery consumption if a bot runs frequently. (2) The abundant usage of SMS and mobile network would lead to high charges which would cause users' attention. (3) The changing network state and IP address makes it hard to establish an efficient P2P-structured botnet.

Aiming at the challenges mentioned above, with the development tendency of mobile botnet, this paper presents a mobile botnet model based on SMS-HTTP protocol and centralized structure, and designs an intelligent bot program model, which gives the bots more autonomy to improve the robustness of entire botnet.

2 Propagation of Bots

The first step to establish a mobile botnet is to infect the goal smartphones. Currently all the propagation means can be divided into two classes, one is technological means, such as vulnerability exploitation, and the other is non-technological means and the most popular one is social engineering means, which is used by most of existing botnets. For example, masters send short messages containing malicious links or disguise bots as attractive applications. In Android, the most popular means is to upload bots to application stores or integrate them into ROM packages. In fact, most of researchers on mobile botnet don't focus attention on the propagation of bots.

Therefore the social engineering means are still the most popular and effective means to propagate bots from the perspective of costs and efficiency, and so they are in our mobile botnet model. The following lists the most possible ways adopted by masters.

1. Integrate bots to customized ROMs.
2. Counterfeit popular applications and publish them to irregular places (forum etc.).
3. Disguise a bot as a normal application with normal functions and publish it to application stores.

3 C&C Channel

Compared with viruses and Trojans, botnets have the unique component – the so-called C&C (Command and Control) channels, which are responsible for transmitting commands for masters. In a way the C&C channel is the core of a botnet because it connects masters and the controlled bots just like a bridge. Generally speaking, the C&C channel contains three aspects [13]:

Protocol masters and bots use commonly. For instance, the most common ones in traditional botnets are IRC and HTTP. For smartphones, they have their unique protocols that PCs don't have, and the most common is SMS (Short Message Service, it's actually a kind of service and here we regard it as a protocol that the two sides of communication and telecom operators both abide by). It's widely used by researchers for its timeliness and users' receiving short messages later when offline [7, 10]. On the other hand, Android extremely emphasizes network service and has more convenient ways to access network, so HTTP is also a popular protocol beloved by masters and researchers, which makes the controlling mode be more similar to traditional botnets and be able to take full use of the resources on Internet.

Topology the network structure composed of masters, commands servers and bots. Reference [13] divides all the topologies into four classes – pure centralized structure, pure P2P structure, combined structure and hybrid structure. Most of the existing botnets adopt the pure CS as their topologies, that is, each bot only communicates with the command servers. Besides, there are some researchers who use phone numbers for addressing bots to establish P2P-based botnets [7]. However, bots need to send lots of short messages to maintain the topology, which would lead to fee abnormality. Reference [10] presents a hybrid-structured and SMS-HTTP based botnet model in which command servers and bots are arranged on separate levels – command servers in the same level are connected in a pure P2P structure and pure centralized structure is adopted between command servers and bots. However, the model is staying on the theoretical layer and hard to implement.

Resources the software and hardware that masters use and the intermediate nodes that masters and bots both use, such as the public IRC/HTTP/web 2.0 servers, P2P network nodes and springboard nodes. In mobile botnets, the most commonly used resources include all kinds of web servers on Internet and the infrastructures of operators, such as the picture server and microblog server used in reference [11].

For a mobile botnet, the most important step is to seek a suitable C&C channel. Considering the high expenses, it's not suitable to adopt a P2P-structured topology based on SMS. As for protocols, SMS and HTTP are still the most popular ones and both have respective advantages. SMS has strong robustness and short messages can be received later when phones are offline while HTTP costs less than SMS when transmitting same information, so we can organically combine them together. Besides, considering the strong ability of accessing network of smartphones, masters can take effective use of the free public servers on Internet.

Based on the analysis described above, this paper puts forward a C&C model with SMS-HTTP protocol and centralized-structured topology, as Fig. 1 shows.

In the model, commands can be published in two ways. They can either be transmitted to bots by controlling short messages (messages that containing commands) via tools like group messaging device, or be placed on public cloud servers and then obtained by bots when they access network.

The commands can be published in two ways – online and offline. When a bot can't access network, it can still obtain commands by SMS without any costs, and when connecting to network, the bot then changes to access the specified servers via

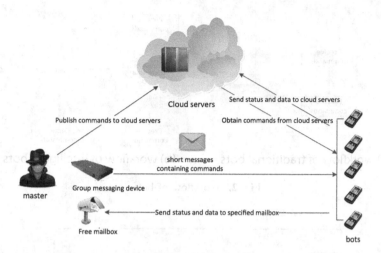

Fig. 1. Design of C&C channel

HTTP. Thus on one hand the design can take full use of the advantages of the two protocols, and on the other hand, it can effectively reduce the cost of masters.

4   Intelligent Bot

After bots obtain the commands, the next step is to execute them immediately, which is very normal. However, users usually have their experience in the status of their phones, such as the stand-by time, power consumption and flow consumption etc. High frequency of bots' activities would easily cause abnormality of the status and cause the attention of users, which is not expected by masters. So bots need to change their working mode.

The best way to avoid abnormality of bots is to attempt to behave normal, given which this paper proposes the concept of "intelligent bots". Different from traditional bots, an "intelligent bot" doesn't execute commands immediately after receiving them. It first forecasts the result of executing the commands on the base of current status of phones. If the result leads to abnormality, bots would store the commands temporarily and execute them immediately otherwise, as Fig. 2 shows.

4.1   Design of Bot

To achieve the goal, masters need to add new modules except attack module and command receiving module. Figure 3 presents the modularized architecture of an intelligent bot.

Monitoring Module. This module takes charge of monitoring the status of phones, including the airplane mode status, connection status of network, remaining battery capacity and charging status and so on. Generally, the module runs regularly to master the up-to-date status.

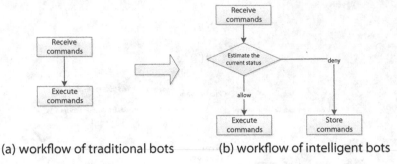

(a) workflow of traditional bots   (b) workflow of intelligent bots

Fig. 2. Workflow of bots

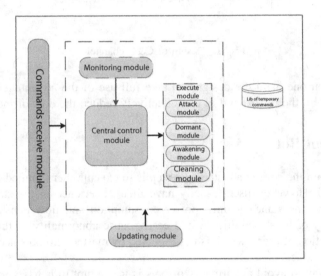

Fig. 3. Architecture of modularized bots

Central Control Module. This module gives the best following instructions according to the current status of phones and receiving commands.

Dormant Module. When the central control module makes a decision that it's not the time to take actions, the dormant module would turn off some functional modules, such as command receiving module and attack module, and only a few modules would be kept alive.

Awakening Module. Contrast with the dormant module, the awakening module takes charge of awakening the modules turned off by the dormant module when the phone is in a safe state.

Updating Module. The module is in charge of updating the bot, including the modules and configuration databases.

Cleaning Module. When the central control module judges that it's not suitable for the bot to stay in the phone any more (For instance, the user of the phone installs a secure software that can discover the abnormality of the bot.), the cleaning module would turn off all the modules and delete all the data related to the bot.

Modularized design has many advantages. On one hand, it contributes to explicit divisions and convenient upgrade. On the other hand, given that Android is faced with a new kind of attack named coordinated attack, in which several applications in Android can cooperate to complete an attack task, each module in the bot architecture can be replaced by a separate application and a more complicated bot is created consequently.

4.2 Disguise of Bot

Most of masters hope that all the bots can survive as long as possible. In order to protect the bots from being discovered easily, it's better for the bots to have a normal identity (for example, bots can disguise themselves as software with normal functions) and then bots can do more things on the phones.

In Android, each software must apply the corresponding permissions if it wants to do something and the application for sensitive permissions would easily cause attention of users and secure software. Nevertheless, a malware can legalize the application by disguising itself as a normal software with normal functions that exactly need the applied permissions.

In the implement of this model, the master disguises the bot as a secure software with several normal functions, in virtue of which the bot get the permissions required to launch attacks. Figure 4 shows the screenshots of the bot.

Fig. 4. Screenshots of bot

5 Defense of Botnet

In this section we will discuss the corresponding defense measures of the mobile botnet model in this paper.

The key link of SMS-based control process is that bots can read each short message the controlled phones receive. As mentioned above, each software in Android must apply the corresponding permission if it wants to read the short messages.

So users had better check the permission lists when installing a software and estimate whether it's necessary for the software to apply it.

Masters' disguising the control commands as spam messages just uses the users' psychology in dealing with spam messages. So instead of simply deleting or ignoring the spam after receiving them, blacklist is a good choice.

Although masters can adopt free cloud servers as commands servers, the domain names of the servers have specified characteristics and defenders can discover them by monitoring the network communication.

Generally speaking, it's hard to discover the bots that are disguised as normal software. Nevertheless, most of the software in Android are written by Java and it's easy to decompile them, and then defenders can slowly examine the source codes purposefully.

In summary, users should download software from regular channels and the software had better go through safety certification. Secondly, remember to pay attention to the permissions each software applies and use security software to limit the unnecessary permissions. Finally, users should develop good habits of using phones to reduce the chance attackers may take use of.

No matter how bots disguise themselves, there are still some characteristics in their behavior. Defenders can design a system that can monitor and record the atomic behavior of all the installed applications in real time, and then analyze the collected behavior information to discover the malicious behavior produced by single application or multiple applications by matching with a rule base.

6 Conclusion

Except for convenience, the rapid development of mobile Internet also brings some security problems. As the extension of botnets in mobile Internet, mobile botnets have emerged and spread to the current popular operating systems and Android is very likely to become the platform of large-scale botnet because of its openness and huge market share. In order to obtain the opportunities in the future battle between attack and defense, it's necessary to study the key technologies of establishing mobile botnets from the perspective of attackers combined with the development tendency of mobile botnets along with the current resources. This paper gives a most conceivable model of mobile botnet and the corresponding defenses. In our future work we'll conduct a simulation verification for the model and design a system that can monitor the behavior of all the applications in Android.

References

1. Apvrille, A.: Symbian worm Yxes: towards mobile botnets. J. Comput. Virol. **8**(4), 117–131 (2012)
2. Porras, Phillip, Saïdi, Hassen, Yegneswaran, Vinod: An analysis of the iKee.B iPhone botnet. In: Schmidt, Andreas U., Russello, Giovanni, Lioy, Antonio, Prasad, Neeli R., Lian, Shiguo (eds.) MobiSec 2010. LNICST, vol. 47, pp. 141–152. Springer, Heidelberg (2010)

3. Wyatt, T.: Security alert: geinimi, sophisticated new android Trojan found in wild. Blog, Dec 2010
4. Felt, A.P., Finifter, M., Chin, E., et al.: A survey of mobile malware in the wild. In: Proceedings of the 1st ACM workshop on Security and privacy in smartphones and mobile devices, pp. 3–14. ACM (2011)
5. Schmidt, A.D., Schmidt, H.G., Batyuk, L., et al.: Smartphone malware evolution revisited: android next target? In: 2009 4th International Conference on Malicious and Unwanted Software (MALWARE), pp. 1–7. IEEE (2009)
6. Mulliner, C., Seifert, J.P.: Rise of the iBots: owning a telco network. In: 2010 5th International Conference on Malicious and Unwanted Software (MALWARE), pp. 71–80. IEEE (2010)
7. Zeng, Y., Shin, K.G., Hu, X.: Design of SMS commanded-and-controlled and P2P-structured mobile botnets. In: Proceedings of the 5th ACM Conference on Security and Privacy in Wireless and Mobile Networks, pp. 137–148. ACM (2012)
8. Singh, Kapil, Sangal, Samrit, Jain, Nehil, Traynor, Patrick, Lee, Wenke: Evaluating bluetooth as a medium for botnet command and control. In: Kreibich, Christian, Jahnke, Marko (eds.) DIMVA 2010. LNCS, vol. 6201, pp. 61–80. Springer, Heidelberg (2010)
9. Xiang, C., Binxing, F., Lihua, Y., Xiaoyi, L., Tianning, Z.: Andbot: towards advanced mobile botnets. In: Proceedings of the 4th USENIX Conference on Large-scale Exploits and Emergent Threats, pp. 11–11. USENIX Association (2011)
10. Geng, G., Chen, D., Gao, H., Zhang, M., Yang, G.: Design and analyze of mobile botnets. J. Tsinghua Univ. Nat. Sci. 51(10), 1329–1334 (2011)
11. Xiaoyi, L., Xiang, C., Donghua, Z., et al.: A mobile botnet based on android System. Comput. Eng. 37(22) (2011). doi:10.3969/j.issn.1000-3428.2011.22.001.
12. Yue, L., Lidong, Z., Hongxia, W., et al.: A mobile botnet based on social network. Comput. Res. Dev. 49(Suppl.), 1–8 (2012)
13. Binxing, F., Xiang, C., Wei, W.: Overview of botnet. Comput. Res. Dev. 48(8), 1315–1331 (2011)

An Improved Common Vulnerability Scoring System Based on K-means

Pingping Liu[1,2(✉)], Zhihong Tian[3,4], Xu Wu[1,2,5], and Wei Liu[1,2]

[1] Key Laboratory of Trustworthy Distributed Computing and Service (BUPT),
Ministry of Education, Beijing, China
liu_ping_yes@163.com, wux@bupt.edu.cn,
lwdaizydream@gmail.com
[2] School of Computer Science, Beijing University of Posts
and Telecommunications, Beijing, China
[3] School of Computer Science and Technology, Harbin Institute of Technology,
Haerbin 150001, China
tianzhihong@hit.edu.cn
[4] Beijing HIT Computer Network and Information Security Technology
Research Center, Beijing, China
[5] Beijing University of Posts and Telecommunications Library, Beijing, China

Abstract. To objectively divide the level of vulnerability severity in Common Vulnerability Scoring System (CVSS), this paper provides a method based on k-means clustering algorithm to improve CVSS and makes it more convictive to evaluate vulnerability. A lot of data as sample are achieved by scoring the severity of the known vulnerabilities according to CVSS, and then these data can be processed by k-means. At last we objectively obtain the ranges of CVSS scores corresponding to every vulnerability severity level, and the results are in keeping with CVSS system basically. So that the proposed method can determine the severity level of a new vulnerability according to the divided scope of CVSS scores objectively.

Keywords: CVSS · K-means · Vulnerability severity · Vulnerability level division

1 Introduction

With the rapid development of Internet, the number of software which is applied to computer information systems is increasing fast, so the insufficient and defects of computer software or other components are also increasing correspondingly. In other words, the amount of vulnerabilities in computer systems is more. By using the vulnerabilities in computer, hacker can do something in our computer such as access without authorization or Denial of Service attack, to damage to your computer, so it is a serious threat.

Due to different vulnerability on the degree of damage to computer information system is different, the quantitative assessment of vulnerability severity can be used to classify vulnerability severity, then according to the priority of vulnerabilities administrator takes some corresponding measures to deal with the existing vulnerabilities, and ensures the safety of system.

Y. Yuan et al. (Eds.): ISCTCS 2013, CCIS 426, pp. 62–69, 2014.
DOI: 10.1007/978-3-662-43908-1_8, © Springer-Verlag Berlin Heidelberg 2014

The goal of this paper is to divide vulnerability severity level objectively in CVSS, so that people get a better understanding about vulnerabilities severity division. This paper takes a lot of CVSS scores as sample and deals with these scores to objectively divide the vulnerability severity level.

2 Relation Work

Now, research institutions and researchers have evaluated vulnerabilities severity in systems from the quantitative or qualitative viewpoint. 1999 Government of Canada provided a document entitled Threat and Risk Assessment Wording Guide to carry out a Threat and Risk Assessment (TRA) for an existing or proposed IT system [1]. This document analyzed vulnerabilities qualitatively, in terms of the severity of impact and the potential exposure to loss, and eventually vulnerability severity is divided into five levels. According to vulnerability exploitation, Microsoft Security TechCenter makes a qualitative analysis about vulnerability severity and eventually vulnerability severity is divided into four levels, including Low, Moderate, Important, Critical [2].

Computer Emergency Response Team (CERT) considered several factors such as information availability and the vulnerability exploitation, to rate the damage to system quantitatively. The result is a number between 0 and 180 that reflects an approximate severity about the vulnerability [3]. YANG Hong-yu proposed a vulnerability severity grey hierarchy analytic evaluation model, which considered several metrics such as access complexity and authentication to analyze vulnerability severity from the quantitative and qualitative viewpoint. Eventually, it achieved vulnerability severity level and a corresponding comprehensive quantitative value [4]. ZHANG Yong-zheng presented privilege-escalating based on vulnerability taxonomy with multidimensional quantitative attribute, which computed the damage value with a simple weighted summation according to three factors: confidentiality, availability, integrity [5].

Above researches, there are some problems about vulnerability severity division. For example, researcher only analyzes vulnerability severity from the quantitative viewpoint, which can't reflect the vulnerability severity level visually and just classifies vulnerability level according to subjective judgment such as in [5] which divided vulnerability severity into five levels subjectively by the range of damage values. It is the same in CVSS where the division of vulnerability is classified subjectively by experts' experiences and knowledge.

3 K-means Clustering Algorithm

Clustering algorithm is a statistical analysis method about dataset classification. K-means is a simple clustering analysis algorithm, which is based on distance between elements as the similarity evaluation metrics [6]. The main idea of the k-means algorithm [7] is: assign k as an input parameter of k-means algorithm, which represents that how many subsets a dataset will be divided into; randomly select k different elements as the center of each subset from the dataset; compute the distances between all of the elements and the center of every subset; put all the elements into a special subset where the element is nearest with the center of this subset; then repeat computing the center of k subsets unless the center of each subset does not change or changes little.

According to the dimension of data, use different formulation to compute the distance between two data. For example, one-dimensional data can be calculated as follows:

$$Dist(x, y) = |x - y| \tag{1}$$

However, multi-dimensional data can use Minkowski distance [6] to be calculated as follows:

$$Dist(x, y) = \sqrt[p]{|x_1 - y_1|^p + |x_2 - y_2|^p + \cdots + |x_n - y_n|^p} \tag{2}$$

Assume that Q represents the center of a special subset, and S represents the sum of the values of all the elements in this subset. N represents the amount of the elements in this subset, so the center of this subset can again be given by:

$$Q = \frac{S}{N} \tag{3}$$

Known from the analysis above, k-means algorithm follow the steps outlined below:

(a) assign k. How many subsets.
(b) initialize the center of every subset. Determine k different center values.
(c) classify elements. Compute the distance between the elements and the center of every subset by formulation (1) or (2), and compare distance with each other to classify elements.
(d) repeat computing the center of each subset by formulation (3) and Stop computing if the center of each subset does not change or changes little, otherwise, turn to step (c).

4   CVSS Scoring Standard

CVSS provides an open framework for communicating the characteristics and impacts of IT vulnerabilities to evaluate IT system. In the CVSS version 2.0 [8], CVSS consists of three groups: Base, Temporal and Environmental. Each group has several metrics and produces a numeric score ranging from 0 to 10, as shown in Fig. 1. In Fig. 1, the base group reflects the intrinsic qualities of vulnerability. The Temporal group reflects the characteristics of a vulnerability that changes over time. The Environment group reflects the characteristics of a vulnerability that is unique to any user's environment.

To calculate the CVSS score, every metric can be given a score according reference [8, 9], as shown in Table 1:

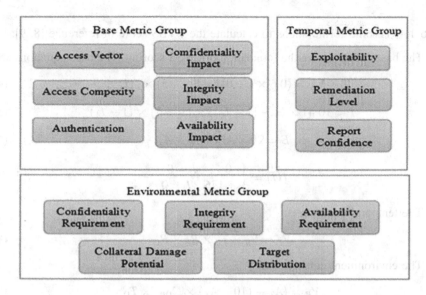

Fig. 1. CVSS metric groups

Table 1. CVSS metrics scoring table

Metrics	Options	Scores
Base metric group (V_B)		
Access vector (A_V)	Local/adjacent network/network	0.395/0.646/1.0
Access complexity (A_C)	High/medium/low	0.35/0.61/0.71
Authentication (A_U)	Multiple/single/no need	0.45/0.56/0.704
Confidentiality impact (I_C)	None/partial/complete	0.0/0.275/0.660
Integrity impact (I_I)	None/partial/complete	0.0/0.275/0.660
Availability impact (I_A)	None/partial/complete	0.0/0.275/0.660
Temporal metric group (V_T)		
Exploitability (T_E)	Unproven/proof-of-concept//functional/ high/not defined	0.85/0.9/0.95/1.0/1.0
Remediation level (R_L)	Official-fix/temporary-fix/workaround/ unavailable/not defined	0.87/0.9/0.95/1.0/1.0
Report confidence (R_C)	Unconfirmed/uncorroborated/confirmed/ not defined	0.9/0.95/1.0/1.0
Environmental metric group (V_E)		
Collateral damage potential (C_{DP})	None/low/low-medium/medium-high/ high/not defined	0/0.1/0.3/0.4/0.5/0
Target distribution (T_D)	None/low/medium/high/not defined	0/0.25/0.75/1.0/1.0
Confidentiality requirement (C_R)	Low/medium/high/not defined	0.5/1.0/1.51/1.0
Integrity requirement (I_R)	Low/medium/high/not defined	0.5/1.0/1.51/1.0
Availability requirement (A_R)	Low/medium/high/not defined	0.5/1.0/1.51/1.0

The below is some formulations to calculate the CVSS score in reference [8, 9]:

(1)   The base equations are the foundation of CVSS scoring. The base equations are:

$$V_B = (0.6 \times I + 0.4 \times E - 1.5) \times f(I) \tag{4}$$

$$I = 10.41 \times (1 - (1 - I_C)) \times (1 - I_I) \times (1 - I_A) \tag{5}$$

$$E = 20 \times A_V \times A_C \times A_U \tag{6}$$

$$f(I) = \begin{cases} 0 & I = 0 \\ 1.176 & I \neq 0 \end{cases} \tag{7}$$

(2)   The temporal equation is:

$$V_T = V_B \times T_E \times R_L \times R_C \tag{8}$$

(3)   The environment equations are:

$$V_E = (A_T + (10 - A_T) \times C_{DP}) \times T_D \tag{9}$$

$$A_T = V_B' \times T_E \times R_L \times R_C \tag{10}$$

$$V_B' = (0.6 \times I' + 0.4 \times E - 1.5) \times f(I') \tag{11}$$

$$I' = \min\{10, 10.41 \times (1 - (1 - I_C \times C_R) \times (1 - I_I \times I_R) \times (1 - I_A \times A_R))\} \tag{12}$$

5   Vulnerability Severity Level Division

Assume there is a vulnerability set V, n elements in total in the set, denoted by $V = \{v_1, v_2,..., v_n\}$ where $v_i(i = 1, 2,..., n)$ represents a special vulnerability. Using CVSS scoring standard to score for every element will obtain a lot of values about vulnerability severity denoted by $S = \{s_1, s_2,..., s_n\}$ where s_i represents a score value which v_i gets according to CVSS, so we can deal with S by k-means clustering algorithm. Assume the set V will be divided into k subsets, and the centers have been initialized, so we can compute the similarity degree among S by Eq. (1) and repeat computing the center of each subset and also classifying the elements of the set S unless the center of each subset does not change or changes little. When we repeat computing the center of each subset, the former center of the set S is denoted by $Qpre = \{p_1, p_2,..., p_k\}$, the latter center by $Qback = \{b_1, b_2,..., b_k\}$, and the change of all the centers can be calculated by error function which is expressed as:

$$ER = \sum_{i=1}^{k} |b_i - p_i|^2 \tag{13}$$

Where b_i and p_i represent the center value of the subset i after computing the center and before respectively.

After processing set S with k-means clustering algorithm, we can get a set which represents the centers of all the subsets, denoted by $Qresult = \{q_1, q_2,..., q_k\}$ where the elements are sorted by size such as $q_1 < q_2 \cdots < q_k$. Take the average of two adjacent elements in set $Qresult$ as the boundary of the scope relating to a special vulnerability severity level. But the lower bound of all the scores is 0 and the upper bound 10, so the score scopes which are corresponding to every type of vulnerability severity level can be given, as shown in Table 2:

We can give k a number such as 3, so the first type is corresponding to the low severity of vulnerability, the second type mediate severity and the third type high severity. Therefore, when a new vulnerability is found, it is easy to judge which type this vulnerability belongs to, because we just need to score the new vulnerability by CVSS, and then get the severity level about the vulnerability according to Table 2.

Table 2. CVSS score interval of each category

CVSS score intervals	Types of vulnerability severity level
$[0, \frac{q_1+q_2}{2}]$	1
$[\frac{q_i+q_{i+1}}{2}, \frac{q_{i+1}+q_{i+2}}{2}]$ $i = 1, 2,..., k - 2$	$i + 1$
$[\frac{q_{k-1}+q_k}{2},10]$	k

6 Application Example

We divide the vulnerabilities of Microsoft products which are described in the Common Vulnerability and Exposures (CVE) database [10] into several categories. Firstly, we score Microsoft vulnerabilities of the recent five years in CVE by CVSS. However, the temporal metrics and environmental metrics change over time, so we take the base score as the CVSS score and then get a set about those vulnerabilities severity from National Vulnerability Database (NVD) [11]. For example, we score the vulnerability CVE-2012-2549 (named MS12-083 in Microsoft), and quantize the base metrics, as shown in Table 3:

By Eqs. (4), (5), (6), and (7), we can figure out $I = 4.9$, $E = 8.6$, $V_B = 5.8$. The score of CVE-2012-2549 is 5.8. The rest of vulnerabilities can be computed similarly.

After analyzing the recent five-year vulnerabilities of Microsoft products, we achieve a set about the CVSS scores of those vulnerability and deal with this set by using k-means clustering algorithm. In order to compare with CVSS system, we give $k = 3$ which represents that those vulnerabilities will be divided into three categories corresponding to three levels of vulnerability severity respectively. We give the initial centers of three subsets denoted by $Qpre = \{2.0, 5.0, 8.0\}$ and the final centers can be computed, denoted by $Qresult = \{2.140, 4.620, 8.823\}$. So we can obtain the scopes about the division of vulnerability severity level of Microsoft products according to Table 2, and give a table to compare with CVSS system, as shown in Table 4:

Table 3. The base metrics scoring of CVE-2012-2549

Metrics	Options	Scores
Access vector (A_V)	Network	1.0
Access complexity (A_C)	Medium	0.61
Authentication (A_U)	No need	0.704
Confidentiality impact (I_C)	Partial	0.275
Integrity impact (I_I)	Partial	0.275
Availability impact (I_A)	None	0.0

Table 4. Compared with CVSS system about the division of vulnerabilities severity

Vulnerability severity level	CVSS score scopes	
	CVSS system	The proposed method
Low	[0.0, 3.9]	[0.0, 3.3]
Medium	[4.0, 6.9]	[3.4, 6.7]
High	[7.0, 10.0]	[6.8, 10.0]

From the table above, we can know the severity level of CVE–2012-2549: Medium. However, the scores arranging from 3.4 to 3.9 are medium level in this paper while low level in CVSS system. Similarly, the scores arranging from 6.8 to 6.9 are high level in the paper while medium level in CVSS system. This is the reason that the level of the vulnerabilities is just judged by the experience of the professional experts in CVSS system and it is a universal method to evaluate vulnerabilities of all the products, however, the method in the paper just aims at Microsoft products and the level of those vulnerabilities is divided objectively by using the known vulnerabilities as sample. But the division in the paper is in keeping with CVSS system basically.

7 Conclusion

The paper takes the known vulnerabilities as the sample data and deals with the CVSS scores set by k-means clustering algorithm and finally divides the level of vulnerability severity objectively. This is an improvement of CVSS system and makes it more convictive. Moreover, the proposed method can divide vulnerability severity into several types as needed. We can repeat computing the center of each type periodically when there are a certain amount of new vulnerabilities, so the proposed method is more dynamic and reasonable. But during the CVSS scoring, the workload is larger as the amount of vulnerability increase. At last, the paper gives a division about the recent five-year vulnerabilities of Microsoft products to verify the proposed method.

Acknowledgements. This work is supported by the Hi-Tech Research and Development Program of China under Grant Nos. 2012AA01A404, 2012AA012506, 2012AA01A401, 2012AA012901.

References

1. Threat and risk assessment working guide. http://www.docin.com/p-105716229.html
2. Security bulletin severity rating system. http://technet.microsoft.com/en-us/security/gg309177.aspx
3. Vulnerability notes database field description. http://www.kb.cert.org/vuls/html/fieldhelp
4. Yang, H., Xie, L., Zhu, D.: A vulnerability severity grey hierarchy analytic evaluation model. J. Univ. Electron. Sci. Technol. China **39**, 777–782 (2010)
5. Zhang, Y., Yun, X., Hu, M.: Research on privilege-escalating based vulnerability taxonomy with multidimensional quantitative attribute. J. China Inst. Commun. **25**, 107–114 (2004)
6. Shao, F., Yu, Z.: Principle and Algorithm of Data Mining. China WaterPower Press, Beijing (2003)
7. K-meansclustering   algorithm.   http://www.cnblogs.com/jerrylead/archive/2011/04/06/2006910.html
8. A complete guide to the common vulnerability scoring system version 2.0. http://www.first.org/cvss/cvss-guide.html
9. Wang, R.: Research on techniques of vulnerability detection and security evaluation based on correlation analysis. Northwest University, pp. 31–34 (2012)
10. Common vulnerability and exposures. http://cve.mitre.org/
11. National vulnerability database home. http://nvd.nist.gov/

A Design of Linkage Security Defense System Based on Honeypot

Gangfu Feng[✉], Chen Zhang, and Quan Zhang

National University of Defense Technology, Changsha, China
marsfgf@163.com, zhan9chen@gmail.com,
quanzhang@nudt.edu.cn

Abstract. Network security is a growing concern today for organizations. Our network faces many new threats and unknown attacks. The traditional defense system can not response to the 0-day attacks. This paper is to design a linkage security defense system based on honeypot technique. The honeypot is a security resource whose value lies in being probed, attacked or compromised. We collect information of attacker and other threats actively with honeypot centered in linkage security defense system. With the information collected, the linkage system will update security system policies and rules in time. Therefore, we are able to improve our network security by the linkage security defense system in real time.

Keywords: Honeypot · Linkage architecture design · Real-time defense system

1 Introduction

Network security is currently one of the most trending topics in the field of computer science. Various type of network attacks increasing. Network security has played a more and more important role in the national economic development and national defense and security fields.

The current network environment leads to growing demand for safety and security is no longer a single demand. It has risen to the anti-virus, access control, encryption, intrusion detection, vulnerability scanning, firewall and other types of security products [1]. Single security technology and products already could not meet users need to network security. Therefore, in this paper, we propose a linkage security defense system based on honeypot and use honeypot as the main body. The system changes the security strategy through the information obtained by honeypot. Make the honeypot and firewall, intrusion detection, intrusion prevention and other to be a linkage network security protection system [2, 3].

This paper is organized as follows: In Sect. 2 we examine traditional network security defense system. In Sect. 3 we provide an overview of the honeypot concept and approaches to their implementation. Section 4 presents the defense system based on honeypot. We then conclude and provide our opinion on the future in Sect. 5.

Y. Yuan et al. (Eds.): ISCTCS 2013, CCIS 426, pp. 70–77, 2014.
DOI: 10.1007/978-3-662-43908-1_9, © Springer-Verlag Berlin Heidelberg 2014

2 Traditional Network Security Defense System

2.1 The Traditional Defense System

Intrusion detection system (IDS) was seen as the center of all security technology by Traditional security system, as intrusion detection in the security system is the focus of decision making. But the firewall and intrusion detection system in traditional linkage system is unable to respond to unknown attack technology, which would have been in a passive position in the new attack techniques cause harm to the system before it can be repaired [4]. Traditional network defense system is shown in Fig. 1.

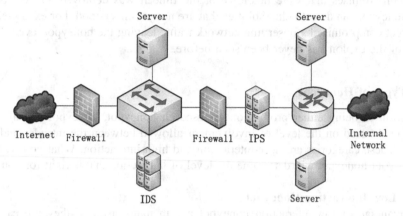

Fig. 1. Traditional network defense system

2.2 The Lack of the Traditional Defense System

The traditional defense system has many shortcomings. First, each part is relatively independent in traditional defense system. Firewall, IDS, IPS and other components just complete their own work. There is no contact between them. This leads to each part in the defense system can play a limited role. For example, firewall can't block the intrusion that discovered by IDS. Second, the defense is passive and can not response unknown attacks. As the vulnerability mining technique is getting mature, 0-day attacks are gradually increasing. The traditional defense system can not block 0-day attacks. Therefore, in many cases, administrator can only find the intrusion after the system has been damaged. The linkage defense system based on honeypot can overcome these problems.

3 Honeypot Technique

3.1 Concepts of Honeypot

Based on the active offense theory, honeypot is a newly arisen technology which is valued by the realm in computer network security increasingly. The amount of useful information provided by IDS is decreasing in the face of ever more sophisticated evasion techniques and an increasing number of protocols that employ encryption to protect network traffic from eavesdroppers.IDS also suffer from high false positive rates that decrease their usefulness even further. Honeypot can help with some of these problems [5].

A honeypot is an information system resource whose value lies in unauthorized or illicit use of that resource. The value of a honeypot is weighed by the information that can be obtained from it. Monitoring the data that enters and leaves a honeypot lets us gather information that is not available to IDS. For example, we can log the keystrokes of an interactive session even if encryption is used to protect the network traffic. To detect malicious behavior, IDS requires signatures of known attacks and often fail to detect compromises that were unknown at the time it was deployed. On the other hand, honeypot can detect vulnerabilities that are not yet understood. For example, we can detect compromise by observing network traffic leaving the honeypot, even if the means of the exploit has never been seen before.

3.2   Types of Honeypot

In addition to being either production or research honeypot, honeypot can also be categorized based on the level of involvement allowed between the intruder and the system. These categories are: low-interaction and high-interaction. What you want to do with your honeypot will determine the level of interaction that is right for you [6].

3.2.1   Low-Interaction Honeypot

The advantage of low-interaction honeypot are in many aspects, they are easy to deploy and maintain, does not require a lot of computing resources to run, and the risk of low-interaction honeypot can be exploited by attackers than running completely capture and control honeypot is much smaller. On the other hand, this is a low-interaction honeypot major drawback. It does not provide a complete interaction. The attacker can not get a true super user shell, so it can not respond to the new attack techniques.

3.2.2   High-Interaction Honeypot

High-interaction honeypot provide a complete interactive system for attackers, which means the honeypot does not emulate any services, features or the underlying operating system. On the contrary, it provides real system and services, and the same as used within the organization today. Therefore, the attacker is able to attack the host and control it completely, which enables administrators to learn more about the tools used by attackers, to better understand the attacker community.

3.3   The Main Techniques in Honeypot

In the honeypot development and deployment process, mainly the following four kinds of techniques will be used.

First, Network spoofing technique. Network spoofing technique is to make honeypot system on the network with the real host system indistinguishable. Currently there are two implementations. Adopt real system that is through safe handling and consistent with the target network environment, which is called the real honeypot. Using the virtual system that is consistent with the target network environment, which is called a virtual honeypot [7].

Second, Attack capture technique. Attack capture technology is to capture the attacker's intrusion. To ensure the accuracy of the data captured attack, completeness and timeliness, the attacker captures general from three levels of data collection. (1) Access control level. (2) Network layer. (3) System level.

Third, the data control technique. Data control technology is to control the attacker access honeypot activities, so as not to use honeypot as a springboard for attacking and harm other host.

Fourth, Analysis and feature extraction. The attack analysis and feature extraction are fused to various attacks, mining data capture, analysis of hacker tools, strategies and motivation, and extract characteristics of unknown attacks [8].

4 The Defense System Based on Honeypot

4.1 Linkage Architecture Design

The linkage security system uses a variety of safety equipment interaction and the linkage response to provide different levels of security protection. This will not only be able to fully play a variety of security mechanisms and security measures function, but also easy to manage, upgrade and deployment. Linkage security protection system architecture is shown in Fig. 2.

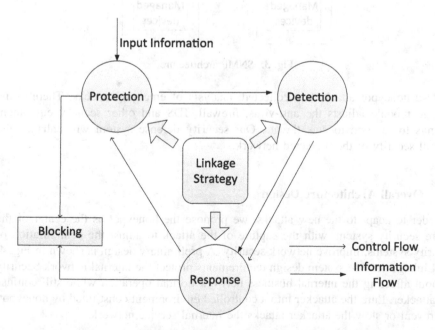

Fig. 2. Linkage architecture

For the linkage between the various components, we use the Simple Network Management Protocol (SNMP) to manage and communicate. SNMP defines convey management information protocol message format and the management station and the device for delivery of messages between agents of order. It provides the underlying framework for most network management system.

SNMP uses connectionless data packet mode, the potential to provide a degree of robustness, even in a high load on the network can continue to process management functions. SNMP uses managers - agent administration model and it's shown in Fig. 3.

We design unified data interface for honeypot, firewall, IDS and other components in the defense system. Construct a linkage management module and use the SNMP protocol for each part information interaction. Then form the honeypot as the center, other network security equipment complement with each other in security defense system.

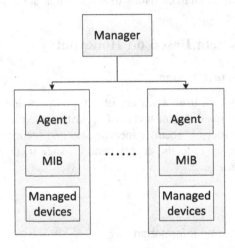

Fig. 3. SNMP architecture

Use honeypot attack data collected, analysis of emerging attacks. Thereby the linkage module adjusts the anti-virus, firewall, IDS and other security equipment settings to respond to new threats. Our security defense system will enhance the overall security of the protected network.

4.2   Overall Architecture Design

In order to adapt to the new attacks, we propose the honeypot as the center of the entire security system, with the capture of the attack to adjust the configuration of security systems, improve network security. A preliminary design is shown in Fig. 4.

Linkage defense system design requirements protect the internal network Security without affecting the internal business network normal operation while still confuse the attacker. Lure the attacker into a controlled environment constituted by honeypot, to prevent or slow the attacker attacks the internal service network.

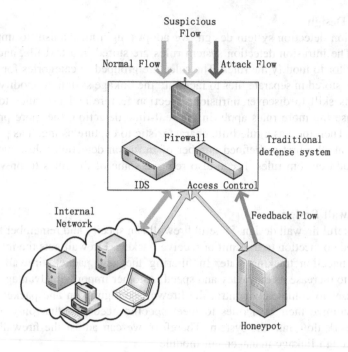

Fig. 4. Linkage security defense system based on honeypot

For normal flow, direct release. If the data do not meet the firewall rules or are identified as malicious data by intrusion detection systems, directly blocking. For suspicious flow, first deliver to the honeypot system. If the honeypot system is damaged, the defense system will feedback block commands. If normal, then it will be forwarded to the protected internal network.

4.3   Each Components Design

4.3.1   Honeypot Design

The honeypot in linkage system achieve three main functions. First is the network data collection. Honeypot is designed to answer network packets that their destination address belongs to honeypot network. Properly configured network Let honeypot can receive messages that sent to the honeypot. If the network data impacts the normal operation of the honeypot system, we have determined to attack data. Second, honeypot should not be identified by attacker. Honeypot will not being exposed when in fingerprint identification is very important. In order to make the honeypot look like the real host when it is scanned and probed, we introduce appropriate modifications in the protocol header before packets sent. It will make packets match the fingerprint recognition software intended operating system features. Third, record attack data and form log. Honeypot can record and report on all agreements and complete the connection attempt to connect logs. It can also be configured to human-readable way to store honeypot system receives all packets [9]. Meanwhile, the service program can also output to the standard error report their honeypot to collect network information.

4.3.2 IDS Design

In the intrusion detection system design, we adopt plugin mechanism to improve its scalability. The intrusion detection system rules are stored in a text file, and we can use a text editor to modify the rules. The rules are grouped in categories for different types and are stored in separate files to facilitate the linkage system to modify its rules [10]. It needs skill to discover intrusion detection feature and use rules to capture them. Because the more rules apply in the real-time detection, the more processing power need. Therefore, as a rule little characteristic to capture as much as possible is very important. We first predefined number of intrusion detection rules, and linkage system can add custom rules. It can also remove some of the rules to prevent false alarms.

4.3.3 Firewall Design

We use a stateful firewall design. Stateful firewall can specify and remember the status of established connection to transmit or receive packets. Firewall gets the information from the connection tracking state. In filtering the new packet, firewall uses the information to increase its efficiency and speed. Another important advantage is that it allows the user to completely control the firewall configuration and packet filtering. We can customize their own rules to meet specific needs, so that only allow our desired network flow into the system. Therefore we can adjust the firewall rules in real-time through linkage management module.

5 Conclusion

In this paper we have designed a linkage security defense system that based on honeypot technique. The system is centered honeypot. The honeypot access to information as a linkage system driven, real-time updates security system policies and rules, and enhance the security systems of the unknown attack response capability.

Honeypot is increasingly deployed in networks. However, they are mostly used passively. Administrators watch what happens once a machine has been compromised. Our design can solve the problem. We collect information on attacker and other threats actively using honeypot in linkage security defense system. We believe honeypot can prove a useful tool in digital forensics investigations.

Acknowledgements. This research project was supported by National Natural Science Foundation of China (No. 61302091).

References

1. Mokube, I., Adams, M.: Honeypots: concepts, approaches, and challenges. In: ACMSE 2007, pp. 321–326. ACM, Winston-Salem (2007)
2. Mairh, A., Barik, D., Verma, K., Jena, D.: Honeypot in network security: a survey. In: ICCCS'11, pp. 600–605. ACM, New York (2011)

3. Krueger, T., Gascon, H., Krämer, N., Rieck, K.: Learning stateful models for network honeypots. In: AISec'12, pp. 37–48. ACM, Raleigh (2012)
4. Biedermann, S., Mink, M., Katzenbeisser, S.: Fast dynamic extracted honeypots in cloud computing. In: CCSW'12, pp. 13–18. ACM, Raleigh (2012)
5. Wang, P., Lei, W., Cunningham, R., Zou, C.C.: Honeypot detection in advanced botnet attacks. Int. J. Inf. Comput. Secur. **4**, 30–51 (2010). Inderscience Publishers, Geneva
6. Portokalidis, G., Bos, H.: SweetBait: zero-hour worm detection and containment using low- and high-interaction. Comput. Netw.: Int. J. Comput. Telecommun. Netw. **51**, 1256–1274 (2010). ScienceDirect, Amsterdam
7. Valli, C.: Honeypot technologies and their applicability as a strategic internal countermeasure. Int. J. Inf. Comput. Secur. **1**, 430–436 (2007). Inderscience Publishers, Geneva
8. Tiwari, R., Jain, A.: Improving network security and design using honeypots. In: CUBE'12, pp. 847–852. ACM, Pune (2012)
9. Kim, H.-G., Kim, D.-J., Cho, S.-J., Park, M., Park, M.: An efficient visitation algorithm to improve the detection speed of high-interaction client honeypots. In: RACS'11, pp. 266–271. ACM, Miami (2011)
10. Niemi, O.-P., Levomäki, A., Manner, J.: Dismantling intrusion prevention systems. In: SIGCOMM'12, pp. 285–286. ACM, New York (2012)

A Modified Single-Channel Blind Separation Method Using EMD and ICA

Jiao Wang[1(✉)], Yulin Liu[2], Zhichao Chao[1], and Wei He[1]

[1] Chongqing Communication College, Chongqing 400035, China
{wangjiao20071991, superchao1982}@163.com,
cqcchw@gmail.com
[2] China Electronic System Engineering Corporation,
Shenyang 110005 Liaoning, China
spliuyl@uestc.edu.cn

Abstract. In view of the traditional blind source separation methods cannot be applied to separate the mixed signal in single-channel communication, a modified single-channel signals blind separation method using Empirical Mode Decomposition (EMD) and Independent Component Analysis (ICA) is proposed in this paper. In our method, EMD is employed to decompose the preprocessed received signal into some non-overlapping Intrinsic Mode Functions (IMF). In order to construct the input matrix of ICA, optimum IMFs are selected based on their energy in time domain. Finally, ICA is applied to extract and recover the source signal from the received signal. Simulation results show that our method has the same performance with the exiting method, while the system running time has been greatly shortened.

Keywords: Single-channel · Blind source separation · EMD · ICA

1 Introduction

With the electromagnetic environment becoming more complex and the communication channel getting worse and worse, conventional communication system faces huge challenge. Therefore, it is significance to research new technology and its implementation method to ensure the quality of communication. Blind Source Separation (BSS) theory, which has been emerging as an efficient tool to isolate the independent components in the signals, provides a new train of thought to solve this problem. It does not need any prior knowledge about each source, only utilizes the general information that all the sources are independent with each other [1].

In most of the suggested solution for blind source separation, when the number of received is no less than the number of signal sources, most algorithm show a good convergence [2–4]. However, in the field of communication signal processing, it has always referred to as a single-channel signal processing technique, where the traditional BSS algorithm cannot used directly in single-channel system. To overcome the problem, researchers have developed many processing methods. An oversampling with tapped delay-lines and Independent Component Analysis (ICA) algorithm is proposed in [5], this method achieves separation of spectrally overlapping MPSK

Y. Yuan et al. (Eds.): ISCTCS 2013, CCIS 426, pp. 78–85, 2014.
DOI: 10.1007/978-3-662-43908-1_10, © Springer-Verlag Berlin Heidelberg 2014

signals, but it suit for the separation with known pulse shapes. Singular Spectrum Analysis (SSA) and BSS method are used jointly in [6], which can solve the single-channel signals separation in electronic reconnaissance. However, this method may fail to separate the mixed signal when the frequency spectrums of source signals are overlapping. A wavelet decomposition method is proposed in [7] to decompose the single-channel signal into different spectral modes. Bogdan Mijovic introduced Empirical Mode Decomposition (EMD) to decompose a single-channel signal into multiple components in Electroencephalogram (EEG) signal processing [8]. Recently, research has been conducted on the application and improvement of EMD for mechanical fault diagnosis and condition monitoring and biomedical signal processing [9, 10]. However, it should be point out that the EMD decomposition consumption time is too long.

In this paper, a modified single-channel blind separation method using EMD and ICA is proposed. The preprocessed signal is decomposed by EMD into Intrinsic Mode Functions (IMF) components. The optimum IMF components which have more than 98 % of the total energy are selected as the input of ICA. The ICA algorithm is then employed to separate the signal components and recover the source signal. Our method switches the single-channel BSS problem into multiple components BSS problem, and greatly reduces the computational time for signal separation.

The paper is organized as follows. In Sect. 2, we introduce the theoretical background of EMD process and ICA algorithm. Next, in Sect. 3, present the proposed our method for a single-channel signal processing. We will show the performance of the proposed method in simulation results in Sect. 4. Conclusions and summarized of the paper is given in Sect. 5.

2   Theoretical Background

2.1   Empirical Mode Decomposition

EMD is a technique to specifically deal with nonstationary and nonlinear signals. EMD decompose signal into a set of IMFs, with each IMF being independent of others [11]. According to the definition of IMF, two assumption should be satisfied: (1) In the whole data sequence, the number of extrema value points and zero crossings may differ by no more than one at most; (2) the local mean calculate by the local maxima and minima is zero. The advantage of EMD is that it derived from the signal to be analyzed itself, without prior knowledge about the signal.

Assume received signal $x(t)$, the procedure for EMD decomposition is shown as follow:

Step1: Find the local maxima and minima of the signal $x(t)$.

Step2: Then the upper envelope and lower envelope are constructed from the maxima and minima, through cubic curve fitting.

Step3: Calculate the mean values $m(t)$ of the upper and lower envelopes. And a new time series $h_1(t)$ can be designated as follows:

$$h_1(t) = x(t) - m_1(t) \qquad (1)$$

Step4: Check whether $h_1(t)$ is satisfied the consumption of IMF. If $h_1(t)$ is not satisfied, repeat the step on (2), (3) until the $h_1(t)$ satisfied the consumption, and then set $c_1(t) = h_1(t)$.

Step5: Separate $c_1(t)$ from $x(t)$ to obtain the residual $r_1(t)$ defined as:

$$r_1(t) = x(t) - c_1(t) \tag{2}$$

Step6: Treat $r_1(t)$ as the original signal and repeat step (1)–(5) until the residual $r_N(t)$ is a monotonic function which no more IMF can be obtained. The EMD decomposition is completed, and then the signal $x(t)$ can be decomposed as follows:

$$x(t) = \sum_{k=1}^{N} c_k(t) + r_N(t) \tag{3}$$

2.2   Independent Component Analysis

Without loss generality, assuming that N sources $s_1(t)$, $s_2(t)$..., $s_N(t)$ are independent with each other and observations $x_1(t)$, $x_2(t)$,..., $x_N(t)$ are obtained by N sensors where each sensor receives a different mixture of source signals. The mixed mode can be expressed as

$$\begin{cases} x_1(t) = a_{11}s_1(t) + a_{12}s_2(t) + \cdots + a_{1N}s_N(t) \\ x_2(t) = a_{21}s_1(t) + a_{22}s_2(t) + \cdots + a_{2N}s_N(t) \\ \vdots \\ x_N(t) = a_{N1}s_1(t) + a_{N2}s_2(t) + \cdots + a_{NN}s_N(t) \end{cases} \tag{4}$$

Equation (4) can be written as:

$$\mathbf{x}(t) = \mathbf{A}\mathbf{s}(t) = \begin{bmatrix} a_{11} & a_{12} & \cdots & a_{1N} \\ a_{21} & a_{22} & \cdots & a_{2N} \\ \vdots & \vdots & \ddots & \vdots \\ a_{N1} & a_{N2} & \cdots & a_{NN} \end{bmatrix} \mathbf{s}(t) \tag{5}$$

where $\mathbf{A}$ and $\mathbf{s}$ are unknown. The task of ICA is estimates the matrix $\mathbf{A}$ and its inverse $\mathbf{w}$, called demixing matrix, to obtain the independent components:

$$y(t) = \mathbf{w}^T \mathbf{x}(t) = \mathbf{w}^T \mathbf{A}\mathbf{s}(t) = \hat{\mathbf{s}}(t) \tag{6}$$

where $\mathbf{w} = \mathbf{A}^{-1}$ and $\mathbf{Y}$ can be considered as estimation of $\mathbf{s}$. However, there is no direct way to compute the demixing matrix because the prior information about the mixing matrix is unknown. The Central Limit Theorem indicates that the distribution of a sum of independent random variable tends to a Gaussian distribution. Thus, a sum of two independent random variables is closer to the Gaussian distribution than a sum of any two random variables. Measuring Non-Gaussianity is used to obtain the independent components. The famous FastICA algorithm [12] is employed in this paper to separate the mixed signals.

3 The Proposed Method

In the traditional ICA algorithm, the number of sensors must be more than the number of the source signals. When there is only one antenna used in communication system, ICA algorithm cannot use directly for source separation in single-channel communication. Therefore, it is necessary to construct the input matrix if one antenna is used to capture the communication signal.

A modified method for single-channel communication blind separation using EMD and ICA is proposed in this paper. Generally speaking, the method proposed in this paper is composed of two steps: EMD decomposition and ICA recovery. EMD is employed to form the input matrix in this paper. And then ICA algorithm is applied to reconstruct the source signal. The idea of this method is shown in Fig. 1:

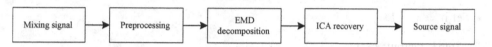

Fig. 1. Block diagram of single-channel blind separation with EMD and ICA

3.1 EMD Decomposition and the Optimum IMFs Selection

EMD is employed to decompose a single complicated series in the time domain into a finite set of IMFs.

The received signal through preprocessing is decomposed by EMD to obtain a set of IMFs. However, the whole set of IMFs as the input matrix of ICA, the enormous amount of calculation is reduces the processing speed of the system. This paper proposed a method to extract the optimum IMFs using energy-based shown in Fig. 2. The detail of selection is described as follow:

Calculating the energy contains all the IMFs of signal decomposed by EMD is given as:

$$E_x = \sum_{i=1}^{N} E_{c_i(t)} \tag{7}$$

where N is the number of all the IMFs, $E_{c_i(t)}$ denotes the energy of the i-th IMF which is calculated as:

$$E_{c_i(t)} = \sum_{k=1}^{L} |c_i(k)|^2 \tag{8}$$

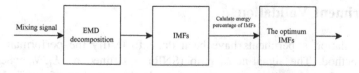

Fig. 2. Block of EMD decomposition and the optimum IMFs selection

where L is the number of the data samples of the i-th IMF. Finally, the energy percentage of the i-th IMF is calculated as:

$$per_i = \frac{E_{c_i(t)}}{E_x} \tag{9}$$

Then we can perform the IMF component selection follow these steps:
Step1: Initialization: n=1, $\xi = 98\ \%$
Step2: Repeat until convergence $(D_n > \xi)$:

- Calculate sum of the first n IMF component signal energy percentage D_n:

$$D_n = \sum_{j=1}^{n} Per_j \tag{10}$$

- Set $n = n + 1$.

Step3: Output: $c_i(t)$ (i = 1, 2,..., n).
Through selecting the optimum IMFs, the size of input matrix can greatly reduce, as well as having the same performance of the whole IMFs as the input.

3.2 ICA Recovery

The task of ICA is to recover the source signal. After EMD, the optimum IMFs have been chosen to construct the input matrix of ICA. First, the ICA algorithm provides us with mixing **M** and demixing matrices **w**, and a matrix of ICs as an output. Then select the interesting signal using prior information, the signal is reconstructed first by multiplying it with the mixing matrix **M** to derive a new IMF set. Finally, sum all the newly derived IMFs to reconstruct the source signal. The block of the source recovery with ICA is shown in Fig. 3.

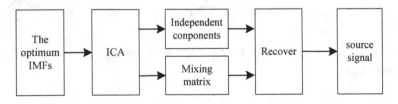

Fig. 3. Block of the source recovery with ICA

4 Experiment Validation

Several simulation experiments have been done to testify the performance of the proposed method. The signal-noise ratio (SNR) is defined by E_b/N_0 where E_b is the variance of communication signal and N_0 is the variance of noise. Here, the performance of the separation is measured by a correlation coefficient between the time series $x(k)$, $k = 1, 2,..., n$, and $y(k)$, $k = 1, 2,..., n$ which is defined as:

$$\rho(x, y) = \left| \sum_{k=1}^{n} x(k)y(k) \middle/ \sqrt{\sum_{k=1}^{n} x^2(k) \sum_{k=1}^{n} y^2(k)} \right| \tag{11}$$

Assume symbol sequence of PSK signal is 1000 bit/s, center frequency is 100 kHz, interference signal is the spot jamming, whose center frequency is 99.5 kHz. When the SNR $= 12$ dB, the time-domain plots of the received signal and the IMFs signals of EMD decomposed are shown in Fig. 4.

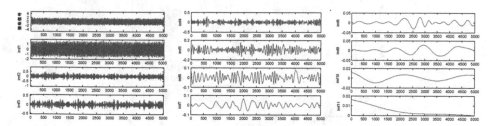

Fig. 4. Received signal and the IMFs signals

Based on the energy percentage of IMFs calculated using (9), the energy percentage of each IMFs are shown in Fig. 5.

As shown in Fig. 5, the energy percentage of c_1 is the 67.2 % which the highest in the whole signal. And the energy percentage of c_2, c_3, c_4 are 20.1 %, 6.6 % and 2.7 %. According to the energy-based, c_1, c_2, c_3 and c_4 are the optimal components which are chosen as the input of ICA. Through the ICA analysis, the source signal can be observed in the IC components in Fig. 6.

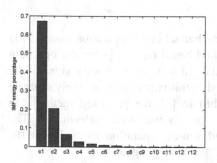
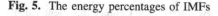
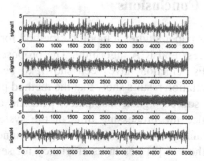

Fig. 5. The energy percentages of IMFs   **Fig. 6.** The recover signal obtain by ICA

Compared with the proposed method in [8], the performance of separation is correlation coefficient and running time of system with 50 times Monte Carlo experiments. The correlation coefficient between separation signal and source signal with variable SNR is shown in Fig. 7. Set the sampling points are 10000. The running time of system is shown in Table 1.

From the figure, conclusions can be given that they have the same performance of separation mixing signal, but the consuming time of the proposed method in this paper is greatly less than the method in [8]. Therefore, the proposed method is superior than the method in [8] for single-channel signal separation.

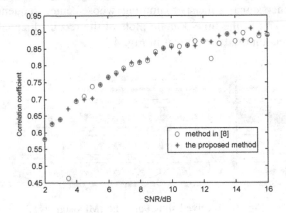

Fig. 7. Correlation coefficient between separation signal and source signal

Table 1. Running time of system (s)

	Proposed method	Method in [8]
The average elapsed time	1.85	10.7

5 Conclusions

This paper studies a modified method for single-channel blind separation using EMD process and ICA algorithm. The proposed method based on energy for the optimum IMFs selection have been shown to be effective in separating mixing signal. The simulation results show that the method proposed in this paper can effectively separate the source signal. Compared with the algorithm in [8], the proposed method can reduce the processing time of the system, as well as the same performance. The advantage of the modified single-channel blind source separation method over the method in [8] lies in its efficiency for separate the mixing signal.

Acknowledgment. This research is funded by the Program for New Century Excellent Talents in University (No. NCET-11-0873), the Program for Innovative Research Team in University of Chongqing (No. KJTD201343), the Key Project of Chongqing Natural Science Foundation (CSTC2011BA2016) and the Program for Fundamental and Advanced Research of Chongqing (No. cstc2013jcyjA40045).

References

1. Hyvarinen, A., Karhunen, J., Oja, E.: Independent Component Analysis. Wiley, Chichester (2001)
2. Huang, Z.C., Yang, X.N., Zhang, X.D.: Communication reconnaissance complex signal separation based on independent component analysis. JT sing hua Univ. (Sci. & Tech.) 50(1), 86–91 (2010)
3. Zhang, Z.Y., Cao, Q.Q., Chen, W.Z.: Blind separation and parameter estimation of multiple frequency-hopping signals. J. Zhejiang Univ. (Eng. Sci.) 39(4), 455–470 (2005)
4. Yu, M., Wang, Y.H., Wang, G.F.: BSS based anti-jamming method for frequency hopping communication against partial-band noise jamming. Syst. Eng. Electron. 35(5), 1080–1084 (2013)
5. Liu, K., Li, H., Dai, X. et al.: Single channel blind separation of co-frequency MPSK signals. In: Proceeding of International Conference on Communication, Internet and Information Technology, November 2006, pp. 42–46 (2006)
6. Yu, N.Y., Ma, H.G., Jiang, Q.B., et al.: SSA and BSS separation algorithm for single-channel signals. Chin. Space Sci. Technol. 33(1), 61–67 (2013)
7. Shao, H., Shi, X.H., Li, L.: Power signal separation in milling process based on wavelet transform and independent component analysis. Int. J. Mach. Tools Manuf. 51(9), 701–710 (2011)
8. Mijovic, B., De vos, M., Gligorijevic, I., et al.: Source separation from single-channel recording by combining empirical-mode decomposition and independent component analysis. IEEE Trans. Biomed. Eng. 57(9), 2188–2196 (2010)
9. Miao, Q., Wang, D., Pecht, M.: Rolling element bearing fault feature extraction using EMD based independent component analysis. In: International Prognostics and Health Management Conference, Denver, CO, pp. 21–23 (2011)
10. Blanco-Velasco, M., Weng, B., Barner, K.E.: ECG signal denoising and baseline wander correction based on the empirical mode decomposition. Comput. Biol. Med. 38, 1–13 (2008)
11. Huang, N.E., Shen, Z., Long, S.R., et al.: The empirical mode decomposition and hilbert spectrum for nonlinear and nonstationary time series analysis. Proc. Roy. Lond. A 454, 903–995 (1998)
12. Hyvarinen, A., Oja, E.: A fast fixed-point algorithm for independent component analysis. Neural Comput. 9(7), 1–5 (1997)

Flexible Mechanism Research of Workflow System Based on SOA

Shaopeng Wang[1(✉)], Yuan Zhang[2(✉)], and Yan Peng[2(✉)]

[1] College of Information Engineering, Capital Normal University,
Beijing, China
wsp000000@163.com
[2] School of management, Capital Normal University, Beijing, China
yuaner.cn@gmail.com, pengyanpy@163.com

Abstract. Flexible mechanism is an important orientation of workflow study. This paper, in the design process of a workflow system based on SOA, studies the flexible mechanism of workflow system from such aspects as system expansion, workflow modeling and workflow running. It proposes various methods based on the three divisions of service granularity, roles and content routing to enhance the flexibility expansion of the system. Meanwhile, it adopts a modeling scheme of flexible workflow based on ECA rules and Web Service and develops a graphical workflow modeling tool based on ECA rules, which enhance not only the flexibility of workflow modeling but also that of workflow running. Through the practical development of the system, the validity of the flexible implementation mechanism proposed in this paper is verified. By combining several flexible implementation mechanisms and applying them in the practical system development, this research lays a good foundation for further studies on the flexibility of workflow system, such as correction examination of workflow modeling and exception handling of workflow running.

Keywords: Workflow · Flexible mechanism · ECA rule · Web service

1 Introduction

With the development of enterprise information technology, workflow management systems (or WFMS) will be ever more important. Workflow management systems are required to provide flexible ways of managing workflows [1]. Many organizations make use of workflow management systems for automating their business processes. Business processes frequently require changes over time. For example, a change in some business practice could require making changes not only to a business process definition, but also to instances of the corresponding schema currently in execution. It is therefore widely recognized that a workflow management system should provide flexible ways of managing workflows [2].

In this paper, the flexible problem of workflow system is described. A flexible mechanism is proposed by designing and completing a workflow system based on SOA. It makes the workflow system more flexible.

Y. Yuan et al. (Eds.): ISCTCS 2013, CCIS 426, pp. 86–92, 2014.
DOI: 10.1007/978-3-662-43908-1_11, © Springer-Verlag Berlin Heidelberg 2014

2 SOA Technology and Flexible Knowledge

2.1 SOA Technology

SOA (Service Oriented Architecture) is a service-oriented architecture [3]. SOA is a service-oriented enterprise systems architecture. It has the properties of loose coupling, high cohesion and open [4]. The service, service registration and agent, service requester, service provider and the related protocol and operation, form the basis of the structure of SOA [5]. The key technologies of SOA include Web Service, XML and so on.

2.2 Workflow System Flexibility

Flexibility refers to the system has the ability to fast response to the changes in the environment, conditions and tasks. The flexibility of workflow refers to it can change the execution paths in the case of not interrupt execution and has the ability to adapt [6].

3 Analysis and Design of Flexible Extension of System

3.1 Flexible Design Based on Service Encapsulation

Compared with the traditional workflow system, workflow system based on SOA encapsulates various functions of the system in the service. It improves the flexibility of system design and implementation.

In the process of service design, the service coupling and the service granularity choice are two fundamental problems. Business service granularity is defined as the number of basic activities included [7]. The relationship between service granularity and system flexibility is shown in Fig. 1.

At present, there is not a specific technical standard to confirm service granularity size. This design uses a service classification method to determine the service granularity. Services are divided into three types: atomic service, synthesis service and composite service.

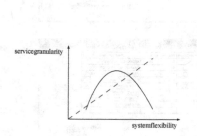

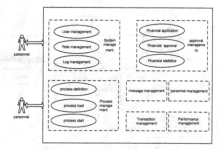

Fig. 1. The relationship between service granularity and system flexibility

Fig. 2. Divide function modules of the financial approval system

Taking the financial approval system in financial integration project for example, this paper realizes the confirmation of service granularity. First of all, the system modules are divided. It is shown in Fig. 2.

Through the design of financial approval service, it illustrates the relationship between the basic service, synthesis service and composite service. It is shown in Fig. 3.

3.2   Flexible Design Based on Roles

By introducing the concept of the role, there is a middle layer between users and system function module. It solves the problem of user status changes and reduces the coupling between user and business activities. Relationships among users, roles and system permissions are shown in Fig. 4.

Taking the financial approval system for example, it illustrates the practical application of flexible design based on role. Relationships among the user, role and permission are shown in Fig. 5.

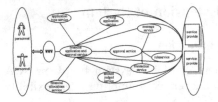

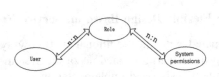

Fig. 3. Designs of financial application and   **Fig. 4.** The relationship between users, roles approval service   and permission system

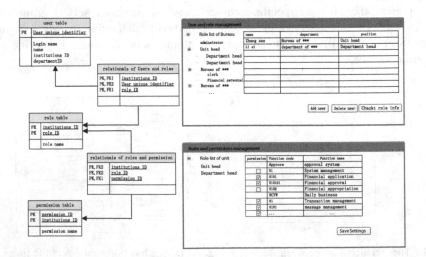

Fig. 5. Design of relationships among the system user, role and permission

3.3   Flexible Design Based on Content-Based Routing

Content-based routing is not using a specific address, but using the content of the message itself to locate and route messages. Content-based routing is implemented by the routing module and service module. Service is the ultimate consumer of the message. The mapping information between the message type and service can make the routing module guide the flow of information. Routing module checks received message content and forwards the message to the different place according to certain rules.

Content-based routing has a routing table. The routing table is used for the address mapping. In the initial state, service address of the routing table is empty. It is shown in Fig. 6.

Routing table updates according to the services provided by the service provider. When increasing service or deleting service, the routing table also updates. When the routing table updates, the service address will have a corresponding change. It is shown in Fig. 7.

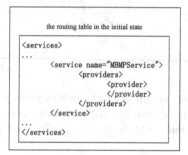

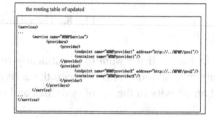

Fig. 6. The routing table in the initial state   **Fig. 7.** The routing table update

4   Design and Implementation of Flexible Workflow Modeling

Workflow model established by WFMC has some disadvantages. For example, it does not support the process of dynamic generation and intelligent flow. To solve these problems, workflow model based on ECA rules is put forward. Workflow model based on ECA rules realizes workflow task automatic routing by implementation of event trigger rules [8]. Workflow model based on ECA rules has some advantages. For instance, it provides a unified description mechanism of the component behavior for system and ensures the correct execution of workflow through the strict event semantics. It also enhances the flexibility of the system [9, 10]. However, workflow model based on ECA rules also has some shortcomings. In order to overcome these shortcomings, this paper presents a flexible workflow model based on ECA rules and Web Service. This model is based on SOA architecture.

4.1   Flexible Support of Workflow Running

Workflow model based on ECA rules and Web Service supports the flexibility of workflow running and has the ability to dynamically modify the workflow. Dynamic modification embodies in the following aspects: adding active nodes, deleting active nodes and changing the routing information of nodes. This paper uses the financial approval process of a government department to reflect the model support workflow running flexible. The financial approval process is shown in Fig. 8.

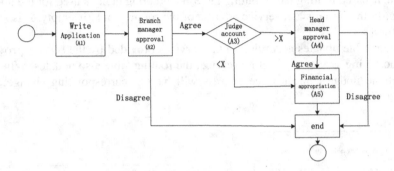

Fig. 8. The financial approval process

In Fig. 8, if we want to dynamically modify business processes, such as joining a temporary activity (A6) between the activity (A1) and activity (A2), we only need to add an activity in the set of activities and modify some rules in the ECA rules library.

4.2   Realization of Graphical Workflow Modeling Tool

Flexible workflow modeling tool is an important part of the workflow system. The objective of graphical modeling tool is to provide a business process design environment which is easy to operate and meets process standards. The graphical modeling tool can reduce the communication between developers and users, improve the design speed of business processes and increase the flexibility of workflow modeling. The system based on the workflow model proposed by this paper develops a graphical workflow modeling tool. It is shown in Fig. 9.

During the design and development process, because most users are unfamiliar with the workflow modeling, complex activities are encapsulated as a Web Service. Complex business logic is not reflected in the graphical process. Business logic is represented by ECA rules. The graphical modeling tool makes ordinary users can use the modeling tool through simple dragging and setting attribute to complete the workflow modeling.

This system through the Web Service technology realizes the communication among the workflow modeling tool, the database and the workflow. When the business process ready to perform, the system through the workflow model defined by XML files obtains the corresponding data from the database to build workflow. The

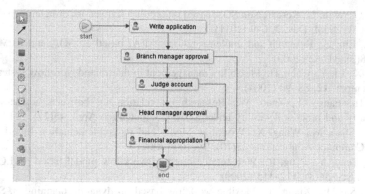

Fig. 9. Flexible workflow modeling tool

workflow instance executes by ECA rules. During the execution of workflow, it calls the corresponding Web Service to execute according to the process definition. This implementation reduces the coupling of each part and increases the flexibility of workflow modeling.

5   Conclusion

The extensive use of workflow technology causes users more attention to the flexibility of the workflow system. Through the design and realization of a workflow system based on SOA, this paper studies the flexible mechanism of the workflow system. The system uses various methods based on service granularity divisions, roles and content routing to increase the flexibility expansion of the system. It also uses the flexible workflow model based on ECA rules and Web Service to enhance the flexibility of workflow modeling and workflow running. Implementation of system functionality verifies flexible mechanisms proposed in this paper. It lays a good foundation for further studies on the flexibility of workflow system, such as correction examination of workflow modeling and exception handling of workflow running.

Acknowledgements. Thanks for the support of Key Laboratory of Trustworthy Distributed Computing and Service (BUPT), Ministry of Education.

References

1. Halliday, J.J., Shivastava, S.K., Wheater, S.M.: Flexible workflow management in the openflow system. In: Proceedings of 4th International Enterprise Distributed Object Computing Conference (EDOC 2001), 4–7 September 2001, Seattle, Washington, pp. 82–92. IEEE Computer Society (2001)
2. Wainer, J., de Lima Bezerra, F., Barthelmess, P.: Tucupi: a flexible workflow system based on overridable constraints. In: ACM SAC'04, pp. 498–502 (2004)
3. IBM: Patterns: service-oriented architecture and web services. IBM RedBooks (2004)

4. Zhang, Q., Wan, L.: Research on SOA-based integration framework of heterogeneous data. Comput. Technol. Dev. **3**, 6–9 (2011)
5. Liu, X., Liu, Z.: Research and implementation of EAI based on SOA and BPM. Softw. Guide **8**(3), 31–32 (2009)
6. Zhang, X., Li, Y., Chen, H.: Flexibility management in distributed workflow system. Appl. Res. Comput. **12**, 88–90 (2004)
7. Chen, H., Fang, D., Zhao, W.: Research on relationship between business service granularity and process flexibility under SOA. Comput. Eng. Appl. **45**(27), 7–10 (2009)
8. Liu, H., Shao, M., Wang, X.: Workflow Model and Its Implementation Based on ECA Rules. Computer Applications **22**(10), 98–100 (2002)
9. He, C., Teng, Y., Peng, R.: Web service oriented workflow model based on ECA rules. Comput. Sci. **36**(8), 112–115 (2009)
10. Shi, Y., Sun, R., Xiang, Y.: Flexible workflow based on dynamic planning. J. Southeast Univ. (Nat. Sci. Ed.) **40**(z2), 258–262 (2010)

Effective Rate Control Algorithm for H.264 Based on Scene Change Detection

Yaoyao Guo[1,2(✉)], Songlin Sun[1,2], Xiaojun Jing[1,2], Hai Huang[1,2],
Yueming Lu[1,2], and Na Chen[1,2]

[1] School of Information and Communication Engineering,
Beijing University of Posts and Telecommunications, Beijing, China
[2] Key Laboratory of Trustworthy Distributed Computing and Service (BUPT),
Ministry of Education, Beijing University of Posts and Telecommunications,
Beijing, China
{guoyaoyao1990,slsun,jxiaojun,
huanghai,ymlu,chn}@bupt.edu.cn

Abstract. The standard rate control algorithm works with all the levels such as the GOP, frame, and unit levels. However, it cannot allocate bits reasonably under the condition of scene change. In this paper, an efficient rate control algorithm to detect scene change and reallocate the channel target bits of H.264 is proposed. The proposed method can detect scene change effectively and change the length of GOP adaptively, so the target bits can be allocated more reasonably than standard rate control algorithm.

Keywords: Rate control · Scene change · H.264 · Adaptively GOP · JVT-G012

1 Introduction

As the compressed video should be transmitted through a limited bandwidth, the rate control is one of crucial technical modules in high quality services, especially for the real time application. Although the rate control algorithm is not part of the video coding standards, a variety of video coding standards recommend the appropriate rate control algorithm as its important role, such as the MPEG-2's TM5 [1], H.263's TMN8 [2], MPEG-4's VM8 [3] etc. In order to meet the bit-rate video transmission applications requirements, many other rate control algorithms are developed on the basis of the above algorithm. Based on the Quadratic R-Q model [4], JVT-G012 [5] proposed a rate control algorithm for H.264/AVC and provided a novel linear model to predict the MAD and that method solved the "chicken-egg" dilemma. This proposal has become the basis for H.264 Rate Control.

Rate control can be categorized into GOP level, frame level and basic unit level in terms of processing unit size. Rate control can be divided into two parts. On one hand, limited bits should be allocated quote to each processing unit, including GOP, frame and coding unit (CU). On the other hand, the quantization parameter (QP) should be calculated to ensure that the output bit rate match the target bit rate well.

Y. Yuan et al. (Eds.): ISCTCS 2013, CCIS 426, pp. 93–99, 2014.
DOI: 10.1007/978-3-662-43908-1_12, © Springer-Verlag Berlin Heidelberg 2014

However, traditional rate control algorithms such as JVT-G012 [5], JVT-H017 [6] and JVT-W042 [7] only consider the complexity of the image itself, and neglect the correlation between each frame in the same GOP when they allocate the resources to each frame in the group of pictures (GOP). For example, when the video sequence has frequently scene change, one frame which contains scene change may have no correlation with the reference frame. If scene change sequences are still processed by the traditional rate control method, which will lead to the waste of coding source and cut down the quality of coding. This paper proposes a method that can detect scene change and revise the length of GOP adaptively in the rate control algorithm. It can save the resources of coding and improve the quality of whole sequence coding effectively.

The rest of the paper is organized as follows. Section 2 introduces the influence of scene change in rate control. Adaptive changing length of GOP is described in Sect. 3. Section 4 presents the experimental results. Finally, we conclude the paper in Sect. 5.

2   The Influence of Scene Change in Rate Control

The bits produced by frame of I, P and B are not the same. In order to improve the channel utilization, a buffer zone is added between the encoder and the channel. However the buffer size and the requirements of communication delay constitute a new contradiction. The purpose of rate control is to resolve this problem.

For an efficient rate control algorithm, one important issue is that bits should be allocated reasonably so that the encoder can obtain the best coding quality. Meanwhile, that situation should be on the condition that bandwidth resources should be made full use of and buffer does not overflow. When scene change occurs in the video sequence, the encoding quality will be affected and the influence depends on the position of scene change frame in the GOP.

Scene change that occurs in I-frame does not have any effect on video coding as I-frame uses intra coding mode. Meanwhile, B-frame uses bidirectional prediction. If one of the two reference frames is in the same scene with it, the prediction precision still can be guaranteed and the quality of video will not be affected very much.

Unlike I and B frame, when scene change occurs in the P-frame, the impact on the current GOP coding quality will be much worse. Because the reference frame is not in the same scene with the current P-frame, inter-prediction coding will be completely ineffective. As a result, Macro-block must go through the RDO (Rate Distortion optimization) mode selection before taking the intra frame coding. Moreover, the optimization process will cost a lot of time. As the majority of macro blocks use intra coding mode, they take up a lot of resources. As a result, the quality of subsequent frames will decline due to the lack of bits.

3   Rate Control Algorithm Based on Scene Change

3.1   Scene Change Detection Algorithm

The principle of scene change detection is as follows: find a variable which represents the correlation between frames and compare it with the threshold value [8]. If it is greater than the threshold, this means scene change has taken place and bits should be reallocated. The traditional way predicting scene change is gray detection. This algorithm is simple but very effective. The pixel's gray value of current frame is compared with the value which is located in the same position in the reconstructed frame. Then the average difference is calculated as follows.

$$\text{Diff} = \frac{1}{W \times H} \sum_{i=0}^{W-1} \sum_{j=0}^{H-1} \left| f_n(i,j) - f'_n(i,j) \right| \tag{1}$$

where $f_n(i,j)$ denotes the gray value of pixel (i, j) in n-th frame. $f'_n(i,j)$ denotes the gray value of pixel (i, j) in n-th reconstructed frame. W and H are the width and height of the frame, respectively. Diff is the average difference. Scene change is detected by calculating the value of Diff through formula (2).

$$\text{Diff} > T_{sc} \tag{2}$$

where T_{sc} is threshold value, which decides the accuracy of scene change detection. According to the experience, it is set to a fixed value. However, According to the characteristics of different video sequences, scene change is usually divided into three types, namely abrupt, melting and fading [9, 10]. It doesn't work on melting and fading if threshold is set to a fixed value. Then a flag is used to indicate the type of scene change, it is calculated by the following formula:

$$flag = \begin{cases} 1 & \text{Diff} < 10 \\ 2 & 10 \leq \text{Diff} \leq 40 \\ 3 & \text{Diff} > 40 \end{cases} \tag{3}$$

where Diff is average difference of gray. When the value of Diff is less than 10, we consider that a interrupt scene change take place. The value of Diff is between 10 and 40 means that a melting or fading scene change take place. Others means that the video sequence is normal.

Figure 1 is the output which uses the gray detection to monitor the sequence. Video Sequence is composed of five different sequences, which are akiyo, bus, foreman, mother_daughter and news. The figure shows that the value of Diff will increase obviously when the scene change takes place.

3.2   Adaptive Reorganization of GOP

When scene change takes place and the scene change frame is P-frame coincidentally, the space correlation is more important than the time correlation. The scene change frame is set as I-frame because the majority of the Macro-blocks in P-frame will use intra coding after RDO. And a lot of coding time is saved after taking this measure. The number of I-frame in the sequence must be kept at the same level so as to avoid consuming more bits. The algorithm of paper is shown as follows.

(1)   If an interrupt scene change takes place, we terminate current GOP and set the type of scene change frame as I-frame [11]. The coming GOP will be

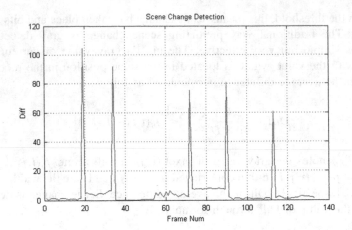

Fig. 1. Scene change detection

compensated by the remaining bits. The actual length of GOP is L_a and the target length of GOP is L_t. When the GOP is coded properly, it means that $L_a = L_t$. The other condition is that the GOP is terminated in the situation of interrupt scene change (flag = 1) which will lead to $L_a < L_t$. The actual bits that current GOP consumes are R_a:

$$R_a = R_p - B \times \frac{(L_t - L_a)}{F} \tag{4}$$

where B is the bandwidth, F is the frame rate. R_p is the allocated bit at the beginning of this GOP. The remaining bits will be allocated to the subsequent two GOPs. The target length of subsequent GOP is L_{tmp}.

$$L_{tmp} = L_t - L_a \tag{5}$$

$$L_t = \begin{cases} L + L_{tmp}/2 + L_{tmp}\%2 & \textit{the first GOP after scene change} \\ L + L_{tmp}/2 & \textit{the sec GOP after scene change} \\ L & \text{else} \end{cases} \tag{6}$$

where L is the default length which is set at the beginning. After the length of next GOP is determinated, the bits reallocated are as follows:

$$R_a = R_p + B \times \frac{L_t}{F} \tag{7}$$

After reconstructing GOP, the remaining bits and frames are reallocated to the next two GOPs. Meanwhile, the number of I-frame is not increased. So the algorithm proposed in this paper has good adaptability for frequent scene change sequence.

(2) If a melting or fading scene change is on the way, the current GOP is given extra bits which are determined by the formula as follows:

$$R_a = R_a + R_{left}/(2 * F_{left}) \tag{8}$$

where R_a is the bits that current GOP remains. R_{left} is the remaining bits of the whole sequence. Fleft is the number of remaining frames.

4 Experiment

In order to validate the algorithm proposed in this paper, JM11.0 is used as simulation platform. The proposed algorithm is compared with JVT-G012 at coding bit rate and coding quality. Coding bit rate is measured by error between target coding bits and actual coding bits. Coding quality is measured by PSNR. The configure file used in the experiments is encoder_baseline.cfg. Table 1 presents the main coding parameter.

Table 1. JM configuration

Coding parameter	Set value	Meaning
IntraPeriod	10	Period of I-frame
InitialQP	32	Initial QP
RDOptimization	1	RDOQ
RateControlEnable	1	Enable rate control
Bitrate	9600000	Bitrate (bps)

Table 2. Bit rate comparison

Sequence	Target bit rate (kbps)	Actual bits		ΔIERRORI	
		JVT-G012	Proposal	JVT-G012	Proposal
1	96	89.81	97.57	6.19	1.57
	128	119.67	129.70	8.33	1.7
	196	183.12	197.53	12.88	1.53
2	96	90.16	96.99	5.84	0.99
	128	120.08	128.68	7.92	0.68
	196	183.68	195.65	12.32	0.35
3	96	94.05	96.35	1.95	0.35
	128	123.03	130.33	4.97	2.33
	196	186.69	200.64	9.31	4.64

Experimental sequences are composed by standard testing sequence. The target bitrate is set as 96 kbps, 128 kbps, 192 kbps, respectively. The result of bit rate comparison and PSNR performance comparison are shown in Tables 2 and 3.

From Table 2 we can find that the proposed algorithm has better performance in controlling the accuracy of produced bits than the traditional method.

Table 3. PSNR performance comparison

Sequence number	Target bit rate (kbps)	Average PSNR		Increase
		JVT-G012	Proposal	
1	96	36.74	38.87	2.13
	128	38.42	39.67	1.25
	196	41.47	41.96	0.49
2	96	39.42	39.85	0.43
	128	40.97	41.32	0.35
	196	43.15	43.41	0.26
3	96	35.71	36.95	1.24
	128	37.86	38.2	0.34
	196	40.44	40.77	0.33

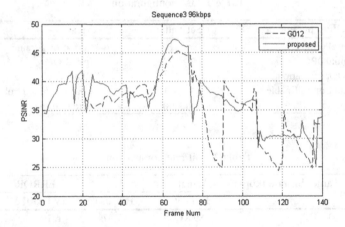

Fig. 2. PSNR comparison of sequence "3"

Table 3 shows that the PSNR performance comparison under different bandwidths. We can find that our algorithm has better PSNR under restricted bandwidth. Our algorithm acquires 0.76 dB higher than JVT-G012 in average PSNR increase.

Meanwhile, Fig. 2 give the result of comparison that sequence 3 is processed by proposed algorithm and JVT-G012, respectively. It shows that proposed algorithm has a better PSNR compared to G012 when scene change sequences are processed.

5   Conclusion

To solve the problems of traditional algorithm processing scene change sequences, this paper uses traditional gray detection to detect scene change frame and proposes a method to identify the type of scene changes and reallocate resources to the remaining GOPs and frames. The experimental results show that the proposed rate control scheme does much better than the recommended rate algorithm of H.264. The average PSNR gain can be up to 0.76 dB for scene change sequence. Moreover, our algorithm provides small mismatch between the target bit rate and the actual bit rate.

Acknowledgement. This work is supported in part by NSFC 61143008, National High Technology Research and Development Program of China (No. 2011AA01A204), the Fundamental Research Funds for the Central Universities.

References

1. ISO/IEC JTC1/SC29/WG11. MPEG test model 5 (TM5) (1993)
2. ITU-T/SG15. Video coder test model (TMN8) (1997)
3. ISO/IEC JTC1/SC29/WG11. MPEG-4 video verification model v18.0 (VM8) (2001)
4. Chiang, T., Zhang, Y.: A new rate control scheme using quadratic rate distortion model. IEEE Trans. Circ. Syst. Video Technol. 7(2), 287–311 (1997)
5. Li, Z.G., Pan, F., Lim, K.P., Feng, G., Lin, X., Rahardja, S.: Adaptive basic unit layer rate control for JVT. Joint Video Team of ISO/IEC MPEG and ITU-T VCEG, JVT-G012r1 (2003)
6. Institute of Computing Technology: Proposed Draft of Adaptive Rate Control for JVT-H017.doc. The Meeting: Geneva, 20–26 May 2003
7. Leontaris, A.: Rate control reorganization in the Joint Model (JM) reference software. Joint Video Team of ISO/IEC MPEG and ITU-T VCEG, JVT-W042, April 2007
8. Luo, L.J., Zhou, C.R., He, Z.Y.: A new algorithm on MPEG-2 target bit-number allocation at scene changes. IEEE Trans. Circ. Syst. Video Technol. 7(5), 815–819 (1997)
9. Lupatini, G., Saraceno, C., Leonardi, R.: Scene break detection: a comparison. In: Eighth International Workshop on Continuous-Media Databases and Applications, pp. 34–41 (1998)
10. Lienhart, R.: Reliable transition detection in videos: a survey and practitioner's guide. Int. J. Image Graph. 1(3), 469–486 (2001)
11. Lee, J., Shin, I.H., Park, H.W.: Adaptive intra-frame assignment and bit-rate estimation for variable GOP length in H.264. IEEE Trans. Circ. Syst. Video Technol. 16(10), 1271–1279 (2006)

Another Improvement of LMAP++:
An RFID Authentication Protocol

Anqi Huang[✉], Chen Zhang, and Chaojing Tang

College of Electronic Science and Engineering,
National University of Defense Technology, Changsha, China
{angelhuang.hn,zhangchen,tangchaojing}@gmail.com

Abstract. Radio Frequency Identification (RFID) Systems have been deployed in a variety of fields. With widespread application, RFID systems raise a plenty of security and privacy issues, among which the authorized communication between reader and tags is concerned by researchers primarily. In order to adapt the resource constraint, lightweight mutual authentication protocols are designed to secure the tag/reader authentication. In this paper, we propose an improving RFID authentication protocol based on LMAP++ protocol. The proposed protocol guarantees the tag anonymity, untraceability and synchronization.

Keywords: RFID · LMAP++ · Mutual authentication protocol

1 Introduction

RFID (Radio Frequency Identification) has characteristics of high-accuracy, long-period and easy operation [1]. Nowadays, it is widely used in storage, logistics and selling fields [2]. However, the proliferation of RFID systems lead to certain security threats, including eavesdropping, spoofing, counterfeiting, man in the middle, denial of services, physical invasion, traceability and de-synchronization.

The numerous deployments require the low cost of each tag, which results in the limitation of resource-hundreds of bits and limited number of logic gates to store the cryptographic algorithm. Considering the resource constraint, the lightweight cryptographic scheme which uses only bitwise operations (e.g., modular addition, exclusive OR) is a major solution to achieve the data security, while the existed lightweight mutual authentication protocols have been proved not secure enough.

In this paper, we propose an improved version of LMAP++ to realize the mutual authentication between the authorized reader and tags. Furthermore, we also analyze the security of the proposed protocol in terms of traceability and de-synchronization.

The rest of this paper is organized as follows. Section 2 reviews the related work of lightweight authentication protocols. The notations used in our protocol are illustrated in Sect. 3. Then we elaborate the designed protocol in Sect. 4, and security analysis is presented in Sect. 5. In Sect. 6, it is the conclusion of our work.

Y. Yuan et al. (Eds.): ISCTCS 2013, CCIS 426, pp. 100–106, 2014.
DOI: 10.1007/978-3-662-43908-1_13, © Springer-Verlag Berlin Heidelberg 2014

2 Relation Work

Lightweight authentication protocols are the most suitable to the security of low-cost RFID tags. Vajda and L. Buttyan [3] have presented the extremely lightweight challenge-response authentication algorithm, but this protocol can be easily attacked by the adversary. Juels in [4] proposed a pseudonym solution without any hash function. Moreover, there are several lightweight mutual authentication protocols proposed in the literature [5–9], but they have already been broken in [10–16].

In [17], Peris-Lopez et al. proposed a well-known mutual authentication protocol: Lightweight Mutual Authentication Protocol (LMAP), in which it just uses the bitwise operations. They also proposed an extension version of this protocol named LMAP+. However, it has been found very soon that these kinds of protocols do not achieve the claimed security [18]. In 2008, Li proposed the improvement of their protocol called LMAP++ [19], but it also had disadvantages, especially the traceability and de-synchronization attacks [20]. In order to avoid the security threats above, Gurubani etc. proposed an improved version of LMAP++ in [21], but Gildas Avoine and Xavier Carpent found it cannot guarantee the untraceability [22].

We proposed another improvement of LMAP++ which is different from the scheme in [21] to insure the security of tag anonymity, untraceability and synchronization.

3 Notations

The proposed protocol is a lightweight RFID authentication protocol that only uses simple bitwise operations: bitwise XOR ($\oplus$) and addition mod $2^m - 1$ (+), instead of hash function or multiplication. The used notations in this paper are listed in Table 1 as follow.

4 Improved Protocol

4.1 Supposition of Design

The RFID system is constituted by three parts: the database, the reader and the tags. We consider the channel between the database and the reader is secure, while the

Table 1. Notations

$ID_{tag(i)}$	A 96-bit unique tag's identifier
$PID^{(n)}_{tag(i)}$	A 96-bit pseudonym of tag i ($1 < i < N$) in the nth successful session, $PID \in \{0, 1\}^{96}$
$Kj^{(n)}_{tag(i)}$	A 96-bit secret key$j$ (j= 1,2,3) of tag i and reader in the nth successful session, $Kj \in \{0, 1\}^{96}$
r	A 96-bit random number generated by reader, $r \in \{0, 1\}^{96}$
A, B, C	Messages transferred between the reader and the tag, $A,B,C \in \{0, 1\}^{96}$
X‖Y	The concatenation of X and Y
(X)n	The nth bit of X
$\oplus$	XOR operation
+	Addition mod $2^m - 1$

wireless channel between the reader and the tag is insecure, in which the mutual authentication of the reader and tag should be completed. Our protocol uses the pseudonym identifiers (PIDs) to conceal the tag information. So the tags must be written with its unique ID (in ROM), its pseudo-ID (in EEPROM) and certain keys (K_1, K_2, K_3) for authentication. These kinds of information are also recorded in a table of database to be indexed by the reader.

Before the operation of authentication, the system is initialized. On one hand, it is the tag initialization. As the EPC Gen2 RFID tag, a word in tag has $L = 96$ bits. For a tag, the unique ID is static, but the pseudo-ID and three keys are updated after every time of successful authentication. Therefore, a tag needs 96-bit ROM and 384-bit EEPROM. On the other hand, the database should also be initialized. The owner of tags builds a central database to store the tag information, in which a row [PID, ID, K_1, K_2, K_3] is stored for every tag. All the N tags' information are listed in a table with 5NL-bit size.

4.2   Protocol Description

The protocol can be split in three main stages: tag identification, mutual authentication and updating of pseudonym and keys. In the way of bitwise operations, the most difference between the proposed protocol and the former ones is the addition mod $2^m - 1$ instead of addition mod 2^m. The process has shown in the Table 2 as below.

Tag Identification: This stage is the same as LMAP++. Before the starting of mutual authentication, the reader has to identify the tag. Initially, the reader will send a *hello* message to the tag i, which is responded by the tag's pseudo-ID. When receiving the *PID*, only the authorized reader has access to search the database, finding the corresponding keys ($K = K1\|K2\|K3$) for tag i. These keys are indispensable in the next authentication procedure.

Mutual Authentication: Through exchanging the messages between the reader and tag, the authorization of the reader and tag can be authenticated. At the beginning of this stage, the reader generates a random number r. With the known $K1$ and $K2$, the reader generates the messages A and B which then are sent to the tag. After receiving the messages A and B, the tag calculates $r1$ and $r2$ from A and B respectively. If $r1$ equals to $r2$, the reader can be authenticated on the tag side. If not, the tag will send an arbitrary message C' to the reader. This process is also similar to the LMAP++. Upon obtaining the right r ($r = r1 = r2$), the tag responds the massage C which differs from LMAP++, and the reader calculates the ID with the assistance of $K3$ and PID. If the ID exists in the database, the tag is regarded as authorized one. If the ID is not valid, the authentication protocol is aborted. In this approach, the tag unique identifier is transmitted securely.

Updating: After the reader and tag have been authenticated mutually, the updating of pseudonym and keys should be carried out on both the reader and the tag sides as above equations in Table 2. Compared with LMAP++, the updating of *PID* has been improved. The advantages of this improvement will be stated in the next chapter. The key numbers ($K = K1\|K2\|K3$) in the n + 1 run are updated in the similar way of LMAP++.

Table 2. The nth Protocol Run

Tag Identification:

Reader → Tag: Hello

Tag → Reader: PID

Mutual Authentication:

Reader → Tag: A||B

Tag → Reader: C

where:

$A = PID_{tag(i)}^{(n)} \oplus K1_{tag(i)}^{(n)} + r$

$B = PID_{tag(i)}^{(n)} + K2_{tag(i)}^{(n)} \oplus r$

$C = PID_{tag(i)}^{(n)} + ID_{tag(i)} \oplus K3_{tag(i)}^{(n)} + r$

For LMAP++:

$A = PID_{tag(i)}^{(n)} \oplus K1_{tag(i)}^{(n)} + r$

$B = PID_{tag(i)}^{(n)} + K2_{tag(i)}^{(n)} \oplus r$

$C = (PID_{tag(i)}^{(n)} + ID_{tag(i)} \oplus r) \oplus (K1_{tag(i)}^{(n)} + K2_{tag(i)}^{(n)} + r)$

Updating:

$PID_{tag(i)}^{(n+1)} = PID_{tag(i)}^{(n)} \oplus r + (K2_{tag(i)}^{(n)} + K3_{tag(i)}^{(n)} + ID_{tag(i)})$

$K1_{tag(i)}^{(n+1)} = K1_{tag(i)}^{(n)} \oplus r + (PID_{tag(i)}^{(n+1)} + K2_{tag(i)}^{(n)} + ID_{tag(i)})$

$K2_{tag(i)}^{(n+1)} = K2_{tag(i)}^{(n)} \oplus r + (PID_{tag(i)}^{(n+1)} + K3_{tag(i)}^{(n)} + ID_{tag(i)})$

$K3_{tag(i)}^{(n+1)} = K3_{tag(i)}^{(n)} \oplus r + (PID_{tag(i)}^{(n+1)} + K1_{tag(i)}^{(n)} + ID_{tag(i)})$

(+: addition mod $2^m - 1$)

For LMAP++:

$PID_{tag(i)}^{(n+1)} = (PID_{tag(i)}^{(n)} + K1_{tag(i)}^{(n)}) \oplus r + (ID_{tag(i)} + K2_{tag(i)}^{(n)}) \oplus r$

$K1_{tag(i)}^{(n+1)} = K1_{tag(i)}^{(n)} \oplus r + (PID_{tag(i)}^{(n+1)} + K2_{tag(i)}^{(n)} + ID_{tag(i)})$

$K2_{tag(i)}^{(n+1)} = K2_{tag(i)}^{(n)} \oplus r + (PID_{tag(i)}^{(n+1)} + K1_{tag(i)}^{(n)} + ID_{tag(i)})$

(+: addition mod 2^m)

With the purpose of synchronization, the proposed protocol adopts the same mechanism in [19]. The status bit s is both in the reader and the tag to indicate the protocol success or not. Set s = 0, if the authentication protocol is completed. Otherwise, s is set to 1. Only in the condition of s = 0, the updating process will be operated.

5   Security Analysis

The proposed protocol not only provides the data confidentiality but also defends the traceability and de-synchronization.

Data Confidentiality: The information-sending mechanism of our protocol guarantees the users privacy. The tag sends the massage C hiding the static identifier by random number r and secret key K3, which makes the nearby eavesdroppers cannot distinguish the tag identifier even though they capture the massages.

Traceability Defense: LMAP++ in [19] defines the massages A, B, C as in Table 2. If we consider only last significant bit (LSB), the addition mod 2^m can be replaced by bitwise XOR. Therefore, in the LMAP++, the tag will be traced by the adversary through the last significant bit of tag unique ID as below.

$$(ID_{tag(i)})_0 = (A)_0 \oplus (B)_0 \oplus (C)_0 \oplus (PID_{tag(i)}^{(n)})_0 \tag{1}$$

The proposed protocol redesigns the massage C which uses the K3 to avoid above threat. In addition, we apply the addition mod $2^m - 1$ but not addition mod 2^m as well. Even for the last significant bit, the result of addition mod $2^m - 1$ cannot be treated as bitwise XOR, so the attacker is not able to know the ID through the transmitted massages.

De-synchronization Defense: The main aim of this attack is to convince the tag and reader to update their common parameters (PID, K1, K2, K3) to different values. The authentication in the next run will not be successful because of the different parameters. For the LMAP++, the attacker toggles the LSBs of A, B and r. In the massage of C, the attacker tampers the r to $r' = r + 1$ and transmits to the reader. Because of the same results of $r \oplus r$ and $r' \oplus r'$, the reader still completes the authentication but it regards the r' as the r. As a result, the reader and the tag uses r' and r respectively to update the PID and keys. The different updated values will trigger the unsuccess of the future transaction.

Our designed protocol uses the random number r only once in massage C to avoid the same results of using r and r'. In essence, this kind of attack make use of the LSB of each massage and treat all the operation into bitwise XOR in these LSBs. The weakness of addition mod 2^m leads to the possibility of threat. The proposed protocol alters the addition operation to addition mod $2^m - 1$, curtailing the threat from LSB.

6   Conclusion

In this paper, we present improvement of LMAP++, a low-cost RFID mutual authentication protocol. This improved protocol inherits the security quality of LMAP++: data confidentiality, tag anonymity and mutual authentication. The abilities against traceability and de-synchronization are provided as well. These capabilities are owing to the improving equations and the change of addition operation.

Acknowledgement. This research was supported by National Natural Science Foundation of China No. 61302091.

References

1. Want, R.: An introduction to RFID technology. IEEE Pervasive Comput. **5**(1), 25–33 (2006)
2. Wen, H.: 2007 RFID development analysis. Chinese Electronic, 2008:50–54

3. Vajda, I., Buttyan, L.: Lightweight authentication protocols for low-cost RFID tags. In: Proceedings of UBICOMP'03 (2003)
4. Juels, A.: Minimalist cryptography for low-cost RFID tags (extended abstract). In: Blundo, C., Cimato, S. (eds.) SCN 2004. LNCS, vol. 3352, pp. 149–164. Springer, Heidelberg (2005)
5. Sadighian, A., Jalili, R.: AFMAP: anonymous forward-secure mutual authentication protocols for RFID systems. In: Third IEEE International Conference on Emerging Security Information, Systems and Technologies (SECURWARE 2009), pp. 31–36 (2009)
6. Sadighian, A., Jalili, R.: FLMAP: a fast lightweight mutual authentication protocol for RFID. In: 16th IEEE International Conference on Networks, New Delhi, India, pp. 1–6 (2008)
7. Chien, S.: A lightweight RFID authentication protocol providing strong authentication. IEEE Trans. Dependable Secur. Comput. 4(4), 337–340 (2007)
8. Peris-Lopez, P., Hernandez-Castro, J.C., Tapiador, J.M., Ribagorda, A.: Advances in ultralightweight cryptography for low-cost RFID Tags: gossamer protocol. In: Chung, K.-I., Sohn, K., Yung, M. (eds.) WISA 2008. LNCS, vol. 5379, pp. 56–68. Springer, Heidelberg (2009)
9. Peris-Lopez, P., Hernandez-Castro, J.C., Estevez-Tapiador, J.M., Ribagorda, A.: EMAP: an efficient mutual-authentication protocol for low-cost RFID tags. In: Meersman, R., Tari, Z., Herrero, P. (eds.) OTM 2006 Workshops. LNCS, vol. 4277, pp. 352–361. Springer, Heidelberg (2006)
10. Safkhani, M., Naderi, M., Bagheri, N.: Cryptanalysis of AFMAP. IEICE Electron. Express 7(17), 1240–1245 (2010)
11. Safkhani, M., Naderi, M., Rashvand, H.: Cryptanalysis of AFMAP. Int. J. Comput. Commun. Technol. 2(2), 182–186 (2010)
12. Bárász, M., Boros, B.: Passive attack against the M2AP mutual authentication protocol for RFID tags. In: First International EURASIP Workshop on RFID Technology, Vienna, Austria, September 2007
13. Cao, T., Bertino, E., Lei, H.: Security analysis of the SASI protocol. IEEE Trans. Dependable Secur. Comput. 6(1), 73–77 (2009)
14. Hernandez-Castro, J.C., Tapiador, J.M.E., Peris-Lopez, P., Quisquater, J.-J.: Cryptanalysis of the SASI ultralightweight RFID authentication protocol with modular rotations. Technical report arXiv:0811.4257, Nov 2008
15. Li, T., Deng, R.H.: Vulnerability analysis of EMAP - an efficient RFID mutual authentication protocol. In: Second International Conference on Availability, Reliability and Security – ARES 2007, Vienna, Austria, April 2007
16. Phan, R.C.-W.: Cryptanalysis of a new ultralightweight RFID authentication protocol - SASI. IEEE Trans. Dependable Secur. Comput. 6(4), 316–320 (2009)
17. Peris-Lopez, P., Hernandez-Castro, J.C., Estevez-Tapiador, J.M., Ribagorda, A.: LMAP: A real lightweight mutual authentication protocol for low-cost RFID tags. In: Proceedings of RFIDSec06 Workshop on RFID Security, Graz, Austria, 12–14 July 2006
18. Li, T., Wang, G.: Security analysis of two ultra-lightweight RFID authentication protocols. In: IFIP SEC 2007, Sandton, Gauteng, South Africa, May 2007
19. Li, T.: Employing lightweight primitives on low-cost RFID tags for authentication. In: VTC Fall, pp. 1–5 (2008)
20. Safkhani, M., Bagheri, N., Naderi, M., Sanadhya, S.K.: Security analysis of LMAP++, an RFID authentication protocol. In: 2011 International Conference for Internet Technology and Secured Transactions (ICITST), pp. 689–694 (2011)

21. Gurubani, J.B., Thakkar, H., Patel, D.R.: Improvements over extended LMAP+: RFID authentication protocol. In: Dimitrakos, T., Moona, R., Patel, D., McKnight, D. (eds.) IFIPTM 2012. IFIP AICT, vol. 374, pp. 225–231. Springer, Heidelberg (2012)
22. Avoine, G., Carpent, X.: Yet another ultralightweight authentication protocol that is broken. In: Hoepman, J.-H., Verbauwhede, I. (eds.) RFIDSec 2012. LNCS, vol. 7739, pp. 20–30. Springer, Heidelberg (2013)

A New Approach to Decrease Invalidate Rate of Weak Consistency Methods in Web Proxy Caching

Chen Chen[1,3], Qingyun Liu[1,3(✉)], Hongzhou Sha[2,3],
Zhou Zhou[1,3], and Chao Zheng[1,3]

[1] Institute of Information Engineering, Chinese Academy of Science, Beijing, China
{chenchen,liuqingyun,zhouzhou,zhengchao}@iie.ac.cn
[2] Beijing University of Posts and Telecommunications, Beijing, China
shahongzhou@nelmail.iie.ac.cn
[3] National Engineering Laboratory for Information Security Technologies,
Beijing, China

Abstract. With the growing demand for accelerating large scale web access, web proxy cache is widely used. To make full use of computing resource and bandwidth of proxy cache nodes, weak cache consistency is the best choice in most cases. Traditional refreshing methods like Adaptive TTL will cause high invalidate rate of web pages. We introduce a new effective way to decrease the invalidate rate of frequently queried objects in weak consistency scheme. Based on Zipfs law, our method focuses on giving the hotspot objects more priorities during cache refreshing process, which reduces the invalidate rate on hotspot objects by paying less concentration on the less frequently queried objects.

Keywords: Web proxy cache · Invalidate rate · Weak consistency

1 Introduction

Nowadays the scale of the World Wide Web is growing explosively, and web proxy cache is widely used. Its well known that transparent proxy caches like Squid can only maintain a weak consistency. TTL (Time-To-Live), Adaptive Time-To-Live, Client Polling and Piggyback Invalidation are popular weak consistency mechanisms. TTL and Adaptive TTL mechanism use timers based on modification-time to update cached pages, making a stable invalidate rate relatively. They cannot take advantage of real-time cache accessing behavior C limiting the invalidate rates dependency on the server modification time uncontrollably. And the objects which are less of worthy in cache updating process occupy large burden on the limited bandwidth and computing resources. The client polling mechanism will update cache items periodically, but making a high invalidate rate when the updating period is too long. It will also make a heavy burden on performance when the period is set to too small. And piggyback

Y. Yuan et al. (Eds.): ISCTCS 2013, CCIS 426, pp. 107–114, 2014.
DOI: 10.1007/978-3-662-43908-1_14, © Springer-Verlag Berlin Heidelberg 2014

invalidation mechanism calls for more cooperation between proxy caches and web servers, which is not applicable in transparent proxy caches. Among all of the above weak consistency mechanisms, we found a way of improving the traditional weak consistencies performance by using the distribution of user accessing behavior on traditional effective Adaptive TTL or TTL methods. Furthermore, we also introduce an estimating method for hotness calculation, based on the exponential hotspot raising assumption.

2   Related Work

Breslau et al. [1] described that the Zipfs law is implemented in the web caching area naturally. And Spanoudakis et al. [2] made a new approach on the invalidate rate improvement, focusing on the prediction of more accurate updating timer compared with the widely adopted Adaptive TTL method. Gwertzman and Seltzer [3] proposed the Adaptive TTL method, which can produce an invalidate rate less than 5 % - a big improvement among weak consistent schemes. While Cao [4] made experimental comparison among Adaptive TTL, Polling-every-time and Invalidation methods, showing that invalidation method is the most recommended protocol, which could make the best performance either on network traffic and workload, or on the invalidation rate. But the invalidation method introduced more burden on the complexity between cache server and the resource server - which does not fit for the proxy cache environment, especially when the proxy cache is transparent from the content. Moreover, Li et al. [5] developed the lease algorithm in mobile network, which can balance both space and control message usages among strong consistency strategies like polling-every-time and invalidation. Krishnamurthy and Wills [6] presented the Piggy-back methods, better than many traditional methods, which gave us an pruning recommendation in algorithm selection. Barish [7] gave us an outline view of the existing web caching techniques, including proxy-caching, proxy caching and transparent caching, which are all our interests. Wang [8] made a remarkable description over each aspects of web caching, and introduced the weak consistency mechanism especially.

3   EW (Enhanced Weak Consistency) Model

The Adaptive TTL method can guarantee 5 % invalidate rate at most, but with the increasing scale of the World Wide Web, 5 % also means a large amount of data. As its known to all, web querying behaviors obey the Zipfs law, which shows a long tail effect on Web objects querying. In most of the implementations about web proxy caching, objects with higher frequency are more worthy of caching, which could easily cause burdens in caching computation. What we care about is to make traditional weak consistency algorithms like Adaptive-TTL more effective in the hotspot web objects and reduce the invalidate rate especially on hotspot objects, increasing the average refreshing frequency on hotspot objects in order to reduce the invalidation rate selectively. We introduce a hotness aware queue, each time when object in cache is visited, it will be operated on its measurement, and when the measurement goes over the threshold, the object will be pushed into the updating queue, which is sorted by update timer, generated by Adaptive TTL method. Theres a watching thread outside the queue to check whether the first update time is up over and over. Whenever it is confirmed that the first object in updating queue is out of date, the object will be updated from the original Web server, the thread will also check objects form the second to the end to refresh objects. Updating methods worst time complexity is O(n). But on average there're no more computation requirements than the Adaptive TTL method. In most of the cases, Web objects' frequencies obey the Zipfs law C an exponent cumulative distribution of frequency. And in web cache environment, we should consider more characteristics of web objects such as web access behaviors including recency, frequency and web objects properties including size, cost or latency and type of objects etc. Based on the unbalanced distribution, there'll be less than 40 % of the objects attending the updating process experimentally, and with a tolerance on the invalid rate on the objects that are less worthy of caching, the global invalidate rate of Adaptive-TTL will reduce to 2 % at most. First of all, we are going to talk about the qualification measurement of judging whether an object is worthy of caching or not.

3.1   Summarize of Frequency Measurement

One of the core jobs of hotness estimation is the appropriate measurement of objects characteristics. We should give objects with larger frequency bigger priorities. Our implementation is to use the frequency information in the exponential assumption later talked about.

3.2   Types of Web Objects

From qualitative analyses of the modification periods of web objects, we conclude an experiential frequency list in Table 1.

The most frequently modified objects are more likely to be those web objects with less modification cost, such as the text formatted object like HTML. And the binary objects like flash, voice and video objects are the less likely to be changed - the modifications on such objects are usually redirected to new addresses. Moreover, the type of the objects can easily be recognized by the

Table 1. Experiential Frequency level of different object types

Type \ Size	Small	Large
HTML	Most	Moderate
Script	Moderate	Moderate
Other Text	Moderate	Least
Binary	Least	Least

URL suffixes or header information of the objects. We could give each type a weight separately related to the modification frequency above.

3.3 Cost and Size of Web Objects

As for the modification cost of large objects is bigger than that of the smaller ones, we estimate that the frequency pattern and the size of objects have inverse relationship. Since it is in the proxy cache environment, internet transmission latency is another important pattern, which not only has relationship with the size of object, but also related to the delay of each objects. We describe the delay by the variable cost, and the frequency of modifications will be directly proportional to $\frac{cost}{size}$. So, we concluded all of the characteristics above to a compound measurement variable a, which is showed below:

$$a = \left(\frac{cost}{size}\right) \cdot weight \tag{1}$$

3.4 Hotness Estimation Model

To simplify the hotness model, we make an assumption that all of the querying hotness are similar to an exponential function exponentially as:

$$C\left(t\right) = a^t \tag{2}$$

where "a" is the compound measurement talked above and "t" is the time. The real-time frequency could be described as $\frac{count}{\Delta t}$, where Δt is the querying period and the count is sampled during the period Δt. Since our goal is to estimate the expected hotness, which could be estimated with Δt, we should give an expression of the variable Δt. Based on assumption, we believe that each time when we make a sampling during the period, the accumulated count has an exponent relationship with t_0 as (3):

$$\Delta t = \log_a \left(1 + \frac{\Delta C_{expect}}{C\left(t_0\right)}\right) \tag{3}$$

In Eq. (3), variable a shows the characteristics of the web objects, t_0 is the query time since the appearance of the cached item, and $C(t)$ is the expected accumulated hit count. Δt is the expecting querying period, and C_{expect} is the expected count sampled in last period while $C(t_0)$ is the last accumulated count. Since we should give an expression of the hotness with real-time sampled frequencies, we will simplify the relationship between t_0 and Δt into Δt-only updating function with the equation below:

$$t_0 = \log_a \frac{\Delta C}{a^{\Delta t} - 1} \tag{4}$$

Plugging (4) into (3), the next expected querying cycle $\Delta t'$ is generated in (5).

$$\Delta t' = \log_a \left(1 + \frac{\Delta C_{expect}}{\Delta C} \cdot \left(a^{\Delta t} - 1\right)\right) \tag{5}$$

Our curiosity is placed on the period, where we can gain the hotness information from it. The hotness could be described either as $\Delta t'$ with a descending comparing order or as $\frac{1}{\Delta t'}$ with an ascending order. Moreover, the promotion threshold assignment could be based on the formula, too.

3.5 Hotness Aware Queue Algorithm

Hotness is measured by the hotness pattern, which could be simplified as frequency. Whenever an object is queried, it will be updated in cache and be checked whether it has the qualification to promote to the Hotness Queue or not. The Hotness maintenance logic is described below:

Algorithm 1. Hotness Maintaining

Input: The key of the target object K_t
Output: The content of the object D_t
  if K_t is in the Cache **then**
    Push K_t into Cache with initial Frequency
    return Not found
  else
    if Object K_t exceeds Threshold **then**
      Push K_t into Updating Queue
    end if
    Update K_t's Frequency
    Find D_t in Cache with K_t
  end if
  return D_t

When an object is put into the updating queue, there should be an updating procedure, described as:

Algorithm 2. Updating

  Initialize the Updating Queue
  while True **do**
    if the 1st Object out of date **then**
      Update the 1st object
      for $i = 2$ to $Size(Queue)$ **do**
        if the ith Object out of date **then**
          Update the ith object
        else
          break
        end if
      end for
    else
      Sleep(timer)
    end if
  end while

In the process, the working thread will check the Hotness Queue over and over until the main process is terminated. The updating period in hotness queue is given by outside Adaptive TTL method or traditional TTL method optionally, which are not our emphasis. In the next section, we will discuss the invalidate rate of this method, and later we will show the efficiency of data reduction based on the distribution.

3.6   Analysis

For most websites, the modification cycle of web object is approximate to constant. Let the modification cycle be T and the refreshing cycle of cached object be Δt, the invalidate rate of each cached objects could be estimated by (6).

$$
rate_{invalid} \leq \begin{cases} \frac{\Delta t}{T}, \Delta t < T \\ \frac{T}{\Delta t}, \Delta t \geq T \end{cases} \tag{6}
$$

According to Zipfs law, we use a distribution expression formula shown in (7), where "i" is the ranking of cached item by frequency, N is the number of all cached objects, and F_i is the relative frequency and hotness of object "i". Since the formula is uniformed, F_i can also be treated as appearance probability of objects.

$$
F_i = \frac{1/i}{\sum_1^N 1/n} \approx \frac{1}{0.96i \cdot \ln 2.22N} \tag{7}
$$

Let the Threshold of objects with more worthy be T, the expected number of refreshed objects N_c is described as:

$$
N_c \leq \frac{1}{0.96T \cdot ln2.22N} \tag{8}
$$

Because of the normalization operation in (7), Nc is also the data reduction scale, and $(1 - N_c)$ of the cached data will not be updated on average, which makes an improvement on performance. Hotter cached items will get smaller refreshing cycle than the original ones, which in fact makes the cache updating process more effective for the hotspots based on the adjusting to the real-time querying behavior. With the same refreshing computing resources, hot objects will get more refreshing opportunities, making a reduction on invalidate rate as well. Meanwhile, the optimization also reduces the wastes of computing power on the objects which are less worthy of caching.

4   Experiment

The dataset is a 30 days web querying log of 56,374,164 lines from a web proxy server, with 16,625,621 lines could be cached, of which 2,705,302 lines are unique. We made a simulation based on the data. With the simulation environment, we can continuously test our algorithms. Our experiment are focused on the data reduction scale of cached data, which has an direct proportion to the reduction rate of invalidate rate.

Since the distribution of data in small cache is distinguished from the whole dataset distribution, especially for the scale of low frequency objects, we make the experiment between long-term querying in total 30-days and the short period distributions in 5 min. The distribution is showed in Figs. 1, 2 and Table 2.

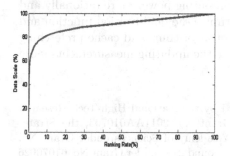

Fig. 1. 30-day CDF

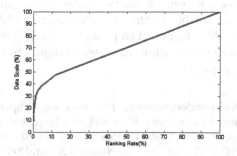

Fig. 2. 5-min CDF

Table 2. Top-4 least frequently accessing CDF comparison

Frequency	30 day count	Percentage (%)	5 min count	Percentage (%)
1	1,962,470	11.80	628	59.81
2	304,530	3.66	77	14.67
3	114,184	2.06	29	8.29
4	63,925	0.38	21	8.00

Obviously, we can figure from the experiment that the reduction on data scale by frequency is more effective in short periods, with a large amount of data with frequency 1. And objects who are put into cache with less frequency are not likely to be accessed again. In the experiment, there was a 60 % reduction by limiting the frequency to 1, where with a higher threshold and more invalid tolerance on less frequent items, we could either gain lower computing power on updating process or the improvement on the performance of invalidate rate C reducing 2.5 or more times of invalidate rate, or achieving a reduction of computing power on refreshing procedures.

5   Conclusion

Weak consistency caching method is one of the most important parts of proxy caching, especially for the web proxy caching area in the big-data world. Although Adaptive-TTL method shows a stable performance on invalidation rate control, when it comes to the unlimited high speed network flow field, 5 % is not a small rate anymore, which is hard to tolerant. Facing the problem of optimizing the invalidate rate of cache weak consistency scheme, we present an EW (Enhanced Weak Consistency) model to optimize the invalidate rate of Adaptive TTL, TTL method and so on based on Zipfs law, decreasing the cache refreshing cycle selectively. Our work mainly focuses on the measurement of web objects, hotness estimation modeling and the invalidate rate estimation. Finally, under the same refreshing calculation resources, we made a reduction of the updating data scale, reducing the invalidate rate of hotspots to about 2 % when we set the promotion threshold to 1. With our work, we can use limited cache spaces and computing power more rationally and controllable. In the next process, we will optimize the qualification function and modify the model to fit for cache replacement algorithms and cache prefetching algorithms, using schedule techniques to make the updating measurements more compatible.

Acknowledgement. This work was supported by the National High-Tech Research and Development Plan 863 of China under Grant No. 2011AA010703, the Strategic Priority Research Program of the Chinese Academy of Sciences under Grant No. XDA06030200, and the National Natural Science Foundation under Grant No. 61070026.

References

1. Breslau, L., Cao, P., Fan, L., Phillips, G., Shenker, S.: Web caching and Zipf-like distributions: evidence and implications. INFOCOM '99, Vol. 1, pp. 126–134 (1999)
2. Spanoudakis, M., Lorentzos, D., Anagnostopoulos, C., Hadjiefthymiades, S.: On the use of optimal stopping theory for cache consistency checks. In: 2012 16th Panhellenic Conference IEEE Informatics (PCI), pp. 327–332 (2012)
3. Gwertzman, J., Seltzer, M.: World wide web cache consistency. In: USENIX Annual Technical Conference, pp. 141–152 (1996)
4. Cao, P., Liu, C.: Maintaining strong cache consistency in the world wide web. IEEE Trans. Comput. **47**(4), 445–457 (1998)
5. Li, X., Qiu, F., Zhou, H., Zhang, H., You, I.: Maintaining strong consistency for the identifier-to-locator mapping cache. In: 2012 IEEE Globecom Workshops (GC Wkshps), pp. 986–991 (2012)
6. Krishnamurthy, B., Wills, C.E.: Study of piggyback cache validation for proxy caches in the world wide web. In: USENIX Symposium on Internet Technologies and Systems, p. 38 (1997)
7. Barish, G., Obraczke, K.: World wide web caching: trends and techniques. IEEE Commun. Mag. **38**(5), 178–184 (2000)
8. Wang, J.: A survey of web caching schemes for the internet. ACM SIGCOMM Comput. Commun. Rev. **29**(5), 36–46 (1999)

An Anomaly Detection Model Based on Cloud Model and Danger Theory

Wenhao Wang[✉], Chen Zhang, and Quan Zhang

School of Electronic Science and Engineering,
National University of Defense Technology, Changsha, China
wangwenhao1986@163.com, zhangchen@hotmail.com

Abstract. In order to solve non-real time problem in traditional intrusion detection technologies, this paper proposes an anomaly detection model based on cloud model and danger theory. First using cloud model as a tool to evaluate the diversity factors between test data and the standard data set, then covert it into signal input of DCA to detect abnormality degree of system. Meanwhile, a dendritic cell algorithm based on data segmented detection is proposed in order to raise real-time response of the system. The paper use KDDCUP99 data sets to validate membership of normal data and detection rate of this model. Experimental results show that the model can effectively distinguish between normal data and abnormal data, and also improve the system anomaly detection capabilities.

Keywords: IDS · AIS · Danger theory · Cloud model

1 Introduction

Inspired by highly parallel, distributed, self-organizing and self-learning feature of biological immune system, Forrest proposed artificial immune system (AIS) in 1994, and introduce self/non-self recognition model [1] to apply for the computer system security protection. Uwe Aickelin, Professor of Nottingham University, combine Danger Theory (DT) which draw constant attention in biological immune theory with AIS, presents a danger theory based intrusion detection method [2]. On the basis of Uwe Aickelin's work, Greensmith abstract the biological immune mechanism of dendritic cells to establish a new immune algorithm—Dendritic Cell Algorithm (DCA) for anomaly detection [3]. DCA does not require additional detector training time, having small calculation amount and taking up little computational resources, so DCA has a natural advantage for dealing with large real-time data stream.

However, how to define "danger" becomes an important issue in the practical application of DT. For example, when the computer system is subject to external intrusion, the system's network traffic and behavior may change with time, then how to judge whether the system is abnormal or not and how to measure the degree of abnormality system become serious problems. Cloud model as an uncertainty mathematical conversion tool, which is designed to transform qualitative concept and quantitative representation, has been widely used in the intrusion detection fields. Weiwei and Deyi [4] used cloud model to implement an intrusion detection method

Y. Yuan et al. (Eds.): ISCTCS 2013, CCIS 426, pp. 115–122, 2014.
DOI: 10.1007/978-3-662-43908-1_15, © Springer-Verlag Berlin Heidelberg 2014

that can detect and collect system-level, network-level and user-level data, and making invasion decisions through the cloud decider. Lowry et al. [5] proposed an intrusion detection method based on multidimensional cloud theory, which defined a number of qualitative rules for reasoning uncertainty, but these rules have no objective criteria and basis. He et al. [6] combined behaviors of host computer with cloud model to define "danger" in the DT, however, the author ignored the dynamic changes of behavioral parameters, meanwhile this method is lack of direct experimental support which has little significance for practical guidance.

To solve the above problems, this paper presents an anomaly detection model which is based on cloud model and danger theory. Backward Cloud Generator is used to generate three data characteristics of normal cloud model- expectations, entropy and hyper entropy. When the test data input, the model will calculate the diversity factor between test data and normal cloud model, then convert it into signal inputs of DCA. If DCA detect abnormality degree of certain period is greater than threshold, system will release inflammatory signals to amplify immune response to shorten the response time, specific chart of the model is shown in Fig. 1.

2   Semantic Foundation of Cloud Model

Cloud model is a linguistic values model between qualitative and quantitative concept, which combining the concept of fuzziness and randomness to reflect the relationship

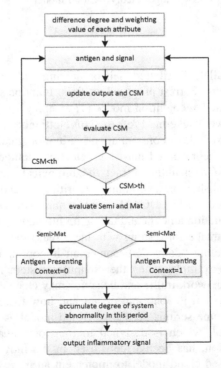

Fig. 1. A flow diagram of dendritic cell algorithm based on data segmented detection

of membership grade among different things. Cloud has been defined in the literature [6], which is mainly characterized by three data characteristics: Expectation (Ex), Entropy (En) and Hyper Entropy (He):

Ex: the expectations of cloud droplets in the whole domain of spatial distribution, which is the most possible point we hope to appear.

En: that qualitative concept of uncertainty, not only contains the concept of ran-dom-ness, but also encompasses the concept of ambiguity. Randomness is reflected in the appearing probability of cloud droplets in that point, while the qualitative fuzzy concept reflects the margin of uncertainty.

He: the uncertainty measure of entropy, reflecting the dispersion degree of cloud membership.

Cloud model as the specific method, can be generated by the software or the solidified hardware. Forward cloud generator or backward cloud generator are two of the most basic algorithm of cloud model. Forward cloud generator obtains the dis-tribution and quantitative data range through linguistic qualitative information, and complete the conversion directly. Backward cloud generator selects a sample data set with certain distribution to convert into linguistic qualitative information. The specific generation algorithm of forward cloud generator and backward cloud generator can be found in [7].

3 Based on Cloud Model and Danger Theory

The model is divided into two modules: the cloud model data processing module and DCA anomaly detection module. The mainly objective of cloud model data processing module is to establish normal cloud model and obtain its three data characteristics. DCA anomaly detection module calculates the diversity factor between normal cloud model and test data, and converts it into input of DCA to detect abnormality of test data.

3.1 Cloud Model Data Processing Module

Traditional data feature extraction methods contain entropy method, the card method, mutual information method, mean-variance method and so on. Due to requirements of data accuracy, backward cloud generator is now generally accepted as the feature extraction method. First of all, backward cloud generator algorithm needs to restore the digital characteristics of cloud model, such as entropy and hyper entropy. The parameters restoring method can use either membership grade, or directly use the property values of normal data, which avoids the uncertainty of membership grade and easy to promote into a higher dimensional. The specific algorithm is described as follows:

As the low computation and extraction feature of Chi-square test method, the paper use Chi-square method to complete the normal data modeling and data char-acteristics extracting. In order to calculate the Chi-square value and the weighting value of each attribute in the normal data. Take X as a matrix set recording the normal data in n rows and m columns, where each row represents one data, each column represents an attribute, i for the i-th data, j represents the j-th attribute. The specific process of normal cloud module feature calculation is as follows:

1. Enter the normal data, calculate the average of the j-th attribute in X:

$$\overline{X_j} = \frac{\sum_{i=1}^{n} x_{ij}}{n} \tag{1}$$

2. Using backward cloud algorithm to calculate each entropy of attribute cloud model in training data, the other two cloud model features can be extracted by the following formula:

$$Ex_j = \frac{\sum_{i=1}^{n} x_{ij}}{n} = \overline{X_j} \tag{2}$$

$$En_j = \sqrt{\frac{\pi}{2}} \times \frac{\sum_{i=1}^{n} |x_{ij} - Ex_j|}{n} \tag{3}$$

$$He_j = \sqrt{\frac{\sum_{i=1}^{n} (x_{ij} - Ex_j)^2}{n-1} - En_j^2} \tag{4}$$

3. Repeat steps 1 and step 2, complete each characteristic calculation of the other attributes cloud in the training data, to establish the normal data model. So as to complete the modeling process by backward cloud algorithms.
4. Calculated for each chi-square value of the column properties, see formula (5)

$$CS_j = \frac{(x_{ij} - \overline{X_j})^2}{\overline{X_j}} \tag{5}$$

5. By using the normalization formula, to calculate the weighting value of each attribute separately

$$P_j = \frac{CS_j}{\sum_{j=1}^{m} CS_j} \tag{6}$$

3.2   DCA Anomaly Detection Module

After the modeling of normal data, cloud model data processing module will produces three data characteristics - expectations, entropy and hyper entropy, DCA anomaly detection module first utilizes these characteristics to calculate the diversity factor between test data and normal cloud model. Secondly, according to different meanings of data's properties, DCA convert these diversity factors into different signal types, concrete signal implications and the process of DCA can be found in [8]. The difference degree of each attribute is done through backward cloud generator algorithm [9] under X condition. The backward cloud generator algorithm is as follows:

6. Generate normal cloud model based on the entropy and hyper entropy of random number:

$$Rn = NormalRandom(En_j, He_j) \tag{7}$$

7. Calculate the membership grade and difference degree of the input test data, taking the expectations as the center, as the standard deviation to produce the normal random number:

$$\mu_{ij} = \exp\left[-\frac{x_{ij} - Ex_j^2}{2Rn^2}\right] \tag{8}$$

$$\sigma_{ij} = 1 - \mu_{ij} \tag{9}$$

Traditional DCA focuses on process abnormities of data stream, ignoring the relationships in the data stream. But under the actual network circumstances, the intrusion behavior is usually centralized and targeted, if the computer is being invaded, then the evil data will be significantly increased comparing to the previous period. So the system alert level should be raised in this period data flow, just as the human body immune system. When a body organization is subjected to large-scale invasion of non-self antigens, cells in this region will immerse a lot of unnatural deaths and release dangerous signal to alert the body and amplify danger signal by inflammatory signals. Moreover, during the period when the body has a low degree of abnormality, the body generates inflammatory signals to suppress dangerous inflammatory signal generation. This inflammatory signal acts role of adjusting immune responses, so as to balance the body's immune process. The new algorithm can improve system's real-time response, if the degree of abnormality within a certain time significantly increased, the system will enhance concern of data flow in this period, reducing the system response time. The specific algorithm process is shown in Fig. 1.

4 Experimental Results and Analysis

The paper selects KDDCUP99 [8] data sets as the experimental data set. This data set is recognized as a practical network security audit data set, many intrusion detection and research papers are based on the data set. The experiment has two parts: data feature calculation and dendritic cell algorithm based on data segmented detection.

4.1 Data Feature Calculation

Experiment Select 1000 normal data to establish normal cloud model. After using formula (2−4), we get three attributes: expectation, entropy, hyper entropy, experiment content and simulation results are as follows:

It can be seen from the above, the lower membership of data attributes is, the lower weight percentage is. In the actual conditions, some properties of normal data may also be quite different from standard data set, so these properties should be little influence on the entire data, the share of weight factors should also be small (Fig. 2).

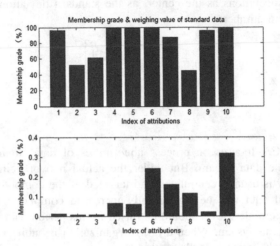

Fig. 2. Standard data set membership degree and the weight factor distribution histogram

4.2 DCA Segmented Detection Based on Data

Experiment selects normal data and intrusion data by simulating actual network environment, the first 300 is normal, the next 10 is attack signal of type pod, the next 50 is attack signal of type imap, the next 100 is normal, the final 100 is attack signal of type guess_passwd. Meanwhile, Experiment selects data segment length is 50, the inflammatory signal = 1.2, when DCA detect MCAV is more than 70 % of the overall number of antigens, which means the degree of abnormality exceeds the safe

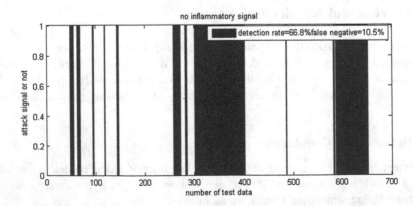

Fig. 3. The dendritic cell algorithm without inflammatory signal

level, system will start inflammatory signal to amplify PAMP. If MCAV is smaller than 30 %, system will start inflammatory signal to amplify SS, the specific results as shown below (Figs. 3 and 4):

It is obvious that the dendritic cell algorithm with inflammatory signal has better detection rate than traditional DCA, and reduces false negative rate. Experiment shows the anomaly detection model in this chapter can raise the ability of detecting abnormality.

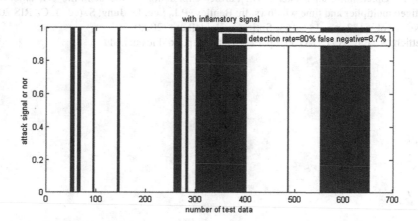

Fig. 4. The dendritic cell algorithm with inflammatory signal

5   Conclusion

DCA is currently still in the process of continuous improvement, the applicability of this algorithm become significant constraints on its development. How to select antigen and signals as input parameters, how to enter the standard normalization process and how to determine the threshold are still needed to solve in DCA. This paper create a standard cloud model by selecting the normal data, and detect data by segment, experiment shows the anomaly detection model can improve detection rates, effective reflects the degree of data abnormality.

References

1. Forrest, S., Perelson, A.S., Allen, L., et al.: Self-nonself discrimination in a computer. In: Proceedings of 1994 IEEE Computer Society Symposium on Research in Security and Privacy 1994, pp. 202–212. IEEE (1994)
2. Aickelin, U., Bentley, P.J., Cayzer, S., Kim, J., McLeod, J.: Danger theory: the link between AIS and IDS? In: Bentley, P.J., Hart, E., Timmis, J. (eds.) ICARIS 2003. LNCS, vol. 2787, pp. 147–155. Springer, Heidelberg (2003)
3. Greensmith, J., Aickelin, U., Cayzer, S.: Introducing dendritic cells as a novel immune-inspired algorithm for anomaly detection. In: Jacob, C., Pilat, M.L., Bentley, P.J., Timmis, J.I. (eds.) ICARIS 2005. LNCS, vol. 3627, pp. 153–167. Springer, Heidelberg (2005)

4. Weiwei, Z., Deyi, L.: Intrusion detection using cloud mode. Comput. Eng. Appl. **39**(26), 158–160 (2003)
5. Lowry, C.A., Woodall, W.H., Champ, C.W., et al.: A multivariate exponentially weighted moving average control chart. Technometrics **34**(1), 46–53 (1992)
6. Yang, H., Dong, H., Liang, Y., et al.: Definition of danger signal in artificial immune system using cloud method. Comput. Eng. Appl. **42**(10), 34–45 (2006)
7. Li, D., Meng, H.: Membership clouds and membership clouds generators. Comput. R&D **32**(6), 15–20 (1995)
8. Gu, F., Greensmith, J., Aickelin, U.: Further exploration of the dendritic cell algorithm: antigen multiplier and time windows. In: Bentley, P.J., Lee, D., Jung, S. (eds.) ICARIS 2008. LNCS, vol. 5132, pp. 142–153. Springer, Heidelberg (2008)
9. Hettich, S., Bay, S.D.: KDD Cup 1999 Data. http://kdd.ics.uci.edu

Generation and Distribution of Decoy Document System

Lei Wang[1(⊠)], Chenglong Li[2], QingFeng Tan[1], and XueBin Wang[3]

[1] Institute of Information Engineering, CAS, Beijing, China
{wanglei64,tanqingfeng}@iie.ac.cn
[2] National Computer Network Emergency Response Technical
Team/Coordination Center of China (CNCERT/CC), Beijing, China
lichenglong@cert.org.cn
[3] Beijing University of Posts and Telecommunications, Beijing, China
wangxuebin@nelmail.iie.ac.cn

Abstract. Currently a lot of the document data are leaked. We designed and implemented a decoy document system, which made up for the lack of traditional protection technology. We researched the document content generating technology, the document distributing technology and the document tracking and locating technology. We tested the system on networks, and our technology was proved to be effective.

Keywords: Document generating · Document distributing · Document tracking and locating · Decoy document

1 Introduction

Currently a lot of data leakages are the document data. The document types are mostly Office documents, PDF documents, CAD documents, with contents about official documents, engineering drawings, employee information, financial statements, and etc. On Sunday November 28th 2010, WikiLeaks—a non-profit organization released 251,287 classified documents of the U.S. State Department, and made a lot of American diplomatic insider public, which was called American diplomatic history "911" [1]. In March, 2011 CERT-Georgia discovered a Cyber Espionage incident, and then published a 27-page report, which said the malware infected at least 390 computers, targeted at government agencies, banks, and critical infrastructure. It searched sensitive documents, and uploaded to some Command and Control Servers, whose keywords included NATO, FBI, CIA, Russia, Georgia [2].

Now, there are many existing technologies to prevent the leakage of classified document. Text Filtering Technology filters transmit data on the host or the network exit, and can be used to prevent sensitive data leaked [3]. But it could not ensure that the classified document be filtered out from a dynamic text flow. Intrusion Detection Technology can only identify specific attack patterns or deviations from known, long-term user behavior. But it works as a standalone part, rather than an integrated defense architecture [4]. Access Control Technology affects the communication between domains, so that its utility is reduced [4]. Encryption and Decryption Technology could not stop legal users from leaking classified data by themselves.

Y. Yuan et al. (Eds.): ISCTCS 2013, CCIS 426, pp. 123–129, 2014.
DOI: 10.1007/978-3-662-43908-1_16, © Springer-Verlag Berlin Heidelberg 2014

To compensate for the insufficient of above techniques, we developed a generation and distribution of decoy document system. In addition, we distributed the different topic decoy documents to the target honeypots, and combined honeypots to capture attacks. Once decoy documents were opened, the attackers could be located and events could be analyzed.

The rest of this paper is organized as follows. Section 2 reviews prior research related to decoy document technology. Section 3 discusses the design and implementation of the system. Section 4 presents the results of our experiments. Section 5 summarizes our conclusions.

2   Related Work

Spitzner described how honeypots can be used to detect insider attack, rather than external attacks [6]. He combined honeytokens, which are some information that attacks are interested in, such as login and password, credit card numbers, medical record, financial account, and so on. But all of them are not true and bogus. These honeytokens are monitored and contribute to trapping attackers and finding some potential eavesdroppers. Jim Yuill introduced an intrusion-detection device named honeyfiles, which contained honeytokens [7]. The honeyfiles resided on a file server, and the server sent an alarm to end-users when a honey file was accessed.

Bowen et al. developed a decoy document system to automatically generate decoy files. The decoy files are generated according to selected the decoy document topic. They introduced and formalized a number of properties of decoys as a guide to design trap-based defenses to increase the likelihood of detecting an insider attack [4]. The beacons in the decoy document could trigger an alert when touched.

Ben implemented a Serinus System which could automate the generation of decoy files according to different host environments. The decoy files were generated based on statistics, which gathered on file attributes such as: file names, file sizes, file creation dates, number of images [8].

In addition, Ben Salem and Stolfo presented some effective techniques to deploy decoy documents. They discussed several tradeoffs between the characteristics and effective decoys. Specially, they presented guidelines for making decoy documents more enticing and believable [9].

Most recently, Jonathan et al. presented a new method of generating decoy document contents based automatic translation. They discussed how to use language manipulation to craft decoy content that is more more appealing for adversaries, but normal users can immediately recognize as fake study [10].

Bowen et al. proposed a novel trap-based architecture for enterprise networks that detected "silent" attacks who were eavesdropping network traffic [11]. They generate a lot of believable decoy information which was transported on inner networks. They successfully monitored eavesdropping and exploitation attempts.

Tiago proposed a solution capable of tracking sensitive document within a corporate network. They resorted to an agent installed on the hosts to be monitored that detected and logged the usage of files by potentially dangerous operations, such as copying it to a removable drive or sending it by e-mail as an attachment [12]. The method monitored the transmission path of decoy documents within the enterprise network.

3 System Design

3.1 System Goals

Base on the system we developed, we proposed six core properties for decoy documents. **Believability**: The decoy document and the classified document are as similar as possible, but the decoy document should not contain any sensitive information. The decoy document appears true and is capable of being believed by attacks. **Differentiable**: The decoy document and the classified document are easy to be distinguished by legitimate users, in order to avoid accessing the decoy document in the case of user mistakes. **Detectability**: The decoy document and the classified document are easy to be detected by the protection system on the host or the network exit. **Visibility**: The decoy document is easily found or perceived by attackers, deliberately stored on the place attackers are easy to see, initiative to "leak out" on the network. **Enticing**: The content and title of the decoy document are highly attractive, and are able to arouse hope or desire of attacks. **Traceability**: Once the decoy document is accessed, it is possible to track the target behavior of accessing, and obtain a visitor's information.

3.2 System Structure

Based on the six core properties above, we designed five modules of our system, which generated and distributed documents to targets. It was shown in Fig. 1.

The System Interaction Process Module was used to identify the callers' configure and resolve to system parameters, which was for calling other four sub-modules. The Decoy Type Process Module was designed to generate diverse document type templates based on the parameters, such as: Office Word, Office Excel, PDF, RTF, CAD and TXT. The Decoy Topic Process Module was to generate a variety of document

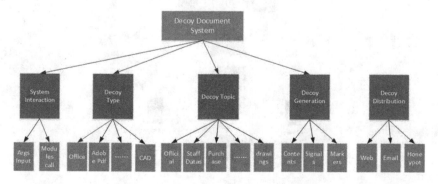

Fig. 1. Decoy document system modules

topic templates, which contained different contents such as Official Documentation, Employee Information, Purchase Order, Financial Statement, Engineering Drawing and etc. Moreover, users could upload documents as topic templates. The Decoy Generation Process Module organized topic contents into an elegant layout. "Beacons" and "Markers" were also added to documents. The Decoy Distribution Process Module supported users obtained documents by email and downloading from webpage according to demand. In addition, we combined honeypots and deployed decoys according to the documentation environment of the honeypot with reference to [8]. The invoking process flow between modules was illustrated in Fig. 2.

3.3   System Implement

Content Generation Technology. We used HoneyToken Technology to generate contents. It filtered keywords from the input data source based on replacement rules [13]. According to mapping rules which was set by user or added by expert, we replaced sensitive data fields. The sensitive data fields were generally identity attributes (identification number, phone number), valuable attributes (credit card number, passwords, financial). Then, we set the paragraph space, text color and size and title of the decoy article. We made the layout of contents just like people edited, but sorted by program.

Distributing Technology. We developed a web server for users to manage decoy documents. It supported configuration, generation, downloading of decoy documents and uploading templates. Furthermore, we implemented a mail server based on Apache James. Users would send email to get desired documents. We also designed a program to transfer files, which distributed the decoy to specified honeypots.

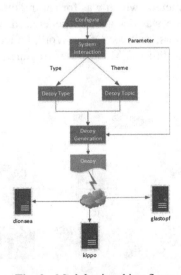

Fig. 2. Modules invoking flow

Tracking and Locating Technology. The embedded "marker" is used by a host or network sensor to detect when documents are loaded in memory or transmitted in the clear. The markers are constructed as a unique pattern of a string. We used a random algorithm to generate a key and a seed. And the key is used by a hash algorithm to encrypt the seed, and then we get the seed's MAC value. Furthermore, we design an algorithm to transform the seed, the key and the MAC value to a string pattern, which looked more real. The string was divided into three parts, hidden in "Subject", "Keywords", and "Category" of the document fields.

Beacon code in decoy documents should be hidden to avoid their easy identification. Once a document is opened, the beacons attempt to silently send an alert token to a centralized server, and we used HTTP protocol to send alerts. In the case of the MS Word and MS Excel document, the vbscript code and a remote image were stealthily embedded. The remote image is rendered but not visible by eyes. In the case of PDF document beacons, the signaling mechanism relies on the execution of the javascript code within the document.

Once triggered an alert event, we used the world map to locate the attacker. We combined all monitoring information from sensors and honeypots, to analyze attacks.

4 Evaluation

We tested the decoys on the hosts and the honeypots. The testers were our lab members but had no knowledge of our system. In addition, we simulated an attack to honeypots, stole documents, sent to the remote end, and opened decoys. The central server captured the whole attack event.

We tested the documents with the most common configurations of operating systems and document viewers. Presented in Tables 1, 2 and 3 below, we tested two document types. For Word and Excel document, we tested the "remote image" and "macro" beacon, and "javascript" beacon for PDF. We found that whether the beacons worked was related to the operating system and the application software. For all operating systems and office softwares, the "remote image" beacon works well. There was one time that the "remote image" beacon did not trigger, that was affected by high network latency. The "macro" beacon just worked well when decoys opened by office 2003. When opened by office 2007 and 2010, it popped up a warning. If allowed by the user, it also worked well. The "javascript" beacon worked well on Mac and Windows platform but not well on Ubuntu platform.

Table 1. Word and excel remote image test results

OS	Application	Tests (remote image)	Triggers
Windows XP/Win7	Office 2003	10	9
Windows XP/Win7	Office 2010	10	10
Mac OS	Office 2003, 2010	5	5
Ubuntu	Open Office	5	5

Table 2. Word and excel macro test results

OS	Application	Tests (macro)	Triggers
Windows XP/Win7	Word 2003	10	10
Windows XP/Win7	Word 2010	10	0
Mac OS	Office 2003	5	5
Mac	Office 2010	5	0
Ubuntu	OpenOffice	5	0

Table 3. PDF beacon test results

OS	Application	Tests	Triggers
Windows XP/Win7	Adobe	10	10
Windows XP/Win7	Foxit	10	10
Mac OS	Adobe	5	5
Ubuntu	Evince	5	0

5 Conclusions

Experiments indicated that the decoy document system worked well. We generated high "believability" decoys. Embedded "beacons" made decoy documents easily detected and "markers" made documents being tracked. The remote image technology worked well on any operating system, no matter the decoy document was opened by any application. The vbscript code popped up a warning when opened by office 2007 and 2010 version, and the javascript code did the same opened by any PDF reader. In our future work, we would break out these limits, and send alerts with no warnings.

Acknowledgements. These and the Reference headings are in bold but have no numbers. Text below continues as normal. This work is supported by National Natural Science Foundation of China (Grant No. 61272500), National High Technology Research and Development Program of China, 863 Program (Grant No. 2011AA01A103 and 2012AA013101), National Key Technology R&D Program (Grant No. 2012BAH37B04), and Strategic Priority Research Program of the Chinese Academy of Sciences (Grant No. XDA06030200).

References

1. http://en.wikipedia.org/wiki/United_States_diplomatic_cables_leak#cite_note-1
2. http://dea.gov.ge/uploads/CERT%20DOCS/Cyber%20Espionage.pdf
3. Oard, D.W., Marchionini, G.: A conceptual framework for text filtering. Technical report, University of Maryland, Maryland (1996)
4. Bowen, B.M., et al.: Monitoring technologies for mitigating insider threats. Columbia University, Department of Computer Science, 28 Aug. 2009. http://ids.cs.columbia.edu/sites/default/files/insider-bookchapter.pdf

5. Bowen, B.M., Hershkop, S., Keromytis, A.D., Stolfo, S.J.: Baiting Inside Attackers Using Decoy Documents. In: Chen, Y., Dimitriou, T.D., Zhou, J. (eds.) SecureComm 2009. LNICST, vol. 19, pp. 51–70. Springer, Heidelberg (2009)
6. Spitzner, L.: Honeypots: catching the insider threat. ACSAC, December 2003
7. Yuill, J., Zappe, M., Denning, D., Feer, F.: Honeyfiles: deceptive files for intru-sion detection. In: Proceedings of the Fifth Annual IEEE SMC Information Assurance Workshop, pp. 116–122, June 2004
8. Whitham, B.: Automating the generation of fake documents to detect network intruders. Int. J. Cyber-Security Digit. Forensics 2, 103–118 (2013)
9. Salem, M. B., Stolfo, S.: Decoy document deployment for effective masquerade attack detection. In: Conference on Detection of Intrusions and Malware and Vulnerability Assessment (2011)
10. Voris, J., Boggs, N., Stolfo, S.: Lost in translation: improving decoy documents via automated translation. In: Workshop on Research for Insider Threat (2012)
11. Bowen, B. M., Kemerlis, V. P., Prabhu, P., Keromytis, A. D., Stolfo, S. J.: Automating the injection of believable decoys to detect snooping. In: Proceedings of the Third ACM Conference on Wireless Network Security, p. 8186 (2010)
12. Mendo, T.: Document flow tracking within corporate networks, Master's thesis, Carnegie Mellon University/Faculdade de Ciências da Universidade de Lisboa, November 2009
13. Bercovitch, M., Renford, M., Hasson, L., Shabtai, A., Rokach, L., Elovici, Y.: HoneyGen: an automated honeytokens generator. Intell. Secur. Inf. 131–136 (2011)

Detecting the DGA-Based Malicious Domain Names

Ying Zhang[⊠], Yongzheng Zhang, and Jun Xiao

Institute of Information Engineering, Chinese Academy of Sciences,
Beijing, China
{zhangying, zhangyongzheng, xiaojun}@iie.ac.cn

Abstract. To achieve the goals of concealment and migration, some Bot Nets, such as Conficker, Srizbis and Torpig, use Domain Generation Algorithm (DGA) to produce a large number of random domain names dynamically. Then a small subset of these domain names would be selected for actual C&C. Compared with normal domain names, these domain names generated by DGA have significant difference in length, character frequency, etc. Current researches mainly use clustering-classification methods to Detect abnormal domain name. Some of them use NXDomain traffic clustering, other researches based on the classification of string features, such as the distribution of alphanumeric characters and bigram. In fact, domain name has strict hierarchy and each domain level has particular regularities. In this paper, the hierarchical characteristic is introduced into the detection process. We divide the domain name into distinct levels and calculate the characteristic value separately. In each level, we use entropy, bigram and length detections. Because of different efficiency in levels, we design the weigh for each level based on their efficiency. Finally, the level characteristic value of domain name is the weighted average value of levels. Our experiments show that the accuracy of the level-based method is higher than 94 %.

Keywords: Domain names · Domain generation algorithm · Malicious · Level · Entropy · Bigram · Length

1   Introduction

Domain Name System (DNS), as one of the core services of Internet, provides mapping and parsing between domain name and IP address. DNS technique can be found in almost all internet applications, such as web surfing and email. However, it involves risk too. In the last ten years, hundreds of network security events have occurred, which has seriously affected people's daily use of the network, causing great harm to the whole society.

Domain Name Generation Algorithm (DGA) [1] is used to periodically generate a large number of domain names which are selected as control nodes. Most Botnets, such as Conficker, Srizbis and Tor-pig, produce a large number of domain names to control the bot which is based on Domain Name Generation Algorithm. Botnets dynamically generate a lot of domain names and specify them as hidden nodes. Above all, exceptional domain research has important theoretical significance and practical value.

Y. Yuan et al. (Eds.): ISCTCS 2013, CCIS 426, pp. 130–137, 2014.
DOI: 10.1007/978-3-662-43908-1_17, © Springer-Verlag Berlin Heidelberg 2014

2   Related Work

There is some relevant literature about the DGA generated domain detection:

Stone-Gross et al. [2] first pointed out the difference between domain fluxing and IP fast-fluxing. Domain fluxing used a domain generation algorithm to generate a large number of domain names. The authors also pointed out Torpig's DGA algorithm adopts the second character of the most popular topic on Twitter every day as a random seed to generate the first domain name. They used the fifth topic's second character to update the domain name. Srizbis also used magic number as random seed to generate domain name. A different set of domains is generated by XOR'ing magic number with the current date. The generated domain name only consists of "q w e r t y u i o p a s d f".

Yadav et al. [3] proposed a detection technique to identify botnets by finding domain names which are randomly generated [4], improved NXDomains and temporal correlation. In first paper, they used an offline dataset from a Tier-1 ISP in South Asia to detect Conficker botnets automatically for evaluating their method. In second paper, they used ISP dataset and DNS logs of a university.

Villamarin-Salomon and Brustoloni [5] compared two methods of identifying botnet C&Cs. In the first method, they identified domains with high query rates or temporally correlated domains. They used Chebyshev's inequality and Mahalanobis distance to identify anomalous domains. In the second method, they analyzed recurring "dynamic" DNS replied with NXDomain responses. Their experiments indicated that the first method was not effective, because several legitimate services used DNS with short time-to-live (TTL) values. Their second method could get better detection and identified suspicious C&C domains.

Overall, some common deficiencies exist in the former researches. Firstly, the rate of false alarm is high. Besides, the instantaneity performance is poor. In addition, a large amount of memory consumption is required during the detection process. Finally, most methods cannot detect multiple types of network attack simultaneous and lose their effect when facing with unknown Anomaly Domain Names.

3   Detection Algorithm

A Domain Name [6] is an identification string that defines a realm of administrative autonomy, authority, or control on the Internet. Domain names, as the representatives of each corporation or institute on the internet, consist of letters, numbers and "dash". Each domain name has several levels. Different levels are separated by "dot".

The probability of the occurrence of each character in normal domain names follows certain distribution. However, when the domain name is faked, the distribution of each character will be extremely different from the normal one. We use entropy to calculate the chaotic stage of the distribution in faked domain names in order to distinguish them from the normal ones. Although entropy can be used to detect each character's frequency of occurrence, it doesn't take the characters' sequence into account. So, we use bigram-detection to measure the probability of occurrence that two characters successively appeared. Besides, the length of each level also obeys certain distribution. In order to improve the accuracy of the detection algorithm, we introduce length value into the detection process as a macroscopic measurement.

3.1 Entropy Detection

Shannon, the founder of information theory, introduced the concept of entropy into his researches. The higher the concentration, the lower the entropy. Each character's probability in one single level can be calculated. If there is M characters in a level, and the probability of character i is P_i. Then, entropy can be explicitly written as follows:

$$D_{entropy} = -\frac{1}{M}\sum_{i=1}^{M} p_i \log_2 p_i \qquad (1)$$

3.2 Bigram Detection

We start and end the character string with "\$" and separate the domain names into bigrams level by level. For example, "google" is separated into "\$g", "go", "oo", "og", "gl", "le" and "e\$". In each level, we record the frequency of every bigram $Cnt_{i,j}$. MAX_{Cnt} is the largest value in this matrix. The Bigram character value of this level is defined as:

$$B_{i,j} = 1 - \frac{\log Cnt_{i,j}}{\log MAX_{Cnt}} \qquad (2)$$

Then the bigram matrix can be calculated:

$$D_{bigram} = \begin{array}{c} \\ a \\ \vdots \\ z \\ 0 \\ \vdots \\ 9 \\ - \\ \$ \end{array} \begin{array}{ccccccc} a & \cdots & z & 0 & \cdots & 9 & - & \$ \\ \left[\begin{array}{cccccccc} B_{1,1} & \cdots & B_{1,26} & B_{1,27} & \cdots & B_{1,36} & B_{1,37} & B_{1,38} \\ \vdots & \ddots & \vdots & \vdots & \ddots & \vdots & \vdots & \vdots \\ B_{26,1} & \cdots & B_{26,26} & B_{26,27} & \cdots & B_{26,36} & B_{26,37} & B_{26,38} \\ B_{27,1} & \cdots & B_{27,26} & B_{27,27} & \cdots & B_{27,36} & B_{27,37} & B_{27,38} \\ \vdots & \ddots & \vdots & \vdots & \ddots & \vdots & \vdots & \vdots \\ B_{36,1} & \cdots & B_{36,26} & B_{36,27} & \cdots & B_{36,36} & B_{36,37} & B_{36,38} \\ B_{37,1} & \cdots & B_{37,26} & B_{37,27} & \cdots & B_{37,36} & B_{37,37} & B_{37,38} \\ B_{38,1} & \cdots & B_{38,26} & B_{38,27} & \cdots & B_{38,36} & B_{38,37} & B_{38,38} \end{array}\right] \end{array}$$

3.3 Length Detection

A domain name's length, as a global assessment variable, also embodies a part of the features. We use the existing data set to record the frequency of length in each level of normal domain names. Suppose in a level, Cnt_i represents the frequency of domain name whose length equals i and Cnt_{MAx} is most frequent length's value. When we detect a suspect domain name's length, we can get its length frequency from our empirical data, and its length character value can be tested by the following formula:

$$D_{length} = 1 - \frac{Cnt_i}{Cnt_{MAx}} \tag{3}$$

While Cnt_i of the suspect domain name equals zero times, it is obvious that such length never occurs in normal domain names; while Cnt_i equals to Cnt_{MAx}, it means such length always appears in normal domain names and its corresponding length character value equals zero. To sum up, D_{length} refers to the possibility of abnormal domain name, the closer to 1, the more likely it is.

3.4   Domain Name Detection

The first step is to train the normal domain name set. After training, we can get the entropy character value, bigram character value and length character value of each level from the normal data set. The average of each index is noted as $A_{normally}^{entropy}, A_{normally}^{bigram}$ and $A_{normally}^{length}$. And the level character value is worked out as the three indexes' weighted average.

$$\begin{cases} A_{normally}^{level} = \alpha A_{normally}^{entropy} + \beta A_{normally}^{bigram} + \gamma A_{normally}^{length} \\ \alpha + \beta + \gamma = 1 \end{cases} \tag{4}$$

Finally, we can calculate the domain names' integral character value.

$$A_{normally} = \frac{1}{N} \sum_{i=1}^{N} A_{normally}^{level_i} \tag{5}$$

The second step is to train the other three abnormal domain name sets. The process is similar to the training of the normal one. After this step, suspect domain names can be selected by comparing their integral character value with the criterion. Once the integral character value is out of the threshold, this domain name is considered as a fake name.

4   Results

In this section, we evaluate the three level-detection methods; then we compare the detection accuracy of domain names generated by three common DGA algorithms like Conficker, Torpig, and Srizbis. In addition, we will briefly introduce our test data set.

4.1   Data Set

For our analysis, we use an ISP DNS data as the normal data set. This data contains 36863040 domain names in one hour traffic. The abnormal data sets are generated by three different domain name algorithms which are Conficker, Torpig, and Srizbis. A domain name generated by Conficker usually has four to ten characters for each level and their top-level domain utilizes the 110 standard names. Torpig uses the most popular words from Twitter as random seeds. And Srizbis uses certain numbers as random seeds, by doing XOR operation with the current date to generate new domain names.

4.2   Evaluation of Entropy Detection

Entropy detection can show the difference of frequency of each character between normal domain names and suspect ones. According to the statistical result, in normal domain names, the five vowels "a, e, i, o, u" appear most frequently; among the Consonants, "c, m, n, s, p, q" have the highest frequency, while "j, z" hardly turn up. In addition, numbers occur in normal domain names too, but with a comparatively low frequency.

It is extremely explicit that the domain names generated by DGA are quite different from the normal ones. First, none of Conficker, Torpig, and Srizbis uses numbers in their domain names. Second, the probability of each letter's is different. In Conficker, the most frequent letters are "c, m, o" and the other letters have a similar distribution. In Torpig, "h, x" have extremely high frequency. In Srizbis, only fourteen letters occurred in the domain names which are "q w e r t y u i o p a s d f" (Fig. 1).

4.3   Evaluation of Bigram Detection

Bigram value can reflect the distribution of adjacent characters. According to the experiment result, firstly, we get a same obvious conclusion that there is no number utilized in DGA generated domain names. In addition, the frequency of bigram is

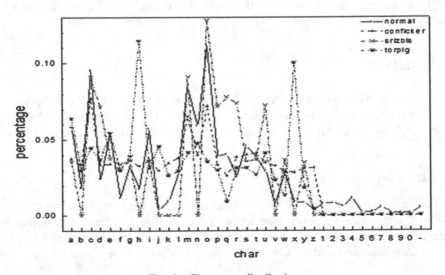

Fig. 1. Characters distribution

quite different too. Taking the bigrams beginning with "a" as an example, in normal domain names, it is highly frequent that 'a' is followed by 'i', 'o', 'p'; while bigrams, such as "ae", "aq", seldom appear.

However, it is extremely different from the DGA generated domain names. In Conficker, 'a' usually turns up at the end of character strings. In Torpig, the frequency of "ai", "ap" are quite low, while "ag", "an", "ar", "ay" are comparatively high. In Srizbis, nearly half of the letters have never been used, while the rest is with an even frequency. The same situation occurred in the other bigrams' detection process. Therefore, we can use Bigram value to evaluate the validity of a domain name (Fig. 2).

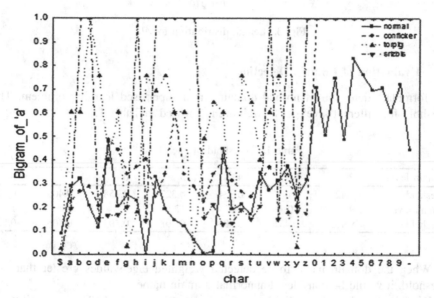

Fig. 2. Bigram of 'a'

4.4   Evaluation of Length Detection

The result of length detection is apparent too. Taking the detection of Second-level domain name as example, in the normal domain names, the most frequent length of SLD is two and five, and with longer length, the frequency decreases. Among the three kinds of domain name algorithms, Conficker is the only one that considered the length of the character string in the second level. But, the length value of Conficker is so even that without certain tendency. In Torpig and Srizbis, their SLDs have fixed lengths which are eight and nine (Fig. 3).

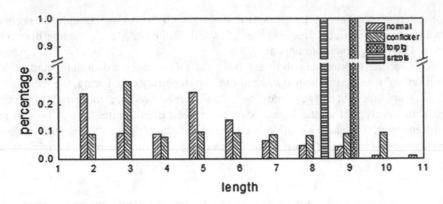

Fig. 3. Length distribution for all

4.5   Evaluation of Domain Detection

We formulate detection of normal domains as a supervised learning problem. The threshold for different level get by training is showed in Table 1:

Table 1. Threshold of each level

Domain level	2	3	4	5	6	7	8
Threshold	0.421	0.403	0.334	0.327	0.358	0.405	0.423
Domain level	9	10	11	12	13	14	15
Threshold	0.452	0.451	0.53	0.398	0.503	0.506	0.553

When the domain name to be detected weighted eigenvalues greater than the threshold, it would be considered abnormal domain name.

We test the detection efficiency of our detection method. The probability of normal domain were judged as normal is 96.2 %. Three kinds of DGA recognition accuracy are high. The detection accuracy of domain names generated by Conficker reaches 94.3 %. 93.5 % of domain names generated by Torpig algorithm can be correctly identified. Detection accuracy for Srizbis algorithm is 90.1 %.

5   Conclusions

In conclusion, this paper introduced a level-based domain name detection algorithm, which can discriminate the suspect domain names with a high accuracy. The level detection contains three character values which measure the character distribution, bigram distribution and the length separately. By combining the three character values, we can determine the threshold of each level's synthetic character value. The result of our experiment shows the level-based domain name detection algorithm can achieve very high detection accuracy.

6 Future Work

It is universally acknowledged that DGAs are not constant algorithms. Just like Conficker, some DGAs have improved their algorithms in both aspects of domain name generation and query program design. This paper limited to extend the efficiency of domain name detection from the level's perspective. In the future, improvement can also be made in the realm of random seeds selection and random algorithm design.

References

1. Domain generation algorithm. http://en.wikipedia.org/wiki/Domain_generation_algorithm
2. Stone-Gross, B., Cova, M., Cavallaro, L., Gilbert, B., Szydlowski, M., Kemmerer, R., Kruegel, C., Vigna, G.: Your botnet is my botnet: analysis of a botnet takeover. In: Proceedings of the 16th ACM Conference on Computer and Communications Security, CCS'09, pp. 635–647. ACM, New York (2009)
3. Yadav, S., Reddy, A.K.K., Reddy, A.N., Ranjan, S.: Detecting algorithmically generated malicious domain names. In: Proceedings of the 10th Annual Conference on Internet Measurement, IMC '10, pp. 48–61. ACM, New York (2010)
4. Yadav, S., Narasimha Reddy, A.L.: Winning with DNS Failures: strategies for faster botnet detection. In: Rajarajan, M., Piper, F., Wang, H., Kesidis, G. (eds.) SecureComm 2011. LNICST, vol. 96, pp. 446–459. Springer, Heidelberg (2012)
5. Villamarin-Salomon, R., Brustoloni, J.: Identifying botnets using anomaly detection techniques applied to DNS traffic. In: 5th Consumer Communications and Networking Conference (2008)
6. Domain name. http://en.wikipedia.org/wiki/Domain_Name

Microblog Sentiment Classification Based on Supervised and Unsupervised Combination

Shaojie Pei[1](✉), Lumin Zhang[1], Aiping Li[1], and Yusha Liu[2]

[1] School of Computer, National University of Defense Technology,
Changsha, China
chenyue24psj@gmail.com

[2] Department of Optical Engineering, Zhejiang University, Hangzhou, China

Abstract. Millions of users are sharing their views and opinions in microblog everyday, which makes sentiment classification in microblog be an important and practical issue in social networks. In this paper, we combined the conversional supervised algorithm with unsupervised methods to conduct sentiment analysis. Specifically, we divided the content into two parts: those with emoticons and those without emoticons, and use multiple optimization for the two different parts. Practical evaluation shows that our methods could perform effectively and efficiently for this attracting problem.

Keywords: Sentiment classification · Naive Bayes · Semantic similarity · Microblog

1 Introduction

With the rapid development of social network, microblog has become a popular and valuable social media to analyze user's opinions. Sentiment analysis, also known as opinion mining, aims to analyze people's attitude, viewpoint and feelings to entities, such as products, services, organizations or individuals, events, topics, and their properties [1]. Due to its important application, many research have conducted on this hot topic. Typically, there are two types of methods for sentiment classification. One is using supervised learning algorithm, like Naive Bayes, Support Vector Machine, etc. The other one is unsupervised algorithm based on rules or corpus dictionaries. We will briefly introduce those previous work in Sect. 2.

In this paper, we combine these two methods to perform sentiment analysis in Chinese microblog. Particularly, we divide messages into two types, those with emoticons and those without emoticons. Emoticon is a kind of sentiment symbol to directly express user's feelings or moods. It becomes more and more popular in Chinese microblog such as SINA Weibo, and plays increasing important role in sentiment classification. For emoticon messages, we designed an emoticon model to directly classify the orientation into anger, fear, sadness, happiness, like, disgusted, surprise. For those messages without emoticons, we proposed

Y. Yuan et al. (Eds.): ISCTCS 2013, CCIS 426, pp. 138–145, 2014.
DOI: 10.1007/978-3-662-43908-1_18, © Springer-Verlag Berlin Heidelberg 2014

a classification model combining Naive Bayes algorithm with dictionary-based methods to perform the final analysis. The main contribution of this paper is as follows:

(1) We proposed a framework for the problem of sentiment analysis in microblog and used a combination method to tackle the problem. We also paid more attention to the important emoticons appearing in messages.
(2) Using 21256 real messages in SINA Weibo, we performed practical experiments for our algorithm, and the result shows that our approach could perform effectively and efficiently.

The rest is organized as follows. In Sect. 2, we will briefly introduce previous related work. In Sect. 3, we detail our models and methods. The experiments are shown in Sect. 4 and we conclude our work in Sect. 5.

2   Related Work

Supervised learning methods, such as Naive Bayes or Support Vector Machines. Pang et al. [2] used supervised learning to classify movie reviews into two classes, positive and negative, and showed that using unigrams as features in classification performed quite well with either Naive Bayes or SVM. Zheng and Ye [3] conducts an exploring research on sentiment analysis to Chinese traveler reviews by Support Vector Machine algorithm.

As for unsupervised learning, [4] proposed a unsupervised classification method for document by building emotional vocabulary list. Reference [5] is a typical method of this technique. Given a review, the algorithm computers the average sentiment orientation (SO) of all phrased in the review based on point-wise mutual information measures, and classified the review as positive if the average SO is positive and negative otherwise. In addition, lexicon-based method, which uses a dictionary of sentiment words and phrases with their associated orientations and strength, and incorporates intensification and negation to compute a sentiment score for each document, is also widely used.

3   Classification Model Construction

3.1   Definition

We firstly make some definitions as follows.

Definition 1. $D = (d_1, d_2, d_3 \cdots, d_n)$: microblog archive flow, $d_i = \{w_1, \cdots, w_n, e_1, \cdots, e_n\}$: a microblog with $w_1, \cdots, w_n$ represents the vocabulary obtained after preprocessing, $e_1, \cdots, e_n$ represents emoticons in a microblog.

Definition 2. $feature\_words = \{w_i | w_i \in d_i \text{ and } w_i \in lexicon\}$ represents a set of feature words obtained from a preprocessing microblog without emoticons. Here dictionary represents emotional lexicon.

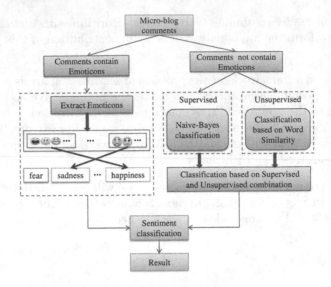

Fig. 1. Microblogs sentiment classification process.

Definition 3. $C = < c_1, c_2, \cdots, c_m >$: *emotion vector, where c_k represents emotion. The message d is provided, then we should detect the emotion c_k from a microblog, $c_k = \arg\max\limits_{c_i \in C} P(c_i | d)$.*

In this paper, the microblogs were divided into two parts, microblogs with emoticons and non-emoticons. For the microblogs with emoticons, we use emoticon model for the emotional classification. While for the microblogs without emoticons, we propose a classification method combining the characteristics of Naive Bayes based on emotional lexicons and the classification method based on semantic similarity of Hownet, respectively. The method and procedure is demonstrated in Fig. 1.

3.2 Emoticonal Classification for Microblogs with Emoticons

The emoticons can directly demonstrate reviewers emotional tendencies in microblogs. Zhao et al. [6] categorized the emoticons into different sentiments would make the tweets divided into different emotion classes. In this paper, we made the emoticons belong to one of the 7 types. For a microblog containing many emoticons, the emoticons always represent the same emotion, thus the emoticons usually belong to the same emotional type. In order to realize the classification for microblogs with emoticons, firstly, we extract the emoticons, then find the corresponding mapping emotional types. So far, we can obtain the emotional classification. For a microblog with emoticons, $d_i = \{w_1, \cdots, w_n, e_1, \cdots, e_n | n \geq 2\}$, the emotional classification method is demonstrated in formula (1).

$$C_{emo}(c_i, d) = \{c_i | c_i \in C, (e_1 \cdots e_n) \to c_i\} \tag{1}$$

3.3   The Emotional Classification for Microblogs Without Emoticons

Native Bayes Classification Based on Emotional Lexicon. In this paper, when refers to the emotional classification for microblogs without emoticons, Naive Bayes method firstly is used to build the microblog emotion classifiers [7]. Bayes classification is a kind of prior probability based on assumptions and a learning method calculating the probability of each key under the condition of a given assumption.

A microblog without emoticons can be expressed as $d_i = \{w_1, \cdots, w_n\}$, and so for the microblogs without emoticons, after the preprocessing extraction for the feature words, the feature words gather can express as $feature\_words = \{w_i | w_i \in d_i \ and \ w_i \in lexicon\}$, and its emotional categories are $C = \{c_i | i = 1, 2, 3, 4, 5, 6, 7\}$, under the condition of feature words are independent to each other, the classification method based on Naive Bayes for non-emoticons microblogs as shown in formula (2).

$$
\begin{aligned}
C_{Bayes} &= \arg\max_{c_i \in C} Bayes(c_j, d) \\
&= \arg\max_{c_i \in C} \{P(c_j) \textstyle\prod_{i=1}^{n} P(w_i, c_j)\}
\end{aligned}
\tag{2}
$$

$Bayes(c_j, d)$ represents the probability of microblog d classified based on Naive Bayes and belonged category, c_j. $P(c_j)$ represents the prior probability of type c_j. $P(w_i, c_j)$ represents the posterior probability that w_i belongs to category c_j. The prior probability $P(c_j)$ is obtained according to the prior estimation from the training corpus. The calculation method of the estimation is shown in formula (3).

$$
P(c_j) = \frac{message(c_j)}{\sum_{c_j \in C} message(c_j)}
\tag{3}
$$

Here, $message(c_j)$ represents the microblogs belong to category c_j. The posterior probability $P(w_i, c_j)$ represents the probability that the feature word w_i, belongs to category c_j, and can be estimated by the calculation in the training corpus. The calculation method of the posterior probability is shown in formula (4), (5). Here, $weight(w_i, c_j)$ represents the weight of w_i in the category c_j.

$$
P(w_i, c_j) = \frac{weight(w_i, c_j) + 1/N}{\sum_{i=1}^{n} weight(w_i, c_j) + 1}
\tag{4}
$$

$$
N = \sum_{c_j \in C} \sum_{i=1}^{n} weight(w_i, c_j)
\tag{5}
$$

The Emotional Classification Based on Lexical Semantic Similarity of HowNet. In this paper, when refers to the emotional classification of non-emoticon microblogs, we also use the classification method based on the lexical semantic similarity. Liu and Li [8] proposed a similarity calculation method based on Hownet. By using Hownet semantics and primitive similarity calculation method realized text orientation analysis [9], a new emotional classification based on Hownet lexical semantic similarity is proposed in this paper.

For two Chinese vocabulary w_1 and w_2, if w_1 has n concepts: $S_{11}, \cdots, S_{1n}$. w_2 has m concepts: $S_{21}, \cdots, S_{2m}$. The similarity of the vocabulary w_1 and w_2 is the maximum for the similarity of each concept, as demonstrated in formula(6).

$$Sim(W_1, W_2) = \max_{i=1..n, j=1...m} Sim(S_{1i}, S_{2j}) \tag{6}$$

In this way, the problem of the similarity between two words is due to the similarity between two concepts. The overall similarity of the semantic expression of the two concepts is demonstrated in formula (7).

$$Sim(S_1, S_2) = \sum_{i=1}^{4} \beta_i \prod_{j=1}^{i} Sim_j(S_1, S_2) \tag{7}$$

Here, $\beta_i (1 \leq i \leq 4)$ s an adjustable parameter, and $\beta_1 + \beta_2 + \beta_3 + \beta_4 = 1$, $\beta_1 \geq \beta_2 \geq \beta_3 \geq \beta_4$. $Sim_1(S_1, S_2)$ represents the similarity of two concepts for the first independent primitive description; $Sim_2(S_1, S_2)$ represents the similarity of two concepts for the other independent primitive description; $Sim_3(S_1, S_2)$ represents the similarity of two concepts for the related independent primitive description; $Sim_4(S_1, S_2)$ represents the similarity of two concepts for the symbol independent primitive description.

Since all the concepts ultimately come down to primitive, so the similarity calculation of primitive is the basis of that in concepts, as shown in formula (8).

$$Sim(p_1, p_2) = \frac{\alpha}{d + \alpha} \tag{8}$$

Among them, p_1 and p_2 expresses two primitives. d, a positive integer, is the length of the path between p_1 and p_2 in the primitive hierarchy. α is an adjustable parameter.

After preprocessing to non-emoticons microblog, it can be expressed as $d = \{w_1, \cdots, w_n\}$, emotional categories $C = \{c_i | i = 1, 2, 3, 4, 5, 6, 7\}$. In the case of feature words are independent to each other, the classification method for non-emoticons microblogs is demonstrated in formula (9).

$$C_{sim} = \arg\max_{c_i \in C} Sim(c_i, d)$$
$$= \arg\max_{c_i \in C} \sum_{j=1}^{n} Sim(c_i, w_j) \tag{9}$$

Here, $Sim(c_i, d)$ is the similarity between the microblog, $d = \{w_1, \cdots, w_n\}$, and the emotional category c_i. $Sim(c_i, w_j)$ is the similarity between the vocabulary w_j contained by microblog d and category c_i, namely the maximum similarity between the vocabulary w_j and every emotional words c_{ij} in the emotion c_i. The calculation equation is shown in formula (10).

$$Sim(c_i, w_j) = \max\{Sim(c_{ij}, w_j) | c_{ij} \in lexicon \& c_{ij} \rightarrow c_i\} \tag{10}$$

The Combination of Emotion Classification of Native Bayes and Lexical Semantic Similarity. In this paper, based on the combination of emotional classification of Native Bayes and lexical semantic similarity of Hownet, We proposed a classification method combining the supervised and unsupervised algorithm, and used a parameter β to adjust the weight between the two methods, the calculation equation is shown in formula (11).

$$C = \arg\max_{c_i \in C}\{\beta * Bayes(c_i, d) + (1 - \beta) * Sim(c_i, d)\} \tag{11}$$

4 Results and Discussions

4.1 Dataset

In this paper, corpus is formed by Chinese 2013 $NLP\&CC$ technology evaluation test data, 21256 Microblogs. We pretreated corpus by some procedures (Lexical Analysis, The removal of punctuation and stop words), got 4786 Microblogs as the training sample, Finally. We use the lexical ontology proposed in [10]. The corpus contains 7 categories, including 389 anger words, 1179 fear words, 2314 sad words, 1967 happy words, 11107 likeable words, 10282 disgusted words, 228 surprise words.

4.2 Evaluation Methods

The microblog emotional discrimination is calculated using precision, recall and F-measure. The equations are demonstrated in formula (12)–(14).

$$\Pr ecision = \frac{\#correct(emotion = c_i)}{\#proposed(emotion = c_i)} \tag{12}$$

$$Recall = \frac{\#correct(emotion = c_i)}{\#gold(emotion = c_i)} \tag{13}$$

$$F\text{-}measure = \frac{2 \times \Pr ecision \times Recall}{\Pr ecision + Recall} \times 100\,\% \tag{14}$$

Here $\#gold$ is the artificial labeled number, $\#correct$ is the number matched between the submit results and the labeled results, $\#proposed$ is the submit results number.

The average precision, recall and F-measure of the Macro was acted as evaluation index, and the equations are demonstrated in formula (15)–(17).

$$Macro\_\Pr ecision = \frac{1}{6}\sum_{c_i} \frac{\#correct(emotion = c_i)}{\#proposed(emotion = c_i)} \tag{15}$$

$$Macro\_Recall = \frac{1}{6}\sum_{c_i} \frac{\#correct(emotion = c_i)}{\#gold(emotion = c_i)} \tag{16}$$

$$Macro\_F\text{-}measure = \frac{2 \times Macro\_\Pr ecision \times Macro\_Recall}{Macro\_\Pr ecision + Macro\_Recall} \times 100\% \quad (17)$$

The equations of Micro-average precision, recall and F-measure are demonstrated in formula (18)–(20).

$$Micro\_\Pr ecision = \frac{\sum_{s_i} \#correct(emotion = s_i)}{\sum_{s_i} \#proposed(emotion = s_i)} \quad (18)$$

$$Micro\_Recall = \frac{\sum_{c_i} \#correct(emotion = c_i)}{\sum_{c_i} \#gold(emotion = c_i)} \quad (19)$$

$$Micro\_F\text{-}measure = \frac{2 \times Micro\_\Pr ecision \times Micro\_Recall}{Micro\_\Pr ecision + Micro\_Recall} \times 100\% \quad (20)$$

Here c_i is one of the 7 sentiment categories.

4.3   The Combining Analysis of Naive Bayes and Semantic Similarity of Hownet

In the experiment, the weight parameter β of formula (11) is 0.5. The test results are demonstrated in Fig. 2 and Table 1.

Through the combination of the two methods, only the surprise and like classification results are slightly lower, 79.41 %, 79.55 %, respectively. Others are over 80 %. The average precision and F-measure is 83.41 % and 70.41 %, respectively. Considering the Macro and Micro average, the accuracy and the recall rate is approximately 83 % and 60 %, respectively. And the F-measure is improved greatly.

The experiments demonstrate that the precision, recall and F-measure of the Macro-average and Micro-average is best by using the combination of the Naive Bayes classification and semantic similarity of Hownet. So the combination of the two methods is better than any kind of the independent method.

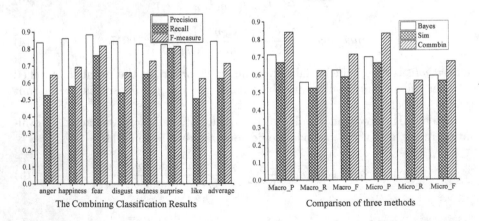

Fig. 2. The Combining classification results.

Table 1. The Combining Classification Results (Macro&Micro)

	Precision(%)	Recall(%)	F-measure(%)
Macro	83.40	61.64	70.89
Micro	82.78	56.14	66.91

5 Conclusions and Future Work

In this paper, we proposed a combination methods for sentiment analysis in Chinese microblog. For emoticon messages and non-emotion messages, we use different strategies to optimism the process. The practical evaluation shows that our algorithm could effectively detect user's sentiment orientation.

References

1. Bing, L.: Sentiment analysis and opinion mining. In: Hirst, G. (ed.) Synthesis lectures on Human language Technologies, vol. 5, 1st edn., pp. 1–167. Morgan & Claypool, San Rafael (2012)
2. Pang, B., Lillian, L., Shivakumar, V.: Thumbs up? sentiment classification using machine learning techniques. In: Proceedings of the ACL-02 Conference on Empirical Methods in Natural Language Processing, pp. 79–86 (2002)
3. Zheng, W., Ye, Q.: Sentiment classification of Chinese traveler reviews by support vector machine algorithm. In: Third International Symposium on Intelligent Information Technology Application, pp. 335–338 (2009)
4. Li, T., Xiao, X., Xue, Q.: An unsupervised approach for sentiment classification. In: 2012 IEEE Symposium on Robotics and Applications (ISRA), pp. 638–640 (2012)
5. Turney, P.D.: Thumbs up or thumbs down? Semantic orientation applied to unsupervised classification of reviews. In: Proceedings of the 40th Annual Meeting on Association for Computational Linguistics, pp. 417–424 (2002)
6. Zhao, J., Dong, L., Wu, J., Xu, K.: Moodlens: an emoticon-based sentiment analysis system for chinese tweets. In: Proceedings of the 18th ACM SIGKDD International Conference on Knowledge Discovery and Data Mining, pp. 1528–1531 (2012)
7. Mitchell, T.M.: Machine Learning. Machinery Industry Press, Beijing (2003)
8. Liu, Q., Li, S.: Word similarity computing based on How-net. Int. J. Comput. Linguist. Chin. Lang. Process. **7**(2), 59–76 (2002)
9. Zhu, P., Fei, B., Fan, S.: Semantic-based text topic sentiment orientation analysis (2012)
10. Linhong, X., Hongfei, L., Yu, P., Hui, R., Jianmei, C.: Constructing the affective lexicon ontology. J. China Soc. Sci. Tech. Inf. **27**(2), 180–185 (2008)

A Prefetching Mechanism Based on MooseFS

Xiaohong Shi[1], Ying Ji[2,3(✉)], Hui Xie[2,3], and Yueming Lu[2,3]

[1] Qihoo 360 Technology CO. Ltd., Beijing 100025, China
sxh@360.cn
[2] School of Information and Communication Engineering,
Beijing University of Posts and Telecommunications, Beijing, China
[3] Key Laboratory of Trustworthy Distributed Computing and Service (BUPT),
Ministry of Education, Beijing, China
jiying87@163.com, xh070180@sina.com,
ymlu@bupt.edu.cn

Abstract. The MooseFS (MFS) distributed file system doesn't have a prefetching operation for reading large files. It has affected the performance of reading files. Aiming at this problem, we improve the performance of sequential reading process for MFS. We present a prefetching mechanism: when the client sends the sequential data reading request to the chunkserver, MFS activates the prefetching mechanism. MFS improves the amount of transferred data for each time from the original 128 KB to 4 MB, and uses the timestamp to empty the cache. The experimental results show that for large file reading operation, the improved MFS (MFS-prefetch) shortens the operating time and response time, and improves the throughput of MFS.

Keywords: MFS · Prefetching mechanism · Reading performance

1 Introduction

With the rapid development of Internet, big data is also attracting more and more attention. Data generated on the Internet has an exponential growth every day [1]. In order to store such a massive data, distributed file systems come into being.

As the open source implementation of GFS [2], MFS is used for the large-scale and distributed cluster environment. It supports a large number of data and large files accessible applications. It is built on a large number of cheap PCs. MFS provides consistency guarantees and fault tolerance mechanisms, along with simple and effective file replications, but it doesn't optimize the process of reading a big file.

MFS inherits the structural characteristics and working pattern of GFS. MFS includes a metadata server, multiple chunkservers (data servers) and multiple clients [3]. The metadata server is responsible for storing all the metadata in the server's memory. The metadata records the name, size, storage location and any other attribution of files. The chunkservers are used to store the files. The client is used to send all kinds of operation requests to metadata server. It also establishes a connection with a chunkserver to receive data.

MFS data-reading principle [4] is shown as Fig. 1. When the client needs to read data from the MFS, the client firstly requests to the metadata server to obtain the

Y. Yuan et al. (Eds.): ISCTCS 2013, CCIS 426, pp. 146–153, 2014.
DOI: 10.1007/978-3-662-43908-1_19, © Springer-Verlag Berlin Heidelberg 2014

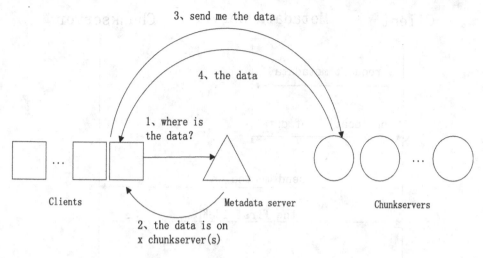

Fig. 1. The reading principle of MFS

metadata and parsing the metadata for the chunkserver where the file data stays. Then the client sends a data-read command to the chunkserver and the chunkserver returns the required file data.

Although this kind of distributed frame structure has been widely used, but there is an obvious shortcoming during the reading operation in this kind of distributed file system. That is there is no acceleration mechanism for data reading. We propose a prefetching mechanism based on it. The experimental results show that we greatly improve the reading performance.

2   Prefetching Mechanism

MFS data-reading operation has to be through fuse kernel [5]. MFS data-reading mechanism is shown as Fig. 2. After building a connection between the client and the chunkserver, the chunkserver begins to transfer data. Firstly, the chunkserver sends a 128 KB data block to the client. After the client receives the data block, the client sends a reading data request to the chunkserver. Then the chunkserver continue sends a 128 KB data block to the client. The process is repeated until the data transfer is completed.

From the MFS data-reading process, we can see that for dozens of megabytes or larger files, the chunkserver transfers data in units of 128 KB. This kind of transfer method undoubtedly slows down the speed of the data-reading operation. It has affected the reading performance of the whole file system.

Aiming at this shortcoming, this paper presents a prefetching mechanism [6], as it is shown in Fig. 3. After building a connection between the client and the chunkserver, the chunkserver begins to transfer data. The chunkserver firstly transfers the first 128 KB data block to the client. After the client receives the data block, the client sends a reading data request to the chunkserver. If the chunkserver detects that the data block the client requests is next to the first data block, the chunkserver starts the

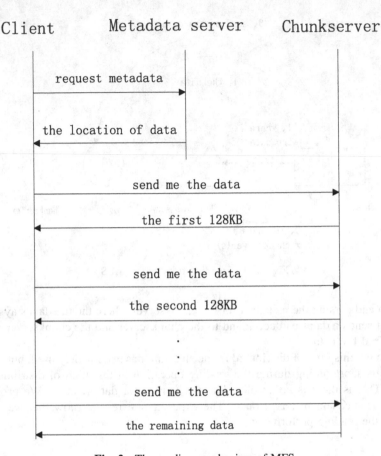

Fig. 2. The reading mechanism of MFS

prefetching mechanism. It begins to transfer the next 4 MB data block until the entire file data is transferred completely.

The data structure for the code of prefetching mechanism is as follows:

```
typedef struct _prefetchbuff_t {

    uint32_t inode;//buffer belongs to this inode - - key
    uint32_t index;//buffer belongs to this chunk index
    uint32_t version;//buffer belongs to this chunk version
    uint32_t offset;//buffer offset in this chunk
    uint32_t size;//buffer size in this chunk
    time_t expiretime;//buffer expire time in seconds
    uint8_t *buff;//buffer
    struct _prefetchbuff_t *next;//next in hashtable
} prefetchbuff_t;
```

The whole process for the client reading the data is shown as Fig. 4. When the client reads the data, it firstly check whether there is prefetched data in its memory.

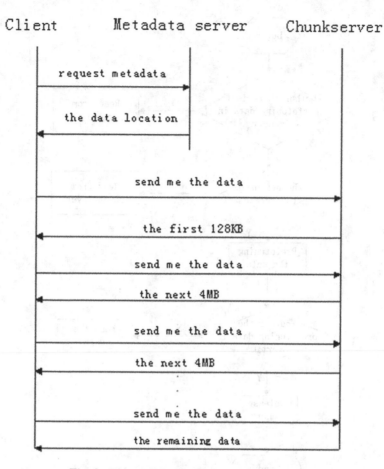

Fig. 3. The reading mechanism of MFS-prefetch

If there is, read the data from its memory directly. If there isn't, the chunkserver determines whether prefetching data according to the data the user requires. If there is no need to prefetch the data, the chunkserver transfers the data as the original manner. If the system activates the prefetching mechanism, the chunkserver transfers the data as the manner introduced above. After the client reads the whole data, the client needs to determine whether the prefetching data in its memory is overtime (we set it 30 seconds). If the data in memory is not timed out, the data is reserved. If the data has timed out, the system releases the memory space. A complete data-reading process is end.

3 Experimental Results and Analysis

The test environment uses a cluster which is made up of five IBM3630M4 servers (d01, d02, d03, d04, d05). These servers are connected via 1000 MB Ethernet switch. Each server is configured as a quad-core Intel E5-2407 processor, 2.2 GHz frequency,

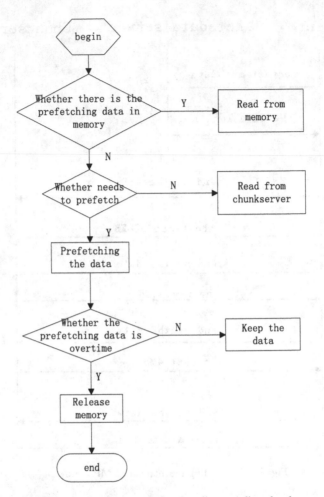

Fig. 4. The whole process for the client reading the data

1066 MHz bus frequency, 10 MB cache, 4 GB DDR-3 memory and 2 TB 7200 rpm SAS drives. d01 is the metadata server of MFS, and d02, d03, d04, d05 are both the chunkserver and the client.

We use d05 as a client to test the "cp" operation time. "cp" operation means the client get a data from MFS. We get a number of data with different sizes and calculate the elapsed time. The experimental result is shown as Fig. 5.

As can be seen from the test result, for reading a file, if the file size is less than 10 MB, the operation time for MFS and MFS-prefetch is almost the same. But for a file more than 50 MB, the operation time for MFS-prefetch is much less than that for MFS. MFS-prefetch shows a distinct advantage. This is because MFS-prefetch prefetches the data in 4 MB increments. When the file size is less than 10 MB, the prefetching operation is made only 1–2 times, so the effect is not that obvious. But when the file size exceeds 50 MB, the time of getting a file for MFS-prefetch is only about one-tenth of the time for MFS. The performance has been greatly improved.

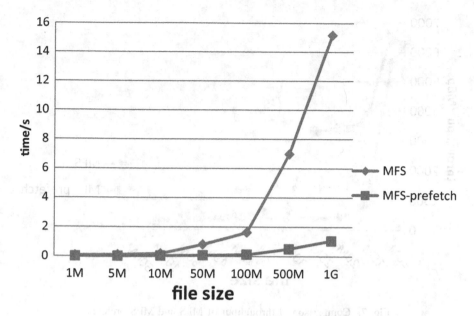

Fig. 5. Time consuming comparison of cp operation of MFS and MFS-prefetch

For the indicators of response time and throughput [7], we use Vdbench—a file system testing tool to test our distributed file system. The test method is that sequentially reading 2500 files with a specified size from MFS and MFS-prefetch, and then calculating the average response time and throughput. The test results are shown as Figs. 6 and 7.

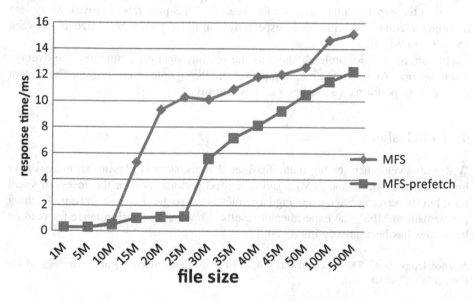

Fig. 6. Comparison of response time of MFS and MFS-prefetch

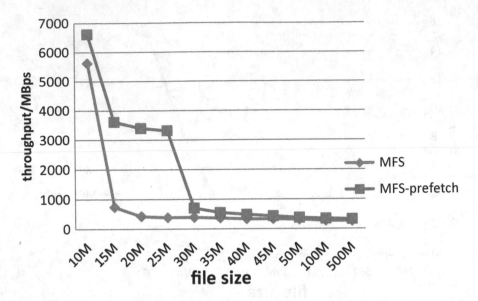

Fig. 7. Comparison of throughput of MFS and MFS-prefetch

Response time refers to the delay, it means that the time from the data transfer command is received to the transmission is started. We can see from Fig. 6 that the response time for MFS-prefetch is shorter. Because for MFS, the client must send a reading data command each time a 128 KB data block is transferred through the network. But for MFS-prefetch, the client sends a reading data command only after a 4 MB data block is transferred. The average response time will be greatly reduced.

From the experimental result we can see that MFS-prefetch improves the system throughput compared with MFS, especially for those files whose size is between 15 MB and 30 MB.

In summary, MFS-prefetch shortens the reading operation time and the average response time. At the same time, it improves the throughput of the system. The system data-reading performance has been greatly improved.

4   Conclusion

With the development of big data, distributed file system is playing an increasingly important role [8]. Although MFS shows a good performance for the access of small files, but its performance for reading large files is not so good. So we add a prefetching mechanism to MFS. The experimental results show that the performance for reading large files has been greatly improved.

Acknowledgement. This research was supported by National Science and Technology Major Project 2012ZX03002001.

References

1. http://www.csdn.net/article/a/2011-05-19/298203
2. Ghemawat, S., Gobioff, H., Leung, S.T.: The Google file system. In: SOSP '03 Proceedings of the Nineteenth ACM Symposium on Operating Systems Principles, vol. 37, Issue 5, pp. 29–43, Dec 2003
3. Yu, J., Wu, W., Li, H.: DMooseFS: design and implementation of distributed files system with distributed metadata server. In: 2012 IEEE Asia Pacific Cloud Computing Congress (APCloudCC)
4. http://www.cnblogs.com/oubo/archive/2012/05/04/2482893.html
5. Installing MooseFS Step by Step Tutorial. http://www.moosefs.org/
6. Yang, J., Jiang, F., Li, L.: Optimal design of file system on embedded system. Comput. Technol. Its Appl. **12**, 141–144 (2007)
7. http://www.51testing.com/?uid-88979-action-spacelist-type-blog-itemtypeid-5864
8. Rajaraman, A., Ullman, J.D.: Mining of Massive Datasets. Cambridge University Press, Cambridge (2011)

Improving the Efficiency of Storing SNS Small Files in HDFS

Ganggang Zhang[✉], Min Zuo, Xinliang Liu, and Fan Xia

School of Computer Science and Information Engineering,
Beijing Technology and Business University, Beijing, China
just_send@163.com,
{zuomin,liuxinl,xiafan}@btbu.edu.cn

Abstract. Users of the SNS produce files every day, which makes it face a great demand for file storage. HDFS is such a good system to meet the demand. Files produced by SNS users are always small, but the HDFS is designed to store big files. When we use HDFS to store files in SNS directly, something bad will happen. This paper proposes a novel method to store SNS files in HDFS by merging all files of the same user to one single file. The method is evaluated by experiments conducted on files produced by SNS users and has a better performance than the original HDFS.

Keywords: Cloud computing · HDFS small files storing · Social network site

1 Introduction

As we know the main trend of Internet application is oriented to users, the users produce various kinds of files when they use these applications. Social Network Site, known as SNS, is such a typical Internet application. SNS is a place where users can publish private or semi-private information [1]. Sites provided such services are well known as MySpace, Facebook, Twitter etc. Users can produce all kinds of information, and view information produced by their friends.

The file types produced by the users in SNS mostly contain pictures, text, and office documents [2]. With the rapid growth number of users in the SNS, file storage need grows incredibly at the same time. Especially, files produced by users in SNS are always small, normally with a size less than 10 MB. The traditional storage system will fail to deal with these huge file storage needs of performance and stability.

Basic idea of this paper is to merge all files produced by the same user into one single file, and combine the file's location meta-data into the filename to improve the performance of file writing and reading operations.

2 Background

2.1 Hadoop Distributed File System

With the rapid growth of Internet, all kinds of services of Internet blooms well, especially with the coming of Web 2.0, many companies such as Google, Yahoo,

Y. Yuan et al. (Eds.): ISCTCS 2013, CCIS 426, pp. 154–160, 2014.
DOI: 10.1007/978-3-662-43908-1_20, © Springer-Verlag Berlin Heidelberg 2014

started their big data platform. Features of these platforms mainly include: scalability, stability.

The key point of big data platform is the distributed file system. Nowadays, the most famous distributed file systems are Google File System, Hadoop Distributed File System which is known as HDFS, and Amazon's S3 File System [5].

The HDFS cluster provides global file storage services, consisting of the DataNode and the NameNode. Files stored in HDFS are divided into parts of block, and the size of the block is set to 64 MB. Every block will be backup to several DataNode [6].

NameNode is one server which is used to manage HDFS's file meta-data and information of the files' directory tree. Also, NameNode manages the configuration information of HDFS such as **block replica factor** and **block size** [6].

2.2   Description of SNS User Files

In the social services that provided by the SNS, users can produce pictures, audios and office documents. Single size of these files is small, usually less than 10 MB. Imaging daily active users amount reaches 100,000 and assuming each active user produces at least five small files (the file size average value 2 MB). That is to say the system will deal with at least 500,000 times, about 950 GB files, of writing requests and even more reading requests.

2.3   The Small Files Problem

Each file block occupies 150 bytes of memory space in HDFS, when the file size exceeds a block capacity, the size of the meta-data will be extended with the file size accordingly. When the HDFS deals with a large number of small files, the meta-data will occupy a considerable amount of memory space. If we want to store a file about 10 GB in HDFS, this file will be split into 160 blocks for storage, which means the file meta-data will take up 24 KB of the NameNode's memory. But if we want to store 105,000 small files (totally 10 GB), each file will occupy one file block in the DataNode, and about 150 bytes in NameNode's memory for their meta-data. Meta-data stored for these small files will take up about 15 MB of NameNode's memory. Clearly, huge number of small files stored in HDFS will take up most resources.

3   Design

3.1   File Access Patterns in SNS

Before further discussions, we will take consideration into some access patterns of SNS' files.

Some of the file's meta-data from the same user are always the same, such as the file owner, access privilege. Therefore, we can optimize the meta-data of files belongs to the same user to decrease the waste of NameNode's memory.

Usually, SNS will provide the access approach based on web browser, and users may produce files and browse others' files through the web browser. Thus, we must also take the web request into consideration.

3.2 Design Meta Information for Block

We have added three attributes in the meta-data as following.

- **remaining**, which is used to record the remaining capacity of the block;
- **deleted**, which is used to record the deleted capacity of the block;
- **last_inserted_at**, which is used to record the file block's latest created time.

3.3 Design of the Filename

The filename which is returned from DataNode contains the information of the file's location. The structure of the filename is given in Fig. 1.

```
$block_id$_offset_length.ext
```

Fig. 1. Filename structure

As we can see, the filename begins with $, and the file's block id is placed between two $ symbol. We can find the file location with the filename's block id and the position of file stored in the block.

4 File Operations

In this part, we will explain the file's operation logic, including how we write a file, how we read a file, and how we delete a file.

4.1 Write Operations

The writing process is presented as following (Fig. 2).

1. Find available block. The client sends the file writing request to the NameNode. The NameNode tries to find a block in all the blocks belonged to the user which satisfies all the requirements of the request out. If the NameNode got such a block, it sends the block id to client, or the NameNode will return a newly generated block id to the client.
2. Writing file content. The client sends a writing request to the DataNode which was returned from the NameNode. When the DataNode receives the writing request from a client, the DataNode will build the meta-data for the file and write the file content into the target block.

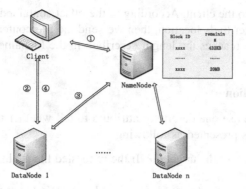

Fig. 2. File write operations

3. Notify the NameNode. When the file writing operation is completed, the Da-taNode is responsible to send the meta-data of the block to NameNode.
4. Notify the client with the constructed filename. After all operations are finished, the DataNode will send the structured filename which contains the location information, which can be seen in the Fig. 1, to the client.

4.2 Read Operation

The process of file reading is described as following (Fig. 3).

1. Locate the DataNode. The client starts the query to the NameNode for the server's location of the block id which is contained in the filename.
2. Query cache. The DataNode will first query the cache for the target block, if the target block exists in the cache, then we will turn to (3), or we will turn to (4).
3. Read the block. The DataNode reads the block and writes it into the cache. The cache replacement policy here takes the least recently used (LRU) algorithm.

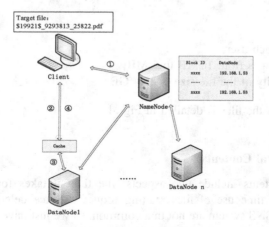

Fig. 3. File read operations

4. Returns the file to the client. According to the offset contained in the filename, we can find the target file's location, then we send the file content to the client until the sent file size reaches the length described in the filename.

4.3 Delete Operation

In the meta-data, we use one descriptor attribute to tell whether the file is valid. File deletion procedure is presented as following.

1. Verify the validity of the target file. If the requested file is already invalid, we can ignore the request.
2. Invalidate the file. If the target file is valid, the DataNode changes the status of the file to invalid, then reports the invalided file size to the NameNode.
3. Notify the NameNode. The NameNode receives the information reported from the DataNode, the NameNode updates the value of deleted file size for the specified block.

5   Evaluation and Results

5.1   Experimental Environment

This experimental environment consists of five hosts, one host is used for the NameNode, and the remaining four are used for the DataNode. Each host is equipped with Pentium-4 processor, 2 GB DDR3 RAM and a 160 GB HDD. The operating system is installed with Ubuntu 10.04. The Java version is 1.6.0, and the Hadoop version is 1.1.2. The block replica factor is configured with the default value 3, and the file block size is set to the default value, 64 MB.

5.2   Dataset

- 100 web users;
- 1000 files for each user;
- The file size ranges from 10 KB to 5 MB;
- The total capacity of the file size is 25.4 GB.

    Distribution of the files is detailed in Fig. 4.

5.3   Experimental Contents

Experimental contents include two aspects: the time it takes for the file writing requests, and the time use of files reading requests. Since deleting and updating operations in the SNS system are not that common, so we just have file's reading and writing for testing.

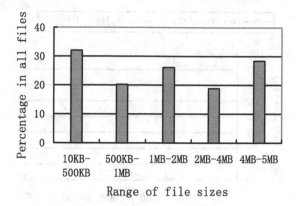

Fig. 4. Experimental files' distribution

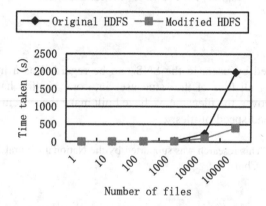

Fig. 5. Time taken for write operation

Time Taken for File Writing. In this study, the files of each user will be stored into HDFS with equal possibility. We recorded the writing time cost of both original HDFS and modified HDFS as file's count increases. The result is illustrated in Fig. 5.

Through the result, we can clearly see that the modified HDFS is faster to write a large amount of small files. The result also points out that with the increase in the number of files written, the modified HDFS's writing time cost can be greatly reduced. That is because the original HDFS will take more time to allocate blocks and more I/O operations to replicate the blocks.

Time Taken for File Reading. In this study, we read all the 100 users' files in an equal possibility. We record the reading time cost in both the original HDFS and modified HDFS with growth of file count, the result is illustrated in Fig. 6.

From the results, we can see that the time cost of modified HDFS has been reduced significantly compared to the original HDFS. Especially, with the increase of the number of files, the difference becomes more and more big. This is because the modified HDFS file block's caching mechanism decreases the I/O time cost of block's reading operations.

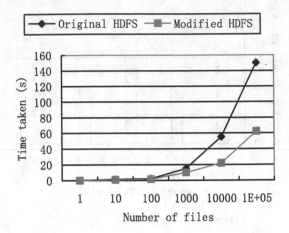

Fig. 6. Time taken for file read operation

6   Conclusion

Small files produced by users in the SNS can be regarded as a huge amount. Our method by merging all files of the same user into one big file has an encouraging performance. Moreover, the filename we have built make the system cost less memory and improve the read speed of files.

Acknowledgement. This research was supported by the National Natural Science Foundation (No. 61170113), P.R. China.

References

1. Boyd, D.M., Ellison, N.B.: Social network sites: definition, history and scholarship. J. Comput. Mediat. Commun. **13**, 210–230 (2008)
2. Yi, C., Deng, W.: Analysis based on user browsing behavior to obtain user interest. Comput. Technol. Dev. **5**, 37–39 (2008)
3. Dong, B., Qiu, J., Zheng, Q., Zhong, X., Li, J., Li, Y.: A novel approach to improving the efficiency of storing and accessing small files on Hadoop: a case study by PowerPoint files. In: Proceedings of IEEE International Conference on Services Computing, pp. 65–72, Miami, FL, USA, July 2010
4. White, T.: The small files problem (2009). http://www.cloudera.com/blog/2009/02/the-small-files-problem
5. White, T.: Hadoop: The Definitive Guide, 2nd edn., pp. 41–45. O'Reilly Media/Yahoo Press, Sebastopol (2009)
6. HDFS Architecture Guide (2009). http://hadoop.apache.org/common/docs/current/hdfs_design.html

A Highly Efficient Indoor Localization Scheme Based Only on Mobile Terminal

Di Wu[1], Xing Li[1], Yongmei Sun[1(⊠)], Yuefeng Ji[1], Jie Mao[2],
and Yingting Liu[2]

[1] State Key Laboratory of Information Photonics and Optical Communications,
Beijing University of Posts and Telecommunications, Beijing 100876, China
{justice,ymsun,jyf}@bupt.edu.cn, iluhcm@163.com
[2] Gansu Electric Power Corporation Information & Communication Company,
Lanzhou, 730050 Gansu, China
mseer@163.com, ytliu@xidian.edu.cn

Abstract. Indoor localization has been paid more and more attention in recent years. However, current localization based on mobile terminal requires remote server. In this paper, a highly efficient indoor localization scheme based only on mobile terminal is proposed. In this scheme, popularized Wi-Fi hot spots are used to generate RF (radio frequency) fingerprint, built-in sensors of the mobile terminal are used to measure displacement of users, and a novel movement filtering algorithm is presented to improve localizing accuracy by taking displacement into account. Without remote server and Internet connecting, the proposed scheme can realize low delay, low energy consuming and secure indoor localization. Experimental results show that this scheme increases the localizing accuracy compared with traditional method.

Keywords: Indoor localization · Mobile terminal · RF fingerprint · Wi-Fi · Sensor

1 Introduction

With the development of our society, location based service (LBS) becomes a kind of service which greatly facilitates human's life and create a great deal of commercial interest. As the key technology, localizing mobile target efficiently and accurately makes sense. While outdoor localization is dominated by methods via satellite (GPS is the most popularized method), it doesn't work well indoor due to poor satellite signal. As a result, indoor localization is a great field for researchers to explore in. In recent research, RF (radio frequency) fingerprint method is in the main stream.

In traditional RF fingerprint method, researchers usually adopt a structure that mobile terminal works as client to collect information and computers work as server to process data and send results to client. In this method, well access to mobile data network is necessary while mobile phone doesn't work smart.

In this paper, a highly efficient indoor localization scheme based only on mobile terminal is proposed. This scheme consists of three parts: Wi-Fi-based fingerprinting localization module, step-and-heading module and accurate localizing phase by

Y. Yuan et al. (Eds.): ISCTCS 2013, CCIS 426, pp. 161–168, 2014.
DOI: 10.1007/978-3-662-43908-1_21, © Springer-Verlag Berlin Heidelberg 2014

adopting movement filtering algorithm. Nowadays, Wi-Fi hot spots are popularized because of low cost and easy deployment, while accelerometer and oriental sensor are embedded in most of the smart mobile phones to calculate walking distance and orientation. Wi-Fi-based fingerprinting localization module gets rough result and step-and-heading module gets displacement of the user. A novel algorithm is presented to improve the performance of localization by using displacement to revise the rough result from Wi-Fi-based fingerprinting localization module. In addition, low delay, low energy consuming and secure indoor localization is realized because all the work is conducted only by mobile terminal. As a result, the scheme is symbolized as highly efficient. In short, a great number of people will benefit from the scheme, and the number will continue to rise as the smart phone market is expanding in the foreseeing future.

The rest of the paper is organized as follows. Related work is discussed in Sect. 2. Section 3 presents the principle of the scheme. Experimental results and analysis are included in Sect. 4. We conclude the work in Sect. 5.

2 Related Work

All the known wireless indoor localization methods can be classified into two categories: model-based method and fingerprinting-based method.

2.1 Model-Based Method

In this method, researchers get locations based on geometrical models. The prevalent log-distance path loss (LDPL) model, builds up a statistical function between RSS values and RF propagation distances [1, 2]. These approaches save the measurement efforts at the cost of decreasing localization accuracy. Apart from power-distance mapping, Time of Arrival (ToA) [3], Time Difference of Arrival (TDoA) [4], and Angle of Arrival (AoA) [5] have brought alternative perspectives to characterize geometric relationship between signal transmitters and receivers.

2.2 Fingerprinting-Based Method

The main idea is to fingerprint the surrounding signatures at every position in the target localizing areas and then build a fingerprint database. The location is then estimated by mapping the measured fingerprints against the database. Most of these techniques utilize the RF signals such as RADAR [6], Horus [7], improved upon RADAR, LANDMARC [8], Active Campus [9], Zee [10], LiFs [11]. Surround Sense performs logical location estimation based on ambience features including sound, light, color, Wi-Fi, etc. All these approaches require site survey over target localizing area to build a fingerprint database.

3 Proposed Scheme

3.1 Outline of the Scheme

The overview of our scheme is presented as the flow chart shows (Fig. 1). The scheme consists of Wi-Fi-based fingerprinting localization module, step-and-heading module and accurate localizing phase by adopting movement filtering algorithm. Wi-Fi-based fingerprinting localization module gets rough result and step-and-heading module gets displacement of the user. A novel algorithm is presented to improve the performance of localization by using displacement to revise the rough result from Wi-Fi-based fingerprinting localization module.

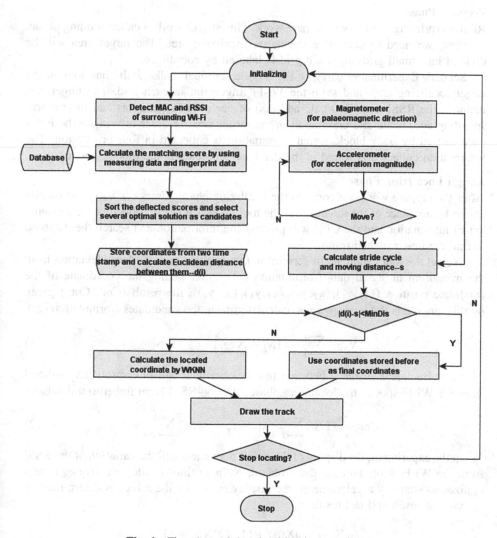

Fig. 1. Flowchart of the algorithm in our scheme

Data is stored in database within the system and data processing is done by CPU embedded in the mobile terminal. As all the work is conducted in the mobile terminal, low delay, low energy consuming and secure indoor localization is realized. The reasons are as follows: first of all, users get localizing result with low delay (in tradition, high-delay occurs due to the limit of network speed); secondly, battery energy of the mobile terminal will not be overused by communicating with remote server; Last but not least, users never need to worry that their privacy is leaked on the Internet.

3.2 Wi-Fi-Based Fingerprinting Localization Module

Prepare Phase
RF fingerprinting needs some prepare work. This step of work is called training phase.

First, we need to determine the target localizing area. The target area will be divided into small grids and each grid is labeled by coordinate.

Second, Experimenter carrying the mobile terminal walks with conscious in the target localizing area, and store the Wi-Fi fingerprint in each grid. The fingerprint includes the RSSI and ID (MAC address) of each Wi-Fi hot spots and their corresponding coordinate and orientation in the target area. In order to weaken the influence caused by body block, signal information is collected in four orientation. The information collected is stored in the database provided by the mobile phone.

Rough Localizing Phase
After the prepare work, we come to the localizing phase. Users can carry the mobile phone to any place of the target area. The mobile phone keeps collecting the surround Wi-Fi information and the CPU will process the information and search the database to find the best-matched result.

We get the four candidate fingerprint in the database with the least deviation from the measurement signal data (formulation (1)). After getting the coordinate of the candidate position $((x_1, y_1), (x_2, y_2), (x_3, y_3), (x_4, y_4))$, the result (Cor_x, Cor_y) given by this module is the average value calculated from the candidates (formulation (2)).

$$V_n = \sum_{j=1}^{m} \left(Lv_j - Avg_j \right)^2, i \in [1, N] \tag{1}$$

V_n —Euclidean distance between the measurement and fingerprint; Lv_j —RSSI from the Wi-Fi spot in the localizing phase; Avg_j —RSSI from fingerprint database.

$$Cor_x = (1/k) \sum_{j=1}^{k} x_j; Cor_y = (1/k) \sum_{j=1}^{k} y_j \tag{2}$$

In the experiment, the display of the result fluctuates with the variation of the RSSI from the Wi-Fi spot. To ease the problem, Kalman filter is adopted. If user is recognized as static by accelerometer, the display shown on the screen is determined by the current result and last result:

$$X(n)' = aX(n) + (1 - a)X(n - 1) \tag{3}$$

$X(n)'$—display shown on the screen; $X(n)$ —current result; $X(n - 1)$ —last result; a —weight determines the importance between the current and last result;

3.3   Step-and-Heading Module

In the step-and-heading module, accelerometer and oriental sensor are used to calculate moving distance and orientation.

During the walk in target area, we assume that the movement is uniform motion during short time period (k seconds). We use accelerometer to detect the acceleration and record it. The cycle of the walking every k seconds can be got by using acceleration information. We adopt the unbiased estimation of the autocorrelation function to calculate (formulation (4)).

$$\text{Corr}_{xx}(m) = \frac{1}{N - |m|} \sum_{n=1}^{N-1-|m|} x_N(n) * x_N(n + m), m \in [1, N] \qquad (4)$$

The total number of peak values of the correlation is associated with q time spots. If the peak value is less than 0.1, we consider it as static to weaken the influence of the noise. For sake of the same reason, we eliminate the first and the last peak value during the period. The cycle is calculated by formulation (5).

$$Cy = \sum_{i=3}^{q-1} (Mc_i - M_{C_{i-1}}) \Big/ q - 3 \qquad (5)$$

The cycle multiplied by the walk step length leads to the result of moving distance (formulation (6)).

$$\text{Dis} = (T * St)/Cy \qquad (6)$$

Combined with the orientation got from oriental sensor, we can get the moving condition in this module.

3.4   Accurate Localizing Phase by Adopting Movement Filtering Algorithm

Result got from the Wi-Fi module is rough due to noise and other interference in the environment. A novel algorithm is presented to improve the performance of localization by using displacement to revise the rough result from Wi-Fi-based fingerprinting localization module. The algorithm is as follows:

1. Four candidate results(expressed in coordinate form) from Wi-Fi localization module are recorded in set O={A1, A2, A3, A4};
2. After the user have walked k seconds, another four candidate results are recorded in another set R={B1, B2, B3, B4};
3. Process the data from sensor and transfer the moving distance and orientation into the change in coordinate which is symbolized as Dis;
4. Select every element in set O and R separately and get the Euclidean distance between them. Thus we get 16 pair of results (formulation (7));

$$\text{EuDis}_k = \sqrt{(x_{pi} - x_{fj})^2 + (y_{pi} - y_{fj})^2}, k \in [1, 16], i, j \in [1, 4] \qquad (7)$$

5. Calculate the absolute value between the EuDis_k and Dis and get the minimum figure. The corresponding result Bn from set R is what we seek for;
6. Substitute the result for Bn if the minimum figure is less than the threshold value we set.

4 Experiment

4.1 Overall of the Experiment Environment

The localizing system is shown in Fig. 2. Experiment is conducted in an office building and the plane structure map is shown in Fig. 3. Southwest point is the origin of coordinates. Each pair of coordinate stands for a reachable grid.

There are at least 8 Wi-Fi hot spots and at most 22 ones can be detected, which meet our demand. The black point in the Fig. 3 is an example of walk trace.

The smart phone applied in the experiment is Huawei C8813 (Android 4.1.2, dual core 1228 MHZ, 4 GB ROM). Although only mobile phone is used in this experiment, we believe the scheme can be applied to tablet PC without significant change.

4.2 Experiment Conduct

In the training phase, the shape and size of the grid influence the accuracy of the result. In this experiment, the grid is shaped into square with length of 1.2 m. In order to ease the noise, we record at least five times in each position and store the average value. This phase is time consuming and needs patience.

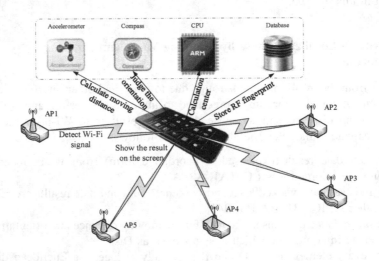

Fig. 2. Structure of the localizing system

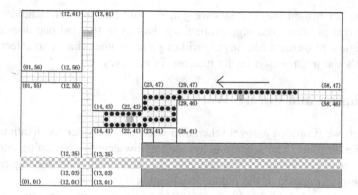

Fig. 3. Experimental environment

Table 1. Localizing data of the two method

Location error	1 m (%)	2 m (%)	3 m (%)	4 m (%)
Wi-Fi only	30	65	80	92
Our scheme	40	75	92	94

In localizing phase, experimenter walks in usual style and gets the real time result. To evaluate the performance of the scheme, we get another set of results by simulating traditional localizing method, which is called Wi-Fi only method. The two set of results will be discussed in the following part.

4.3   Experiment Result

As shown in the Fig. 3 and Table 1, our scheme improve the accuracy of the localizing result. It works much better than traditional method especially within 1m. A large scale of increase in accuracy (33 % increase margin within 1 m and 92 % within 3 m) validate the function of our scheme (Fig. 4).

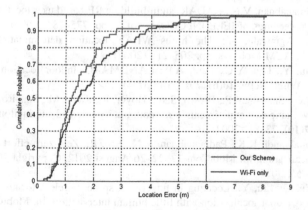

Fig. 4. Comparison of the performance between Wi-Fi only method and our scheme.

After further insight into the data we get, we find that the four candidate results include the real position with high probability. However, the real one doesn't match best sometimes. Movement filtering algorithm gains another chance to select the true result. That's the main reason of the increase in accuracy

5 Conclusion and Future Work

In this paper, we proposed a novel scheme to accomplish indoor localization only by using mobile terminal. The scheme is low delay, low energy consuming and secure. Experiment was conducted to validate that the movement filtering algorithm can improve the performance of the indoor localization.

However, some drawbacks still remain. We may need appropriate method to deal with the noise leading to the fluctuation of the RSSI and find a way to store data more efficiently if applied to a large scale place.

Acknowledgement. This work is supported by Major Program of National Natural Science Foundation of China under Grant No. 61190114, Science and Technology Project of State Grid Corporation under Grant No. 52272313039L, No. 52272313039Q.

References

1. Chintalapudi, K., Padmanabha Iyer, A., Padmanabhan, V.N.: Indoor localization without the pain. In: Proceedings of ACM MobiCom, pp. 173–184 (2010)
2. Lim, H., Kung, L.C., Hou, J.C., Luo, H.: Zero-configuration indoor localization over IEEE 802.11 wireless infrastructure. Wirel. Netw. **16**(2), 405–420 (2010)
3. Youssef, M., Youssef, A., Rieger, C., Shankar, U., Agrawala, A.: Pinpoint: an asynchronous time-based location determination system. In: Proceedings of ACM MobiSys, pp. 165–176 (2006)
4. Priyantha, N.B., Chakraborty, A., Balakrishnan, H.: The cricket location-support system. In: Proceedings of ACM MobiCom, pp. 32–43 (2000)
5. Niculescu, D., Nath, B.: Ad hoc positioning system (APS) using AOA. In: Proceedings of IEEE INFOCOM, vol. 3, pp. 1734–1743 (2003)
6. Bahl, P., Padmanabhan, V.N.: RADAR: an in-building RF-based user location and tracking system. In: Proceedings of IEEE INFOCOM, vol. 2, pp. 775–784 (2000)
7. Youssef, M., Agrawala, A.: The horus WLAN location determination system. In: Proceedings of ACM MobiSys, pp. 205–218 (2005)
8. Ni, L.M., Liu, Y., Lau, Y.C., Patil, A.P.: LANDMARC: indoor location sensing using active RFID. Wirel. Netw. **10**(6), 701–710 (2004)
9. Griswold, W.G., Shanahan, P., Brown, S.W., Boyer, R., Ratto, M., Shapiro, R.B., Truong, T.M.: ActiveCampus: experiments in community-oriented ubiquitous computing. Computer **37**(10), 73–81 (2004)
10. Rai, A., Chintalapudi, K.K., Padmanabhan, V.N., Sen, R.: Zee: zero-effort crowdsourcing for indoor localization. In: MobiCom'12, 22–26 August 2012. Copyright 2012 ACM 978-1-4503-1159-5/12/08
11. Yang, Z., Wu, C., Liu, Y.: Locating in fingerprint space: wireless locating in fingerprint space: wireless indoor localization with little human intervention. In: MobiCom'12, 22–26 August 2012. Copyright 2012 ACM 978-1-4503-1159-5/12/08

A Zones-Based Metadata Management Method for Distributed File System

Xiaowei Xie[1,2(✉)], Yu Yang[1,2], and Yueming Lu[1,2]

[1] School of Information and Communication Engineering,
Beijing University of Posts and Telecommunications, Beijing, China
[2] Key Laboratory of Trustworthy Distributed Computing and Service (BUPT),
Ministry of Education, Beijing, China
xxwei1988@163.com, 18575358@qq.com, ymlu@bupt.edu.cn

Abstract. It is challengeable for the single server to manage the large metadata in MooseFS which is full of small files. This paper proposes a zones-based metadata management (ZMM) method for distributed file system. ZMM changes a single metadata server into a cluster, which includes a zone server and several sub-metadata servers. We tested ZMM in the platform named SandBox and the results shown that the throughput of writing and reading metadata was improved by using ZMM compared with using the single metadata server in MooseFS. With the increase of sub-metadata servers, the throughput of writing and reading metadata was improved as well.

Keywords: ZMM · Distributed file system · Sub-metadata server · ZMM-based sandbox

1 Introduction

With the development of cloud computing, the scale of data is increasing. The file system in a single PC can't support such mass data storage and the large-scale parallel I/O operations. There is an urgent need of a kind of large capacity, high reliability and easy scalable distributed file system. Currently, the industry has developed several distributed file systems based on a variety of architectures.

An important research is the metadata management technologies in distributed file systems [1]. In distributed file systems, more than 60 % of operations are associated with metadata [2]. The efficiency and effectiveness of metadata processing will affect the performance of the entire file system directly [3, 4].

Distributed file systems separate metadata and data. The architecture of most distributed file systems uses a single server, called metadata server, to store metadata and uses a cluster, including several data servers, to store files data. Metadata is stored in the memory of the metadata server in order to enhance the writing and reading speed.

Famous distributed file systems, like GFS (Google File System) [5], HDFS (Hadoop Distribute File System) [6] and MooseFS [7], use the single metadata server architecture.

When such kind of distributed file system has a large number of concurrent accesses, the limitation of the single metadata server will be very obvious. At the same

Y. Yuan et al. (Eds.): ISCTCS 2013, CCIS 426, pp. 169–175, 2014.
DOI: 10.1007/978-3-662-43908-1_22, © Springer-Verlag Berlin Heidelberg 2014

time, with the surging of the metadata, the distributed file system needs a lot of memory space. As a result, the performance of the whole distributed file system will be very poor. The single-metadata-server architecture will be the bottleneck of the distributed file system.

One way to solve this problem is to expand the single-metadata-server architecture to a multi-metadata-servers architecture. However, the metadata management in the multi-metadata-servers architecture is challengeable. Hash and the sub-tree partition are two common methods for the metadata management in the multi-metadata-servers architecture.

Hash [8] means making file directories, names or other relevant-attribute values as keys, calculating corresponding hash values through hash functions, and creating mapping tables between hash values and the locations of metadata. The advantage is that it is easy to achieve load balance, and also supports highly concurrent access. But it increases the difficulty of some operations (readir etc.). At the same time, when distributed file systems increase or decrease one metadata server, the hash value will be changed, and all metadata needs to be re-distributed, which will cause a lot of metadata migration, thereby increase the overhead of distributed file systems.

Sub-tree [9] segmentation method is to divide the metadata tree into metadata sub-trees, then the metadata sub-trees are assigned to metadata servers. Each metadata server manages one or more metadata sub-trees. Sub-tree segmentation is very simple. The metadata tree can optionally be split, so the metadata can be easily distributed into different metadata servers. But it is not easy to implement metadata storage load balance for this method.

2   ZMM

ZMM is Zones-Based Metadata Management Method. ZMM is a kind of multi-metadata-servers architecture. The zone in ZMM is defined as the collection of some metadata.

2.1   Structure of ZMM

The structure of ZMM is shown in Fig. 1. In the ZMM, there are one zone server and several sub-metadata servers. The zone server and the sub-metadata servers have different functions.

Sub-metadata servers have two functions. One is to store metadata. In the ZMM, metadata tree is split into many metadata sub-trees, and each of the sub-trees is a zone. All the zones are assigned to different sub-metadata servers. The other one is to count the total number of directories in one zone. When the number of directories in one zone reaches max number, distributed file systems cannot create new directories in the zone and will create a new zone in other sub-metadata servers randomly, which contributes to achieve load balance in sub-metadata servers.

Zone server is used to manage and organize the scattered zones located at different sub-metadata servers. Zone server also has two functions. One is to number zones.

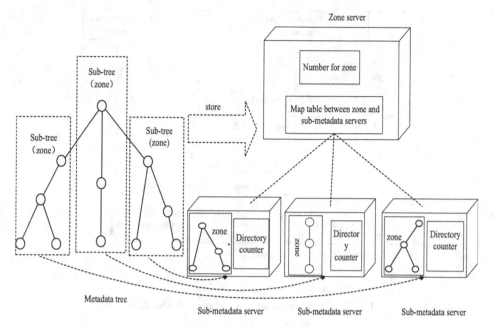

Fig. 1. Structure of ZMM

The number of one zone is globally unique and is the head part of one metadata number. All the metadata in the same zone has the same zone number. The other one is to offer inquiry services through a map table which records the location (sub-metadata server IP and port) of zones.

2.2 Workflow of Operations on Metadata

Operations on metadata include read operation and write operation.

For read operation, the workflow and communication process between servers are shown in Fig. 2. When a client reads metadata, firstly ZMM will access the parent metadata of the target metadata. If the target metadata and its parent metadata are in the same sub-metadata server, which is called Local, the sub-metadata server x will complete the read operation and reply to the client. If the target metadata and its parent metadata are not in the same sub-metadata server, which is called Remote, the sub-metadata server x will analysis the number of the target metadata and get the zone number, secondly the sub-metadata server x will send a packet to the zone server to find the location of the zone through the map in the zone server, thirdly sub-metadata server x will send a packet to sub-metadata server y which stores the target metadata to request for the read operation, at last sub-metadata server y completes the operation and replies to client step by step.

For write operation, workflow and the communication process between servers are shown in Fig. 3. When a client creates a file, ZMM will directly create the file. When a client creates a target directory, ZMM will access the parent metadata of the target

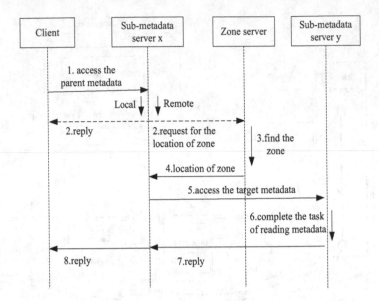

Fig. 2. Communication process of read operation

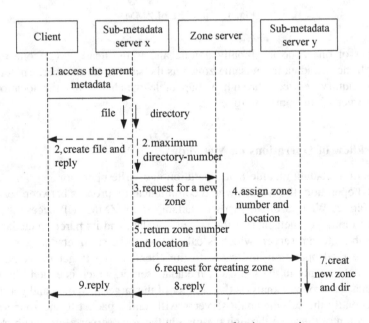

Fig. 3. Communication process of write operation

directory and check the maximum directory-number of the zone which contains the parent metadata. If the total number of the directories in the zone is less than the maximum directory-number, the sub-metadata server x will directly create the directory, but if not, firstly the sub-metadata server x sends a packet to the zone server to request for creating a new zone, secondly the zone server assigns a new zone number and location, thirdly sub-metadata server x sends a packet to the specified sub-metadata server y to create a new zone, at last the sub-metadata server y creates the target directory and replies to the client step by step.

3 Experimental Results and Analysis

ZMM is implemented on the SandBox. In order to verify the performance of ZMM, this paper tests the throughput of writing and reading metadata in MooseFS and ZMM-based SandBox and compares the results. The throughput is measured by operations per second (ops).

MooseFS is a distributed file system. Its system architecture is the same with google file system (GFS). MooseFS consists of one metadata server (master), many data servers (chunk servers) and clients. MooseFS separates metadata and data. Metadata is stored in the only metadata server, and data is distributed in the data servers. Metadata is organized in the memory of the metadata server. ZMM-based SandBox is also a distributed file system. Its metadata management method is ZMM.

Test environment consists of nine IBM 3650M4 servers. Each server contains two high-performance processors, 64 GB memory and four 300 GB 15 K HDD. These servers are connected with each other through High-speed Gigabit Ethernet.

Firstly, this paper tests the throughput of reading and writing metadata in MooseFS. Test method is that the number of clients and the number of each client's threads are two variables. Then fix one variable and change the other one and test ops until the ops is stable. The results are shown in Tables 1 and 2. Through Tables 1 and 2, the maximum write processing capacity of MooseFS is about 3100 ops and the maximum read processing capacity of MooseFS is about 3100 ops.

Secondly, this paper tests the reading and writing throughput of ZMM-based SandBox by the same method above-mentioned. When there is only one sub-metadata server, the maximum of write processing capacity is about 2530 ops and the maximum of read processing capacity is about 2800 ops. When there are two sub-metadata servers, the maximum of write processing capacity is about 4900 ops and the maximum of read processing capacity is about 5300 ops. When there are three sub-metadata servers, the maximum of write processing capacity is about 7200 ops and the maximum of read processing capacity is about 7800 ops. When there are five sub-metadata servers, the maximum of write processing capacity is about 11000 ops and the maximum of read processing capacity is about 12000 ops. The results are shown in Fig. 4.

Table 1. The write performance of MooseFS

Clients ops threads	1	2	3	4	5	6	7
1	684	980	1250	1481	1623	1771	2356
10	1107	1676	2045	2278	2293	2542	3000
20	1238	1695	2238	2388	2492	2623	3220
50	1265	1766	2380	2439	2564	2578	3017
100	1261	1818	2298	2583	2555	2957	3111

Table 2. The read performance of MooseFS

Clients ops threads	1	2	3	4	5	6	7
1	689	1086	1492	2040	2336	2739	3088
10	1153	1578	1923	2222	2205	2678	2741
20	1250	1652	2033	2000	2132	2752	2777
50	1412	1976	2279	2688	2741	3116	2904
100	1428	1960	2307	2298	2398	2637	2602

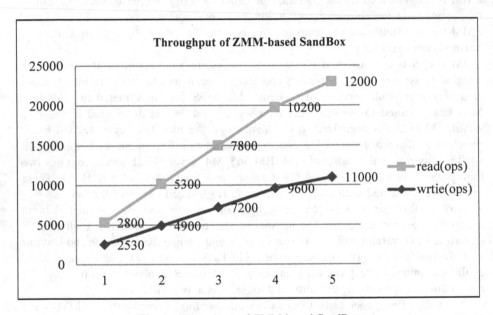

Fig. 4. Throughput of ZMM-based SandBox

In Fig. 4, when there is only one sub-metadata server in ZMM-based SandBox, the maximum of read and write processing capacity is less than MooseFS, but when there are more than one sub-metadata servers, the maximum of read and write processing capacity is more than MooseFS, and with the increase of sub-metadata servers, the maximum of read and write processing capacity is improved linearity. So, ZMM is effective.

4   Conclusion

This paper proposes a new metadata management called ZMM and implements it on ZMM-based SandBox. From the results of test, the performance of ZMM-based SandBox is better than MooseFS and with the increase of sub-metadata servers in ZMM-based SandBox, the performance is improved linearity.

Acknowledgement. This research was supported by National 863 Program (No. 2011AA01A204).

References

1. Wang, J., Feng, D., Wang, F., et al.: MHS: a distributed metadata management strategy. J. Syst. Softw. **82**(3), 2004–2011 (2009)
2. Ousterhout, J.K., Costa, H.D., Harrison, D., et al.: A trace-driven analysis of the Unix4.2 BSD file system. In: Proceedings of the 10th ACM Symposium on Operating Systems Principles (SOSP'85), vol. 12, pp. 15–24 (1985)
3. Pei, X.: Study on metadata management strategy in distributed file system, Wuhan, China (2010)
4. Patil, S.V., Gibson, G., Lang, S., et al.: Giga+: scalable directories for shared file system. In: PDSW'07: Proceedings of 2nd International Workshop on Petascale Data Storage, pp. 26–29 (2007)
5. Ghemawat, S., Gobioff, H., Leung, S.T.: The google file system. In: SOSP'03: Proceedings of the Nineteenth ACM Symposium on Operating Systems Principles, New York, NY, USA, pp. 29–43 (2003)
6. Shafer, J., Rixner, S., Cox, A.L.: The Hadoop distributed filesystem: balancing portability and performance. In: Proceedings: ISPASS 2010, Houstan, TX, pp. 122–133. IEEE (2010)
7. MooseFS, 20 Aug 2012. http://www.moosefs.org/
8. Brandt, S.A., Xue, L., Miller. E.L., et al.: Efficient metadata management in large distributed file system. In: Miller, E., Meter, R.V., (eds.) Proceedings of the 20th IEEE/11th NASA Goddard Conference on Mass Storage Systems and Technologies, pp. 290–298. IEEE Computer Society, San Diego (2003)
9. Morris, J.H., Satyanarayanan, M., Conner, M.H., et al.: Andrew: a distributed personal computing environment. Commun. ACM **29**(3), 184–201 (1986)

Survey on Data Recovery for Cloud Storage

Xiaohong Shi[1], Kun Guo[2,3(✉)], Yueming Lu[2,3], and Xi Chen[2,3]

[1] Qihoo 360 Technology CO. Ltd., Beijing, China
`sxh@360.cn`
[2] School of Information and Communication Engineering,
Beijing University of Posts and Telecommunications, Beijing, China
[3] Key Laboratory of Trustworthy Distributed Computing and Service (BUPT),
Ministry of Education, Beijing, China
`{guokun,ymlu,chenxi0115}@bupt.edu.cn`

Abstract. Cloud computing provides people with lots of convenient services. Computing and storage of data are transferred from the local mobile terminal to the cloud server. Putting everything in the Cloud brings people convenient, but it also cause more various insecurity that cloud storage solutions must face at the same time. Much work has been done to solve the challenges. In this paper, we focus on the data recovery for cloud storage, present a comprehensive survey of existing problems and their current solutions on data recovery issues, discuss data security technologies of the data storage and recovery in cloud and describe some key factors and their role in data recovery.

Keywords: Cloud computing · Cloud storage · Cloud monitoring · Data security · Data recovery

1 Introduction

Cloud Computing is a services increasing, usage and delivery model based on the Internet. It provides online, dynamic, and scalable virtualization resources and services, which contain computing, storage and networking through the Internet. Cloud computing has the characteristics of integrated server clusters, on-demand services, network dependency, resource virtualization, centralized computing, shared server with multi-tenancy and so on based on the definition and services model of cloud computing. Because of these new characteristics, the security of cloud computing, which is always considered as data security for cloud storage, is facing new challenges unlike the traditional server computing [1–3].

With the rapid development of the information society as well as the growing number of global operations, a huge business data has become the core of global business connections and data storage security becomes particularly important. When the data that is not used temporarily but important, it will be stored in cloud storage.

Cloud stores the user data using distributed file system, which has a large number of disks. Distributed file system, the disk quality, the server quality, the number of copies and other information is opaque to the users. So the users are faced with unreliable data storage, disclosure of personal privacy, calculating opacity and other threats. It needs physical, logical, and personnel access control policies.

Y. Yuan et al. (Eds.): ISCTCS 2013, CCIS 426, pp. 176–184, 2014.
DOI: 10.1007/978-3-662-43908-1_23, © Springer-Verlag Berlin Heidelberg 2014

Data security issues of cloud storage exist because of lack of authentication, authorization and audit control, weak encryption algorithms, weak keys, risk of association, unreliable data center, and lack of disaster recovery [1]. The approaches for the issues may include data protection, data location, data segregation, data integrity, confidentiality and availability, data breaches, long-term viability, data recovery and so on [4]. Many papers, such as [5–9], have taken detail solutions for some the issues, which include data privacy and the network attacks, but there are less papers focusing on the solutions for data recovery with respect to the former. With accelerated growing of the data, the approaches that ensure the data not to be lost are becoming more and more important. This paper mainly focus on the related technology of data recovery, which ensure that when the failure happen to the stored data, the service of the lost data can be continued for another way. The data backup and recovery protocols and the technology of isolating stored data and copies need to be studied.

In this paper, we focus on the data storage and recovery level security issues, present a survey of existing problems and their current solutions on data recovery, discuss data security technologies of the data storage and recovery in cloud and describe some key factors and their role in data recovery.

2 Approaches of Data Storage Security

2.1 Failures of Cloud Storage

The failures in cloud storage can happen at any time. At June 2010, because of a software vulnerability in a Cisco switch, data center of Hosting.com had a downtime for few hours [10]. At April 2011, it is reported by Amazon that Elastic Block Store (EBS) volumes were out of working. As a result, Amazon's EC2 and RDS services went down for four days [11]. The failures are not only caused by the accidental application damage, but also the natural disasters and other things. Table 1 shows the classification of these failures [12].

They give a risk to the data availability in cloud storage for users. We will try to prevent these failures to happen, but there is always something not perfect that can make cloud storage down. So how to do can make sure that the failures would take little cost from us is becoming more and more important. The object is that when the data stored in cloud storage in one place is down, and the data stored in another place can take its place quickly. Thus, the services would be not interrupted for a long time due to the failures.

2.2 Data Recovery Technology in Cloud

There is a lot of user data in cloud and the cloud provider need to protect the reliability of all the user data. So the data redundancy storage and recovery technology and dual server cluster data storage technology are proposed.

Table 1. Classification of cloud storage failures

Reasons	Descriptions	Possible solutions
Human error	Unexpected faults of human in daily operations on the storage systems cause unplanned downtime.	Human works with an intelligent error detection system to supplement their own operations, thereby reducing the error rate. Strengthen human on the aspect of operation skills training.
Inherent characteristics of components in storage systems and software vulnerability	It determines that every system has a mean time to failure (MTTF), so the system may has an unexpected downtime.	The storage system need maintenance regularly and another back-up system will be running instead of the main system in maintenance.
Bad operational conditions	Every system all need an appropriate running environment including humidity, temperature, altitude, dust and so on. When any of the environment factors is out of tolerable range, the rate of system failures will rise.	A monitoring system for running environment factors is needed. The environment of main system need to be adjusted regularly and it need other assistance system to maintain appropriate running environment, such as air condition, dust remover and so on.
Natural disasters	The place where the storage systems are located is suffering a natural destructive disaster such as earthquake, tsunami and so on. The system will be breakdown instantly. The disasters are beyond the system handle range for human.	A parallel site that is far away from the main site in distance is needed. When main site is ruined, the back-up site will be running instead of the main site to compensate for downtime losses

(1) data redundancy storage and recovery technology

In order to improve the reliability of user data in cloud, data redundancy storage and recovery technology is needed. The data redundancy storage technology include two parts, which are server cluster and distributed file system. Server cluster is a group of high-performance servers, which are connected with each other by high-speed high-performance switches. And these servers can communicate with other servers with high speed. Distributed file system can store mass data files and each data file has multiple copies. As is shown in Fig. 1, these copies are stored and distributed in different servers in the server cluster, avoiding the loss of data files because of a single server failure.

When servers or network equipment failures occur in the cloud, some copies of the original data file will malfunction. To ensure services in the cloud to be not interrupted, the cloud distributed file system can automatically duplicate the copies lost and store these copies in servers of the cluster, and make the new copies to provide services.

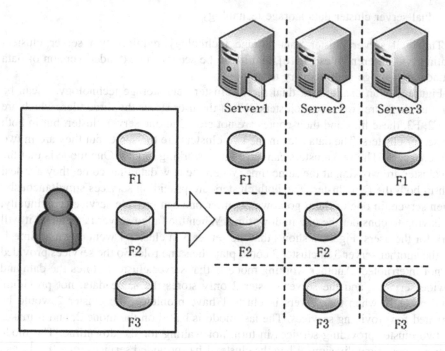

Fig. 1. Data file multi-copy storage technology

It can be seen in Fig. 2 that there are three files F1, F2, F3 with one original file and one copy file respectively. When the server 3 go into downtime, the copy of file F1 and F3 will malfunction. In order to make the two copies continue to provide available online services, cloud distributed file system duplicate the copies of file F1and F3, and the new copies will be stored in the server 2 and server 1. When the file duplicating and storing are finished, cloud distributed file system activates the two new copies, and they will provide online services just like before.

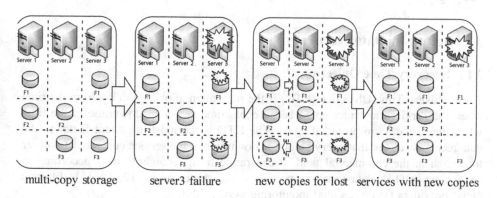

multi-copy storage   server3 failure   new copies for lost   services with new copies

Fig. 2. Online data recovery technology

(2) dual server cluster data storage technology

The dual server cluster data storage technology requires two server clusters locating two different sites [4, 16], and it can be seen as an extended version of data redundancy storage and recovery technology.

Figure 3 is an example of dual server cluster data storage technology. It can be seen that there are two server clusters. When the user stores the three files, which are F1, F2, F3, these files and their copies are not stored in one server cluster, but in both two server clusters. The data files in the two clusters are the same, but they are in two different place. The two clusters can have three working modes. One mode is that the two cluster are working at the same time. When the new data files come, they are deal with in both the two cluster. The both clusters are providing services simultaneously. When servers in one of them go down, another one can provide services continually, not having to consider the one in downtime. When the failed server is mended, it will work for the users. Figure 3 shows that the server 3 in cluster 1 went down at time 1, and the another server 3 in cluster 2 could play the same role. So the services provided are not interrupted. Another working mode is that server cluster1 stores the data and provide services, and the server cluster 2 only stores the same data, not providing services. Only when the servers in cluster1 have problems, the cluster 2 would be activated for providing services. The last mode is based on the mode 2, and it makes the two cluster providing services in turn, not waiting for the downtime. The mode takes a way of time division. When the cluster 1 has provided services for a fixed time, it will rest and the cluster 2 will be working for another time segmentation. It is periodic and the resting cluster could be maintained. But they are storing data files all the time for protecting data.

The three modes have their own advantages and disadvantages. From the perspective of services interruption time, the mode 1 is best, almost not having the downtime for the entire system. The mode 2 takes second place and the mode 3 have the longest services interruption time. But from the perspective of maintaining cost, the mode 3 has the least cost, the mode 2 takes the second place and the mode 1 has the most cost. The services interruption time could cause the users addition cost. How to get a compromise between the two different costs is the next point worthy for studying.

3 Factors in Data Recovery

3.1 Recovery Time Objective

The Recovery Time Objective (RTO) is the maximum allowable delay from the time when the services are interrupted because of some server in downtime to the time when the services are provided again. The RTO is the most important factor in the data recovery, due to that every second in downtime of the service cost the data owner too much in the commercial field. It can range from seconds to days according to service types [13], data recovery protocols and strategies [3, 12, 14–18], different cloud providers [19], the cloud monitoring system [20].

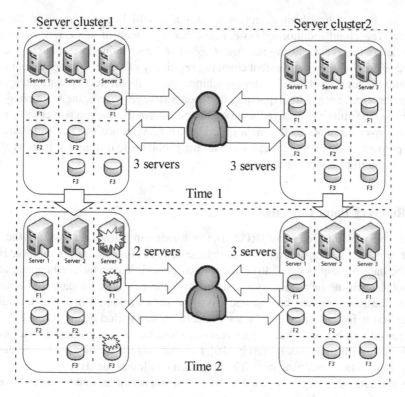

Fig. 3. Dual server cluster data storage technology

The service types decide what kind of data protection should be taken appropriately to have an efficient maintaining and lower cost. The approach called service differentiation divides all services to different class according to Quality of Service (QoS), including high class with key protecting and low class with general protecting. The cost of different class is distinguished.

The protocols and strategies mainly focus on reducing the recovery time and the cost of data recovery. Generally, the two factors can be not achieved at the same time, just like the dual server cluster data storage technology. Many studies evaluated the recovery strategies to find the best promise between time and cost. However the RTO may changes in different time model proposed by different services providers, causing the little error to the strategies. So the standard model for the data recovery should be established.

The cloud monitoring system play an important role in the data recovery. Because the recovery time include the time for failure detection and the time for restoring services. If the failure of the server happened, causing the loss of data files for services, and the backup server knew nothing about that and did not take any solution, the downtime would be extended. So the faster a failure is detected, the sooner the data recovery is finished. The common method is the heartbeat detection technology, which make the server for providing services sends a data message to other server as a backup periodically, informing that it still work normally. Once the backup server no longer receive the heartbeat detection message, it will begin to proceed the data recovery. The cloud monitoring system also can be aware of some risk event happening before the event causing the downtime of servers. Though the natural disasters are hard to predict, the environment changing regularity of servers, some of the human errors and the running state of system machines can be monitored by warning system. If some abnormal events are happening to the data storage system, the warning system will take some solutions to solve the problem and inform the backup server to be ready for taking over the work of the main one. Thus, it may reduce the rate of failures. In these approaches, none of them can solve all the problems in different situations alone, the issues should be studied further.

3.2   Recovery Point Objective

The Recovery Point Objective (RPO) is the maximum allowable loss for the data storage from the server failure. The downtime always comes with no symbol. However, the data backup is carried out for a fixed period. When failure happens at the time point when the new backup is just finished, there will be no data loss actually. Because the lost data can be restored from the data backup. But when the failure happens just before the time point when the data backup period begins, the whole data in the period will be lost. That is the worst situation. Bermbach proposed an approach of dividing big files into small ones in [16], because that the smaller the stored data is, the less time data transferring cost. The approach can lower the data transferring time during the data recovery, and what is the most important is that it have a precise recovery point with an appropriate backup period.

4   Conclusion

As described in the paper, a survey of existing problems and their current possible solutions on data recovery issues are presented, and the data security technologies of the data storage and recovery in cloud and some key factors in data recovery are discussed either. Though some solutions can solve the problems of data recovery to a certain degree, there are still many issues to be study further, which include the compromise of RTO and the recovery cost, the successful transferring of heartbeat message, the energy cost reducing, the efficient layout for main site and second site, the risk aware mechanism, the efficient classification with QoS, the appropriate data recovery model and strategies, the consensus problem of local and remote backup site and so on. So there are yet many practical problems which have to be solved, hoping the article can shed light on the research in this field.

Acknowledgement. This research was supported by National Science and Technology Major Projects (No. 2012ZX03002001), P. R. China.

References

1. Modi, C., Patel, D., Borisaniya, B., et al.: A survey on security issues and solutions at different layers of cloud computing. J. Supercomput. **63**(2), 561–592 (2013)
2. Rong, C.M., Nguyen, S.T., Jaatun, M.G.: Beyond lightning: a survey on security challenges in cloud computing. Comput. Electr. Eng. **39**(1), 47–54 (2013)
3. Che, J.H., Duan, Y.M., Zhang, T., et al.: Study on the security models and strategies of cloud computing. Procedia Eng. **23**, 586–593 (2011)
4. Subashini, S., Kavitha, V.: A survey on security issues in service delivery models of cloud computing. J. Netw. Comput. Appl. **34**(1), 1–11 (2011)
5. Wang, Y.J., Zhao, S.J., Le, J.: Providing privacy preserving in cloud computing. In: International Conference on Test and Measurement, vol. 2, pp. 213-216 (2009)
6. Mowbray, M., Pearson, S.: A client-based privacy manager for cloud computing. In: Proceedings of the Fourth International ICST Conference on Communication System Software and Middleware, COMSWARE'09, Dublin, Ireland, 16–19 June 2009
7. Lin, D., Squicciarini, A.: Data protection models for service provisioning in the cloud. In: Proceeding of the ACM Symposium on Access Control Models and Technologies, SACMAT'10, Pittsburgh, Pennsylvania, USA, pp. 183–192 (2010)
8. Abbasy, M.R., Shanmugam, B.: Enabling data hiding for resource sharing in cloud computing environments based on DNA sequences. In: Proceedings of the 2011 IEEE World Congress on Services, SERVICES'11, pp. 385–390 (2011)
9. Stolfo, S.J., Salem, M.B., Keromytis, A.D.: Fog computing: mitigating insider data theft attacks in the cloud. In: IEEE Symposium on Security and Privacy Workshops, San Francisco, CA, pp. 125–128 (2012)
10. Sourya: Should you be concerned? A list of recent cloud computing failures—intuit goes down (2011). http://www.cloudtweaks.com/2011/06/should-you-be-concerned-a-list-of-recent-cloud-computingfailures
11. Metz, C.: Amazon outage spans clouds 'insulated' from each other (2011). http://www.theregister.co.uk/2011/04/21/amazon_web_services_outages_spans_zones/fromeachother
12. Wiboonrat, M.: System reliability of fault tolerant data center. In: The Fifth International Conference on Communication Theory, Reliability, and Quality of Service, Chamonix, France, pp. 19–25 (2012)
13. Wiboonrat, M.: An empirical IT contingency planning model for disaster recovery strategy selection. In: IEEE International Conference on Engineering Management, Europe, Estoril, pp. 1–5 (2008)
14. Singha, R.: A multi-site disaster recovery solution based on IP storage networking. In: International Conference on Information and Computer Networks vol. 27, pp. 139–142 (2012)
15. Wiboonrat, M., Kosavisutte, K.: Optimization strategy for disaster recovery. In: 4th IEEE International Conference on Management of Innovation and Technology, Bangkok, pp. 675–680 (2008)
16. Bermbach, D., Klems, M., Tai, S., et al.: Metastorage: a federated cloud storage system to manage consistency-latency tradeoffs. In: 2011 IEEE International Conference on Cloud Computing (CLOUD), Washington, DC, pp. 452–459 (2011)
17. Alhazmi, O.H., Malaiya, Y.K.: Evaluating disaster recovery plans using the cloud. In: 2013 Proceedings of Annual on Reliability and Maintainability Symposium (RAMS), Orlando, FL, pp. 1–6 (2013)
18. Xiang, F., Liu, C.Y., Fang, B.X., et al.: Novel "rich cloud" based data disaster recovery strategy. J. Commun. **6**, 92–101 (2013)

19. Wood, T., Cecchet, E., Ramakrishnan, K.K., et al.: Disaster recovery as a cloud service: economic benefits & deployment challenges. In: 2nd USENIX Workshop on Hot Topics in Cloud Computing, Boston, MA, pp. 1–7 (2010)
20. Aceto, G., Botta, A., Donato, D.W., et al.: Cloud monitoring: a survey. Comput. Netw. **57**(9), 2093–2115 (2013)

The Evaluation of Service Trustworthiness Based on BP-Neural Network

Yue Li[1,2(✉)], Qingyang Gao[1], and Jørgen Bøegh[1,2]

[1] School of Information and Communication Engineering,
Beijing University of Posts and Telecommunications, Beijing, China
{liyuelaura, gqy8013}@gmail.com, jorgen@bupt.edu.cn
[2] Key Laboratory of Trustworthy Distributed Computing and Service (BUPT),
Beijing, China

Abstract. With the development of Internet, business models of offline service rendering and online service promotion and evaluation developed. But how to evaluate the service trustworthiness has not attracted great attention and much research. We build a Service Trustworthiness Evaluation Model based on outlier detection, user clustering and BP-Neural Network. In this paper, we use real data of trustworthy community to prove our assumption. Results of practical experiments show that the Service Trustworthiness Evaluation Model proposed in this paper can objectively reflect service trustworthiness. At the same time, it has significance for other evaluation systems.

Keywords: Trustworthiness · Data mining · BP-Neural network

1 Introduction

In the field of Internet, the algorithms for application search in application stores are becoming mature but the system for the evaluation and ranking in application still needs to be studied [1]. The same defect existed in the evaluation and recommendation of the entity service industry.

This comes from the existing evaluation mechanism, which is a calculation model simply based on user ratings. There is a defect in it because different kind of people may have different preferences in different services. So the linear evaluation model based on user evaluation numbers is not trustworthy.

In this paper, we use real data of trustworthy community as research background for the purpose of building a multidimensional trustworthiness evaluation model based on user history data and user evaluation. This new evaluation model can be more accurate and objective for describing the trustworthiness by using the BP-Neural Network widely used in data mining. At the same time we combining user using history data and evaluation data to compute the value.

2 Service Trustworthiness Evaluation Model

In the course of traditional data mining, Neural Network algorithms are usually used for classification and Pattern Recognition. In this paper we use BP-Neural Network for

Y. Yuan et al. (Eds.): ISCTCS 2013, CCIS 426, pp. 185–190, 2014.
DOI: 10.1007/978-3-662-43908-1_24, © Springer-Verlag Berlin Heidelberg 2014

reference. Changing input data values make the evaluation results more objective. Based on this new improved algorithm, this paper builds a whole new multidimensional trustworthiness evaluation model.

Considering the sensitivity of training set and input data in Neural Network algorithms, we added a data pretreatment module during the model building. A Euclidean distance algorithm is used to identify the outliers in user evaluation data. It can exclude affect of not objective user data on neural network calculation result and we use this method to filter these data.

At the same time, we note that different users have preference for different types of services. It can be seen that it is necessary to classify services and users. Therefore we can give different effect weight based on different types of services and user history data [2].

In conclusion, we build a Service Trustworthiness Evaluation Model (STEM) based on an improved algorithm and data processing procedure. Through use of practical data in contrast experiment, the calculation results in the new STEM are shown to be more accurate than the older one, which is just based on user evaluation data. It can be the new standard of service trustworthiness evaluation.

2.1   Algorithm Flow

STEM divides the treatment process into three steps shown as Fig. 1. First step is data cleaning and outlier identification. Second step is clustering and assigning weight. The third step is computing by neural network algorithm and outputting results.

First of all, process original user evaluation data and identify outliers. Trustworthy service community is a network information sharing platform. Some of the evaluation data is obviously not objective. These data may come from extreme users or some cheating users who submit false data for their individual interests. This situation also happens in other platforms. We use the following method: firstly get data computer can calculate by discrete treatment, and secondly calculate all Euclidean distance and identify suspicious outliers [3].

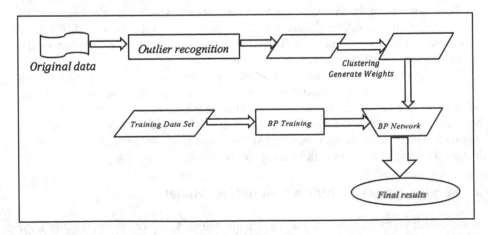

Fig. 1. Algorithm flow

Table 1. Euclidean distance calculation results

User ID	Value	Distance value
01	1	8.8881944173
02	2	6.2449979983
03	4	4.3588989435
04	3	4.3588989435
05	5	6.2449979983
06	5	6.2449979983
07	3	4.3588989435
08	5	6.2449979983
09	4	4.3588989435
10	3	4.3588989435

The calculation results, including cheating user data are shown in Table 1. This table shows ten groups of user evaluation data and we calculate all the Euclidean distance for each value. We excluded the outliers whose distance value to other nodes is greater than a certain threshold. As is shown, the User ID 01 distance value is obviously greater should be excluded.

In the second step, we assign different weights for different types of services by classifying different users [4]. Based on users' usage data in the different service types we use a k-means algorithm to clustering users [5]. We use the different types of services for each user using historical data as clustering basis and get user sets. Based on usage times given by the trustworthy service community to the certain service type, we assign weights arrays for every user set to different service types. As shown in Table 2, we use k-means to clustering users by time column and give weight for every user set.

The third step, calculate service trustworthy value. We train the BP-Neural Network by trustworthy internal user data as training sets [6]. During the training process, the BP-Neural Network may adjust the weights according to the existed network node results. The training process will not stop until the error is within the convergence condition [7]. Then, we calculate trustworthiness value of other services using service description data, service communication data and efficiency data as neural networks input, as shown in Fig. 2.

Table 2. User usage data

User ID	Value	Time
02	2	3
03	4	9
04	3	6
05	5	15
06	5	8
07	3	3
08	5	5
09	4	1
10	3	2

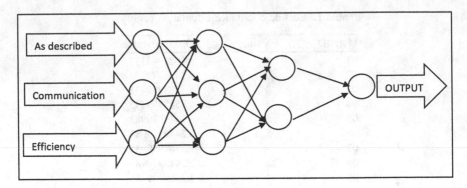

Fig. 2. BP-Neural network data flow

2.2 Pseudo Code of Core Algorithm

The pseudo code of the core algorithm is show in Fig. 3. There are six steps needed to finish the system.

3 Experiments and Comparison

In order to verify the validity of the model presented above, we get a sample data set from a trustworthy service community database, and conduct a blind questionnaire among internal users about the service data. Answers of internal users are more trustworthy and can be used as a trustworthiness reference.

```
//Main Program
1. ReadInData (Original Data);
//read the training data and the
//sample data from database
2. DataSets = excludeOutlier();
//use Euclid algorithm to compute the
//distance of the data items
//find the outliers, and delete them
3. userWeights[][]=ClusterAndGernera
   teWeights();
//according to the type of the service
//and the user evaluate data
//generate the weights of the service
4. TrainBPNetwork(TrainingDataSet)
//train the BP Network and save the
//weights of the network
5. computeWithTheBPnetwork(SampleDat
   aSet);
//input the sample data set, to
//compute the result
6. printAndSave();
```

Fig. 3. Pseudo code

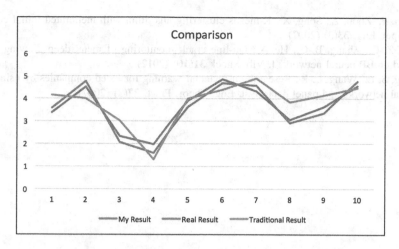

Fig. 4. Comparison results

As a comparative group, we use the average value that we get from the traditional evaluation model with the same sample data sets.

We use a line graph to make the results more visual. Comparison results are shown as Fig. 4.

4   Conclusion

In this paper we put forward a new STEM combined with the outlier identification user clustering and BP-Neural Network algorithms. And we give examples of the use of trustworthy community. Experiments have shown that this new STEM can be used for service evaluation and the results are much more trustable than for a traditional algorithm. At the same time, this new method of trustworthiness evaluation has significance in the field of B2C item evaluation or entity service evaluation.

Acknowledgements. This paper is supported by The National Natural Science Foundation of China (Grant No. 91118002), and 863 Program (Grant No. 2011AA01A204).

References

1. Zhang, X.-X., Xiao, H.-M., Fan W.-G.: The Evaluation of B2C E-Commerce Site. In: Henan Science **24**(6) (2006)
2. Zhang, J., Hu Ming, Wang Bo: Empirical study on electronic public service evaluation by using optimal fuzzy cluster models. Ind. Eng. J. **16**(2) (2013)
3. Jiang, F., Du, J.-W., Sui, Y.-F., Cao, C.-G.: Outlier detection based on boundary and distance. Acta Electron. Sin. **38**(3) (2010)
4. Li, T., Wang, J.-D., Ye, F.-Y., Feng, X.-Y., Zhang, Y.-D.: Collaborative filtering recommendation algorithm based on clustering basal users. Syst. Eng. Electron. **29**(7) (2007)

5. Yuan, F., Zhou, Z., Song, X.: K-means clustering algorithm with meliorated initial center. Comput. Eng. **33**(3) (2007)
6. Luo, Z.-G., Zhang, B.-G., He, X.: On-line crack monitoring of metal deep drawing parts based on BP neural network. J. Vib. Shock **31**(10) (2012)
7. Yang, S.-E., Wang, L.-P.: Research on financial warning for listed companies by using BP neural networks and panel data. Syst. Eng. Theor. Pract. **27**(2) (2007)

Research on Trustworthy Sensor Network Based on Zigbee Technology

Shuaisen Wang[1,2]([✉]), Jørgen Bøegh[1], and Jincui Yang[1,2]

[1] School of Software Engineering, Beijing University of Posts
and Telecommunications, Beijing, China
wss81@bupt.edu.cn, jorgen_boegh@yahoo.dk,
jincuiyang@sina.com
[2] Key Laboratory of Trustworthy Distributed Computing and Service (BUPT),
Ministry of Education, Beijing, China

Abstract. This article introduces a trustworthy sensor network construction scheme based on a trustworthy node selection method. With this scheme, sensor networks will be safer and more reliable. This sensor network is based on Zigbee technology and selects corresponding appropriate pattern of networking. The nodes of Zigbee sensor network will be chosen using a node credibility formula. According to the setting scenarios, the result of simulation will be shown. Through this article, sensor network will be more useful in future application.

Keywords: Trustworthy · Sensor network · Zigbee · Cluster network · Node credibility

1 Introduction

In recent years, sensor networks are increasingly being used for data collection, information processing, wireless communications and other fields, thus getting closer to our real life. However, due to large numbers of nodes in sensor networks densely distributed in an area, the information must be passed through the multi-hop relay in order to reach the destination, and the nodes exposed are vulnerable to attack. Therefore it is necessary to build trustworthy secure sensor networks. However the trustworthy secure scheme of current sensor networks is still in research and far away from being practically applied.

Zigbee technology is a short-range wireless communication technology, mainly used in the field of automatic control and remote control. It can be embedded in a variety of devices. Its low-power, low-cost, low-delay, high capacity features make it easy to build a short-range wireless sensor network. While it works in unlicensed bands and can easily be used close to our daily life in promotion area. In the trustworthy area, Zigbee has a variety of measures [1] to ensure that, for example the AES-128 encryption algorithm, data integrity check and authentication functions. However, these measures still have some shortcomings and can only ensure security to a certain extent.

This article introduces a trustworthy sensor network based on Zigbee technology and this sensor network is formed in cluster type. The nodes of this sensor network

Y. Yuan et al. (Eds.): ISCTCS 2013, CCIS 426, pp. 191–197, 2014.
DOI: 10.1007/978-3-662-43908-1_25, © Springer-Verlag Berlin Heidelberg 2014

will be chosen using a trustworthy node selection method. The first part of the article proposes the concept of trustworthy and the basis of building trustworthy sensor network. The second part gives a presentation of sensor network and Zigbee technology, and proposes the formula for node credibility. In the end, the result will be proven by Matlab simulation software.

2 A Trustworthy Node Selection Method Based on Zigbee Sensor Network

2.1 Definition of Trustworthy

The so-called trustworthy mainly refers to a relationship of trust, that is trustees trust those who are trusted. Those who are trusted need to be credible [2], including availability, reliability, security, robustness, testability, maintainability, and so on. On the other hand, the credible extent needs to be measured to determine whether to trust(the value of the measure is called credibility). This article presents the concept of building trustworthy sensor network to solve security issues of Zigbee sensor networks. Through measuring the credibility of Zigbee sensor network nodes to choose credible nodes, the trustworthy sensor network based on Zigbee technology will be built.

2.2 Sensor Network and Zigbee Technology

A sensor network is a wireless network in a certain area by deploying sensors, data processing unit and communication unit nodes through wireless communication so that they can form in a self-organizing way [3]. As a new short-range two-way wireless communication technology, Zigbee can realize wireless networking and control of small and cheap devices. Based on IEEE 802.15.4, it can achieve coordinate communication among thousands of tiny sensors. These sensors transfer data through radio waves from one sensor to another in the manner of relay, and only require very little energy. In this point of view, the communication efficiency of Zigbee is pretty high [4].

According to the difference of performance, there are two types of devices in Zigbee networks [5]. One type is full function device(FFD), known as the master device, which acts as the role of network coordinator, and can communicate with any type of devices in the network. Another device is a reduced function device(RFD), known as the slave device, which can only communicate with the master device, and can't act as the coordinator of the network.

At the same time, Zigbee has three patterns of networking: star network, mesh network, cluster network [6] (Fig. 1).

(1) In star network, a central node called Zigbee coordinator controls the whole network, and it is responsible for the establishment and maintenance of the network. The other nodes are called end nodes, and can communicate directly with the central nodes.

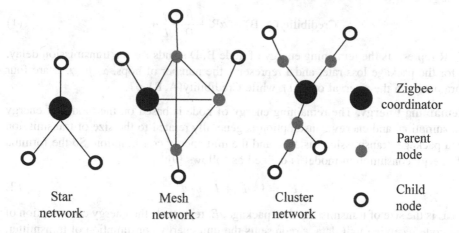

Fig. 1. Three patterns of Zigbee networking

(2)   In mesh network, a more flexible topology can be shown, and the network is established with no restrictions on the shape. The communication between nodes executes optimal path policy.

(3)   In cluster network, Zigbee coordinator is not only responsible to the establishment and maintenance of the network, but also responsible to address assignment of the network nodes. In this network structure, the parent node has a routing function and can communicate directly with child nodes, other parent nodes and the coordinator. But the child node can only communicate with its unique parent nodes.

In summary, cluster network is composed of star network and mesh network. It is energy saving, easily scalable, also can make data transmission more efficient, rapid and reliable. Furthermore, it can be more suitable for building trustworthy sensor network. Depending on the network structure, using the formula of node credibility to measure the credibility of the next node, the next node will be decided, and then the entire Zigbee sensor network will be determined.

2.3   Trustworthy Node Selection

The credible nature of node is the research base of sensor network node security measuring. The credibility of node can be calculated through the sampling of node delay, package loss rate, remaining energy, bandwidth and other indicators [7]. In the node for data transmission, high credibility nodes will be selected as the next hops to improve the security of data transmission, and then the entire trustworthy sensor network will be determined. According to the definition of network performance metrics by IPPM [8], this article selects the following indicators to define node credibility: delay, package loss rate, hop and the remaining energy. Delay, package loss rate and hop are inverse proportional to the credibility of node, and the remaining energy is proportional to it. The credibility of node can be defined by the following formula:

$$\text{Credibility}(A, B) = \alpha R + \frac{\beta}{D} + \frac{\gamma}{L} + \frac{\delta}{J} \tag{1}$$

R represents the remaining energy of node B, D stands for the transmission delay, L for the package loss rate, and J represents the number of hops. α, β, γ, δ are four parameters in the interval of $(0,1)$, while $\text{Credibility}(A, B) < 1$.

Remaining Energy. The remaining energy of node is based on the model of energy consumption, and energy consumption is generally related to the size of transmission data package, transmission distance and the unit energy consumption. So the formula of energy consumption model is defined as follows [9]:

$$E_C = L \cdot E_i + L \cdot \varepsilon \cdot d^3 \tag{2}$$

L is the size of transmission data package, E_i represents the energy consumption of the node receiving unit data, ε represents the unit energy consumption of transmitter, and d stands for the transmission distance.

Transmission Delay. Traditional network delay is usually acquired in the upper layer. For Zigbee network, the transmission delay is short, so the delay of a node can be measured by presetting timer. When the package reaches the node, start the timer. When the package is sent to the next node: stop the timer. The transmission delay of a node is now shown in the timer.

Package Loss Rate. When the data package is transmitted in sensor network, each node has a package received confirmation process. The data package will be considered lost when the node has sent the data package and it has not reached the next node within a certain delay θ. The timer can also be used to measure package loss rate. First preset threshold φ to the timer, then start the timer of node N when node M sends data package. The data package will be considered lost when the data package hasn't reached node N before the timer threshold φ. The package loss rate can be obtained by monitoring a large number of sample data packages.

Hop. The number of hops can be acquired by sending Hello packages. First set K to the number of hops in Hello packages, the source node send the packages, and then the number of hops between all the nodes receiving the Hello packages and source node is K.

As is shown in Fig. 2, according to Zigbee cluster network, the node as the next hop whose credibility is high will be chosen in the use of the formula of node credibility, and finally the whole trustworthy sensor network will be decided [10].

3   Experiment

The simulation experiment will test the proposed theory of this article, and the simulation scenarios are set as follows: 100 identical sensor nodes are randomly distributed within 500m*500 m area, and the initial energy of each sensor node is 1 J. Build sensor network in trustworthy node selection method and traditional method, and ensure that both two sensor networks have 50 nodes. By taking specific behavior

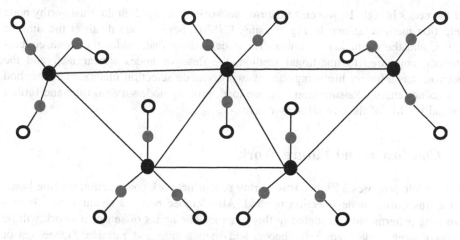

Fig. 2. Zigbee cluster network

to simulate malicious attacks, such as black hole attack, wormhole attack, DOS attack, and so on [11], the number of survival nodes will be measured every once in a while. The security and credibility of sensor network will be evaluated by the number of nodes survived.

As is shown in Fig. 3: The sensor network built based on traditional method (shown in Fig. 3 using TM), begins node death at the time of 100 s, and the death rate

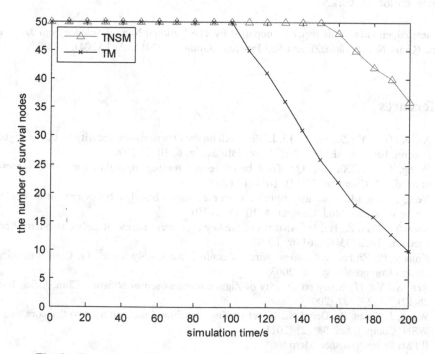

Fig. 3. Comparison of the two methods in the number of survival nodes

of the nodes is high. However, the sensor network built based on the trustworthy node selection method (shown in Fig. 3 using TNSM), begins node death at the time of 150 s, and the death rate is lower. These data show that, under the same circumstances, compared to traditional method, the dead of nodes appear later and the network has a longer life using the trustworthy node selection method. This method can reduce energy consumption, balance load, prolong node survival time and further extend the life of the overall sensor network.

4 Conclusion and Future Work

This article proposes a Zigbee trustworthy sensor network construction scheme based on a trustworthy node selection method. Also Zigbee network features and its networking patterns are considered in this scheme. The nodes of sensor network will be chosen using node credibility theory, and then a safe and reliable Zigbee sensor network will be built. An experiment was carried out by Matlab software, and it demonstrates that this method is safe and reliable compared to traditional methods. However, it still has some shortcomings. More factors of affecting the security of sensor network should be considered, and the stability of the network is still a question.

As a new technology of building sensor network, Zigbee has become increasingly close to our daily life. Nowadays more and more new applications are in urgent need of enhancing security requirements, so it is very necessary to strengthen the security of Zigbee sensor network.

Acknowledgements. This paper is supported by The National Natural Science Foundation of China (Grant No.911180002), and 863 Program (Grant No. 2011AA01A204).

References

1. Xu, X., Gao, Y., Zhang, W., Li, J.: Research on data transmission security tactics of Zigbee network based on IEEE 802.15.4. Net Info Secur. **6**, 10–12 (2009)
2. Wang, C., Jia, X., Lin, Q.: Trust based secure routing algorithm for wireless sensor networks. J. Commun. **29**(11), 105–112 (2008)
3. Ye, Q., Zhou, M.: A security authentication mechanism based on behavior trust in wireless sensor networks. Mod. Comput. **4**, 10–15 (2010)
4. Zhou, G., Han, Z., Hu, N.: Analysis of the key agreement sheme of zigbee standard. Appl. Electron. Tech. **33**(10), 61–69 (2007)
5. Kinney, P.: Zigbee technology: wireless control that simply works. In: Communications Design Conference, vol. 2 (2003)
6. Ren, X., Yu, H.: Study on security of Zigbee wireless sensor network. Chin. J. Sci. Instr. **28**(12), 2132–2137 (2007)
7. Wang, J., Chen, Z., Deng, X.: Novel routing algorithm based on trustworthy core tree in WSN. Comput. Sci. **38**(12) (2011)
8. IPPM: IP Performance Metrics

9. Liu, Y.: Trust Model for Wireless Sensor Networks Based on Hierarchical Trust Management. Taiyuan University of Technology, Taiyua (2012)

10. Liu, B., Chen, H., Wang, H., Kong, X.: A trusted security scheme of wireless sensor networks. Comput. Digital Eng. **41**(7), 1129–1133 (2013)

11. Zhang, Q.: Research on Nodes Credibility Technology in Wireless Sensor Network Environment. Nanjing University of Posts and Telecommunications (2011)

Research of Digital Campus Construction Based on Cloud Computing

Lilei Lu[⊠], Yanhong Shang, Yaping Ge, and Jinli Qu

Computer Science Department, Tangshan Normal University, Tangshan, China
{lilei_lu2013,yanhong_shang}@163.com,
{yping_g,qjli_2000}@126.com

Abstract. Based on the actual investigation of some specific primary and secondary schools in Hebei Province, Inner Mongolia and Beijing, this paper analyzes the current main problems existed in digital campus construction especially in primary and secondary schools. Considering the powerful advantages of cloud computing and its existing application in digital campus construction, this paper proposes a loosely coupled architecture of digital campus cloud platform model based on SaaS and SOA. Cloud computing is mainly used to build the software architecture in this model. The model has been proved to be effective and efficient in the construction of digital campus in primary and secondary schools of Inner Mongolia telecommunication.

Keywords: Digital campus · Cloud computing · Saas · SOA · Cloud platform

1 Introduction

Education informatization is one of the main signs of a national education modernization level [1]. Medium and Long-term Education Reform and Development Plan (2010−2020) issued by Chinese government proposes: Speed up the process of education information, deploy education information network ahead of time. Promote the construction of digital campus and to 2020 digital education service system covers all types of schools in cities and countryside.

In such circumstances, some provinces have made great efforts to strengthen basic education informatization construction and improve digital campus construction in order to promote the development of education with information technology. In recent years, nationwide digital campus construction has carried out certain work and obtained great achievement in some provinces and cities, but the general level is still low.

Through the actual investigation to specific schools especially to some primary and secondary schools in Hebei Province, Inner Mongolia and Beijing in the past years, as well as joint research with some education experts, we believe that the general education informatization level of the domestic information technology is not high. The current main problems are listed as follows:

General level backward, focusing on hardware and ignoring software. The investigation and research performed indicates that it is common phenomenon to focus on hardware construction rather than software construction in many organization units which has started to implement informatization whether in Beijing or in

Y. Yuan et al. (Eds.): ISCTCS 2013, CCIS 426, pp. 198–204, 2014.
DOI: 10.1007/978-3-662-43908-1_26, © Springer-Verlag Berlin Heidelberg 2014

provinces. In most Chinese primary and secondary schools, computer applications are restricted to the office automation and routine processing [2]. Thus it is a waste of hardware if computers are only used for such simple applications instead of advanced network technology application to perform teaching, learning and management.

Lack of specialized technical personnel, deficiency of management capacity. As has been shown in the investigation, there are no specialized technical personnel in most of primary and secondary schools. For example, computer teachers work as part-time technical personnel in Jining No.1 Middle School of Inner Mongolia. They are only responsible for computer hardware maintenance, network opening and operating system maintenance. And there is the same situation in small cities and remote places. The problem lies in that part-time computer teachers are often incapable of building information system, management and maintenance. This leads to low utilization in hardware. Even in Beijing, resource utilization is low in many schools.

Large investment and poor effect. In recent years the investment to education in-formatization is gradually increased. However, on the one hand, most investment are mainly used to buy hardware such as computers and network devices; on the other hand, in traditional informatization method, single school can not support the infor-matization construction of larger investment. Thus, the informatization construction just stays at Web sites level in many cases.

Low level of informatization services. Under the current circumstances of focusing on hardware construction, software resources are often incomplete, personnel training is not enough. This leads to the poor system compatibility and scalability and results in not fully used investment. Meanwhile, under the circumstances of informatization construction without orderly and organizational management in recent years, there exist independent functional systems based on different platforms and different architectures, resulting in islands of information and business barriers.

These existing problems do not coordinate with the current application level of information technology throughout society and the latest level of the network tech-nology development. So it is essential to accelerate the construction of digital campus. How to build an efficient digital campus has become more and more essential to make full use of all kinds of modern technology and equipment such as computers, network in order to achieve ideal education effect.

Cloud computing technology has brought new opportunities for efficient digital campus construction including not only universities but also primary and secondary schools [2]. It can help to solve those problems mentioned above as appropriate.

2 Overview of Cloud Computing Technology in Digital Campus Construction

Cloud computing refers to both the applications delivered as services over the Internet and the hardware and systems software in the data centers that provide those services [3].

Its core idea is a network connection of computing resources with unified management and scheduling, constitute a computational resources to pool user service according to the needs and provide network resources, known as "cloud" [1]. Cloud computing is an extensive and deep application of SOA (Service-Oriented Architecture) from the perspective of architecture. Because of its special advantages, it has more and more extensive applications. Cloud computing technology has the following privileges in the digital campus construction:

(1) **Integrating resources, reducing cost.** Cloud computing includes three modes. The use of private cloud can integrate all kinds of resources such as servers, storage system and provide united services. Thus it can improve the resource utilization especially hardware and can lower the cost of purchase new hardware.

(2) **Improving informatization service level.** The use of cloud computing can implement united development, united data center, united operational management and united platform maintenance and provide many kinds of services such as computing, storage and application. Users can acquire the cloud resources or services according to their needs. So there is great promotion in informatization service level.

(3) **Reducing security risks.** Because of the highly concentrated resource integration and united management and united services, cloud computing applications don't require the deployment of a large infrastructure at client's location, which eliminates or drastically reduces the upfront commitment of resources [4]. This can reduce the clients' security risk.

Just as same as its general application, cloud computing's application in digital campus construction usually includes three layers which are IaaS (Infrastructure as a Service), PaaS (Platform as a service) and SaaS (Software As A Service) from bottom to top, as shown in Fig. 1. It is also a basic framework in digital campus construction. Detailed components or functions can be increased or decreased to every layer according to actual application.

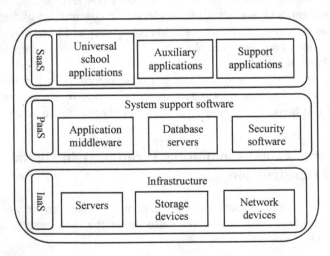

Fig. 1. A basic framework of digital campus cloud platform

3   A Digital Campus Cloud Platform Model Based on SAAS and SOA

As has been mentioned above, now we know that cloud computing digital campus usually consists of three layers from bottom to top. SaaS lies in the application layer. Considering the scale and ease of use in actual application, we proposes a simplified digital campus cloud platform model based on SaaS and SOA, which focuses on the application interface or software application. The cloud platform of digital campus construction model includes six layers, as shown in Fig. 2. They are basis platform layer, data resource layer, business support layer, function support layer, application system layer and user layer from bottom to top. The detailed structure is shown in Fig. 3.

A. Basis platform layer. This layer provides devices and all kinds of application environment support for all tops of layers. It consists of network and communication system, host storage and backup systems, information security system, operating system, terminal devices.

B. Data resource layer. This layer is to build the globally shared data sets and the purpose is to manage the global database and dataset [5]. Data resource layer consists of user authentication database, business database, communication database, education resource database, billing database and other database. This layer provides support for business support layer.

C. Business support layer. This layer is based on a loosely coupled SOA business system architecture and it is built on a combination of a number of loosely coupled components and unified defined interfaces. This can bring convenience for unified data processing services and unified communications interaction between different business systems through a flexible business system. It makes relative isolation of business processes and achieves business run independently. Thus it can lead to a

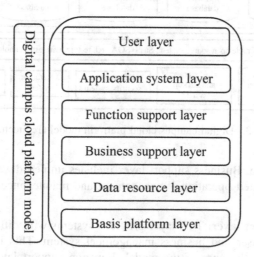

Fig. 2. Digital campus cloud platform layers

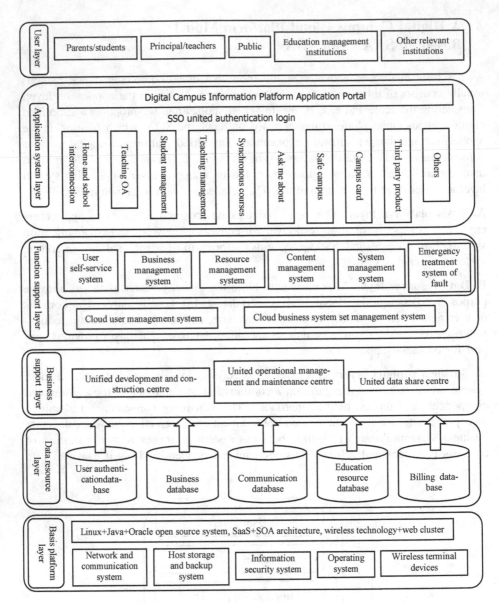

Fig. 3. Digital campus cloud platform model architecture

more quick response. Business support layer includes unified development and construction center, united operational management and maintenance center and united data share centre.

D. Function support layer. This layer provides systems with different function and support for cloud user and business management system. This layer and business support layer forms the core of the model. Function support layer includes digital campus services function and support function, as shown in Fig. 3. Digital campus services include user self-service, business management, resource management, content management and system management system and Emergency treatment system of fault. Support function includes cloud user management system and cloud business system set management system.

E. Application system layer. This layer is a cluster of application functions and a portal of digital campus information platform application. It provides united authentication for single sign-on login (SSO). It can be increased other application functions when it is necessary in future.

F. User layer. This layer provides friendly interface for different types of users. Users include parents and students, principal and teachers, public, education management institutions and other relevant institutions.

4 Application

The digital campus cloud platform model has been referenced and implemented during the course of the digital campus construction for Inner Mongolia telecommunication primary and secondary school by Zhongkeyu Science and Technology Limited Company. The implementation result showed that the use of the model has acquired good application result and provided satisfactory services. To some degree, it helps to improve information management level, to reduce overall investment, to improve informatization management level and device utilization. On the whole, it can help to solve the problems mentioned at the beginning of this paper.

5 Conclusions

Construction of digital campus is of great importance in education informatization process. How to build efficient digital campus is a challenging work. The emerging cloud computing technology can afford an effective solution for digital campus construction and help to construct effective and efficient digital campus model. With cloud computing, we succeeded in constructing a digital campus cloud platform. However, how to fully exert its role and integrate existing resources deserves further research.

Acknowledgement. This work is supported by Tangshan Normal University (No. 2013E04), additional materials are kindly provided by Beijing Zhongkeyu Science and Technology Limited Company.

References

1. Zhao, Q.: Application study of online education platform based on cloud computing. In: 2012 2nd International Conference on Consumer Electronics, Communications and Networks (CECNet), pp. 908–911. IEEE (2012)

2. Cai, Y.: The research and application of SaaS in educational information system based on educational metropolitan area network. In: 2010 International Conference on Educational and Information Technology (ICEIT), vol. 2, pp. V2-508−V2-510. IEEE (2010)
3. Armbrust, M., Fox, A., Griffith, R., et al.: A view of cloud computing. Commun. ACM **53**(4), 50–58 (2010)
4. Carraro, G., Chong, F.: Software as a service (SaaS): an enterprise perspective. MSDN Solution Architecture Center (2006)
5. Junhua, Z., Lin, W., Xin, G., et al.: Study of digital campus construction based on "SOA+ cloud". In: 2012 7th International Conference on Computer Science and Education (ICCSE), pp. 1903–1907. IEEE (2012)

Multi-layer CAPTCHA Based on Chinese Character Deformation

Tingting Wang[1,2]([✉]) and Jørgen Bøegh[1]

[1] School of Software Engineering, Beijing University of Posts
and Telecommunications, Beijing, China
getingting@126.com, jorgen_boegh@yahoo.dk
[2] Key Laboratory of Trustworthy Distributed Computing and Service (BUPT),
Ministry of Education, Beijing, China

Abstract. The main function of CAPCHA is to prevent malicious programs from register or login, malicious irrigation, bag breaking and other
network attacks. Most of the current graphic CAPTCHA's are generated based
on numbers or letters by using a random function and then perform distortion
or add viscosity curves. These graphic CAPTCHA's can easily be identified
by user, but provides an opportunity for malicious software attack website system. This paper puts forward an algorithm based on multiple layers to
generate random Chinese character CAPTCHA's which has a variety of
deformation features. We apply it to dynamic webpage, to ensure the security
of land check.

Keywords: CAPTCHA · Chinese character · Deformation

1 Introduction

The rapid development of computer network and e-commerce not only bring a great
convenience to people's life, but also change the traditional way of life of people. At
the same time, the network has brought great convenience and opportunities for
people. The problem of network security has increasingly become the focus of
attention. It is one of the important factors that threaten the development of network
applications.

In addition to meeting the basic function that users need, network application
system also provides a safe environment for users, the user login is the first barrier of
system security. Especially for Internet banking system security, it is particularly
important. How to design a website with a secure login authentication procedure is the
main issue discussed in this paper.

CAPTCHA (Completely Automated Public Turing test to tell Computers and
Humans Apart [7]), which is commonly used for land check at present. Its main
function is to prevent malicious programs from register or login, malicious irrigation,
bag breaking and other network attacks. Because CAPTCHA is easy to realize, it has
been widely used in system in large-scale network.

The principle of CAPTCHA is to randomly choose some character code in the
form of a picture and present it in the software verification interface or verification

Y. Yuan et al. (Eds.): ISCTCS 2013, CCIS 426, pp. 205–211, 2014.
DOI: 10.1007/978-3-662-43908-1_27, © Springer-Verlag Berlin Heidelberg 2014

page. When users complete input operation and submit the form, then compare the user's input code with the CAPTCHA character stored in the server session [3]. When the two are the then the submitted information is valid, otherwise we must refuse it.

Most of current graphic CAPTCHA's are generated based on a fixed set of numbers and letters by using a random function and then perform distortion or add viscosity curves. These graphics CAPTCHA's can easily be identified by a user, but provides an opportunity for malware attack. The emerging voice CAPTCHA and video CAPTCHA need high technology support, hence the popularizing is difficult for now.

This paper puts forward an algorithm based on multiple layers to generate random Chinese CAPTCHA's which has a variety of deformation features [8]. We apply it to dynamic web page to ensure the security of land check.

2   Design and Implementation of CAPTCHA Generation

The main flow of this algorithm is shown as Fig. 1:

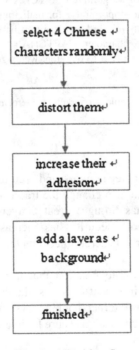

Fig. 1. Algorithm flow

2.1   Randomly Generated Characters

We first have to select candidate characters. Because English and numeric characters are relatively simple, too much deformation will make the user identification difficult. Hence, English characters are only suitable for small deformation, but this also makes segmentation and recognition for easier a computer program. The structure of Chinese characters is more complex, some deformation will not cause too much difficulty for identification by humans. In addition, segmentation and identification it is more difficult for computer programs. Therefore we choose Chinese characters as the CAPTCHA character.

In order to facilitate the user identification CAPTCHA, we select 500 Chinese characters, which are composed of one to eight strokes, as the CAPTCHA generation library. When validating the CAPTCHA, randomly select 4 Chinese characters among these candidates. The program uses Chinese character code by section position to represent the 500 Chinese characters. Use hashset to store them, where the key is the number (coded by section position) and the value is the Chinese character.

The normal format Chinese character in our program is shown in Fig. 2.

Fig. 2. Normal format

2.2   Design and Implementation of Deformation

In order to increase the recognition difficulty, we need to increase the feature libraries to provide the CAPTCHA with different characteristics. Feature values used in this paper include the following two main aspects:

1)   For each Chinese character randomly setting CAPTCHA different display properties, namely preset multiple fonts;
2)   Increase the random value verification code of Chinese characters deformation, so that each character has different deformation results.

In the deformation, we set the effects including random distortions and increased adhesion.

2.2.1   Random Distortions

In order to increase program recognition difficulty without distorting human recognition, we only distort Chinese characters randomly left up down and right. We apply distorting picture method: first generate a picture in the program, then write each Chinese character into a picture and distort the picture [6]. Lastly splice them into a complete picture.

In order to make the different distortions effective for each character, and not to influence each other in the process of deformation, we distorted the images generated for each individual character, and then assembled them into a complete picture.

After distortions through the above steps, the CAPTCHA example is as shown in Fig. 3.

供 诞 亏 五

Fig. 3. Twist effect

2.2.2   Increasing Adhesion

Increasing adhesion is increasing the compactness between the Chinese characters, hereby bringing segmentation barriers to the program. In order to ensure that each character deformation does not affect the others in the deformation process, each picture of a character are spaced farther. For the sake of increasing the characters' compactness felling, before adhering characters, we must remove the blanks. Based on image analysis, we found that the colors on the edge of the contact zone between text and background should neither be the background color nor the word color but a somewhere in-between color.

Using this feature, it is easy to delineate out blank areas' coordinate range between two characters, and then remove the blank part between characters, thereby shorten the whole CAPTCHA image's width. The specific algorithm is as follows:

The location of pixel points on the horizontal axis which has not the background color as the width marker value of the character, record the width of 4 markers character value. Then eliminated the blank part between characters, and at the same time, shortened the pattern width. The steps of the algorithm are as follows:

(a) Mark flag as false, used for identification the starting position character pixel width;
(b) For each pixel in the picture of CAPTCHA image:
    If flag is false, and this column contains the character pixels which are not all the background color, then save the transverse coordinate of this column as the start value of a character's width and the flag value is true;
    If flag is true, and this column does not contain character pixels which are all background colors that are blank, then save the transverse coordinate of the previous column as the start value of a character's width and the flag value is false;
(c) For the first 3 Chinese characters:
    If there is a blank area in the width of the character and the next character in, remove the blank portion, according to the interval width recalculation all the start value of the behind characters' width;
(d) Return to the picture. After these steps, effect is shown in Fig. 4.
    We can see from the figure that after the above steps, character spacing in the picture is greatly reduced. We can also make them more crowded by removing

Fig. 4. Remove the blank area

part of the derivative color of the character and background transfer part. The derived color in the peripheral edge of the character of the subject about 1 to 3 pixels, and removing these derived colors will not affect the character body and user identification. In the system codes, in order to make the characters crowding, I use character's width starting value generated from the last process, then put every character's width starting value increased by 2 pixels, and the ending value reduced by 2 pixels, the same with deleting characters in the first 2 columns and the last 2 columns of pixels. The results of treatment are as shown in Fig. 5.

Fig. 5. Further congestion treatment of CAPTCHA

2.3 Multiple Layers Design

In order to further increase the difficulty of program recognition, we use a multiple layers design that is adding an interference layer to the above CAPTCHA.

Use the image generated by the above methods as the foreground layer, the interference layer are used to confuse the string validation in the CAPTCHA. The string of the foreground layer and the background layer are chosen from the same candidate character set. This increases the similarity between the layer and the background layer prospects. In order to make the interference information of the background layer appear, we need to set a certain transparency on the foreground layer, generally the transparency is around 50 %, to make automatic recognition the verification string information of CAPTCHA difficult for malware.

The interference layer is composed of Chinese characters which have random length, position, color, font and slope, and it is also taken from the same candidate character set, thus increasing the similarity between interference string and verification string. This makes it more difficult for malware to distinguish, hereby reducing the possibility of successful attack on the network application system. At the same time, because of the transparency of different regions of the foreground layer is random, color depth of interference string shown in the graphic CAPTCHA are different, compared with the traditional CAPTCHA which use noise image, grid image, and random line texture image as the information interference. This interference layer can not only achieve the same identification effect for both real users and malicious program, but is also more conducive for real users to distinguish between verification code strings and interference string, and hence real users can quickly identify the correct code information.

2.3.1 Interference Layer Formation
The number, position, inclination and color of the Chinese characters in the interference layer are controlled by random() function. We define the number of

interference layers of Chinese characters between $1 \sim 3$. The character pitch is determined by the size of each character and the CAPTCHA image. Then use the cycle structure, set each randomly generated character random position, colors and slope, and by setting the flag to prevent those characters coincide. Finally save these generated interference strings as a layer object.

2.3.2   The Foreground Layer Formation

In order to increase the recognition difficulty for the malware, we need to set the foreground transparency. The foreground layer transparency is to be achieved through redrawing and color adjustment. The algorithm generating the foreground layer with linear transformation transparency is as follows:

(a) Read the picture;
(b) For every pixel in this picture:
       Change its Alpha randomly;
(c) Return image with JPEG format;

The Aloha in this code is the picture's transparency, which is between 40 % and 60 %. Each pixel's transparency is random.

2.3.3   Layer Synthesis

After generating the interference layer and the foreground layer, merge the two layers together.

It uses the Java Graphics class implementing the synthesis [9] of a certain transparency foreground layer and interference layer, thus generating a complete graphic CAPTCHA. After synthesizing the CAPTCHA is shown below (Fig. 6).

Fig. 6. The CAPTCHA after synthesizing

3   Multi-layer CAPTCHA Based on Chinese Character Deformation Identification Probability Analysis

In order to analyze the safety of multi-layer CAPTCHA based on Chinese character deformation, we use an open source CAPTCHA identification tool PWNtcha to compare identification probability, the result are as shown in Table 1.

As shown in Table 1, the probability of PWNtcha identifying image CAPTCHA was only 62 %. It is the most difficult CAPTCHA to recognize in the tested image CAPTCHAs. Experiments show that, multi-layer CAPTCHA based on Chinese character deformation has higher security, and is convenient for users to use.

Table 1. Identification result

CAPTCHA species	Identification probability (%)
687c	100
9906	90
区原任这	80
供诞丂互	62

4 Conclusions

This paper describes a basic idea, method and algorithm of a multi-layer CAPT-CHA based on Chinese character deformation. We use java beans technology, apply the CAPTCHA generated by this algorithm to JSP, and obtained the quite ideal effect. Multi-layer CAPTCHA based on Chinese character deformation technology does not only prevent the computer program of automatic identification, but also has good prospects for the development of practical application system, such as Internet Banking, social website and so on. In order to increase the attacker in the CAPTCHA cracking difficulty, and how to design and develop a more highly secure CAPTCHA, relevant researchers need further study and research.

Acknowledgement. This paper is supported by The National Natural Science Foundation of China (Grant No. 91118002), and 863 Program (Grant No. 2011AA01A204).

References

1. Stallings, W.: Cryptography and Network Security: Principles and Practice. Prentice Hall, New Jersey (1998)
2. Anderson, R., Needham, R.: Robustness Principles for Public Key Protocols. In: Coppersmith, D. (ed.) CRYPTO 1995. LNCS, vol. 963, pp. 236–247. Springer, Heidelberg (1995)
3. Cookie source code. http://www.cookiecentral.com
4. Kormann, D.P., Rubin, A.D.: Risks of passport single sign-on protocol. Comput. Netw. **33**, 51–68 (2000)
5. Li, Y., Qiufeng, W., Yuan, M.: PKI: Foundation for the construction of the security of E-commernce. Comput. Eng. Appl. **10**, 45–67 (2001)
6. Zhang, W., Xu, B., Xu, L.: Study on the Technology of Security of Page Web 11, 158–161 (2000)
7. Moy, G., Jones, N., Harkless, C.: Distortion estimation techniques in solving visual CAPTCHAs (2004)
8. Ahn, L.V., Blum, M., Langford, J.: Telling Humans and Computers Apart (automatically) or How Lazy Cryptographers do AI. CMU Press, Pennsylvania (2002)
9. Zhang, Z., Yin, S.: Based on Servlet graphic verification code research and implementation (2009)
10. Xiong, R., He, X.: Study on common method of image fusion (2009)

Filtering Training Data When Training Feed-Forward Artificial Neural Network

Krishna Moniz[1(✉)] and Yuyu Yuan[2]

[1] University of Montana, Missoula, MT, USA
krishnamoniz@live.nl
[2] Beijing University of Posts and Telecommunications, Beijing, China

Abstract. This article introduces a simple filter to the basic implementation of the feed forward artificial neural network. The filter chooses the frequency at which to use training data based on reliability of the provided training example. We posit that the inclusion of this filter will improve the effectiveness of the neural network during actual usage. However, implementation and testing shows that filtering training data for reliability does not significantly improve the effectiveness of the neural network.

Keywords: Neural network · Training data · Artificial neural network · Basic neural network · Randomized filter · Forward neural network · Supervised learning · Basic implementation

1 Introduction

A feed forward neural network tries mimicking the behaviour of interconnected artificial neurons similar to the ones found in the human brain. The basic implementation for this artificial neural network has been around since the 1980's. However, due to various factors its usage became less popular during the 1990's and did not come back into vogue until the early 2010's.

Generally, an artificial neural is trained using supervised learning, where we provide an untrained neural network with a set of input and known outputs. During training, the network learns how to recognize output from unknown inputs. If we choose to train a network using supervised learning, we face the problem of finding reliable training data. Real life teaches us that it might be hard to come by a large quantity of indisputably reliable input and output pairs. We would therefore benefit from a method that allows us to include unreliable training data (i.e. data were we are not a 100 % sure that the provided output is the best fit for the given input) during the training phase.

We propose adding a simple filter to the basic implementation of the feed forward neural network in order to mitigate the negative effect of using unreliable training data.

The decision to limit the research scope to feed forward neural networks was based on the implementation constraints. However, we see no reason why the approach cannot be extended to any linear optimization problem. Our approach requires the filtering of input data prior to submission to the neural network and a

Y. Yuan et al. (Eds.): ISCTCS 2013, CCIS 426, pp. 212–218, 2014.
DOI: 10.1007/978-3-662-43908-1_28, © Springer-Verlag Berlin Heidelberg 2014

neural network is merely connected graph of nodes. The value of the nodes is determined by fixed sigmoid function, in our case $f(x) = \frac{1}{1+e^{-x}}$ and the value of the connections is determined by linear optimization function (Rumelhart et al., 1986).

2 Basic Neural Network

Below we introduce the concept neural network and show that training is done by means of linear optimization.

A neural network is a set of perceptrons in a weighted directed graph. A perceptron represents an artificial representation of a neural node with n inputs and one output (Rosenblatt and Papert, 1969).

The value of the perceptron is equal to the logistic regression of the summation of the previous nodes times the weights of the incoming connection.

$$a^{(1)} = \frac{1}{1 + e^{-(\sum_{i=0}^{n} w_i x_i)}} \tag{1}$$

Here $a^{(1)}$ represents the value of the perceptron (i.e. the output), x is a vector representing the values of input nodes, w is a vector representing the weights of the of the connections from the input nodes to the perceptron. The (1) superscript of the a and w values indicate that this is the second layer of the neural network. Note that this notation gives us the freedom to denote the input layer x as $a^{(0)}$. Using this modified notation, we can rewrite our perceptron result as (where k denotes the layer of the network):

$$a^{(k)} = \frac{1}{1 + e^{-(\sum_{i=0}^{n} w_i^{(k)} a_i^{(k-1)})}} \tag{2}$$

This general form of a perceptron is shown in Fig. 1.

In a neural network, we combine perceptrons in a directed graph with information flowing from the original inputs to the final outputs. See Fig. 2 for a complete neural net. In the figure, layer $a^{(0)}$ represents the input layer and layer $a^{(3)}$ represents the output. The value of each node is determined by the sigmoid function and the weight of each connection is determined during training (supervised learning).

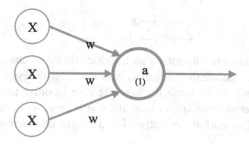

Fig. 1. A single perceptron with 3 input nodes (n = 3)

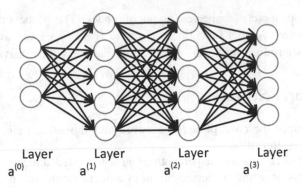

Layer $a^{(0)}$ Layer $a^{(1)}$ Layer $a^{(2)}$ Layer $a^{(3)}$

Fig. 2. Possible configuration of a 4 layer neural net with 3 input nodes and 4 output nodes

The neural net also contains an extra "bias node" in each layer, which we have excluded from the figure. The bias node is added to each layer to cope with the fact that during training, both the weights and the node values are changed. The bias node, is connected to all the nodes in the next layer, but none in the previous layer and it always emits 1. The purpose is pretty straightforward and therefore we have chosen to exclude further discussion on the node in the rest of the explanation of the network.

In order to determine the weight of the connections, we train the set by means of back propagation of errors a method introduced by Rumelhart et al. in the early 1980s.

Back propagation is a supervised learning method were we run a training set containing inputs and corresponding outputs through the neural network. During each run, we calculate the cost of keeping the existing weights and change the values of the weights to result in a lower cost on the next run. This cost can be interpreted as the difference between the output produced by the neural network and the output expected by the training example.

To quantify that, let us assume to run a training set with m samples through a net with K+1 layers, thus givens us layers 0 to K. Note that the first layer ($a^{(0)}$) is the input layer and the last layer $a^{(K)}$ is the output layer. A single example is denoted by (x_c, y_c), where x_c is the input vector (equal to $a^{(0)}$) and $y_c^{(k)}$ is the expected output vector at layer k. The actual output of the neural network is $a^{(K)}$. Note that $a_c^{(k)}$ and $y_c^{(k)}$ are vectorized representations at each layer. The values at each layer are determined by back propagating from the output layer.

For our network, the error then becomes:

$$E = \sum\nolimits_{c=0}^{m} \sum\nolimits_{k=1}^{K} \left(a_c^{(k)} - y_c^{(k)} \right)^2 \tag{3}$$

Our job then becomes to minimize this E, which do by means of gradient descent. This means we must calculate the partial derivative of E with respect to each weight in the network. Let's look at the math for a single case in order to understand what is going on. Note that because we are looking at a single case, we exclude the subscript c from our notation. The partial derivative for a single connection of a single case becomes:

$$\frac{\partial E}{\partial w_i^{(k)}} = \frac{\partial E}{\partial y_i^{(k)}} a_i^{(k-1)} \tag{4}$$

Where i denotes the vector component. In other words $a^{(k)} = \left[a_1^{(k)}, a_2^{(k)}, a_3^{(k)}, \ldots, a_n^{(k)} \right]$. Furthermore, $\frac{\partial E}{\partial y_i^{(k)}}$ is the differential of the node, which is:

$$\frac{\partial E}{\partial y_i^{(k)}} = \frac{\partial E}{\partial a_i^{(k)}} a_i^{(k)} \left(1 - a_i^{(k)} \right) \tag{5}$$

The $\frac{\partial E}{\partial a_i^{(k)}}$ term is just the summed effect of the previous nodes on the current node, thus:

$$\frac{\partial E}{\partial a_i^{(k)}} = \sum_i \frac{\partial E}{\partial y_i^{(k+1)}} \cdot w_i^{(k+1)} \tag{6}$$

Note that for the output nodes ($k = K$) we just use the difference from the expected value, namely $\frac{\partial E}{\partial a_i^{(K)}} = (a_i^{(K)} - y_i^{(K)})$

The ability to determine the cost of each weight at of the network for each example independent of the other samples gives us a very simple method of implementing gradient descent. Namely, change each weight by an amount proportional to the cost of the current implementation (i.e. proportional to $\frac{\partial E}{\partial w_i^{(k)}}$).

$$w_i^{(k)}(t) = w_i^{(k)}(t-1) + \Delta w_i^{(k)}(t) \tag{7}$$

To speed up the process, we can use acceleration implementation and thus change each weight based on the momentum of the previous change. This gives us:

$$\Delta w_l^{(k)}(t) = -\varepsilon \frac{\partial E}{\partial w_i^{(k)}(t)} + \alpha \Delta w_i^{(k)}(t-1) \tag{8}$$

Where t is incremented by 1 every time we go through the set of training data. The constants ε and α are fixed and in our implementation set to $\varepsilon = 0.7$ and $\alpha = 0.9$

As in all optimization problems, we continue to train the network until the error E falls below predetermined threshold (in our implementation set to 1.000).

3 Proposed Algorithm

It the independent effect that each training example has on the neural network that allows us an opportunity for filtering input data. Namely, during each successive run of a training example, we can train the model with the example.

We posit that questionable data points can be used to train the network, but should be used less often then clearly correct data points.

H_o: Making usage of training example during training dependent on their reliability will result in a better trained neural network

The basic implementation of back propagation looks something like this:

```
// for each example in the training set
for(c = 0; c < m; c++)
{
    // for each layer in the network
    // (except the input layer k=0)
    for(k = K; k > 0; k-- )
    {
        // for each connection in the layer
        for(i = 0; i > n; i++)
        {
            // calculate the change in the weight
            deltaWeight =  calculateChangeInWeight();
            // update the weight
            weights[k][i] += deltaWeights;
        }
    }
}
```

Our modification introduces a single filter before each step in the optimization:

The filter function useThis Example() is a randomized probability function, whose likelihood of returning true is directly determined by the likelihood of the training being correct.

```
// for each example in the training set
for(c = 0; c < m; c++)
{
    // filter each example by likelihood of being
    // correct
    if(useThisExample(trainingdata[c]))
    {
        for(k = K; k > 0; k-- )
        {
            . . .
        }
    }
```

As we stated in the introduction, we assume that quality of the network should improve if it was trained with more reliable data.

4 Experiment

Our experiment consists of three different implementations of the basic neural network. All three implementations received the same training and testing data.

The training data consists of a set of Chinese tones recordings. Each example has:

- A normalized pitch recording (x). Consisting of 100 data points with each point having a value between 0 and 1. $x_c = [x_1, x_2, x_3, ..., x_{100}]$
- The Chinese tone (y) that this represents. This is a 4 dimensional vector where each dimensions represents one of 4 tones. The values are between 0 and 1. $y_c = [y_1, y_2, y_3, y_4]$
- A reliability factor (r) indicating how likely this that this pitch recording correctly represents the given Chinese tone. The factor is a scalar between 0 and 1. Where 1 represents 100 % sure that it is correct.

The three implementations are as follows:

- A basic neural network with no filtering
- A neural network which excludes all questionable data points. In other words, the filter returns false if $r < 0.7$.
- A neural network with a randomized filter function. note: rand is a random value between 0 and 1

$$filter = \begin{cases} false & random\ number > r \\ true & random\ number \le r \end{cases}$$

The neural network was a 3 layer network with 75 nodes in the input layer, 25 nodes in the hidden layer and 4 nodes in the output layer.

Results and discussion
The training data is as follows

	# of points	Min reliability	Avg reliability	Max reliability
All data	6223	0.0000	0.6481	1.0000
Output = 1	1573	0.0000	0.6732	1.0000
Output = 2	1430	0.0003	0.4576	1.0000
Output = 3	1267	0.0002	0.6864	1.0000
Output = 4	1953	0.0000	0.7425	1.0000

During training we got the following test results using the training data

	Σ error	Correct guesses	Incorrect guesses
No filtering	2.0892	4417	1806
Exclude unreliable points	2.9477	4126	2097
Randomized filter	2.9993	4368	1855

Finally we used the trained neural network on fresh testing data and received the following:

	Σ error	Correct guesses	Incorrect guesses	Ratio %
No filtering	1.9461	1286	227	85
Exclude unreliable points	2.9483	1258	255	83
Randomized filter	2.0000	1299	214	86

As the data shows, the three different training methods yielded similar results. The randomized filter did give the best results, but the sum of error was higher than that of the net trained without a filter. Further, the ration improvement of less 1 % does not merit the additional effort of including the filter.

Hence our hypothesis H_o is false.

One thing worth mentioning is that completely excluding "unreliable" data from the training set yielded the worst result. Hence we do learn that you are better off including questionable data in training set, thus providing the net with more data points than excluding them completely.

5   Conclusion

We found using a randomized filter did not significantly improve the quality of the neural network. However, we did discover that the network performed better than if we had completely ignored the data. Therefore we suggest that future implementations of the basic neural network remain unmodified (i.e. the filter is unnecessary), but that programmers feel free in to include data is not 100 % reliable when training their artificial neural network.

References

Rosenblatt, L., Papert, S.: Perceptrons. MIT, Cambridge (1969)
Rumelhart, D., Hinton, G., Williams, R.: Learning representations by back-propagating errors. Nature **323**, 533–536 (1986)

Security Risk Assessment of Mobile Internet Under Cloud Computing Mode

Luping Chen, Yongzhen Guo[✉], and Feng Zhou

China Software Testing Center, Beijing, China
yzguo@cstc.org.cn

Abstract. With the development of cloud computing and internet and the wide combination of them, internet mobile internet security issues under the cloud computing mode become more and more significant. Compared with the traditional internet security problems, the new one could cause much more serious destructions, so it is necessary to pull out the mobile internet security risk evaluation method based cloud computing mode as soon as possible. This passage has analyzed deeply of the technological characteristics, service's modes and new appeared security issues of mobile internet under the cloud computing mode. Combined with current information security risk evaluation methods, the passage also provides new mobile internet security risk evaluate method. This method includes assets identification, threat identification, fragility identification, existed security measures confirmation and risk computing.

Keywords: Cloud computing · Mobile internet · Security Risk Assessment · Judgment matrix

1 Security Risk of Mobile Internet Under Cloud Computing Mode

With a surge of construction on 3G network and fast popularity of intelligent terminal, mobile internet technology and service have been developed rapidly. At a business level, scales for applications such as social networks, search engines continue to grow. Meanwhile, new mobile internet business like weblog and mobile map emerge one after another. Intelligent terminals based on different operation systems bloom together. Open operation systems of intelligent terminals are able to install and unload third-party software. Mobile internet contains attributes like network integration, intelligent termination, and application diversification and opens platform, etc. However, this is a big threat to maintain national security, stabilization of public order and people's rights.

1.1 Security Risk of Cloud Computing Business Systems

Cloud computing is a new computing model build on distributed computing, network computing and parallel computing. It is a new method of shared infrastructure, which faces super-large scale distributed environment and provides data storage as well as network services. The advantages of cloud computing like convenience, economy and expansibility attract many IT companies putting their strategies on it. But there are

Y. Yuan et al. (Eds.): ISCTCS 2013, CCIS 426, pp. 219–226, 2014.
DOI: 10.1007/978-3-662-43908-1_29, © Springer-Verlag Berlin Heidelberg 2014

many critical problems, especially the security problem when considering security issues based on cloud computing happened occasionally. Survey results of Gartner in 2009 showed more than 70 % of interviewed CTO thought the reason why not employ cloud computing recently was data security and privacy. Besides, a gust of security events from cloud computing innovators such as Amazon, Google in recent years heightened people's fear [1].

All of these security events indicate that secure problem has become the most important one in cloud computing development. Research institution Gartner has released a report named Cloud Computing Security Risk Assessment. Seven risks include: access of privileged users, reviewability, data position, data isolation, data recovery, survey support and long-term severability have been listed.

1.2 Mobile Internet Security Risk

With the large scale commercialization of 3G and continuous popularization of intelligent terminals in our country, mobile internet comes to be familiar and used by people gradually. As data demonstrated, the number of mobile phone user is more than 1 billion in 2012, among the group there are at least 0.38 billion people hold a smart phone. Other than this huge group of users, applications which adapt to the mobile environment are also staying in a rapid growth For instance, there are more than 150 thousand applications in Apple App Store and the number is increasing 12 % per month at the mean time. Google's Android market just follows by with current application quantity more than 40 thousand and increasing with a rate of 68 % per month [2].

The mobile internet is now in a status of fast booming, but because of its technological characteristics and potential tremendous economy interest, mobile internet is now facing series of new problems to be solved apart from traditional internet security issues. For example, some disguised base stations exist in many areas of China, These disguised stations which based on host computers and laptops are built by criminals. They provide even better signals in a limited region therefore the telecommunication carriers' signals will be suppressed. Consequently, the mobile terminals will be induced to choose the disguised base stations first and the disguised base stations are able to pretend to be any number, send short messages to mobile phone users without monitoring, and the quantity can reach 50 thousand per hour. This way has already been the new method for criminals to send fraudulent and advertisement messages, which indicates a huge threat.

Just like internet tide in the late 90s, mobile internet is changing our life step by step. It is becoming an indispensable part of people's life. To deal with various of security issues in mobile internet, set up risk assessment aiming at mobile internet security is imperative.

2 Identification of Security Risk in Mobile Network Under Cloud Computing Mode

Confidentiality, integrity, availability, authority, reliability, and audit are six security properties of asset evaluation.

Value of assets in risk assessment is not measured by their economic value, but by degree of assets match with six security properties above, or degree of effects when those security properties have not been achieved.

2.1 Asset Identification

Assets of the mobile internet refer to valuable resources in the mobile internet services. Assets of the mobile Internet can also be divided into hardware, software, data and so on.

Asset valuation bases on the importance of a variety of assets to assessment information system. Considering social influence, business value and service availability, assign value for six security attributes, and take rating method to divide those attributes into five grades. In this hierarchy, 5, 4, 3, 2, 1 stand for very high, high, medium, low and very low respectively. Selecting the highest value among six attributes values for this asset and mapping this value to five levels, the higher the level, the more important of the asset [5].

2.2 Threat Identification

Threat is a kind of factor which has the possibility of potential damage to assets, and it is objectively existed. Factors cause threat can be divided into artificial factors and environmental factors.

Threat identification is mainly about the frequency that threat occurs in similar situation. In most cases, it is the possibility for threat's occurrence. Through the existing data and experience [5].

Threat frequency can be predicted according to the threat showed in past security issues report and its frequency, or experience of experts.

2.3 Vulnerability Identification

Vulnerability means weakness exists in asset itself. Threat can cause harm only when it makes use of asset vulnerability.

According to the scale of the mobile internet, whether to allow access from privileged user and character identification for censorship of mobile internet, data location, data isolation measures, data recovery measures and long-term survivability can all lead to vulnerability of security issues.

Severity of vulnerability can be rated by hierarchy. Different levels represent different severity of assets vulnerability, the higher the level, the greater the vulnerability severity [5].

2.4 Confirmation on Existing Security Measures

During the identification of fragility, evaluator should confirm the effectiveness of taken security measures. The security measurement confirmation should evaluate its effectiveness, it means whether it can reduce system's fragility and withstand threats.

Effective security measures should be kept to avoid unnecessary work and capitals brought by duplicate implementation of the security measures. Confirmed improper security measures need to be considered that whether they should be cancelled or refined, or substituted by more proper security measures [5].

Security measures can be divided into two ways, preventive and protective. Preventive security measures are able to reduce the possibility of security issues caused by vulnerability for making use of threats, such as intrusion detection system; protective security measures can reduce influence of organization or system security issues.

There is connection between existed security measures confirmation and fragility identification. Generally speaking, the utilization of security measures will reduce the fragility on system technology and management. But the security measures confirmation doesn't need to be like fragility identification procedure which specifies to fragility of each asset and component. It is an integration of a category with concrete measures, and it is used to provide basis or reference to work out risk processing plan.

3 Analysis of Mobile Internet Security Risk Under Cloud Computing Mode

3.1 Risk Calculation Theory

After completion of asset identification, threat identification, vulnerability identification, as well as confirmation of existing security measures, appropriate methods and tools will be adopted to determine the possibility of threat and severity of threat caused by vulnerability. To get the effect of threat needs combining the possibility of threat and the severity of the threat. Then the final risk value could be calculated through the effect of threat and threat and the mobile Internet on asset value. Its principle diagram is shown in Fig. 1.

3.2 Risk Calculation Method

In risk assessment, risk factors involved in risk calculation generally are: assets, threat and vulnerability. As pointed in risk calculation principle, combination patterns of these factors are as follows: threats and vulnerabilities determine the possibility of a security incident, assets and vulnerabilities determine loss of security incident, possibility of security events the and loss brought by security issues determines risk value [4]. A norm form of risk value calculation is given below:

$$\text{Risk Value } R(A) = F(A, T) = F(A, G(V, Sv, D, Sd))$$

A: assets of the mobile Internet, T: effect of threat, F: calculation function of risk value, V: probability of vulnerabilities occurrence, D severity of vulnerability, Sv: effect of existing security measures on reducing threats occurrence, Sd: effect of existing security measures on reducing damage of threats, G: calculation function of threat effect.

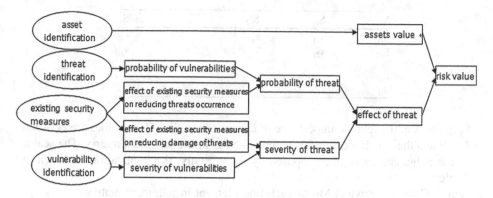

Fig. 1. Risk calculation theory

1.   Calculation of Asset Value

For asset information of any item A, six attributes should be considered: Availability Ava(A), confidentiality Conf(A), integrity Inte(A), Authority Auth(A), reliability Rel(A) and audit Aud(A). For information assets, the six properties have no difference of importance. Therefore, we can take the average of the six as a value of information assets V(A) for item A. That is:

$$V(A) = [Ava(A) + Conf(A) + Inte(A) + Auth(A) + Rel(A) + Aud(A)]/6$$

2.   Threat Impacts

For a threat T_i, corresponding weak spot set can be represented as $Vi = (V_{i1}, ..., V_{im})$, which, possibility of any weak spot V_{ij} be used by threat T_i is probability $P(V_{ij})$ and its possible severity of destruction or seriousness of weak point V_{ij} is D_{ij}.

The influence degree of a threat is the mathematical expectation of probability of all its corresponding vulnerabilities occur and their severity:

$$E(T_i) = \sum_{j=1}^{m} E(V_{ij}) = \sum_{j=1}^{m} (P(V_{ij}) * D_{ij})$$

3.   Existing Security Measures Impacts

Considering existing security measure S, including reducing impact of probability for threats occurrence Sv and reducing impact of probability for threats destruction Sd.

Assuming there are l existing security measures, their effects on the vulnerability V_{ij} which consists threat T_i are different. The weight of each existing security measure could be calculated by judgment matrix [3].

The calculation steps are as follows:

- step 1. Structures the judgment matrix for existing security measures of every vulnerability. The judgment matrix shows the relative importance degree between existing security measures for a vulnerability.

V_{ij}	S_{i1}	S_{i2}	...	S_{il}
S_{i1}	s_{11}	s_{12}	...	s_{11}
S_{i2}	s_{21}	s_{22}	...	s_{21}
$\vdots$	$\vdots$	$\vdots$		$\vdots$
S_{il}	s_{11}	s_{12}	...	s_{11}

Spq: For Vij, the relative importance of factors Sip to Siq. Their values are between 1 to 9 and their reciprocals, which are the scales of the judgment matrix. The scales of the judgment matrix are proposed by Saaty firstly, the implication is shown in Table 1.

- step 2. Calculate product Mp of each line element in judgment matrix:

$$M_p = \prod_{q=1}^{l} s_{pq} \, p = 1, 2, 3 \ldots l$$

- step 3. Calculate the l-th root of Mp:

$$\overline{W_p} = \sqrt[l]{M_p} \quad p = 1, 2, 3 \ldots l$$

- step 4. Normalize the vector $\left(\overline{W_1}, \overline{W_2}, \ldots, \overline{W_l} \right)^T$:

$$W_p = \frac{\overline{W_p}}{\sum_{q=1}^{l} \overline{W_q}}$$

Wp is the weight of existing security measure.

This calculation method as above is used to calculate the weights on reducing impact of probability for threats occurrence Sv and reducing impact of probability for threats destruction Sd. The values of Sv and Sd are limited between 0 to 1.1 stands for having no effect and 0 stands for having complete effect.

Table 1. The scale and its desceiption

Intensity of importance	Explanation
1	Two activities contribute equally to the objective
3	Experience and judgment slightly favor one activity over another
5	Experience and judgment strongly favor one activity over another
7	An activity is strongly favored and its dominance is demonstrated in practice
9	The evidence favoring one activity over another is of the highest possible order of affirmation
2, 4, 6, 8	Intermediate values between the two adjacent judgments
Reciprocals of above nonzero	If activity p has one of the above nonzero numbers assigned to it when compared with activity q, then q has the reciprocal value when compared with p

Under influence of existing security measures, if threat Ti happens, resulted impact is:

$$E(T_i) = \sum_{j=1}^{m} E(V_{ij}) = \sum_{j=1}^{m} \left(\left(P(V_{ij}) * \sum_{p=1}^{l} (W_{ip} * Sv_{ip}) \right) * \left(D_{ij} * \sum_{p=1}^{l} (W_{ip} * Sd_{ip}) \right) \right)$$

After considering safety control measures, risk value R(A) of asset A is:

$$R(A) = A * \sum_{i=1}^{n} E(T_i) = A * \sum_{i=1}^{n} \sum_{j=1}^{m} E(V_{ij})$$

$$= A * \sum_{i=1}^{n} \sum_{j=1}^{m} \left(\left(P(V_{ij}) * \sum_{p=1}^{l} (W_{ip} * Sv_{ip}) \right) * \left(D_{ij} * \sum_{p=1}^{l} (W_{ip} * Sd_{ip}) \right) \right)$$

4 Security Risk Evaluation of Mobile Internet Under Cloud Computing Application Mode

4.1 Judgment of Risk Value

Evaluators should calculate risk value for each asset according to the adopted risk calculation method, set up risk value range for each level according to distribution of risk value, and implement risk level processing to all results. Each level represents corresponding severity [5].

For unacceptable risk, risk treatment should be designed according to vulnerability of the risk. Risk treatment plan should explicitly explain the security measures for vulnerability compensation, expected effect, implementation condition, schedule and responsibility division, etc. The choice of security measures should consider two aspects, namely, management and technology. Meanwhile, selection and implementation of safety measures shall refer to related information security standards.

4.2 Residual Risk Evaluation

After choosing the proper security measures for unacceptable risk, there can be a revaluation in order to confirm the effectiveness of security measures and judge whether the residual risk is reduced to an acceptable level. The residual risk evaluation can be implemented by the procedure this norm form provides, as well as can be cut within a proper range. Generally speaking, the goal for security measures implementation is reducing vulnerability and possibility of security issues. Therefore, the remaining risk evaluation can start from the vulnerability evaluation, to compute the risk value after contrasting of the vulnerability condition between before and after the implementation of security measures.

After choosing appropriate security measures for some risks, if the result of residual risk is still in an unacceptable range, we may consider whether to accept the risk or to further increase the corresponding safety measures.

5 Conclusion

This paper has analyzed deeply of the technological characteristics, service's modes and new appeared security issues of mobile internet under the cloud computing mode [6]. Combined with current information security risk evaluation methods, the passage also provides new mobile internet security risk evaluate method. This method includes assets identification, threat identification, fragility identification, existed security measures confirmation and risk computing.

Acknowledgement. This paper is a part of research achievement of "Research on mobile Internet security issues under the application mode of cloud computing (No. 2012ZX03002003-005)", which is one of project of National Science and Technology Major Project "Next-generation Broadband Wireless Mobile Communication Network".

References

1. Feng, D.G., Zhang, M., Zhang, Y., Xu, Z.: Study on cloud computing security. J. Softw. **22**(1), 71–83 (2011). (in Chinese)
2. Yang, Y., Lai, Y.: The security issues under the cloud computing environment. Comput. Knowl. Technol. **5**(16), 4154–4156 (2009). (in Chinese)
3. Saaty, T.L.: A scaling method for priorities in hierarchical structures. J. Math. Psychol. **15**(3), 234–281 (1977)
4. Yue, Y., Yue, S.: Method based on numerical analysis for information security assessment. Comput. Eng. Des. **27**(3), 404–410 (2006). (in Chinese)
5. GBT 20984-2007, Information security technology— risk assessment specification for information security
6. Cai, Y.F.: Information systems security risk assessment model based on cloud computing. Chin. Manage. Inf. **012**, 75–77 (2010). (in Chinese)

Business Impact Analysis Model Based on the Analytic Hierarchy Process

Jizeng Guan[1,5], Xiaolu Zhu[2,5(✉)], Mingtao Lei[4,5], Jianyi Liu[2], and Cong Wang[3,4,5]

[1] Global Data Solution Ltd., Beijing, China
guanjizheng@gds-services.com
[2] School of Computer Science,
Beijing University of Posts and Telecommunications, Beijing, China
{zhuxiaolu, liujy}@bupt.edu.cn
[3] Automation School of BUPT,
Beijing University of Posts and Telecommunications, Beijing, China
wcong@bupt.edu.cn
[4] School of Software Engineering,
Beijing University of Posts and Telecommunications, Beijing, China
leimingtao1@163.com
[5] Key Laboratory of Trustworthy Distributed Computing and Service (BUPT),
Ministry of Education, Beijing, China

Abstract. BIA (Business Impact Analysis) is an important basis for the organization to carry out the construction for business continuity management. The conclusions of BIA will affect the effectiveness of implementation of business continuity management plan. The major content of BIA is to determine the disaster recovery objectives of the business systems in organization. But most of the existing BIA methods are using the qualitative analysis method and expert evaluation method, which lack of sufficient theoretical support and quantitative scientific computing. The purpose of this paper is to apply mature AHP (Analysis Hierarchy Process) to BIA. BIA can really be used in guiding the implementation of the organization's business continuity management plan through the index system and scientific computing.

Keywords: Business impact analysis · Business continuity management · Recovery time objectives · Recovery point objective · Analytic hierarchy process · Business recovery priority · Disaster recovery

1 Introduction

With the improvement of dependency level of information systems for organization and the promotion of centralization of data storage and processing, the size and the complexity of information system of organization's data centers becomes increasingly higher. The data center failure and business break down caused by unexpected incidents will cause the organization being able to provide services for outside, therefore how to guarantee the organization's information security and business continuity operation is an key responsibility. The purpose of established the system of disaster

Y. Yuan et al. (Eds.): ISCTCS 2013, CCIS 426, pp. 227–234, 2014.
DOI: 10.1007/978-3-662-43908-1_30, © Springer-Verlag Berlin Heidelberg 2014

recovery and business continuity management is to improve the organization's ability of resisting disaster, reduce the losses of the business system caused by the disaster and the adverse effects on the organization and society, and ensure the safety of the business operation and recovery [1].

The major content of BIA is to determine the disaster recovery objectives of the organization's business systems. The disaster recovery objectives include the disaster recovery target and priority of the disaster recovery for the business systems. The disaster recovery priority is an important basis to develop the disaster recovery strategy, but currently this work just relies on the experience of consultants or organization's internal business workers, mostly depends on the scenario of the disaster. This method of completely relied on the experience and human judgment analysis will inevitably lead to lack of scientific conclusion of BIA.

In response to the problems of BIA methodology, this paper will establish the model of disaster recovery priority analysis using the mature analysis hierarchy process (AHP) to make BIA tend to scientific and rational through the method which combined with qualitative analysis and computing.

2   The General Flow of the Business Impact Analysis

BIA is determined the disaster recovery objective of the information system and provided the basis for the strategy of disaster recovery through the analysing of the business function, relationship and the losses and influence of organization when the business function lose efficacy The implementation process of BIA is shown in Fig. 1:

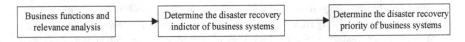

Fig. 1. The implementation process of BIA

(1) Business functions and relevance analysis

This step is carried on to determine the business function list through business functions, transaction features, transaction channel and relevance incidence relation of organization's information systems. The analysis of business functions is distributed into two stages:

First step: analysing business characteristics, which consist of volume of business, daily and key operating period and business function characteristics. This is an important basis for determining RTO of business systems.

Second step: analysis of business incidence relation. Business incidence relation is direct or indirect interactive relation between the various businesses, which consist of business data flow, interactive session, interactive characteristics, interactive channel and so on. The dependence between businesses will be determined through analysis of business incidence relation.

(2) Determine the disaster recovery targets of business systems

The disaster recovery targets of business system mean disaster recovery time objective (RTO) and recovery point objective (RPO) of business systems. The targets will be used as an important basis for determining a disaster recovery technology strategy.

(3) Determine the disaster recovery priority of business systems

The disaster recovery priority of business systems means the recovery order when disaster occurs. The priority will be used as an important basis for determining a business recovery strategy.

3   Business Interrupt Impact Analysis Model Based on AHP

3.1   Establishment of Business Interrupt Impact Evaluation Index System

The business interrupt impact evaluation index system is an important manifestation of accuracy and scientific of BIA. The losses caused by business systems interrupt will be considered when determining the disaster recovery priority of business systems. The analysis of financial and non-financial losses caused by business systems interrupt will be need Financial losses also means economic losses caused by business interrupt, including direct and indirect economic losses. The direct economic losses includes: loss of assets, loss of incomes, increase of additional cost, fines for supervise agencies and so on. The indirect economic losses includes: loss of expected income, loss of business opportunities, the affective of market share etc. While non-financial losses means non-economic losses caused by business interrupt, including impacts such as social, political, Social and public image, cooperation partner etc.

3.2   Establishment of AHP Evaluation Model

3.2.1   Obtain Evaluation Score

According to above index system, the questionnaire of BIA should be designed. When the questionnaire is designed, the option can be designed based on the parameters required by the evaluation index. There is a certain relationship between business interruption impact level and the index score, as shown below: $score = k \times impact$, that is to say the index score is in proportion to the interruption impact level. Therefore, In the design of each index score, the score can be divided into five grades according to the degree of importance caused by business interruption, as shown in Table 1:

Table 1. The define of the interruption impact and index score

The interruption impact	Index score
Business interruption has no effect on the organization	0
Business interruption has smaller effect on the organization	1
Business interruption has important effect on the organization	2
Business interruption has serious effect on the organization	3
Business interruption has very serious effect on the organization	4

The Delphi expert opinion is available in the acquisition of index score [2]. The Delphi method is a subjective qualitative analysis method, which is used most commonly in system evaluation. It can be used for the establishment process of prediction and evaluation index system. On the request of nonoccurrence horizontal linkages, experts' opinion can be collected independently in an anonymous way. By induction, feedback and correction method, the opinion tends to be convergent. The aim is to try to eliminate external interference and reduce error and disagreement in the survey.

3.2.2   Determine the Weights of Evaluation Indexes Using AHP

(1) *The basic principle of AHP*

AHP is a systems analysis method combined with qualitative analysis and quantitative computing proposed by U.S. operational research experts Satty [3]. AHP embodies the basic characteristics of the human mind, namely decompose and judgment. So it has the feasibility, effectiveness and reliability advantages. AHP is a simple method of decision-making and is particularly suitable for the questions, which are difficult to be dealt with using quantitative analysis completely.

AHP first level problem into the evaluation index layer (the lowest level), the criterion layer (intermediate layer) and the target layer (top layer) according to the nature of the problem and the general objective of the problem. The weights of evaluation indexes can be determined through the importance of the lower to the upper layer [4, 5].

(2) *Determine the weights of evaluation indexes*

Stage 1: Structure pair-wise comparison judgment matrix

    Define parameters:

    [1]   judgment matrix: $A_{n \times n}$;

    [2]   amount of the indexes: n;

    [3]   name of indexes: $Index_1, Index_2, Index_3, \cdots, Index_{n-1}, Index_n$;

    [4]   the importance of $Index_i$ to $Index_j$: a_{ij}; and the importance of $Index_j$ to $Index_i$: $a_{ji} = \frac{1}{a_{ij}}$.

The pseudo-code as follows:

```
1:    i=1,j=i
2:    for i=1;i<n;i++
3:        for j=i;j<=n;j++
4:            switch (the importance of Index_i to Index_j){
5:                we can get a_ij and a_ji
6:            }
7:        endfor
8:    endfor
```

Stage 2: Calculate the eigenvector and the max eigenvalue

```
9:    for i=1;i<n;i++
```

$$10: \quad w_i = \frac{1}{n} \sum_{j=1}^{n} \frac{a_{ij}}{\sum_{i=1}^{n} a_{ij}} \text{//calculate the eigenvector}$$

11:    endfor

12:    $\lambda_{max} = \frac{1}{n}\sum_{i=1}^{n}\frac{\sum_{j=1}^{n}a_{ij}w_i}{w_i}$ //calculate the max eigenvalue

Stage 3: Consistency check of judgment matrix

13:    $C.I. = \frac{\lambda_{max}-n}{n-1}$.//calculate the consistency index

14:    $C.R. = \frac{C.I.}{R.I.}$.   //calculate the consistency ratio

15:    if C.R.<0.1

16:    the consistency of the judgment matrix A is acceptable;

17:    else

18:    the consistency of the judgment matrix A is unacceptable, and the judgment matrix should be corrected appropriately;

19:    endif

Stage 4: Consistency improvement of judgment matrix

When the judgement matrix does not have a satisfactory consistency, a modified reference should be given using the improved algorithm as follows [6]:

20:    for i=1;i<n;i++

21:    for j=i+1;j<=n;j++

22:    $c_{ij} = \frac{a_{ij}}{w_i\sum_{i=1}^{n}a_{ij}}$ // $C = (c_{ij})_{n\times n}$ is the induced matrix of A

23:    If(c_{ij}>max)

24:    $max = c_{ij}; k = i; l = j$

25:    endif

26:    endfor

27:    endfor

28:    $a_{kl} = a_{kl} - 1$ and $a_{lk} = \frac{1}{a_{kl}}$

29:    goto the first step to calculate w_i until C.R.<0.1

So far, the work of achieving the weights of evaluation index system is done.

3.3   Determine the Business Recovery Priority

Assuming that set of index score is $\{a_1, a_2, \cdots, a_n\}$ and the weights of evaluation indexes is $\{\lambda_1, \lambda_2, \cdots, \lambda_n\}$ according to the above content, the business system interruption impact assessment score is $result = \sum_{i=1}^{n} a_i \times \lambda_i$.

Every business system of the organization has a corresponding interruption impact assessment score. The ultimate target of BIA can be achieved according to the score and the relationship between the business systems. And the target is business recovery priority level.

4 Experiments

We select business interruption impact assessment index system as shown in Table 2 through BIA for some company's existing business systems.

Table 2. Business interruption impact assessment index system

Index code	Index name	Index code	Index name
A	Interrupt time period impact	G	Involved area
B	The number of affected departments	H	The proportion of disruptions
C	The number of associated systems	I	The company's reputation
D	Alternative means	J	Maintenance costs
E	Maximum tolerance interrupt time	K	Maintenance complexity
F	Maximum tolerable data loss time		

The degree of importance of the various indexes is classified as follows:

(1) Interrupt period impact, maximum tolerance interrupt time, maximum tolerable data loss time;
(2) The number of affected departments, the company's reputation;
(3) The number of associated systems, alternative means, involved area, the proportion of disruptions, maintenance costs, maintenance complexity.

The degree of importance of the various indexes is: (1), (2), (3) internal indicators are equally important; while the importance of external indexes is: (1) > (2) > (3). So, the judgment matrix is shown in Table 3:

Table 3. The judgment matrix of the importance of the indexes

	A	B	C	D	E	F	G	H	I	J	K
A	1	3	5	5	1	1	5	5	3	5	5
B	1/3	1	3	3	1/3	1/3	3	3	1	3	3
C	1/5	1/3	1	1	1/5	1/5	1	1	1/3	1	1
D	1/5	1/3	1	1	1/5	1/5	1	1	1/3	1	1
E	1	3	5	5	1	1	5	5	3	5	5
F	1	3	5	5	1	1	5	5	3	5	5
G	1/5	1/3	1	1	1/5	1/5	1	1	1/3	1	1
H	1/5	1/3	1	1	1/5	1/5	1	1	1/3	1	1
I	1/3	1	3	3	1/3	1/3	3	3	1	3	3
J	1/5	1/3	1	1	1/5	1/5	1	1	1/3	1	1
K	1/5	1/3	1	1	1/5	1/5	1	1	1/3	1	1

We can get the normalized weight values of each index using AHP algorithm, as shown in Table 4:

We select six business systems to assess from the organization's existing business systems, which are: Integrated business system (IBS), Online banking system (NBS),

Table 4. The normalized weight values of each index

Index name	Weight	Index name	Weight
Interrupt time period impact	0.2004	Involved area	0.0356
The number of affected departments	0.0925	The proportion of disruptions	0.0356
The number of associated systems	0.0356	The company's reputation	0.0925
Alternative means	0.0356	Maintenance costs	0.0356
Maximum tolerance interrupt time	0.2004	Maintenance complexity	0.0356
Maximum tolerable data loss time	0.2004		

OA system(OA), SMS platform (SMS), Group union website (GUW), Online Training System (OTS). The evaluation score of index can be got by collecting questionnaires using Delphi experts method, as shown in Table 5:

We can get the business interruption impact assessment scores through compu-tations between the index score in Table 5 and the weights in Table 4. The scores are shown in Table 6:

Table 5. The evaluation score of index

Systems / Index name	IBS	NBS	OA	SMS	GUW	OTS
Interrupt time period impact	4	4	3	3	2	2
The number of affected depart-ments	4	3	3	3	0	2
The number of associated sys-tems	4	3	1	3	0	0
Alternative means	4	4	2	4	1	2
Maximum tolerance interrupt time	4	4	2	3	1	1
Maximum tolerable data loss time	4	4	2	3	1	1
involved area	4	4	2	4	1	2
The proportion of disruptions	4	4	2	3	1	1
The company's reputation	4	4	2	4	1	0
Maintenance costs	4	4	2	3	1	1
Maintenance complexity	4	4	2	3	1	1

Table 6. The business interruption impact assessment scores

System	IBS	NBS	OA	SMS	GUW	OTS
Score	3.9992	3.8711	2.2569	3.1631	1.0721	1.2358

Thus we can get the sort of business interruption impact assessment scores: $IBS > OBS > SMS > OA > OTS > GUW$, and considering the relationship of business systems and the actual situation, we can get the sort of business recovery priority: $IBS > OBS > SMS > OA > OTS > GUW$.

5   Conclusions

According to the organization's objective demand of disaster recovery for business system, this paper proposes a model of the interruption impact analysis of business systems by using AHP algorithm to ensure the organization's business continuity. As the existing analysis methods of BIA are carried out by human judgment and qualitative analysis also being lack of certain scientific basis, while this paper proposes a method to carry out BIA by using AHP algorithm, which combine quantitative analysis and scientific calculation rather than qualitative analysis, so the conclusions are more scientific, more objective, more distinct and more comprehensive. The proposed model provides a reference for the organization managers when implementing disaster recovery. When disaster occurs, the managers can realize the business recovery priority clearly, prevent the risks during disaster recovery implementation process by the wrong priority order and ensure that the business systems can be restored smoothly and can provide services continually.

Acknowledgements. This work is supported by the Key Laboratory of Trustworthy Distributed Computing and Service (BUPT), and Program for The National High Technology Research and Development Program of China (863 Program 2012AA012600, 2012AA012606), and Beijing Higher Education Young Elite Teacher Project (YETP0448).

References

1. Xiao, W., Zhang, B., Chen, X.: A business sort algorithm based on RTO. Chin. Inf. Secur. **1**, 104–106 (2010)
2. Tian, J., Zang, P., Wang, K., Wang, Y.: The integrating model of expert's opinion based on Delphi method. Syst. Eng. Theor. Pract. **24**(1), 57–62 (2004)
3. Saaty, T.L.: Modeling unstructured decision problems—the theory of analytical hierarchies. Math. Comput. Simul. **20**(3), 147–158 (1978)
4. Cao, G., Xing, J., Tu, G.: Grey method with use of an analytic hierarchy process for performance evaluation of flue gas desulfurization technology. Proc. Chin. Soc. Electr. Eng. **26**(4), 51–55 (2006)
5. Luo, S., Liao, R., Wang, Y., Liu, L.: Fuzzy synthetic evaluation of power transformer condition with variable weights. High Voltage Eng. **33**(8), 106–110 (2007)
6. Wu, Z., Zhang, W.G., Guan, X.J.: A statistical method to check and rectify the consistency of a judgment matrix. Syst. Eng. **20**(3), 67–71 (2002)

Trust and Trustworthiness in Human Behavior and IT Services - Concepts, Definitions and Relations

Jørgen Bøegh(✉)

School of Software Engineering, Beijing University of Posts
and Telecommunications, Beijing, China
jorgen_boegh@yahoo.dk

Abstract. This paper discusses trust and trustworthiness as human and social phenomena and shows how these concepts can be translated into trust and trustworthiness for IT services, providing an objective measure of IT trustworthiness. In contrast, the user's trust is subjectively derived from the service trustworthiness in combination with the user's perceived risk related to the transaction.

Keywords: Trust · Trustworthiness · IT services · Neurobiology · Social science · Measurement

1 Introduction

Trust and trustworthiness are important concepts in human life. The ability to decide who is trustworthy is essential; during the human history it has often been a matter of life or death. Today people face the same problem the world of IT services. This is a completely different environment and here the human intuition does not work well. There is an urgent need for finding solutions to help people to evaluate the trustworthiness of IT services.

There are many papers discussing trust and trustworthiness from different perspectives, see for example [1, 7, 12, 15, 22, 32, 35, 36, 40] for surveys. However, there is no general consensus about the definitions of these fundamental terms. Without agreed definitions it is difficult to find a commonly acceptable solution to the trustworthiness problem of IT services. The approach in this study is to investigate the underlying mechanisms for trust and trustworthiness in human life and thereby derive definitions applicable in the IT world.

This paper first reviews recent results in neurobiology that partly explain the human intuition related to trust and trustworthiness. Then social aspects of trust and trustworthiness are discussed. The discussion includes the difference between trusting people who are already known and people who are unknown. Then the difference of trust between people who are equals and unequal in power is analyzed.

Trustworthiness is often achieved by means of social structures like families, companies or states. Social structures provide social control or systems that can enforce trustworthiness by sanctioning breaches. Trustworthiness can be enhanced by

Y. Yuan et al. (Eds.): ISCTCS 2013, CCIS 426, pp. 235–251, 2014.
DOI: 10.1007/978-3-662-43908-1_31, © Springer-Verlag Berlin Heidelberg 2014

legal mechanisms. Here the use of contracts and insurance is discussed. This is followed by an analysis of the reasons for being trustworthy, including the risk of punishment and loss of reputation. Finally it is argued that there is no need for trust without the existence of risk and the possibility of betrayal.

The survey of the human and social sides of trust and trustworthiness leads to suggestions for definitions of the two concepts. The proposed definitions are both consistent with human intuition and suitable for Internet technology. It is demonstrated that trustworthiness can be derived objectively whereas trust is a subjective, individual property.

2 The Human Brain

The history of human life goes more than 2 million years back in time. The first Homo's lived in Africa as far as we know. At certain times in history some of the different human species emigrated to Europe and Asia. About 100.000 years ago our direct ancestors, the Homo sapiens, went out of Africa and started a long journey to conquer the world. We may ask why the Homo sapiens have been so successful. A large part of the answer is related to the human brain.

The 2 million years of evolution has provided humans with a brain that in many respects is superior to the brain of any other living organism. This remarkable evolution has primarily been related to the social behavior of humans [38]. This happened in a complex and dynamic interplay between two opposing factors. The first is that groups can provide better security from enemies and disasters, better mate choice, and more reliable food. The second factor is that mates and food are available also to competitors from within the group.

This is the reason why humans have developed mechanisms for behaving in two different ways. One is mechanisms for working together and helping others, even without a direct reward. The other is mechanisms for lying, cheating, manipulating and forcing others to behave in an involuntary manner by use of threats or intimidation or some other form of pressure or force.

Understanding other people in a social interaction is not a trivial matter. Each individual is a source of ambiguous and complex information. However, when meeting someone for the first time, people are quick to make evaluations of the person and understand the intentions of that person. People actually make relatively accurate and persistent evaluations on the basis of rapid observations.

Deciding whether a stranger is trustworthy is one of the most important decisions routinely faced in social environments. Perceived trustworthiness determines whether to approach or avoid the person. In most part of human history this decision could mean the difference between life and death. This is why trustworthiness evaluation is a built-in function of the human brain.

2.1 Neurons

Human survival has depended on accurate social judgments. Decoding social information requires a highly sophisticated brain. The human brain is like an extremely powerful and complex computer. The brain should not be compared with a large general purpose computer. It is more like a cluster of many highly specialized integrated circuits. Different cognitive processes are carried out in different areas of the brain. This means that we can perform many tasks at the same time and at a very high speed.

The human face is without doubt most important when evaluating another person. The face provides a large variety of important social signals. It can tell if the person is old or young, male or female, sad or happy, angry or scared, and so on. The brain has a specialized area, called the amygdala, important for processing information of the face [11]. The amygdala is an almond-shape set of neurons located deep in the brain. The processing is very fast, less than 100 ms. This is enough time to form an impression of a stranger. If more time is available it will not significantly change the evaluation, only make the person more confident. This also explains why it is said that the first impression is so important.

When meeting another person the brain automatically evaluates the face on multiple trait dimensions. It is shown that two orthogonal dimensions are almost sufficient to describe face evaluations [37]. These dimensions can be described as valence/trustworthiness and power/dominance. They account for more than 80 % of the evaluation. Attractiveness and other traits can be derived fairly well as linear combinations of these two.

The trustworthiness dimension has been studied in detail [11, 41]. The studies measured how the amygdala responds to properties of the person's face. It is remarkable that humans largely base trustworthiness evaluation of a person on characteristics of the person's face. There is a high degree of consensus among people when evaluating trustworthiness of others. Minor individual differences in trustworthiness evaluation can be explained by the combination of the amygdala output with other information to form the final evaluation.

2.2 Hormones

Hormones also influence trust and trustworthiness. When a person gets the feeling being trusted by another person, then it increases the level of the neuropeptide Oxytocin (love hormone) in the blood [4, 24]. The effect of this increase is that the person becomes more willing to trust others. Hence a rise in oxytocin in the brain reduces the natural reservation over interacting with a stranger. What happens is that the amygdala responds to the change of oxytocin level. By using oxytocin administrated as nasal spray it is possible to causes a substantial increase in trust among people. Further it has been observed that untrustworthy persons often have a high level of oxytocin. Increasing the level will have only a small effect and hence not increase trustworthiness noticeable.

On the other hand, when men feel they are distrusted they experience a rise in dihydrotestosterone, a derivative of the testosterone hormone [42]. Elevated levels boost the desire for physical confrontation. This explains why men have an aggressive response to not being trusted. Women do not show such reactions.

3   Forms of Trust

The concepts of trust and trustworthiness can take many different forms and can appear under many different circumstances. Therefore the same trust model cannot be used for all situations. Different aspects are analyzed in the following sections.

3.1   Who to Trust

We can start to look at who we trust. First of all, people may trust people they already know. People will usually trust the persons closest to them. This includes in particular a person's partner and intimate friends. That may be a person's wife, whom he trusts to take care of his children when he is out, to prepare food for him when he comes home, and to refrain from infidelity when he is not there. He trusts his neighbors to look after his home when he goes out and not use the opportunity to steal from him. He trusts his friends or colleagues when hunting and working in the farm. Nowadays people extend their trust in many directions, for example to the staff in the kindergarten and the teachers in the school to educate their children.

People also trust other people they don't know. In modern society in big cities, people are generally surrounded by unknowns. For example, people trust strangers on the street to give directions, and they trust taxi drivers in a city unfamiliar to them to bring them safely to their hotel. People may trust a used car dealer not to sell them a "lemon", and they trust the plumber to repair the sink according to good workmanship. The reason the trust the car dealer or the craftsman may be that they have been recommended by people already being considered trustworthy.

The cases discussed are clearly different. Trusting already known people is based on previous experience whereas trusting strangers is based on intuition, i.e. the human built-in trustworthiness evaluation algorithm of mainly facial properties, or based on recommendations. A common denominator of the situations is that trust can be understood as a method of reducing social complexity [28]. In this way trust creates a feeling of predictability.

An extreme case is that people sometimes trust declared enemies: when a defeated man shows surrender with the white flag then he trusts that he will not be shot by his enemy. Another example is a duel, which is an arranged engagement in combat between two gentlemen (in Japan between Samurai's) in accordance with agreed-upon rules. Duels are mainly fought to restore one's honor by demonstrating a willingness to risk one's life for it. A duel is based on a code of honor and the participants trust each other to follow the rules, i.e. to behave in a predictable manner.

3.2   Equals and Unequals

In some situations trust is between equals; that is a relation between two persons or between two organizations that are roughly equal in power. This situation has been studied extensively in western philosophy. There are rules that are expected to be followed. The model of trust is either based on a "gentleman's agreement" or "men of honor" concept where the two parties are expected to follow some non-written principles of conduct. These approaches work well inside a specific culture or in a closed community, but often break down when dealing across such borders.

Trust can also be a relation between two unequal parties, for example between father and son, husband and wife, employer and employee, master and slave, between a large company and a customer, or between a country's government leaders and the citizen. In some cased the relation may be based on trust, for example a son trusts his father to protect him against dangers, the employee trusts the employer to pay the salary each month, and the customer trusts the bank to invest his money in safe stocks. The trust relation can be in both directions. In some cased trust is not sincere but due to reliance on the more powerful party or even due to being forced to obey the stronger party.

3.3 Trust and Reliance

People rely on public transport for going to work every day, and they rely on the mobile phone to keep in touch with business associates. When driving a car people rely on other drivers to obey the traffic rules and stop at the red light. When people get sick they rely on doctors and prescribed medicine. They rely on the dentist when they have a toothache and they rely on a mechanic when the car has problems. A disabled person relies on relatives or professional care takers. Baier [3] has made a distinction between trust and reliance by saying that trust can be betrayed, whilst reliance can only be disappointed. Also Holton [17] discusses this issue in detail. The main difference is that Baier is mainly concerned with the relationship between two people whereas Holton is considering ternary relationships (person, person, action); however, their conclusions are similar. The role of emotions in trust has also been highlighted by for example [25] and some researchers have found that trust can be considered consisting of behavioral elements, cognitive elements and affective elements [26].

3.4 Trust and Belief

There is a need to distinguish between trust and belief. Belief in its many forms has played and still plays a large role in human societies. One particular form is religious belief [17]. Religion can briefly be described as a collection of cultural and social norms. It provides views of the world, for example explaining natural phenomena and social as well as personal situations. Religion differs from private belief in that it relates to a group of people. It is not well understood from a cognitive psychological point of view why there seems to be a universal propensity toward religious belief.

It is interesting that in 1956 the United States adopted "In God We Trust" as the official motto. The motto today appears on US coins and paper currency. There is a controversy over whether this is a religious statement or not.

Ideologies are related to religions as they also function as prepackaged units of interpretation of basic human understanding of the world, such as how to avoid threats to life and welfare, and how to maintain interpersonal relationships. Another example is astrology. Astrology consists of a number of belief systems which hold that there is a relationship between astronomical phenomena and events in the human world, for example that the time and date of birth can predict the fate and destiny of a person.

4   Enhancing Trustworthiness

Trustworthiness of individuals may be enhanced by means of social structures. Examples of social structures are families, companies, villages, or states. Social structures provide social control or systems that can enforce trustworthiness by sanctioning breaches. Means include moral codes and religious laws. In states the control structure is institutionalized in the form of legal systems, courts and police forces aiming at ensuring compliance.

4.1   Contracts

Use of contracts is another approach to enhance trustworthiness. Contracts have existed for a long time. They are described thoroughly in the Code of Hammurabi, the Babylonian law code, dating back to about 1772 BC. Nearly half of the Code of Hammurabi deals with matters of contract. It gives provisions for the terms of a transaction and it establishes the liability of a builder for a house that collapses and property that is damaged while left in the care of another. Contract enables people to make explicit what they count on another person to do, in return for what, and should they not do just that, what damages can be extracted from them. Contracts work because they are sanctioned by a powerful entity, the state, which enforces fulfillment by means of legal systems.

Contracts are useful both between equal partners and in unequal relations. Much thought has concentrated on the morality of relationships between those who are roughly equal in power to determine the rules and to instigate sanctions against rule breakers. The advantage of a contract is that it is explicit. This explicitness makes breach easy to establish, and the damages or penalties can be decided with a reasonable show of justice. Another advantage of contracts is the security they offer the trusting party. They make it possible to decide to trust but also to trust with minimal vulnerability. This is good for those who do not like to take risk. Contract limits the area of trustworthiness to what is covered by the contract. Contracts also protect the trustee from unreasonable claims from the trustor. Again we have a ternary relationship (trustor, trustee, action).

There is a need for clarification of terminology. In this paper and in the software literature in general, the trustee is the entity/person that is trusted (the object of the action) and the trustor is the entity/person that trusts. In legal terminology the sequence is reversed (because it refers to the noun trust, rather than the verb trust).

4.2   Insurance

Insurance is closely related to risk. Actually, the main purpose of insurance is to lower risk. Hence, lowering risk will increase our willingness to trust. The function of a cup-bearer is an example of insurance. The position was held by an officer of high rank in royal courts. His duty was to serve the drinks at the royal table. Due to the constant fear of plots and intrigues, only a person regarded as thoroughly trustworthy could hold this position. The cup-bearer guarded against poison in the king's cup, and was often required to swallow some of the wine before serving it.

Today insurance companies have a similar role. Insurance is defined as the equitable transfer of the risk of a loss, from one entity to another, in exchange for payment. It is a form of risk management primarily used to hedge against the risk of a contingent, uncertain loss. It is possible to buy insurance for almost anything. However, insurance does not necessarily imply higher trustworthiness. It can though be argued that if a company is willing to insure a service, then the insurance company must have conducted a trustworthiness evaluation of the service provider and found the trustworthiness acceptable relative to the existing risk.

5 Reasons to be Trustworthy

There are several motives for a person to be trustworthy. One reason can be an inherent, genetic property of a person; the person simply desires to be trustworthy. Other reasons may be caused by social needs or social pressure. Some important cases are discussed in the following sections.

5.1 Internal Morals

Some people are simply trustworthy by nature. They have a natural desire to behave in a trustworthy manner. In this case trustworthiness is an inherent, genetic property of a person. Cultural, educational and religious influence may influence people in the direction of trustworthy behavior.

5.2 Love and Sympathy

Trustworthiness and trust can sometimes be explained by sympathy or love [16]. The two aspects are related but not identical. According to [13] the experience of love can be divided into three partly overlapping stages: lust, attraction, and attachment. Lust is the feeling of sexual desire. Attraction determines what partners mates find attractive. Attachment involves sharing a home, undertaking parental duties, providing mutual defense, etc. and involves feelings of safety and security. Like trust, love is regulated by the release of different hormones in the brain. Lust is a short time effect, lasting a few weeks or months. Attraction normally lasts from one to three years whereas attachment lasts for many years.

The conditions necessary to develop sympathy begin with the creation of a small group of socially dependent individuals. The individuals in this community must have a relatively long lifespan in order to encounter opportunities to react with sympathy. For example, the creations of social hierarchies are associated with the onset of sympathy in human interactions. Trust based on love or sympathy is characterized as emotional based trust [26]. In these situations people make a strong emotional investment and hence abuse of trust will create similar strong emotions.

5.3 Punishment

A classical view is that fear of punishment is a main reason for a person to be trustworthy. If there is a high probability for detection and punishment will exceed the possible gain, then most people will act in a way that we will consider as being trustworthy [9]. This behavior is of course related to the social control discussed above.

5.4 Reputation

The fear of getting a bad reputation is another motivation for being trustworthy. This works in relatively closed environments where services are provided to the same group of users repeatedly or in an environment where existing user feedback is available to potential new users. Fear of losing a reputation may actually be the best enforcer of trustworthiness.

6 When to Trust

When we speak about trust and trustworthiness there are two conditions that must be present. The first condition is that there is a risk: if there is no risk, there is no need to trust. The other condition is that there is a possibility of betrayal and an intention to harm; otherwise it is only a question of competence (ability).

6.1 Risk

Risk is a combination of the probability that something will go wrong and the magnitude of harm if it actually goes wrong. The willingness to take risk depends on individuals. For most people taking risk it is asymmetric about a reference point. People tend be risk averse when they perceive themselves to be in the domain of gain, and risk seeking in the domain of loss [39]. Firstly, people generally prefer to be certain of receiving $100 rather than taking their chance at a 50:50 gamble of getting $200 or nothing. Secondly, people generally prefer to take their chances at a 50:50 gamble of losing $200 or nothing rather than being certain of losing $100. Obviously, losses loom larger than gains in most people's mind.

Risk propensity describes the likelihood that a person will take risk. It has been shown that risk propensity is relatively stable, although domain dependent, and strongly related to personality as defined by the Big Five personality traits [30]. There is a significant correlation between risk propensity and high scores in extraversion and openness, and low scores in neuroticism, agreeableness and conscientiousness. It is found that men generally are more willing to take risks than women. Furthermore, young men generally take more risks than older men.

If there is no risk then there is no need to trust [8]. Hence, there is a relation between trust and risk [23], but the exact relation is not obvious and needs further study.

6.2 Betrayal

"Et tu, Brute?" In year 44 BC, the Roman dictator Julius Caesar was attacked and killed by a group of senators, including Brutus, Caesar's close friend. The quotation, in English "And you, Brutus", is used in Western culture to signify the utmost betrayal.

In [5] it is argued that a positive probability of betrayal is a prerequisite for trust. This position limits the scope of the concepts of trust and trustworthiness, both with respect to scope of service and service provider. For example, we rely on the safety and reliability of an airplane, but if the airplane crashes due to a technical problem we will not claim that we have been betrayed. It is only when there is a specific intention to act against the best interest of the user that we talk about betrayal. Hence a machine cannot betray a user. Therefore the term 'trustworthiness' is not appropriate when speaking about an aircraft [6]. Instead we use the concepts of 'dependability'.

Researchers from the dependability area often apply the so called SSR view. SSR covers the three characteristics "Security", "Safety", and "Reliability". Similarly, [2] suggests five characteristics "Availability", "Reliability", "Safety", "Integrity", and "Maintainability". It is concluded that trustworthiness and dependability covers equivalent concepts. In fact, a substantial amount of work on trust has been carried out from this viewpoint and it has found its way into standardization, see for example [18]. It should be noticed that the dependability view represents a property based definition approach.

We follow the view of [5, 6] that it is useful to distinguish between dependability and trustworthiness. The distinction is actually part of the human conception of trustworthiness and was observed by [5]. They found that people are less willing to take a risk when the source of the risk is another person rather than nature. Since being subject to betrayal causes great emotional effects, people seem to possess a considerable betrayal aversion.

6.3 Exceptions

It is not always appropriate to be trustworthy. Being trustworthy means fulfilling obligations, but [3] gives the example of a person who came to do some garden work as promised when at the same time his father was dying at home. The person may be trustworthy, but he obviously made a wrong prioritization. In [16] there is a discussion related to a servant who trusted his master. However, the master turned out not to be trustworthy. The servant finally realizes that "trust can be stupid and, when it seemingly justifies action or inaction, even culpable".

7 IT Services

Many of the issues discussed above are also relevant for IT services. In the context of this paper, a service of a system is its behavior as it is perceived by its user. IT services are characterized as services based entirely on the use of Information Technology. For example, an e-mail service is entirely based on IT. An e-shopping service may include a web site from where to select goods and perform payment transactions, and in addition delivery of goods. Selection and payment are IT services whereas delivery is not an IT service.

In many situations the transactions can be considered to be between strangers. This means that the user and the service provider have limited knowledge of each other. For example, when shopping on the Internet, the details of the Web-shop such as ownership and physical location may be unknown to the buyer, and similarly the buyer is unknown to the shop.

Often IT services represent transactions between unequals. This is the situation when an individual does e-shopping, or when a small company uses an e-service provided by a large company. The opposite situation also exists, where a large organization uses the e-services of a small company.

Contracts are used for IT service provision, for example in the form of service level agreements (SLA's). In this case it is often a relationship between equals. The contract typically specifies what service is provided and the quality of this service. In practice, SLA's mainly protect the service providers rather than the users. Insurance is not commonly used for the IT services.

Reputation systems are much studied, see for example [12, 22, 36] for surveys. There are basically two types of reputation systems: centralized and distributed. A centralized system relies on a "reputation centre" that collects and derives reputation scores from every user of the IT services, and makes these scores publicly available. In a distributed system there is no central "reputation centre". Instead, each user of an IT service simply records the opinion about each experience with the IT service, and provides this information on request to other users.

According to [34], reputation systems must possess at least three properties to operate effectively:

- Long-lived entities that inspire an expectation of future interaction
- Capture and distribution of feedback about current interactions
- Use of feedback to guide trust decisions

Reputation systems are used in practice. One of the best known examples is that used by the eBay auction web service [33]. This system is based on manual feedback from users. Manual feedback is subjective by nature and in particular negative feedback turns out to be difficult to handle appropriately. When managed by the IT service provider, reputation systems are used to give the users an impression of trustworthiness. An independently managed reputation system strongly encourage IT services to perform according to user expectations.

When using IT services, the user often has a real risk. For example when involved in a transaction involving payment of goods before they have been delivered. There is also a real possibility of betrayal. Betrayal implies an intention to act against the interest of another person. So it is not the software as such that betrays, but the people responsible, who decide the functionality of the software.

8 Definitions of Trustworthiness

There are several definitions of trustworthiness in the literature. The goal of this paper is to reach a definition, which complies with the human intuition and the social concepts discussed in the previous sections and which is also suitable for IT services. The following definition from [29] is close to fulfill this goal.

Definition: Trustworthiness is the demonstrated ability of the trustee to perform a specified action while adhering to a set of stated principles (integrity) and acting in the best interest of the trustor (benevolence).

This definition has two parts. The first component is about competence and ability to perform a specified action. Since trustworthiness does not cover all matters, the definition emphasizes "specified actions". For example, a doctor may have the competences to do heart surgery, but probably not to repair a car.

Ability is an objective property. The doctor has passed an examination at university and some practical tests in a hospital. In other words, this part of the definition is about compliance with specifications.

The second component of the definition is about character, i.e. being honest, fair and predictable. This component can be split into two parts. The first part is about behaving according to (high) moral values. This is about integrity. Integrity is concerned with character, i.e. being honest and predictable, and with behaving according to agreed moral values. It means that the trustee will act according to stated and commonly agreed principles for conducting the action or service in question. A service provider can be very competent, but may not be honest. Therefore "integrity" is a necessary part of the definition. Integrity is an objective property because it is possible to check whether or not "a set of stated principles" are followed.

The benevolence part of the definition is problematic. Firstly, it is not immediately part of human intuition as also noted in [29], especially when the two parties do not know each other. Secondly, benevolence is subjective. There is no certainty what is in the best interest of the trustor. The subjectivity of benevolence makes it difficult to use the definition for IT services and what is in the best interest of one trustor may be completely different from what is in the best interest of another trustor.

8.1 Definition for IT Services

In order to reach a definition more useful for IT services, the above discussion suggests that we should slightly modify the formulation in [29] and include only ability and integrity:

Definition: Trustworthiness (of an IT service) is the demonstrated ability of the IT service provider to perform a specified action while adhering to a set of stated principles.

The two parts of the definition "ability to perform a specified action" and "adhering to a set of stated principles" must be precisely described and made available to potential users. This description constitutes the claimed IT service. Service claims include both functional and quality aspects. Ability and integrity can both vary continuously. Trustworthiness should therefore be thought of as a continuum, rather than the trustee being either trustworthy or not trustworthy.

The definition of trustworthiness only depends on the trustee, i.e. the IT service provider; this is in contrast to the original definition in [29]. Their definition also depends on the trustor through the concept of "benevolence".

Trustworthiness is related to moral issues. It requires that the trustor follows specific ethical norms, rules and conventions. The moral issues are included in the set of stated principles. Trustworthiness is also concerned with the trustor's ability to perform the action in question. It is therefore an inherent, dynamic property of the trustee (IT service).

The definition of trustworthiness asks for evidence in terms of "the demonstrated ability". This offers some guidance on how to evaluate trustworthiness. Using the doctor example above, ability can be demonstrated in the form of a university exam and test certificates, or in the form of actual performance, for example measured as survival rate of patients after heart surgery. It follows that trustworthiness evaluation can be split into two (objective) components:

Objective evidence of capability of performing the service while adhering to a set of stated principles.

Historical evidence of how the service has actually been performed relative to claimed performance and stated principles.

The first component represents an initial evaluation. To conduct this evaluation, both the service and the set of principles must be specified. Based on this specification it can be checked whether the service provider can demonstrate the necessary capabilities. The evaluation scheme could follow existing schemes as described in [19] for quality evaluation or in [20] for security evaluation.

The second component represents a continuous evaluation. To conduct this evaluation continuous monitoring of service provision is required. The evaluation is based on measurement of the difference between claimed service and the actual service. Every time the service is provided, this difference is measured.

Combining these two components gives a dynamic expression of the trustworthiness of the service. Hence, trustworthiness is a behavioral concept. It changes over time based on how services are actually performed. This is in contrast to for example software quality, which is a static, inherent property defined as a set of characteristics/attributes that bear on the software's ability to satisfy stated and implied needs of stakeholders [21].

The definition of trustworthiness can be expressed as a "symbolic formula":

$$\text{Trustworthiness} = \text{Capability} + \sum \Delta \text{Performance} \tag{1}$$

The capability represents the initial evaluation. The IT service provider must present the evidence necessary for conducting this evaluation.

Performance represents the behavior of the service. The evaluation is based on measuring the difference between claimed service and the actual service. Whenever a user is using the IT service, this difference is measured.

The formula (1) provides guidelines for how to actually calculate trustworthiness. Related approaches are described in [10, 27].

The definition of trustworthiness applies the "contract" concept in form of service claims. The service claims describes in detail the service offered, the "specified action", and the "set of stated principles" that will be adhered to. The purpose of a contract is to make service claims explicit and to make breaches easy to establish. Furthermore, contracts lower the risk for both trustor and trustee.

The definition of trustworthiness also includes the "reputation" concept. Reputation is established as the users' collective measure of deviations by measuring the difference between claimed service and actual service for each usage of the service. This is in line with the necessary properties of an effective reputation system stated in [34]. Publishing trustworthiness values creates an implicit social control mechanism for ensuring trustworthiness. Fear for losing reputation is actually a strong motivational factor for being trustworthy. The scheme proposed here is a centralized system. The scheme is different from others since it is not based directly on the users' evaluation but on an independent measurement of performance deviations.

8.2   Design for Trustworthiness

In addition to the contract and reputation concepts directly related to the proposed definition, the IT services should follow certain design principles for appearing trustworthy in the view of users. This is similar to the human evaluation of a person's face to decide the level of trustworthiness of that person. For example, [31] identifies four basic principles that communicate trustworthiness of e-commerce Web sites:

- Quality of Web design including professional appearance and clear navigation
- Comprehensive, correct and up-to-date content and product selection
- Connectivity to the rest of the Web; linking to a third party add credibility
- Up-front disclosure of all aspects of the customer relationship like shipping charges

These principles actually comply with the definition of trustworthiness. Principles 1, 2, and 3 are related to ability. They aim to provide an impression of competence. Principle 4 is related to integrity. It provides the set of principles that the service of the Web site will adhere to.

A similar four dimensional framework of features for signaling trustworthiness is proposed in [40]:

- Graphic design - Refers to the graphical design factors on the web site that normally give consumers a first impression
- Structure design - Defines the overall organization and accessibility of displayed information on the web site
- Content design - Refers to the informational components that can be included on the web site, either textual or graphical
- Social-cue design - Relates to embedding social cues, such as face-to-face interaction and social presence, into web interface via different communication media

The human evaluation of trustworthiness of web based services is of course much related to appearance. Following simple design rules can make a big difference. This is similar to how humans use the form of the inner eyebrows, cheekbones, and chin to evaluate the trustworthiness of persons when meeting them for the first time.

In order to cover the design aspect of trustworthiness of IT services, the symbolic formula (1) can be extended with an appearance component.

$$\text{Trustworthiness} = \text{Capability} + \sum \Delta \text{Performance} + \text{Appearance} \quad (2)$$

By identifying a set of design measures based on the rules identified in [31, 40] the "Appearance" component can be defined and calculated using objective evidence.

8.3 Trust

The literature suggests different definitions of trust. An attempt to summarize the different opinions is provided in [14]. Here trust is defined as a particular level of the subjective probability with which an agent assesses that another agent or group of agents will perform a particular action, both before he can monitor such action (or independently of his capacity ever to be able to monitor it) and in a context in which it affects his own action. The definition proposed in [29] is very similar and seems also applicable for IT services. They define trust as follows:

Definition: Trust is the willingness of a party to be vulnerable to the actions of another party based on the expectation that the other party will perform a particular action important to the trustor, irrespective of the ability to monitor or control that other party.

Trust is defined as the expectations of the trustor concerning the actions of the trustee, in other words, as a mental state of the trustee. However, this expectation must partly be derived from knowledge about and understanding of the incentives of the trustor and partly from aspects related to the trustor. These aspects include both external factors such as risk and internal factors such as risk propensity and trust propensity.

Trust is the expectation an individual user has about another party's future behavior based on the history of their encounters. In other words, it is a perception of the user of whether or not the user is willing to apply the service without the user's direct control of the actions performed by the service provider.

When using IT services there is always a possibility of betrayal. The Internet provides a certain degree of anonymity and no direct personal contact. It seems that these factors have a negative influence on some people's morals, making it less conspicuous for them to cheat, steal or betray other people. There are many examples of such malicious behavior on the Internet.

Risks also exist in many situations. IT services may involve confidential information or financial transactions. Here users face the risk of confidential information being misused or money being stolen. Therefore trust is an important element when using IT services.

Trust is individual, hence subjective, for each trustor and depends on trust propensity and risk propensity of the trustor as well as the risk of the action and the trustworthiness of the trustee. The exact interdependencies are not completely clear so further analysis of this definition is needed.

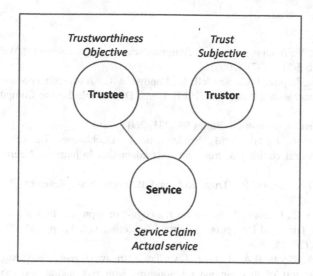

Fig. 1. Trustworthiness, trust, and IT services

Figure 1 summarizes the relationship among the concepts trustworthiness, trust, trustor, trustee, and IT services discussed in this paper.

9 Conclusion

This paper reviews the concepts of trust and trustworthiness from a human perspective, including both the mechanisms in the human brain, and the different social structures and mechanisms involved. It is demonstrated that both individuals and social communities have strong mechanisms that both enforces trustworthiness and support evaluation. These mechanisms have been a major key to the success of the human race. In the IT world these mechanisms do not work well. There is a strong need to design trustworthiness management system that can reestablish the human intuition in the IT world.

The proposed definition of trustworthiness and the scheme for measurement and evaluation of trustworthiness of IT services represents an attempt to translate the human intuitive understanding of trustworthiness to the world of IT services. The next step is to develop the specific measures needed for establishing an IT service behavior trustworthiness management system. This work must be based on a specification language for IT service behavior. The specification language must be able to express both functional and non-functional aspects of service behavior as well as principles for service provision, i.e. the integrity concept. In addition, the components of the evaluation process must be further elaborated. The static part of the evaluation could probably be based on existing standards. The dynamic part must be based on continuous monitoring and measurement. Finally, an exact formula that combines these parts of evaluation into a single expression of service trustworthiness must be derived. In combination, this will lead to a service behavior trustworthiness management system.

References

1. Artz, D., Gil, Y.: A survey of trust in computer science and the Semantic Web. Softw. Eng. Semant. Web **5**(2), 58–71 (2007)
2. Avizienis, A., Laprie, J.-C., Randell, B., Landwehr, C.: Basic concepts and taxonomy of dependable and secure computing. IEEE Trans. Dependable Secure Comput. **1**(1), 11–33 (2004)
3. Baier, A.: Trust and antitrust. Ethics **96**, 231–260 (1986)
4. Baumgartner, T., Heinrichs, M., Vonlanthen, A., Fischbacher, U., Fehr, E.: Oxytocin shapes the neural circuitry of trust and trust adaptation in humans. Neuron **58**, 639–650 (2008)
5. Bohnet, I., Zeckhauser, R.: Trust, Risk and Betrayal, KSG Research Paper Series No. RWP03-041 (2003)
6. Castelfranchi, C., Falcone, R.: Social trust: a cognitive approach. In: Castelfranchi, C., Tan, Y.-H. (eds.) Trust and Deception in Virtual Societies, vol. 11, pp. 55–90. Springer, The Netherlands (2001)
7. Colquitt, J.A., Scott, B.A., LePine, J.A.: Trust, trustworthiness, and trust propensity: a meta-analytic test of their unique relationships with risk taking and job performance. J. Appl. Psychol. **92**(4), 909–927 (2007)
8. Das, T.K., Teng, B.-S.: The Risk-based view of trust: a conceptual framework. J. Bus. Psychol. **19**(1), 85–116 (2004)
9. Dasgupta, P.: Trust as a commodity. In: Gambetta, D. (ed.) Trust: Making and Breaking Cooperative Relations, pp. 49–72. University of Oxford, Oxford (2000)
10. Dillon, T.S., Chang, E., Hussain, F.K.: Managing the dynamic nature of trust. IEEE Trans. Intell. Syst. **19**(5), 79–82 (2004)
11. Engell, A.D., Haxby, J.V., Todorov, A.: Implicit trustworthiness decisions: automatic coding of face properties in the human amygdala. J. Cogn. Neurosci. **19**(9), 1508–1519 (2007)
12. Firdhous, M., Ghazali, O., Hassan, S.: Trust and trust management in cloud computing, Technical Report No: UUM/CAS InterNetWorks TR2011-01, Universiti Utara Malaysia (2011)
13. Fisher, H.: Why We Love: The Nature and Chemistry of Romantic Love. Henry Holt, New York (2004)
14. Gambetta, D.: Can we trust trust? In: Gambetta, D. (ed.) Trust: Making and Breaking Cooperative Relations, pp. 213–238. Oxford University, New York (2000)
15. Hall, S., McQuay, W.: Review of trust research from an interdisciplinary perspective - psychology, sociology, economics, and cyberspace. In: Proceedings of the IEEE 2010 National Aerospace and Electronics Conference (NAECON), pp.18–25 (2010)
16. Hardin, R.: Trustworthiness. Ethics **107**(1), 26–42 (1996)
17. Holton, R.: Deciding to trust, coming to believe. Australas. J. Philos. **72**, 63–76 (1994)
18. ISO/IEC 10181–1:1996 Information technology – Open Systems Interconnection – Security frameworks for open systems: Overview, International Organization for Standardization (1996)
19. ISO/IEC 14598–5:1998 Information technology – Software product evaluation – Part 5: Process for evaluators, International Organization for Standardization (1998)
20. ISO/IEC 15408:2009 Information technology – Security techniques – Evaluation criteria for IT security, International Organization for Standardization (2009)
21. ISO/IEC 25010:2011 Software engineering – Software product Quality Requirements and Evaluation (SQuaRE) – Quality mode, International Organization for Standardization (2011)

22. Jøsang, A., Ismail, R., Boyd, C.: A survey of trust and reputation systems for online service provision. Decis. Support Syst. **43**(2), 618–644 (2007)
23. Jøsang, A., Presti, S.L.: Analysing the relationship between risk and trust. In: Jensen, C., Poslad, S., Dimitrakos, T. (eds.) iTrust 2004. LNCS, vol. 2995, pp. 135–145. Springer, Heidelberg (2004)
24. Kosfeld, M., Heinrichs, M., Zak, P.J., Fischbacher, U., Fehr, E.: Oxytocin increases trust in humans. Nature **435**(2), 673–676 (2005)
25. Lahno, B.: Three aspects of interpersonal trust. Analyse & Kritik **26**, 30–47 (2004)
26. Lewis, J.D., Weigert, A.: Trust as a social reality. Soc. Forces **63**, 967–985 (1985)
27. Limam, N., Boutaba, R.: Assessing software service quality and trustworthiness at selection time. IEEE Trans. Softw. Eng. **36**(4), 559–574 (2010)
28. Luhman, N.: Familiarity, confidence, trust: problems and alternatives. In: Gambetta, D. (ed.) Trust: Making and Breaking Cooperative Relations, pp. 94–107. University of Oxford, Oxford (2000)
29. Mayer, R.C., Davis, J.H., Schoorman, F.D.: An integrative model of organizational trust. Acad. Manag. Rev. **20**, 709–734 (1995)
30. Nicholson, N., Soane, E., Fenton-O'Creevy, M., Willman, P.: Personality and domain-specific risk-taking. J. Risk Res. **8**(2), 157–176 (2005)
31. Nielsen, J.: Trust or Bust: Communicating Trustworthiness in Web Design, Jacob Nielsen's Alertbox, http://www.useit.com/alertbox/990307.html (1999)
32. Ramchurn, S., Huynh, D., Jennings, N.: Trust in multi-agent systems. Knowl. Eng. Rev. **19**(1), 1–25 (2004)
33. Resnick, P., Zeckhauser, R.: Trust among strangers in internet transactions: empirical analysis of eBay's reputation system. In: Baye, M.R. (ed.) The Economics of the Internet and E-commerce, Advances in Applied Microeconomics, vol. 11, pp. 127–157. Elsevier Science, Amsterdam (2002)
34. Resnick, P., Zeckhauser, R., Friedman, E., Kuwabara, K.: Reputation systems. Commun. ACM **43**(12), 45–48 (2000)
35. Ruohomaa, S., Kutvonen, L.: Trust management survey. In: Herrmann, P., Issarny, V., Shiu, S. (eds.) iTrust 2005. LNCS, vol. 3477, pp. 77–92. Springer, Heidelberg (2005)
36. Sabater, J., Sierra, C.: Review on computational trust and reputation models. Artif. Intell. Rev. **24**, 33–60 (2005)
37. Todorov, A., Said, C.P., Engell, A.D., Oosterhof, N.N.: Understanding evaluation of faces on social dimensions. Trends Cogn. Sci. **12**(12), 455–460 (2008)
38. Tooby, J., Cosmides, L.: The psychological foundations of culture. In: Barkow, J., Cosmides, L., Tooby, J. (eds.) The Adapted Mind: Evolutionary psychology and the generation of culture. Oxford University Press, New York (1992)
39. Tversky, A., Kanemann, D.: Advances in prospect theory: cumulative representation of uncertainty. J. Risk Uncertainty **5**, 297–323 (1992)
40. Wang, Y.D., Emurian, H.H.: An overview of online trust: concepts, elements, and implications. Comput. Hum. Behav. **21**, 105–125 (2005)
41. Winston, J., Strange, B.A., O'Doherty, J., Dolan, R.J.: Automatic and intentional brain responses during evaluation of trustworthiness of faces. Nat. Neurosci. **5**(3), 277–283 (2002)
42. Zak, P.J.: The neurobiology of trust. Sci. Am. **298**(6), 88–95 (2008)

A Black-Box Approach for Detecting the Failure Traces

You Meng[1(✉)], Lang Yu[1], Zhongzhi Luan[1], Depei Qian[1], Ming Xie[2], and Zhigao Du[3]

[1] Sino-German Joint Software Institute, Beihang University, Beijing, China
{you.meng, zhongzhi.luan, depei.qian}@jsi.buaa.edu.cn,
yulang94@gmail.com
[2] Tencent Corporation, Shenzhen, China
reganxie@tencent.com
[3] CNPC Research Institute of Safety and Environment Technology,
Beijing, China
duzhigao@cnpc.com.cn

Abstract. Detecting failure traces can help system administrators timely recover from those failures and avoid them afterwards. For system managers, it is not difficult to detect whether a failure is currently occurring, because they only concern about several key measurements. If these measurements exceed the normal threshold, a failure event should be generated. But it is much more complicated to detect the failure traces which represented as failure related events. Because these failure traces may last for quite a long time and effect many components. Furthermore, current distributed system adds and removes new components so quickly that administrators may not have enough time and knowledge to set monitoring threshold for each of them. Based on these problems, we propose our FTD system. We first compare each component's historical state and get outlier states as anomalous event. And then, combined with the failure event that the system provided, we detect the event correlations between failure events and anomalous events as failure traces. A network intrusion benchmark KDD99 is used to evaluate our work and we achieve good performances.

Keywords: Outlying detection · Rule mining · Failure traces · Anomaly

1 Introduction

User level services or components which are at the top of the cloud can easily tell whether they are in good health or not. Because they only concern about several user-related measurements. If these variables act unexpectedly, they will directly generate exceptions. Take the upload service that exists in the Tencent cloud as an example. Many Tencent Corporation's projects use the upload service, and they only concern about the upload related measurements like upload speed or maximum upload thread number. If the average upload speed is much smaller than common, it should generate an exception to show that there may be something wrong with this service. For the failure management system, when receiving this report, the first thing they should do

Y. Yuan et al. (Eds.): ISCTCS 2013, CCIS 426, pp. 252–259, 2014.
DOI: 10.1007/978-3-662-43908-1_32, © Springer-Verlag Berlin Heidelberg 2014

is to find the reasons that lead to this problem. At this time, they may meet several cases: (a) There are only one or two alerts generated from the fundamental components just at that precise time. So these alerts have the biggest probability of having relations with the user level exceptions. (b) Too many alerts or anomalies are generated from various components, and the management system doesn't know which part should be the failure reason. (c) No anomaly is found from any other components around that time. So the management system can't decide the failure traces. We prefer to meet case-a, but actually we always meet the situation of case-b and case-c.

Another point is with the growth of the system scale, too much new hardware, services and components are brought in, and systems that seek to perform failure management can't easily judge whether a new coming fundamental component is in good health or not. Based on these facts, we proposed a system called "FTD" Failure Traces Detecting system) which combines the outlying detection with a rule mining algorithm to detect failure traces. We argue that "FTD" system benefit in detecting failure traces because of several reasons.

- We use grid-based outlying detection methods to detect the anomaly status of each fundamental component in real time. Instead of directly judging normal and abnormal of each status, we score all the states. The data with higher score have lower probability to become failure traces.
- When a user level failure appears, we use rule mining algorithms to detect the correlations between the failure events with the anomalous events.
- In order to avoid the case-b and case-c, a feedback mechanism is built between the rule mining procedures with the anomaly detection procedure. This mechanism allows the system to adjust the anomaly event number according to their anomalous scores and the need of rule mining procedure.

2 Related Work

For large-scale systems, a key challenge facing by their system administrators is to understand failure trends and modes. Many black-box approaches [1–4] are designed to achieve this goal. They treat the monitored system as a black-box and find the probability-based traces between events. But they missed a key issue of how to generate these failures related events? Most of them assume that each component has a completed anomaly detection system and generate anomaly automatically. But in fact, with different event generation strategy, the system may get quite different results.

Many methods are used to detect anomalous state, and most of them are based on the clustering methods [5–7]. These approaches are based on the assumption that the normal statues tend to gather together and the status that far from others should be anomalous status. Quite a lot of methods are proposed to define the word "far" by distance, density, k-means or grid [7]. Other approaches also focus on high dimensioned data anomaly detection [5, 6], distributed outlying [11] and real time outlying detection combined with stream processing [13]. But these detected anomalies only represent that the components of the system may have abnormal behavior, it is difficult to consider the whole system's performances.

The work on finding correlations between failure-related events also attracts much more attention for many years. Several basic ideas are based on time window [13], frequent pattern [8] and call graph [9]. Some work combined these ideas together and point out that the system may change so often and provide a probability-based results [10].

In our work, we didn't focus on the concrete method of detecting anomalous or finding correlations between events, both of them have comparable matured approaches. But when combined with these two approaches together which let the anomalies as the input of correlation detection, we find out that a feedback mechanism is needed to control the anomaly generation process. So we mainly focus on how to let these two processes work together and get good performances.

3   System Model

User level service always generates concrete failure notification when the measurements they concern about act abnormally. So in this paper, we assume that during the failure propagation process, the failure behavior can be at last noticed by the user level service. The FTD system aims to detect the failure traces from the unknown system, which we regard as a black-box.

As shown in Fig. 1, the FTD system mainly in charge of two jobs, generating anomaly events from basic monitored data and find correlations between anomaly events and failure events. The FTD system is an event-based processing system, so all the data are treated as event with an event type and event properties. Without loss of generality, when we refer to an "anomaly" in the following discussion, we mean the abnormal behavior performed by the fundamental components which have the potential to become part of the failure traces. And a "failure" represents the alerts or errors that generated by the user level service, the occurrence of "failure" means there must be something wrong in the system. When we discover a failure and some anomalies have correlations, we referred these anomalies as the traces of this failure.

3.1   The Anomaly Detection

In our approach, the anomaly detection procedure is used to generate anomalous events that symbolize some component may have probability to become part of the failure trace. It inputs the states of each component and output a series of anomalous events in real time. Note that this procedure is designed to detect single component anomaly, complex anomaly that across components will be discussed in the next section.

The system first collects the raw states of each component from the monitored system. If some component's act much differently from its normal historical traces, it will generate events to notify the fact that the component has a potential anomaly. The detailed procedure acts like data classification work. The system the input the

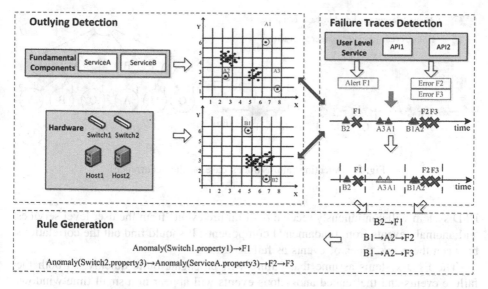

Fig. 1. The whole failure traces detection procedure

monitored data stream of a component and draw all these states into the data space. Based on the assumption that a component works normally in most time, most states that close to each other in the data space should be the normal states. Other states that much "*far*" from others will be considered as a potential anomaly. When a new coming state is recognized as anomaly, a corresponding event will be generated to notify this anomaly. Many algorithms trying to give a better cluster method and try to define the word "*far*" here and they achieve high efficiency. So we directly use a grid-based approach because it can process new added state in real time.

During the grid-based anomaly detection approach, the system adds all the normal historical status into a n-dimensional mesh network. The "n" is property number of the monitored states. For example, if a state only contains two monitored property as CPUUtility and MemUtility, then we draw a 2-dimensional mesh network. Each axis of the mesh is split into several segments by "axis step". So the mesh is assembled by a large number of n-dimensional grids. Each historical state is treated as a vector and mapped as a point in the mesh network. Based on the former assumption, if a grid contains enough points, this grid is a normal grid and all the points in it will be recognized as normal states. Other points will be recognized as anomaly candidates and the system score them by the distance between other normal grids. The points have lower score have more probability to become anomaly. So this procedure continuously input the monitored state and output the state that may become anomaly.

3.2 Detecting the Correlations Between Events

After the anomalous events are generated, the system will find correlations between failure events and anomaly events. Note that when failure behaviors are notices at user level services, events that symbolize the failure will also arrive to the system. So the

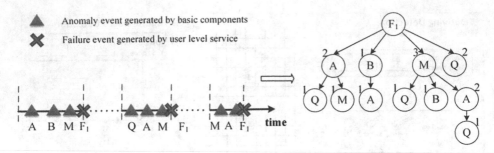

Fig. 2. Detecting failure traces base on the occurrences

FTD system will continuously receive both failure events from the user level services and anomaly events from fundamental components. It should find out the correlations between these two types of events as failure traces.

The FTD systems assume that failure will propagate quite quickly, so both the failure events and the related anomalous events will appear in a small time window. The system is first split the time line into pieces by failure event. Then we list all the possible event sequences of one type of failure. Note that administrators can also define different types of failure based on their behavior. Figure 3 shows a simple example of this process, supposing a type of failure occurs several times. The system extracts the anomalous events around these failures and shows them in the timeline. According to their sequences we can directly get a tree-based event order with occurrence time. Most administrators just request to detect the failure trances that have happened more than a fixed number of times. So the system can directly return them the branches satisfy the requirements.

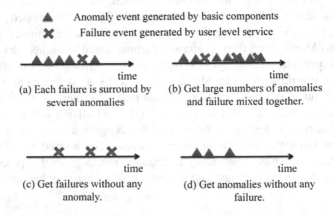

Fig. 3. The four situations that the system may confront when performing event correlation detection

4   Challenges and Feedback Mechanism

The anomalous event inspection procedure generates anomalous events and the correlations between them are detected by failure trace detection procedure. The whole process seems to collaborate quite well, but there is still a big problem of the anomalous event number. Figure 3 lists the four cases that the system may confront in a short time period during the detection process. Case-a and case-b can be easily handled by the time window or frequent pattern finding, but case-c and case-d always exists which tortures the system and administrators. Moreover, the failure traces the system detected are used for understanding the failure mode and failure prediction. So getting the result as Fig. 2 shows which some many types of event (A, B, M, Q) all will lead to failure F_1 is unacceptable for administrator. Because the appearance of these events symbolizes that the failure F_1 has probability to happen.

Note that during the anomaly detection procedure, the system set grid threshold and axis step for each component. As different components have distinct features, we argue that universal anomaly detection parameters can't fit all the components. Moreover this allows the system automatic change a component's anomaly detection parameters to control the anomaly number it generated. Take the failure traces detection of Fig. 2 as an example, the system may use monitoring rule as $A \rightarrow M \rightarrow F_1$, because it has the biggest occurrence time before F_1. But when using this rule to predict failure F_1, we can't guarantee the pattern won't appear in the other segment. This makes the rule of $A \rightarrow M \rightarrow F_1$ achieve a low precision. On the other hand, before failure event F_1, there are still many other anomaly events like Q and B. These events seem to have no contribution to identify the failure which can be recognized as the failure traces of failure F_1, so the system should try to remove the events like this type. So the challenge here is adjusting the parameters of the anomaly inspection procedure to guarantee high precision and recall of all the generated failure traces from failure traces detection procedure.

5   System Implements and Experimental Evaluation

In this section, we describe more implementation detail of FTD and evaluate the performance of it through a number of experiments based on real data of KDDCUP-99. Our primary goal is to help administrators to detect failure traces after a failure has been detected. A grid-based anomaly inspection procedure and a failure traces detection procedure is used to achieve this goal. Moreover, we point out that without a proper anomaly number feedback mechanism, these two procedures can't work well together. So we main focus our evaluation work on the efficiency verification of the feedback mechanism.

The data for evaluating the FTD system is a network intrusion benchmark which published by KDD-Cup in 1999 [12]. It provides a set of network performances related monitored data with the size of 5 million and each data contain 42 monitored items. Most of these states are normal states, while other parts are labeled as intrusion states from 37 types of network intrusion behaviors. During the evaluation process, we first input the monitoring state without anomaly label, and let the system inspects these states and pick up the anomalous status. The grid-based anomaly inspection procedure can at most achieve about 72 % of precision while with 50 % recall at the same time.

Detecting correlations between events can guarantee high recall by selecting the event sequences that always happen before the same type of failure. But the precision which requires these anomalous event patterns shouldn't happen in elsewhere can't be guaranteed. So there are only two ways to avoid this problem, trying to remove the event pattern elsewhere or select another pattern as failure trace. And these two solutions can be achieved by modifying the anomalous event number.

If we directly input these anomalies to detect correlations, the performances of the best five failures traces as shown in Fig. 4(a). But if we add in the feedback mechanism which allows the system automatically change the anomalous event number; we get the best five failure traces' performances shown as Fig. 4(b). While using feedback mechanism, it first tries to raise the precision of an original failure trace by decrease the anomalous event number of the related anomalous event type. This action also reduces the occurrence of these traces by reducing false positive pattern. So the precision of this event sequence will increase. But it also reduces the true positive pattern which decreases the recoil a little. Compared the failure traces No. 1, 2 and 3 between Fig. 4(a) and (b), the precision raises a lot while the recall decreases a little. The traces 4 and traces 5 are replaced by another event pattern because the true positive patterns are reduced too much by the feedback mechanism. But it is clear that after using the feedback mechanism, the overall precision and recall have been raised than before.

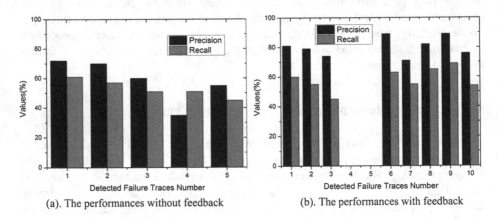

(a). The performances without feedback   (b). The performances with feedback

Fig. 4. The performances of the detected failure traces

6   Conclusion and Future Work

In this paper, we describe a black-box failure detection process including anomaly inspection and event correlation detection. We also point out that directly combines these two parts together can't achieve high efficiency. For anomaly inspection process, each component's behavior is quite distinct and it didn't know how many anomalies should be generated. In event correlation detection process, though it can easily find the event sequence that has the largest precision, the recall can't be guaranteed because of the anomaly number. As a result, we propose a feedback mechanism to allow these two processes negotiate the anomaly number to ensure the detected failure traces' precision and recall. Due to the space limitation, the event type definition problem are no mentioned in this paper, and we just assume each component only have one type of anomaly which is sometimes don't make sense. The feedback mechanism also can be improved in the future.

Acknowledgement. This research was supported by National 863 Program (No. 2011AA01A203), National Natural Science Foundation (61133004), P. R. China.

References

1. Bahl, P., Chandra, R., Greenberg, A., Kandula, S., Maltz, D.A., Zhang, M.: Towards highly reliable enterprise network services via inference of multi-level dependencies, pp. 13–24
2. Aguilera, M.K., Mogul, J.C., Wiener, J.L., Reynolds, P., Muthitacharoen, A.: Performance debugging for distributed systems of black boxes, pp. 74–89
3. Reynolds, P., Wiener, J.L., Mogul, J.C., Aguilera, M.K., Vahdat, A.: WAP5: black-box performance debugging for wide-area systems, pp. 347–356
4. Sigelman, B.H., Barroso, L.A., Burrows, M., Stephenson, P., Plakal, M., Beaver, D., Jaspan, S., Shanbhag, C.: Dapper, a large-scale distributed systems tracing infrastructure. Google research (2010)
5. Aggarwal, C.C., Yu, P.S.: Outlier detection for high dimensional data, pp. 37–46
6. Boudjeloud-Assala, L.: Visual interactive evolutionary algorithm for high dimensional outlier detection and data clustering problems. Int. J. Bio-Inspired Comput. 4(1), 6–13 (2012)
7. Patcha, A., Park, J.-M.: An overview of anomaly detection techniques: existing solutions and latest technological trends. Comput. Netw. 51(12), 3448–3470 (2007)
8. Kim, M., Sumbaly, R., Shah, S.: Root cause detection in a service-oriented architecture, pp. 93–104
9. Tati, S., Ko, B.J., Cao, G., Swami, A., La Porta, T.: Adaptive algorithms for diagnosing large-scale failures in computer networks, pp. 1–12
10. Bronevetsky, G., Laguna, I., de Supinski, B.R., Bagchi, S.: Automatic fault characterization via abnormality-enhanced classification, pp. 1–12
11. Su, L., Han, W.-H., Yang, S.-Q., Zou, P., Jia, Y.: Continuous adaptive outlier detection on distributed data streams. In: Perrott, R., Chapman, B.M., Subhlok, J., de Mello, R.F., Yang, L.T. (eds.) HPCC 2007. LNCS, vol. 4782, pp. 74–85. Springer, Heidelberg (2007)
12. http://kdd.ics.uci.edu/databases/kddcup99/kddcup99.html
13. Wang, P., Wang, H., Liu, M., et al.: An algorithmic approach to event summarization. In: Proceedings of the 2010 ACM SIGMOD International Conference on Management of data, pp. 183–194. ACM (2010)

An Effective Resource Management Architecture in HSE System

Shaolin Qiu[1], Laibin Zhang[2], Yuanqiang Huang[3(✉)],
and Yaming Mao[3]

[1] CNPC Department of Safety Environmental Protection & Energy-Saving,
Beijing, China
[2] China University of Petroleum, Beijing, China
[3] CNPC Research Institute of Safety & Environment Technology,
Beijing, China
{yqhuang,mym}@cnpc.com.cn

Abstract. The HSE information system constructed in China National
Petroleum Corporation (CNPC) in several years ago has not met the demands
of HSE (Health, Safety, and Environment) management improvement. The key
problem lies in that resource management has to be coupled with application
management in its architecture. This paper proposed a design of resource
management architecture to tackle the issues confronted. The proposed architecture design views resource management as an independent task instead of
coupling with application development and management, and make it easier to
achieve scalable resource utilization and application management.

Keywords: Resource management · Architecture · HSE

1 Introduction

HSE System is an IT one which consists of a set of enterprise-class information
technologies for HSE-related risk monitoring and management. CNPC [1] has started
the construction of the HSE System, which is playing a very important role in optimizing the management and business processes, and improving the implementation of
sustainable development strategies in CNPC [2]. However, with newly proposed
strategies of "Resources, Marketing, and Internationalization", the construction of
HSE management has been comprehensively promoted in CNPC. It has been found
that the old HSE System hasn't meet the company's need for rapid HSE business
development in terms of Target, Coverage, and Performance. In other words, the
developing management mechanism of HSE in CNPC has urged the promotion of
HSE System to implement transformation to achieve on-site monitoring and management, and improving report accuracy by the use of new information technologies.

In the following statement, the old HSE system is called as HSE 1.0 and next
generation of it will be called as HSE 2.0. The Fig. 1 shows the function structure of
HSE 1.0:

HSE 1.0 follows a classic architecture design of three-tier structure with the
centralized deployment, as shown in Fig. 2. The architecture design of HSE 1.0 leads

Y. Yuan et al. (Eds.): ISCTCS 2013, CCIS 426, pp. 260–267, 2014.
DOI: 10.1007/978-3-662-43908-1_33, © Springer-Verlag Berlin Heidelberg 2014

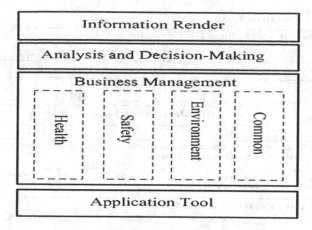

Fig. 1. The function structure of HSE 1.0

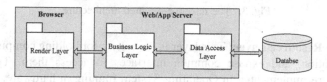

Fig. 2. Three-tier architecture of HSE 1.0

to a business-oriented abstraction, which is very effective in the stage of rapidly developing simple applications. However, as mentioned earlier, with the CNPC's HSE management mechanism developing, coverage of HSE business is expanding and applications are gradually evolving [3]. In this context, we believe that the architecture of HSE 1.0 has been insufficient to meet the newly requirements. In essence, the requirements of business differentiation will eventually be mapped to more fine-grained division and combination of underlying IT resources. Obviously, HSE 1.0 architecture does not present such a fine-grained resource management capabilities.

To address the issues of HSE 1.0, this paper proposes effective resource management architecture for HSE 2.0. In this proposed architecture, IT resources are treated as the first-class element to manage, and the implementation of business is viewed as a combination, sharing and collaboration of IT resources.

2   Overall Design

As mentioned earlier, the key problem of HSE 1.0 is how to tackle resource management problem. Our proposed architecture promotes the importance of resource management [4] by the way of separating resource management from business and making a more sophisticated design instead of relying on traditional Operating System. The purpose is to implement scalable resource management.

According to this idea, the resource-oriented architecture is illustrated in Fig. 3 below:

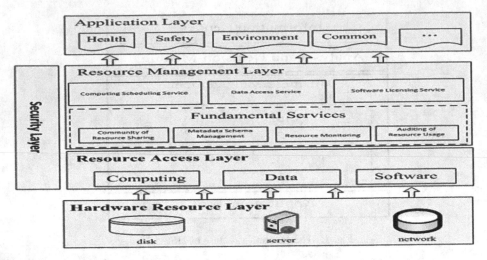

Fig. 3. The resource-oriented architecture

- **Hardware Resource Layer:** This layer is the carrier for holding computation, data, communication, and expose common interfaces to access them. Typically the interfaces are implemented in Operating System running in hardware.
- **Resource Access Layer:** This Layer is designed to achieve higher abstraction of hardware resources, shield the details of the resource usage, and reduce the complexity of access interfaces. In this layer, resources are classified into categories of Computing resource, Data resource and Software resource.
- **Resource Management Layer:** As the core of system, it implements the effective management for distributed resources to provide simplified interfaces for resource utilization by applications.
- **Application Layer:** It contains various HSE-related applications relying on services provided by Resource Management Layer.
- **Security Layer:** It is an indispensable part in HSE system, and interacts with each layer of the architecture. Since the high requirements of confidentiality in HSE business, it makes sure that only authorized user having access to appropriate resources.

3 Details of Implementation

3.1 Resource Access Layer

The purpose of resource access layer is making applications, such as persistently storing monitoring indicators of waste water, waste gas and other pollutants, or generating statistics reports on imported data, are implemented by using IT resources. The interfaces for accessing hardware resource usually implemented by operating system on hardware and computing programs, file systems and database systems on operating system.

Software Servitization. Service refers to a package of access protocol and data in the field of information science. The definition of service includes the layout of access protocol and data format during access in order to do some functions. Usually software can be locally called graphical interface or command line with native support of operating system. But remote users can not access locally installed software without the help of access protocol.

In HSE system, software should provide multiple service forms:

- **Remote Desktop** is the service form that supports remote users to use software like in a local desktop window, allows users to see native GUI that exactly responds to users' operations from remote mouse or keyboard click.
- **Web Portal** is the service form that supports remote users to use software through web browser. It also has a visual graphical user interface, but the GUI could be customized.
- **Remote Terminal** provides remote users a rapid operation window to invoke commands provided by local software, which is ideal for some system management tasks.

OS Virtualization. Traditionally single hardware holds single OS at the same time. The virtualization technology in the level of OS makes it possible that different software on different OS could share the same hardware.

The framework of virtualization consists of Virtual Resource Layer, VM Management Layer and Customization Layer [5]: Virtual Resource Layer consists of virtual machine (VM) supervisors and the corresponding VM instances. VM supervisor is bound to underlying hardware resources, which provides the interface to interact with the underlying hardware while monitoring and manipulating VM instances. VM instance is an instantiated VM image which has ready OS and software. VM Management Layer implements monitoring in the entire life cycle of VM instances with the help of VM supervisor, and support VM deployment and migration. Specifically it has the functions of customized VM image deployment, which provides high reliability and availability support for VM migration and simplified operations of start/monitor/pause/resume/stop for application. When dealing with the same business, VM instances with the same software installed could be gathered to provide more powerful capability. Customization Layer could construct a cluster of VM instances based on resource requirements (eg: CPU number, memory size, software type, etc).

3.2 Resource Management Layer

Resources joined into system through Resource Access Layer may have different access protocols and interfaces. The heterogeneity of accessing makes resources difficult to be managed. The Resource management Layer is proposed with the purpose of shielding this heterogeneity, and decrease complexity of developing and maintaining applications.

3.2.1   Fundamental Services

Community of Resource Sharing

Community of Resource Sharing [6] is a federation among enterprises driven by common interests. Certain confidential files, business data, software licenses, and other resources are only open in certain community. Enterprise as resource provider and user as resource consumer can join several communities, which makes communities overlap. The overlapping of communities makes a more fine-grained resource sharing possible.

Metadata Schema Management

Metadata Schema Management provides storage and maintenance of all kinds of metadata in HSE system. It has to support data storage model in a hierarchical tree-structure, storage of standardized CONSTANTS in CNPC, attribute-based information queries, and replication mechanism to maintain data synchronization of different nodes.

In addition, since metadata could be heterogeneous among different enterprises, it should be allowed that each enterprise maintain its own repository, and the headquarters maintain a global common view of one, while enterprise-level metadata would be synchronized to headquarters periodically.

Resource Monitoring

According to the features of resource heterogeneity, it is necessary to implement a resource monitoring service to understand resource usage and analyze system bottlenecks in HSE system [7]. Taking into account the particularity of HSE business, resource monitoring provides the functions of basic monitoring for universal resource in OS and hardware, and customized monitoring for specific applications. In the design of resource monitoring, it is necessary to follow the principles of self-government by enterprise.

Auditing of Resource Usage

The safety principle in HSE business makes the traceability of resource usage necessary. Auditing service [8] supports both online and offline modes, in which online mode supports real-time monitoring of user behavior to tackle some abnormal situation immediately and offline one provides the ability to trace back what happened before for diagnosis.

3.2.2   Computing Scheduling Service

There are two kinds of computing tasks in HSE system. One is with real-time requirement, such as in-time alerting and processing excessive monitoring data required in Online Monitoring System for Pollution Source. The other is with non-real-time requirement, such as generation of statistical report with larger time span. Essentially these two tasks comply with the same pattern that computing request are packed to be assigned to appropriate nodes to execute. Computing Scheduling aims to solve the problem of mapping between tasks and nodes [9]. It is an efficient method to relieve the imbalance of resource allocation in HSE system.

Computing scheduling service as an important part in Resource Management Layer is with the purpose of adjusting resource difference among enterprises to achieve a certain degree of balance. Through the effective integration of different enterprises' resources, it could possible to provide strong computation capability for upper applications.

Computing request from application is packed into computing task and inserted into Task Queue. The tasks in Task Queue will be managed to match with underlying resource in a First-In-First-Out (FIFO) way. Task Queue is not only a queue, but also a manager with functions of persisting task information and notifying task status.

Resource matching module is responsible for many-to-many matching of tasks and the underlying resources. Specifically, the resource matching module will find appropriate resource nodes from available "resource pool" for each task based on its requirements for function, CPU / memory capacity, OS vendor, etc.

Scheduling decision module achieves one-to-one mapping between task and node. The whole procedure is split into several steps: (1) Weed out invalid nodes from the matched ones. (2) Apply load balancing strategy to assign task to the most appropriate node. (3) Force intervention scheduling to change the original assignment.

3.2.3   Data Access Service
Data access service mainly tackle the problem of data integration to provide a unified logic view of data and access interface for applications [10]. In HSE system, data resource is normally distributed in the two kinds of containers: file system and database.

For data distributed in different databases, a global data view is constructed to provide unified language and protocol for database access. There are several key functions necessary to be implemented: (1) mapping from global query to local queries. The difficulty of mapping lies in semantic heterogeneity of query languages. Data dictionary could be a good choice to help to generate target database's sub-query in mapping; (2) merging query results. After the query results returned from multiple local databases, the information of mapping from global to local in data dictionary is used to combine the results into a global view; (3) caching recent query results to improve the efficiency of subsequent data access; (4) providing access interfaces for application development, database configuration and management.

For data distributed in different file systems, it's necessary to develop a interface for supporting remote file access and management, and shielding the differences of underlying transport protocol. Based on the interface, it could provide a unified file access and storage management service. There are several key functions necessary to be implemented: (1) providing specific protocol to allow files in the local file system could be opened, read, written and closed by remote user; (2) maintaining the mapping between logical file address and physical one; (3) caching recent query results to improve the efficiency of subsequent data access; (4) providing access interfaces for application development, database configuration and management.

3.2.4   Software Licensing Service
In addition to software itself, license for software is also expensive and scarce resource, and even costs much higher than software itself. License is a digital certificate created by software vendors to specify which user can legally use the software.

For those licenses that do not bind to hardware (floating license), their software can be run on any hardware as long as the software has the access to its license. Software licensing service is to achieve the goal of managing software floating licenses scattered in different enterprises in order to save the investing of software in CNPC [11].

Since the ownership of licenses belongs to respective enterprise, it is reasonable to adopt hierarchical management for software license, which includes several components.

Local manager is responsible for the scheduling and allocation of licenses in its own enterprise, and determine which license could be shared by others. Global Information Manager which is independent of any local license management mechanism is responsible for synchronizing information about shared floating licenses in multiple enterprises, including availability status, number, and type of licenses. Router is responsible for message routing of license request and response among multiple enterprises. Given the number of simultaneous software instances with a license normally limited, negotiant allows that user with high priority will get license first when license requests from enterprises conflict. Global Scheduler is required to ensure plenty of floating licenses for some critical applications or users, while make no "starve" on low priority requests as far as possible. Global scheduler with the global view has the most information to do optimal allocation of licenses, and send the license to targets.

3.3 Security Layer

Because of high demand for particularity, security, and confidentiality in HSE business, proposing security layer is vital. Besides security and privacy guarantees offered by IT infrastructure itself in CNPC, the security mechanisms of HSE system should be provided during the communication, authentication and authorization.

The components in HSE system communicate with each other by the way of web service which normally uses HTTP as communication protocol. However message is transferred in the form of plain text by HTTP protocol. To ensure the privacy of the message content, it should offer an alternative that can replace HTTP protocol just like HTTPS [12] which completely encrypt data transferred in communication layer.

Due to the feature of resource-sharing among enterprises in HSE system, how to verify a user's identity is vital. Client should send request with its electronic signature and summary, and the request would be responded until it has confirmed that client's identity has not been forged. With authentication supporting, it is possible to prevent tampering of encrypted messages during transmission, which is effectively to ensure end-to-end security.

Authorization solves another problem that what action a verified user could do even if communication is secured. On server side, pre-configured ACRs (Access Control Rules) are used to determine whether requester has right to execute the operations of which the descriptions are provided by client. With authorization supporting, it is possible to implement the Single Sign-On (SSO) which would be a useful improvement for resource-sharing [13].

4 Conclusion

To support the development of HSE business, HSE system has been built in CNPC in several years. However, with the shift of HSE management paradigm, the old HSE system cannot afford enough flexibility in business upgrading and reconstruction. It results in sophisticated application development with considering more details of resource management, which makes business upgrading more difficult. This paper proposed effective resource management architecture for HSE system. The architecture is characterized by separation of resource management from business management and making the function of resource management served by some independent services. In this paper, we mainly talked about the overall design and functions for proposed architecture and highlight some designs of core components in the architecture.

References

1. Information on http://www.cnpc.com.cn/en/
2. Mao, Y.M., Du, W.D., Lu, C.: The development prospects of HSE software. Environ. Sustain. Dev. **1**, 61–63 (2007)
3. Liu, H., Zhong, X.H., Liu, C., et al.: A Study of the Management and Control System Integration in Oilfield Enterprises Based on Business Process. J. China Univ. Petrol. (Ed. Soc. Sci.) **28**(3), 15–18 (2012)
4. Fleeman, D., Gillen, M., Lenharth, A., et al.: Quality-based adaptive resource management architecture (qarma): a corba resource management service. In: Proceedings of 18th International Parallel and Distributed Processing Symposium, 2004, pp. 116. IEEE (2004)
5. Li, Y., Li W., Jiang, C.: A survey of virtual machine system: Current technology and future trends. In: Third International Symposium on Electronic Commerce and Security (ISECS), 2010, pp. 332–336. IEEE (2010)
6. Kim, K.H., Tchamgoue, G.M., Yong-Kee, J.U.N., et al.: An optimal resource sharing in hierarchical virtual organizations in the grid. IEICE Trans. Inf. Syst. **95**(12), 2948–2951 (2012)
7. Hu, L., Cheng, X., Che, X.: Survey of grid resource monitoring and prediction strategies. Int. J. Intell. Inf. Process. **1**(2), 78–85 (2010)
8. Furlani, T.R., Jones, M.D., Gallo, S.M., et al. Performance metrics and auditing framework using application kernels for high-performance computer systems. Concurr. Comput.: Pract. Exper. (2012)
9. Nesmachnow, S., Cancela, H., Alba, E.: Heterogeneous computing scheduling with evolutionary algorithms. Soft Comput. **15**(4), 685–701 (2010)
10. Fiore, S., Negro, A., Aloisio, G.: The data access layer in the GRelC system architecture. Future Gener. Comput. Syst. **27**(3), 334–340 (2011)
11. Mirabella, R.: License management: how developers control software licensing (2010). Accessed 17 Apr 2010
12. Rescorla, E.: RFC 2818: HTTP over TLS. Internet Eng. Task Force (2000). http://www.ietf.org
13. Ruckmani, V., Sadasivam, G.S.: Integrating an efficient authorization protocol with trigon-based authentication mechanism for improving grid security. In: Das, V.V., et al. (eds.) BAIP 2010. CCIS, vol. 70, pp. 125–129. Springer, Heidelberg (2010)

Energy Efficiency Evaluation of Workload Execution on Intel Xeon Phi Coprocessor

Qi Zhao[✉], Hailong Yang, Guang Wei, Zhongzhi Luan,
and Depei Qian

Sino-German Joint Software Institute,
Department of Computer Science and Engineering,
Beihang University, No.37, Xuanyuan Road, Beijing 100191, China
{qi.zhao,hailong.yang,guang.wei,zhongzhi.luan,depei.qian}@jsi.buaa.edu.cn

Abstract. Although the performance of multi-core processor continues to increase steadily, power consumption with core density at such high level gradually becomes a limiting factor for computing facilities hosting massive servers to expand at even larger scale, especially as we entering the era of many core architecture. In spite of various power management techniques already existed for year, none of them has ever been demonstrated feasible on the real many core platforms since it is until recently the Intel Xeon Phi processor realizes the prospect of many core architecture into product. Along with the Xeon Phi processor, the power management capability has been significantly improved with hardware and software support that the user could analyze the power consumption of the application at fine granularity with sufficient information captured during the runtime by the power monitoring infrastructures implemented on Xeon Phi processor. However, at the time we propose this study, there is no comprehensive investigation to evaluate the power and energy properties of such many core platform when running diverse applications despite of the performance boost.

In this paper, we leverage representative benchmark suites including various parallel workloads, running with OpenMP mode, from diverse domains to evaluate the MIC architecture. With the power measurement ability exposed by Power Management and SCIF interface, the energy can be tracked every 50 ms. The experiments reveal non-intuitive results on the impact of MIC in terms of energy efficiency: (1) for computation intensive workload such as BT and FT in NPB, MC and MD in SHOC, in contrast to our expectation, MIC doesn't keep improving the system energy efficiency with the increasing threads; (2) for memory intensive application such as IS in NPB and DeviceMemory in SHOC, MIC actually deteriorates the system energy efficiency significantly; (3) for EPCC, which is used to investigate overheads of key OpenMP constructs, the workloads suffer energy efficiency decline mostly caused by the high pressures from the communication among cores.

Keywords: Energy efficiency · MIC · OpenMP

Y. Yuan et al. (Eds.): ISCTCS 2013, CCIS 426, pp. 268–275, 2014.
DOI: 10.1007/978-3-662-43908-1_34, © Springer-Verlag Berlin Heidelberg 2014

1   Introduction

The core density of modern processor continuously increases to harvest the recent advances in transistor technology and circuit design, delivering the expected performance scaling for emerging application paradigms such as cloud computing. It is commonly agreed that the promising many core architecture, that transforms each single server into a small HPC, would become ubiquitous in large computing facilities such as datacenters in the near future. In the meanwhile, the power consumption of the many core architecture servers is surging unprecedentedly, which almost reach the ceiling of the power budget within contemporary computing infrastructures at massive scale. Therefore, understanding the application behaviors on many core architecture is essential to manipulate the computing resources in large scale environment energy efficiently. The advent of Intel Xeon Phi processor [1] fulfills the many core architecture as a low hanging fruit at the reach of both industry and academia, which becomes an ideal platform to study the performance benefits as well as the energy efficiency running real world applications. However, a comprehensive investigation on the application behaviors on such architecture is missing, especially from the power and energy perspective.

Furthermore, the fine-grained power management capability enabled on Xeon Phi processor provides a unique opportunity to complement the evaluation on the energy efficiency property of the many core architecture running applications from a wide spectrum of domains. There are sophisticated hardware counters and software APIs supported on current Xeon Phi processors that provide sufficient information to analyze the performance and power characteristics of the applications in real time. And it would be valuable to identify the trade-offs between performance and power consumption running diverse applications realized by the capability of power management supported on Xeon Phi processor. For instance, how to manage the resource allocation for better performance under certain power constraint on the many core architecture. We argue it is the exact time to exploit deeper into the power and energy attributes of the rising many core architecture, thus to reveal useful insights for programmers and administrators to optimize the applications and systems respectively towards more efficient energy usage.

In this paper, we have investigated the power and energy behaviors of diverse applications under different resource settings on the Xeon Phi processor at fine granularity. In sum, our work makes the following contributions:

1. A comprehensive evaluation of power consumption and energy efficiency of MIC is presented with various typical benchmarks.
2. Detailed interpretation of the impact of MIC architecture is complemented based on experimental observations with diverse benchmark suites.

The paper is organized as follows. In Sect. 2 we introduce the approach to measure the power consumption of Phi coprocessor, and Sect. 3 outlines results from our evaluation and analysis in detail. At last, Sects. 4 and 5 discuss the related work and conclude future directions of our research.

2   Power Measurement

We build a Linux shell script to monitor the power consumption of Phi. The precision of the monitoring script is 50 ms, which means, in every 50 ms, we can obtain an average power statistics of Phi during the past 50 ms. The power monitoring script utilizes *MicAccessSDK*, which exposes a set of APIs enabling applications to access the Intel MIC architecture hardware, to collect Phis power parameters. The system management agent running on Phi handles the queries from the host and returns results to the host through the *Symmetric Communication Interface* (SCIF) [2], which is the communication backbone between the host processors and the Phi coprocessors in a heterogeneous computing environment.

Following a successful boot of Phi coprocessor, the primary responsibility of *MicAccessAPI* is to establish connections with the host driver and the coprocessor OS, and subsequently allow software to monitor Phi coprocessor parameters. The host application and coprocessor OS communicate using messages, which are sent via the underlying SCIF architecture using the *Sysfs* mechanism as indicated in Fig. 1 [3].

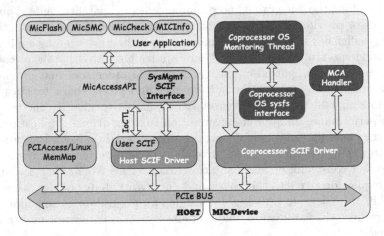

Fig. 1. Intel Xeon Phi coprocessor SysMgmt MicAccessAPI architecture components diagram.

As shown in Algorithm 1, we use this script to obtain power statistics of workloads running on Phi. Meanwhile, with the Linux built-in command, we can also collect the execution time of workloads. Once achieve all these data, we are able to start the evaluation.

3   Evaluation

In this section, we first describe the experimental setup for the evaluation. Then we analyze the results running different benchmarks on the Phi.

Algorithm 1. Power Monitoring Script On Intel Xeon Phi.

Input:
    logfilename: the name of the recorded result file;
Output:
    The formative power statistics result;
1: *fresult* = fopen(*logfilename*)
2: *retVal* = MicInitAPI()
3: **if** *retVal* != MIC_ACCESS_API_SUCCESS **then**
4:    ERROR
5:    return *retVal*
6: **end if**
7: *retVal* = MicInitAdapter()
8: **if** *retVal* != MIC_ACCESS_API_SUCCESS **then**
9:    ERROR
10:    return *retVal*
11: **end if**
12: **while** TRUE **do**
13:    *retVal* = MicGetPowerUsage(&powerUsage)
14:    **if** *retVal* != MIC_ACCESS_API_SUCCESS **then**
15:      ERROR
16:      return *retVal*
17:    **end if**
18:    *fresult*.fprint(*powerUsage*.avePower + " " + dateTime)
19:    *fresult*.flush()
20:    sleep(50ms)
21: **end while**

3.1 Experimental Setup

The experiments have been performed on a Sandy Bridge server with two Intel Xeon Phi 5110 P coprocessor, which has 60 cores and 4 hardware threads per core. The benchmarks are ran on Phi and the power monitor script is ran on host server.

3.2 Evaluation and Analysis

3.2.1 NPB-OMP

NAS parallel benchmarks (NPB) [4] are a set of workloads commonly used to evaluate parallel systems. Here we use the NPB-OMP version to evaluate the energy efficiency of Intel Xeon Phi coprocessor. In order to avoid too long execution time, we carefully choose the appropriate problem size for each workload. Meanwhile, we choose equidistant nine thread number under 240 in order to observe the relationship between the energy related characters and thread number, which is set for the whole evaluation part. The evaluation results are shown in Fig. 2.

Commonly, with increasing threads, the average power would increase and the execution time will decrease. However, as we can see from Fig. 2, some workloads don't act like that. For the power, almost every workload, except *bt* and *cg*,

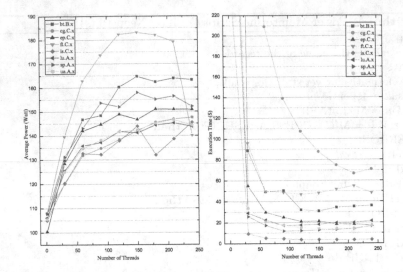

Fig. 2. NPB-OMP evaluation results. The left shows the average power of workload varies with the number of threads. The right shows the execution time of workload varies with the number of threads.

has a decline when number of threads increases. That reveals that using more cores do not always bring high power consumption. For the execution time, we have two observations. Firstly, the execution time drops sharply when the threads increase from 1 to 30 for most of the workloads, except *cg*. Secondly, when threads keep increasing, the execution time is hardly changed for some workloads, such as *is* and *ep*, while the time of the other workloads are on the increase, such as *ft, bt, lu, sp*. This indicates that increasing threads in use will elevate performance. But once it goes beyond the optimal number of threads, it might hurt the performance instead of promoting.

3.2.2 SHOC

The Scalable Heterogeneous Computing Benchmark Suite (SHOC) [5] is a collection of benchmark workloads testing the performance and stability of systems. Its initial focus is on systems containing multi-core processors. We choose seven typical workloads and the evaluation results are in Fig. 3.

From the figure, the average power are similar with NPB-OMP evaluation. *GEMM* is the only different one, which has a relatively stable power consumption when thread number exceeds 30. The execution time for SHOC is quite different with NPB-OMP, which is more diverse. *MD*'s execution time is layered and decreasing with the increasing thread number in general. *Triad* and *Reduction* keep an quite stable execution time when thread number exceeds 30, which means increasing number of thread is not performance beneficial for them. The execution time of *GEMM* and *MaxFlops* stays stable when thread number exceeds 100. *MC*'s execution time drops drastically with increasing number of

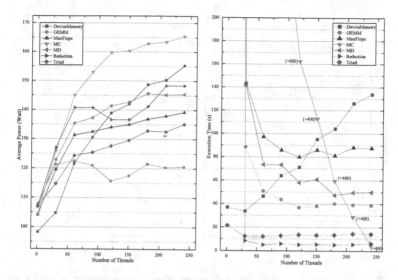

Fig. 3. SHOC evaluation results. The left shows the average power of workload varies with the number of threads. The right shows the execution time of workload varies with the number of threads. MC in the right figure is processed by subtracting 400 for each point in order to be shown in the coordinate domain.

thread while the execution time of *DeviceMemory* increases adversely, which is obvious since the time of memory testing will absolutely increase when raising the number of thread.

3.2.3 EPCC

The EPCC Microbenchmarks [6] are used to investigate overheads of key OpenMP constructs. The micro-benchmarks assess the performance of there constructs and provide a data point for potential parallelization overheads and the scaling behavior in real applications. Figure 4 shows the results.

Syncbench, which measures the overhead of OpenMP constructs that require synchronization, has a slow increasing power and execution time with increasing number of thread. The thread number has a faint effect on both power and execution time. However, *schedbench* has a vigorous increasing in execution time and *arraybench* has a remarkable increasing in power. The power of *schedbench* and the execution time of *arraybench* are relatively stable. From this we know that loop scheduling and array operations might hurt the energy efficiency more than synchronisation on Phi.

4   Related Work

With the development of Intel MIC architecture, a lot of related work on Intel Xeon Phi has done by many scholars and engineers from both academia and

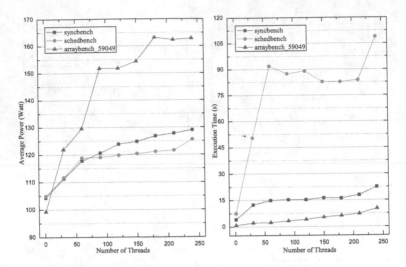

Fig. 4. EPCC evaluation results. The left shows the average power of workload varies with the number of threads. The right shows the execution time of workload varies with the number of threads.

industry. Tim et al. [7] presented an early performance comparison of OpenMP programming on Phi. They applied the Roofline model to investigate the utilization of the architecture and they compared the performance of a Intel Xeon Phi coprocessor system with the performance reached on a large SMP production system. Moreover, performance evaluation of specific benchmarks has been exploited. In [8], the authors used NPB-OMP version to examine the performance of the Phi coprocessor and identified some common issues that may hamper performance. Misra et al. [9] evaluated the Rodinia benchmarks on Phi and they claimed the performance of codes can be enhanced on Phi. Regarding energy, Shao and Brooks [10] from Harvard proposed an instruction-level energy model of Phi. They construct the model based on how energy per instruction scales with the number of cores and the number of active threads per core. Their model is accurate and can be used to identify opportunities to improve energy efficiency. In order to exploit more chances to realize energy efficient computing on Phi, we presented our evaluation work.

5   Conclusion and Future Work

In this paper, we presented detailed evaluation of energy efficiency on Intel MIC architecture - Intel Xeon Phi coprocessor. Using various typical workloads from classical benchmark suits, such as NPB-OMP, SHOC and EPCC, we concluded that different workloads have different behavior leading to different energy efficiency. The optimal energy efficiency thread number highly depends on the characteristic of the workload itself. Using more threads might lead to higher performance, which is the shorter execution time, but it might result in less energy efficient adversely due to the high power. Therefore, our future work will focus on the bottlenecks that can specifically impede energy efficiency on Phi and the method to find out the optimal thread number for workloads to achieve the highest energy efficiency.

Acknowledgments. This work was supported by the National High Technology Research and Development Program ("863" Program) of China under the grant No.2012AA010904.

References

1. Intel Corporation. Intel Many Integrated Core Architecture (Intel MIC Architecture) C Advanced (2013). http://www.intel.com/content/www/us/en/architecture-and-technology/many-integrated-core/intel-many-integrated-core-architecture.html
2. Intel Many Integrated Core Symmetric Communications Interface (SCIF) User Guide. Technical report, Revision 1.01, Intel Corporation (2013)
3. Intel Xeon Phi Coprocessor System Software Developers Guide. Technical report, SKU 328207-001EN, Intel Corporation (2013)
4. Jin, H., Frumkin, M., Yan, J.: The OpenMP implementation of NAS parallel benchmarks and its performance. Technical report, NAS-99-011, NASA Ames Research Center (1999)
5. Danalis, A., Marin, G., McCurdy, C., Meredith, J.S., Roth, P.C., Spafford, K., Tipparaju, V., Vetter, J.S.: The scalable heterogeneous computing (SHOC) benchmark suite. In: Proceedings of the 3rd Workshop on General-Purpose Computation on Graphics Processing Units, pp. 63–74. ACM (2010)
6. Mark Bull, J., O'Neill, D.: A microbenchmark suite for OpenMP 2.0. SIGARCH Comput. Archit. News **29**(5), 41–48 (2001)
7. Cramer, T., Schmidl, D., Klemm, M., an Mey, D.: OpenMP programming on Intel Xeon Phi coprocessors: an early performance comparison. In: Proceedings of the Many-core Applications Research Community (MARC) Symposium at RWTH Aachen University, pp. 38–44, November 2012
8. Vienne, J., Ramachandran, A., Wijngaart, R., Koesterke, L., Shaparov, I.: Performance evaluation of NAS parallel benchmarks on Intel Xeon Phi. In: 6th International Workshop on Parallel Programming Models and Systems Software for High-End Computing (2013)
9. Misra, G., Kurkure, N., Das, A., Valmiki, M., Das, S., Gupta, A.: Evaluation of rodinia codes on Intel Xeon Phi. In: 2013 4th International Conference on Intelligent Systems Modelling Simulation (ISMS), pp. 415–419 (2013)
10. Shao Y.S., Brooks, D.: Energy characterization and instruction-level energy model of Intel's Xeon Phi processor. In: 2013 IEEE International Symposium on Low Power Electronics and Design (ISLPED), pp. 389–394 (2013)

A Covert Channel Bases on CPU Load
in Cloud Computing

Qian Liu[1(✉)], Qianwen He[1], and Yu Zhang[2]

[1] School of Computer and Communication Engineering, University of Science
and Technology Beijing, Beijing, China
hnliuqian@163.com
[2] College of Science, Civil Aviation University of China, Tianjin, China

Abstract. With the development and application of Cloud Computing, all
kinds of products become available for public, but opportunity always along
with challenge. Cloud security has become the key problem of restricting the
development of cloud computing while we benefit from cloud computing.
Virtualization technology is the foundation of cloud computing, its security
mainly is cloud security. Covert channel is about information hiding which
emphasis on the secret of communication. A malicious user on one virtual
machine usually cannot relay secret data to other virtual machines without
using explicit communication media due to shared resource between virtual
machines. The paper has a deep research of covert channel in cloud computing
environment. The channel is working well though experimental tests.

Keywords: Cloud computing · Virtualization · Covert channel · CPU load

1 Introduction

This paper based on the analysis of existing security issues in cloud computing.
Virtual machine provides strong isolation to make sure for its security, but the shared
resource between virtual machine may leads to covert channel. We focus on the study
of covert channel, according to the characteristics of cloud computing virtualization,
analysis of possibility and inevitability of covert channel in cloud computing virtual
environment.

Then, this paper proposes a covert channel based on CPU load. Malicious processes in a virtual machine (or spyware) can change the CPU load time and make it
co-conspirators can detect the change to send secret message using different time to
represent different information. This communication process cannot be detected by
normal security mechanism.

2 Security in Clouding Computing

Since 2006, Cloud Computing was known to the public by Google CEO Eric Schmidt
in the Search Engine Strategies Conference for the first time, Cloud Computing
developed rapidly and become one of most interned technology in industry, academia,
government and so on [1].

Y. Yuan et al. (Eds.): ISCTCS 2013, CCIS 426, pp. 276–282, 2014.
DOI: 10.1007/978-3-662-43908-1_35, © Springer-Verlag Berlin Heidelberg 2014

Typical cloud infrastructure architecture is divided into PaaS (Platform as a Service), IaaS (Infrastructure as a Service) and SaaS (Software as a Service). Virtualization technology provides computing resource scalability, availability, and security of data isolation protection for cloud computing [2]. However, the virtual machines on the same hardware platform still shared hardware resources under the protection of the security policy, which will inevitably lead to information leak. The channel of leak secret message was called covert channel [3].

Research on covert channels is of great significance in both offense and defense [4]. Covert communication is an efficient and reliable way of communication. Information technology can be widely used in national production, financial and economic, national security and other areas [5].

In this paper, we study the CPU load based covert channel lead by cloud computing virtualization shared resources. One of the most convenient resources for covert channels between virtual machines is CPU load, which can be approximated by the amount of time taken for certain computations [6]. Discuss the CPU load covert channel comprehensive, systematic from the basic principles of the channel, where the environment scheduling algorithm, application scenarios, specific communication protocols, error handling, and channel capacity, bit error rate estimation and other aspects.

3   The Covert Channel in Cloud Computing Environment

Cloud computing realizes managing the same hardware and cross-platform virtual machine logic resources though virtualization technology. For example, Xen virtualization platform, covert channels can be divided into covert channel between processes, covert channel between the virtual domain and covert channel between networks [7].

4   Covert Channel Based on CPU Load

4.1   Fundamental Threat Scenario

One of the most convenient resources for covert channels between virtual machines is CPU load, which can be approximated by the amount of time taken for certain computations.

Suppose that there are two processes working on the same CPU virtual machine domain A and domain B as shown in Fig. 1. When process p runs on domain A, the corresponding CPU executing time is t1. When domain A and B running processes p at the same time, because of the CPU shared, the executing time of A is no longer running time t1, but is t2. It can be used to written communications protocol based on the difference in t1 and t2. The receiver receives a bit by measuring how often it can execute unit comp during a standard timespan. If the sender sends bit 1, it repeatedly executes unit comp during a standard timespan. Otherwise, it does not execute any program through out the timespan. When a standard timespan has passed, the receiver compares the number of executions of unit comp with a pre-calculated standard

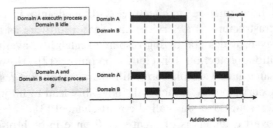

Fig. 1. Changes caused by sharing of the CPU run time

number. If the difference between them is larger than a threshold, the receiver receives bit 1. Otherwise, it receives bit 0.

4.2 The Design of Covert Channel

Covert channel based on CPU load consists of a sender process and a receiver process. Figure 2 shows the structure of the channel.

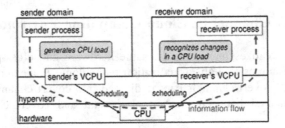

Fig. 2. Structure of covert channel based on CPU load

We assumed that a communication period consists of 64 bits. In one communication cycle, covert channel communicates 64 bits by repeating 1-bit communication 64 times.

4.3 The Communication Protocol of Covert Channel

This paper considers the basis of these factors on the design of the communication protocol. It consists of three phases: synchronization phase, confirmation phase, bit transmission phase. The flow of the communication protocol as Fig. 3 shows:

4.4 Synchronization Phase

The start of arrow in the figure indicates starting the calculation unit, the end of the arrow indicates the end of the calculation. A sender and receiver synchronize as follows. First, the sender creates a specific CPU load pattern that indicates a

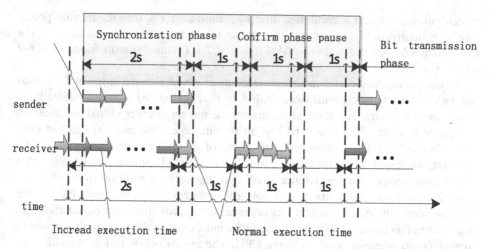

Fig. 3. Flow of communication protocol

communication request. A communication request is represented by executions of unit comp that last for 2 s. The receiver waits for a communication request by repeating an execution of unit comp that takes approximately 0.1 s. When a receiver detects a rise in CPU load, it starts measuring the amount of time that elapses from the rise in CPU load until the fall in the load. If the time is close to 2 s, the receiver judges that the sender is transmitting a communication request.

4.5 Confirmation Phase

In this phase, the sender pauses for a certain period of time, and the receiver calculates how often it can execute unit comp during this period. The number is called standard number, and the period is called standard timespan. Currently, the standard timespan is 1 s. A standard number is used in the bit transmission phase. If the receiver detects a rise in CPU load, it judges that it received a false communication request in the synchronization phase due to CPU usage by processes other than the sender. In that case, the receiver returns to the start of the synchronization phase.

4.6 Bit Transmission Phase

Next, the sender and receiver start the bit communication phase, in which they communicate 64-bit information. The protocol consumes a standard timespan to communicate one bit. The receiver measures the number of executions of unit comp during the standard timespan. If the number is less than 90 % of the standard number, it receives bit 1. Otherwise, it receives bit 0.

5 Discussion and Analysis of Channel's Performance

In order to facilitate covert channel transmission, the test omitting the normal course of work converted to ASCII code manner its bit stream transmission directly.

Synchronization time 3 s, confirmed time 1 s, pause time 1 s, then the transfer phase. The transmission of bits per second, then pause 1 s, so the total time consumed for the transmission 64 bits is $3 + 1+1 + 64 + 63 = 132$ s. Channel transmission rate is 64/ $132 = 0.485$ bit/s.

In this paper, the bit error rate measurements of covert channel based on CPU load are under a variety of circumstances, including changes related properties of both the virtual machine communication, also consider the impact of other virtual machines on a physical machine. Test data is 64 bits bit stream, repeat the test 100 times in each case, observed synchronization and correctness of the data transmission.

First, we tested the transmission capacity of covert channel in the situation that without interference (or interference small). In this case, in addition to sending and receiving processes, there are almost not other process CPU resources. We believe that this ideal situation is minimal disturbance, the approximate that no interference. But even in this case, because the process that must exist in the system, or a desire to control Dom0 occupies nearly 4 % the CPU. The results below as Fig. 4, said:

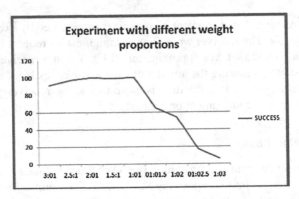

Fig. 4. Experiment with different weight proportions

Changes cause by adjusting the weights between sender and receiver lead to different results. The S: R ratio of the line represents the weight of the sender and the receiver. It can be drawn from the table, when the ratio of the sender and receiver weights is 1:1, CPU load covert channel reach 100 % accuracy. There is no bit error in this situation. This result indicates that, in the ideal case, if the sender and receiver synchronized successfully, then CPU load covert channel has a very high accuracy rate transmission.

Unfortunately, synchronization failed when S:R was not 1:1. When the ratio between weights was increased, the accuracy decreased accordingly. The decrease in the accuracy was prominent when the receiver domain was given a larger weight.

The test results of the work on the multi-core CPU is in the following table. Here, we assign a 4-core virtual machine CPU. The sender and receiver are assigned a different number of VCPU. VCPU and physical CPU are not binding each other, so each VCPU may run on any physical CPU. In order to ensure the unity of variable weights consistent with S: R are set to 1:1, repeat the same transmission 100 times.

Table 1. The test results of different VCPUS

Sender VCPUS	2	3	4	8	6	4	3	1
Receiver VCPUS	2	3	4	8	4	1	2	4
Sucess	0	91	100	4	61	5	8	0
Syn fail	100	9	0	0	39	95	92	100
Bit error	0	0	0	96	0	0	0	0

The result is shown in Table 1. A 100 % success rate was achieved when both the sender and receiver domain had four VCPUs. That was an ideal case because both domains were expected to put loads on all physical cores and interfere with each other. The channel achieved a 92 % success rate when both the sender and receiver had three VCPUs. In that case, synchronization failure occurred only when all receiver processes failed to recognize a communication request. When one or more receiver processes recognized a communication request, they successfully obtained correct bits based on a majority algorithm. When the sender and receiver had two VCPUs, all communication attempts failed. This result was natural because the domain scheduler was likely to assign two distinct physical cores to each domain. When the number of VCPUs in the sender and the receiver were both eight, most communication resulted in bit errors. We assume that the bit errors were caused by competition for physical cores among processes in a receiver group. When the sender and the receiver had a different number of VCPUs, success rates were low. We currently hypothesize that the most influential factor for high success rates is that the number of VCPUs in a receiver domain is close to the number of physical cores, and another influential factor is that the number of VCPUs in a sender domain is close to the number of physical cores.

6 Summary and Future Work

Compared with covert channel in traditional operating systems, networks, databases, covert channel research in cloud computing environment is still in an embryonic stage. As with the traditional host, different network environments, the lack of formal definition, systematic approach to identifying threats metrics and corresponding safety standards in cloud computing covert channel research. This article only discusses the feasibility of the channel, does not study in-depth on how to improve the channel's bandwidth and decrease the error rate. There is a need on how to choose the method of interference and interference factor in limiting covert channels while maintaining the overall system performance.

Acknowledgement. This research was supported by the Fundamental Research Funds for the Central Universities (FRF-TP-13-015A) and the Conjunction Project of Guangdong Province and Ministry of Education on integration of production, education and research (2012B091000052).

References

1. Chen, H.: Research on the technology to enhance the credibility of cloud computing platform. Fudan University, p. 10 (2008)
2. Nance, K., Bishop, M., Hay, B.: Virtual machine introspection: observation or interference? IEEE Secur. Priv. 6(5), 32–37 (2008)
3. Wang, Y., Wu, J., Zeng, H.: The research on covert channel. J. Softw. 21(9), 2262–2288 (2010)
4. Ahsan, K., Kundur D.: Practical data hiding in TCP/IP. In: Proceedings of the ACM Wksp. Multimedia Security, pp. 1–8 (2002)
5. Aviram, A., Hu, S., Ford, B., Gummadi, R.: Determinating timing channels in compute clouds. In: CCSW '10: Proceedings of the 2010 ACM workshop on Cloud Computing Security Workshop, pp. 103–108. ACM, New York (2010)
6. O'Reilly, Programming Amazon Web Services, 15 March 2008
7. Qin, S.: Analysis of covert channel in high security level operating system. J. Softw. 15(12), 1837–1849 (2004)

Adaptive Synchronization of Complex Networks with Time-Varying Delay Nodes and Delay Coupling

Yu Zhang$^{(\boxtimes)}$ and Feiyan Li

College of Science, Civil Aviation University of China, Tianjin, China
121122517@qq.com

Abstract. A novel adaptive synchronization scheme for complex network with time-varying delay and delay coupling is proposed in this paper. Based on Lyapunov stability theory, a linear adaptive controller is designed which can be used in the future practical engineering. Sufficient experimental results on the network synchronization are given to ensure that the dynamic network can synchronize the individual node state in any specified networks. Finally, numerical simulations show the good performance of this proposed scheme.

Keywords: Adaptive synchronization · Time-varying delay · Lyapunov stability theorem

1 Introduction

Nowadays, complex networks have been intensively investigate across fields of science and engineering [1–5], for lots of systems in nature can be described by the model of complex network, such as the Internet, communication networks, word wide web, food web, and so on. In fact, synchronization is a kind of typical collective behaviors and basic motions in nature.

System with time delays is quite ubiquitous in nature. The time delays are usually caused by the tolerance of some reaction itself in communication and epidemic transportation tetrad or by the tolerance of some reaction itself in communication and epidemic, respectively. Therefore, time delays should be modeled in order to simulating more realistic networks. In [6] C. Li and G. Chen introduced complex dynamical network and investigate their synchronization phenomena and criteria. In [7] J. Zhou and T. Chen investigated synchronization dynamics of a general model of complex delayed networks as well as the effects of time delays. In [8], Atay provided synchronization of couples network with coupling delays, and found proper time. Daly may be helpful to synchronization. Of course, there are also some other previous works [9, 10] and so on are introduced in this area.

These works involved mainly focus on delay nodes and global coupling networks with time delay τ, which is usually a constant. Nevertheless, many real networks are not so. Thereby, we study adaptive synchronization of complex network with time-varying delay nodes and delay coupling, which can better explain a variety of dynamic characteristics and provide theoretic references for the control of real networks.

Y. Yuan et al. (Eds.): ISCTCS 2013, CCIS 426, pp. 283–289, 2014.
DOI: 10.1007/978-3-662-43908-1_36, © Springer-Verlag Berlin Heidelberg 2014

The rest of the paper is organized as follows: in Sect. 2 the hypothesis, lemma and model have been proposed. And then, based on Lyapunov stability theory, we study the sufficient condition and corollary of synchronization on networks. In Sect. 3, we give numerical simulations, and the conclusion was presented in Sect. 4.

2   Adaptive Synchronization of Complex Networks with Time-Varying Delay

This section introduces an uncertain complex dynamical model and gives some preliminary definitions and hypotheses. Consider an uncertain nonlinear coupling dynamical network consisting of N identical nodes, which is described as follows:

$$\dot{x}_i(t) = f_1(x_i, t) + f_2(x_i(t - \tau(t)), t) + g_i(x(t - \tau(t))) + u_i \tag{1}$$

For all $t \geq 0$, where $1 \leq i \leq N$, $x_i = (x_{i1}, x_{i2}, \ldots, x_{in})^T \in R^n$ is the state vector of ith node;

$f_k : R^n \times R^+ \rightarrow R^n, k = 1, 2$ are smooth nonlinear function; $g_j : R^m \rightarrow R^n$ are uncertain continuous nonlinear coupling functions, where $m = nN, 1 \leq j \leq N$; The delay $\tau(t)$ is nonnegative continuous functions; $u_i \in R^n$ are the control inputs.

$$x_i(t - \tau(t)) = (x_{i1}(t - \tau(t)), x_{i2}(t - \tau(t)), \ldots, x_{in}(t - \tau(t)))^T$$

$$x(t - \tau(t)) = (x_1(t - \tau(t)), x_2(t - \tau(t)), \ldots, x_N(t - \tau(t)))^T$$

When the network realizes synchronization, there will be $x_1 = x_2 = \ldots = x_N$. At the same time, the coupled control terms will disappear, namely $g_i(x(t - \tau(t))) + u_i = 0, 1 \leq i \leq N$. This will ensure that an arbitrary solution $x_i(t)$ of single nodes is also a solution of the synchronous coupling network.

Take $s(t)$ as the solution of isolated node in network, and assume that the solution is existent and unique, then this solution satisfies:

$$\dot{s}(t, \tau(t)) = f_1(s(t), t) + f_2(s(t - \tau(t)), t)$$

$$s(t - \tau(t)) = (s_1(t - \tau(t)), s_2(t - \tau(t)), \ldots, s_n(t - \tau(t)))^T \tag{2}$$

where $s(t)$ can be generated an equilibrium point, a periodic orbit, a periodic orbit, or a chaotic orbit in the phase apace.

Define error vector as follows:

$$e_i(t) = x_i(t) - s(t), \quad 1 \leq i \leq N \tag{3}$$

Then the objective of controller u_i is to guide the dynamical network (1) to synchronize. That is

$$\lim_{t \rightarrow \infty} \|e_i(t)\|_2 = \lim_{t \rightarrow \infty} \|x_i(t) - s(t, \tau(t))\|_2 = 0, 1 \leq i \leq N \tag{4}$$

According to Eqs. (1) and (2), we have:

$$\dot{e}_i = \tilde{f}_1(x_i, s) + \tilde{f}_2(x_i(t - \tau(t)), s) + \tilde{g}_i(\boldsymbol{x}(t - \tau(t)), s) + u_i \tag{5}$$

where $\tilde{f}_1(x_i, s) = f_1(x_i, t) - f_1(s, t)$

$$\tilde{f}_2(x_i(t - \tau(t)), s) = f_2(x_i(t - \tau(t)), t) - f_2(s, t)$$

$$\tilde{g}_i(\boldsymbol{x}(t - \tau(t)), s) = g_i(\boldsymbol{x}(t - \tau(t)), t) - g_i(s, s, \ldots, s), 1 \le i \le N$$

Make Eq. (5) partly lined at $s(t, \tau(t))$:

$$\dot{e}_i = A(t)e_i + B(t)e_i(t - \tau(t)) + \tilde{g}_i(\boldsymbol{x}(t - \tau(t)), s) + u_i \ 1 \le i \le N \tag{6}$$

where $A(t) = Df_1(s, t) \ B(t) = Df_2(s, t)$ is Jacobin matrix of $f_k(k = 1, 2)$, and $e_i = x_i(t) - s(t, \tau(t))$

In the following, we will give a hypothesis and lemma:

Hypothesis 1. (H1) Assume that there exists a nonnegative constant α, β and $\gamma_{ij}, i, j = 1, 2, \ldots, N$, satisfying

$$\|A(t)\|_2 \le \alpha \|B(t)\|_2 \le \beta, \tag{7}$$

$$\|\tilde{g}_i(\boldsymbol{x}(t - \tau(t)), s)\|_2 \le \sum_{j=1}^N \gamma_{ij} \|e_j(t - \tau(t))\|_2, \ \gamma_{ij} > 0 \tag{8}$$

Remark 1. If (H1) holds, then we get:

$$\left\| (A(t) + A^T(t))/2 \right\|_2 \le \alpha \tag{9}$$

Lemma 1. [11] If x and y are vectors, and ε is nonnegative constant, then the following inequality hold:

$$2x^T y \le \varepsilon x^T x + \frac{1}{\varepsilon} y^T y \tag{10}$$

Theorem 1. Let the hypothetical condition and Lemma are satisfied and $\dot{\tau}(t) < \sigma(\sigma < 1)$. Then the synchronous solution $s(t)$ of uncertain dynamical network (1) is asymptotic stable under the adaptive controllers

$$u_i = -d_i e_i \qquad i = 1, 2, \ldots, N \tag{11}$$

and updating laws:

$$\dot{d}_i = k_i e_i^T e_i = k_i \|e_i\|_2^2, \ i = 1, 2, \ldots, N \tag{12}$$

where $k_i, i = 1, 2, \ldots, N$ are positive constants.

Proof. Consider the Lyapunov candidate as follows:

$$V = \frac{1}{2}\sum_{i=1}^{N} e_i^T e_i + \frac{1}{2}\sum_{i=1}^{N} \frac{(d_i - \hat{d}_i)^2}{k_i} + \frac{1}{1-\sigma}\sum_{i=1}^{N}\int_{t-\tau(t)}^{t} e_i^T(s)e_i(s)ds \qquad (13)$$

where $\hat{d}_i$ $(1 \leq i \leq N)$ are positive constants to be determined.

The derivation of $V(t)$ along the system (6) is:

$$\dot{V} = \frac{1}{2}\sum_{i=1}^{N}(\dot{e}^T e_i + e_i^T \dot{e}_i) + \sum_{i=1}^{N}(d_i - \hat{d}_i)e_i^T e_i$$

$$+ \sum_{i=1}^{N}\frac{e_i^T e_i}{1-\sigma} - \sum_{i=1}^{N}\frac{1-\dot{\tau}(t)}{1-\sigma}e_i^T(t-\tau(t))e_i(t-\tau(t))$$

$$= \sum_{i=1}^{N} e_i^T\left(\frac{A^T(t)+A(t)}{2} - \hat{d}_i I_n + \frac{1}{1-\sigma}I_n\right)e_i + \sum_{i=1}^{N} e_i^T \tilde{g}_i(x(t-\tau(t)),s)$$

$$+ \sum_{i=1}^{N} e_i^T B e_i(t-\tau(t)) - \sum_{i=1}^{N}\frac{1-\dot{\tau}(t)}{1-\sigma}e_i^T(t-\tau(t))e_i(t-\tau(t))$$

$$\leq \sum_{i=1}^{N} e_i^T\left(\frac{A^T(t)+A(t)}{2} - \hat{d}_i I_n + \frac{1}{1-\sigma}I_n\right)e_i$$

$$+ \sum_{i=1}^{N}\frac{1}{2}\left(e_i^T(t-\tau(t))e_i(t-\tau(t)) + e_i^T B(t)B^T(t)e_i\right)$$

$$+ \sum_{i=1}^{N}\sum_{j=1}^{N}\|e_i^T\|_2 \gamma_{ij}\|e_j(t-\tau(t))\|_2 - \sum_{i=1}^{N}\frac{1-\dot{\tau}(t)}{1-\sigma}e_i^T(t-\tau(t))e_i(t-\tau(t))$$

$$\leq \sum_{i=1}^{N} e_i^T\left(\alpha + \frac{\beta^2}{2} - \hat{d}_i + \frac{1}{1-\sigma}\right)e_i + \sum_{i=1}^{N}\frac{1}{2}e_i^T(t-\tau(t))e_i(t-\tau(t))$$

$$+ \sum_{i=1}^{N}\sum_{j=1}^{N}\|e_i^T\|_2 \gamma_{ij}\|e_j(t-\tau(t))\|_2 - \sum_{i=1}^{N}\frac{1-\dot{\tau}(t)}{1-\sigma}e_i^T(t-\tau(t))e_i(t-\tau(t))$$

$$= \left(\alpha + \frac{\beta^2}{2} + \frac{1}{1-\sigma} - \hat{d}_i\right)e^T e + e^T \Gamma e(t-\tau(t)) - \frac{1}{2}e^T(t-\tau(t))e(t-\tau(t))$$

$$- \sum_{i=1}^{N}\frac{1-\dot{\tau}(t)}{1-\sigma}e_i^T(t-\tau(t))e_i(t-\tau(t))$$

$$\leq \left(\alpha + \frac{\beta^2}{2} + \frac{1}{1-\sigma} - \hat{d}_i\right)e^T e + \frac{1}{2}e^T \Gamma^T \Gamma e + e^T(t-\tau(t))e(t-\tau(t))$$

$$- \frac{1-\dot{\tau}(t)}{1-\sigma}e^T(t-\tau(t))e(t-\tau(t))$$

$$< \left(\alpha + \frac{\beta^2}{2} + \frac{1}{1-\sigma} - \hat{d}_i\right)e^T e + \frac{1}{2}e^T \Gamma^T \Gamma e \,(\dot{\tau}(t) < \sigma(\sigma < 1))$$

$$< \left(\alpha + \frac{\beta^2}{2} + \frac{1}{1-\sigma} - \hat{d}_i\right)e^T e + \frac{1}{2}e^T \Gamma^T \Gamma e \,(\dot{\tau}(t) < \sigma(\sigma < 1))$$

where $\mathbf{e} = \left(\|e_1\|_2, \|e_2\|_2, \ldots, \|e_N\|_2 \right)^T$,

$$\mathbf{e}(t - \tau(t)) = \left(\|e_1(t - \tau(t))\|_2, \|e_2(t - \tau(t))\|_2, \ldots, \|e_N(t - \tau(t))\|_2 \right)^T \text{ and } \boldsymbol{\Gamma}$$
$$= (\gamma_{ij})_{N \times N}$$

Since α, β, σ and γ_{ij} $(1 \le i, j \le N)$ are nonnegative constants, one can select suitable constants $\hat{d}_i$ $(1 \le i \le N)$, to make $diag\left\{ \alpha + \frac{\beta^2}{2} + \frac{1}{1-\sigma} - \hat{d}_1, \ldots, \alpha + \frac{\beta^2}{2} + \frac{1}{1-\sigma} - \hat{d}_N \right\} + \frac{1}{2}\mathbf{e}^T \boldsymbol{\Gamma}\boldsymbol{\Gamma}^T$ to be a negative definite matrix. Thus it follows error vector $e_i(t) \to 0$ $(1 \le i \le N)$ as $t \to \infty$. That is the synchronous solution $s(t)$ of uncertain dynamical network (1) is asymptotic stable. The proof is thus completed.

For linear coupling, H1 is naturally satisfied. Thus one get the following corollary.

Corollary 1. Let the hypothetical condition is satisfied, and $\dot{\tau}(t) < \sigma\,(\sigma < 1), g_j :$ $R^m \to R^n$ are uncertain continuous linear coupling functions, where $m = nN$. We also get asymptotic stable under the adaptive controllers (11) and (12).

3 Numerical Simulation

This section presents an example to show the effectiveness of above synchronization criterions. Consider the coupling function $g_i(\mathbf{x}(t - \tau(t))) = \sum_{j=1}^{N} c_{ij}x_j(t - \tau(t))$. Obviously, it satisfied previous hypothetical condition, where c_{ij} is an unknown parameter, the node dynamical function is $\dot{x} = -\lambda x + \gamma x(t - \tau)(1 - x(t - \tau)), \tau = 0.1$. This network is formed by the Logistic system with two balanced points $s_0 = 0$, $s_1 = 1 - \lambda/\gamma$. When $\lambda = 26, \gamma = 104$, the system will begin chaotic state. For simplicity, we investigate the network with ten nodes with time-varying delays, coupling strength between nodes are 0.1, $\tau(t) = 0.1 - 0.02\sin(5t)$.

The dynamical system is described as follows:

$$\dot{x}_{i1} = -26x_{i1} + 104x_{i1}(t - \tau(t))(1 - x_{i1}(t - \tau(t))) + 0.1x_{i-1\,1}(t - \tau(t))$$
$$+ 0.1x_{i+1\,1}(t - \tau(t))$$

$$\dot{x}_{i2} = -26x_{i2} + 104x_{i2}(t - \tau(t))(1 - x_{i2}(t - \tau(t))) + 0.1x_{i-1\,2}(t - \tau(t))$$
$$+ 0.1x_{i+1\,2}(t - \tau(t))$$

$$\dot{x}_{i3} = -26x_{i3} + 104x_{i3}(t - \tau(t))(1 - x_{i3}(t - \tau(t))) + 0.1x_{i-1\,3}(t - \tau(t))$$
$$+ 0.1x_{i+1\,3}(t - \tau(t))$$

When $i = 1$, we can get:

$$\dot{x}_{11} = -26x_{11} + 104x_{11}(t - \tau(t))(1 - x_{11}(t - \tau(t))) + 0.1x_{2\,1}(t - \tau(t))$$
$$+ 0.1x_{10\,1}(t - \tau(t))$$

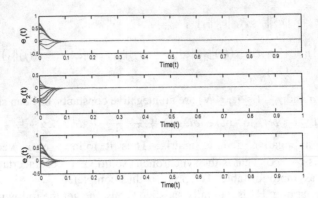

Fig. 1. $k_i = 5$

$$\dot{x}_{12} = -26x_{12} + 104x_{12}(t - \tau(t))(1 - x_{12}(t - \tau(t))) + 0.1x_{2\,2}(t - \tau(t))$$
$$+ 0.1x_{10\,2}(t - \tau(t))$$

$$\dot{x}_{13} = -26x_{13} + 104x_{13}(t - \tau(t))(1 - x_{13}(t - \tau(t))) + 0.1x_{2\,3}(t - \tau(t))$$
$$+ 0.1x_{10\,3}(t - \tau(t))$$

In the same way, when $i = 10$.

Take $s = 1 - \lambda/\gamma = 0.75$ as the goal of synchronization. When $\alpha = 1$, $\beta = 2$, $\sigma = 0.5$ and $\hat{d}_i > 6$, obviously, which satisfies assumption.

As described in Figs. 1 and 2, for the case of identical topological structures, the larger the control strengths $k_i, i = 1, 2, \ldots, N$, the faster the convergence to synchronization.

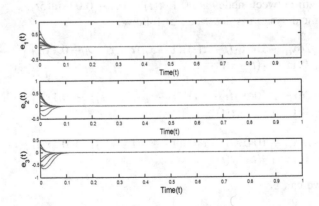

Fig. 2. $k_i = 10$

4   Conclusion

This paper mainly studied the adaptive synchronization of complex network with time-varying delay, which relates to both nodes and coupling. Based on Lyapunov stability theory, the sufficient condition and Corollary of adaptive synchronization were also given to guarantee that the dynamical network synchronizes at individual node state in arbitrary specified network. Finally, the numerical simulations results showed the validity of theory.

References

1. Albert, R., Barabasi, A.L.: Statistical mechanics of complex networks. Mod. Phys. **74**(1), 47–97 (2002)
2. Wang, X., Chen, G.: Complex networks: small-world, scale-free and beyond. IEEE Circ. Syst. **3**(1), 6–20 (2003)
3. Lü, J., Yu, X., Chen, G., Cheng, D.: Characterizing the synchronizability of small-world dynamical networks. IEEE Trans. Circ. Syst. **51**(4), 787–796 (2004)
4. Liu, Y.Z., Jiang, C.S., Lin, C.S., et al.: Chaotic synchronization secure communications based on the Lorenz systems switch. J. Electron. Inf. Technol. **29**(11), 2641–2644 (2009)
5. Zhou, J., Xiang, L., Liu, Z.R.: Synchronization in complex delayed dynamical networks with impulsive effects. Phys. A **384**, 684–692 (2007)
6. Li, C., Chen, G.: Synchronization in general complex delayed dynamical networks with coupling delays. Phys. A **2004**(343), 263–278 (2004)
7. Zhou, J., Chen, T.: Synchronization in general complex delayed dynamical networks. IEEE Trans. Circ. Syst. Reg. Pap. **53**(3), 733–744 (2006)
8. Atay, F., Masoller, F.: Complex transitions to synchronization in delay-coupled networks of logistic maps. Final Version Eur. Phys. **62**(5), 119–126 (2011)
9. Yang, Z.Q., Liu, Z.X.: Adaptive synchronization of uncertain complex delayed dynamical networks. Int. J. Nonlinear Sci. **3**(2), 125–132 (2007)
10. Luo, Q., Wu, W., Li, L.X., Yang, Y.X., Peng, H.P.: Adaptive synchronization re search on the uncertain complex networks with time-delay. ACTA Phys. Sin. **57**(3), 60–65 (2008)
11. Li, P., Yi, Z.: Synchronization analysis of delay complex networks with time-varying couplings. Phys. A **87**(3), 3729–3737 (2008)

Gigabit Ethernet Data Transfer Based on FPGA

Shihong Zhou$^{(\boxtimes)}$ and Lin Yao

School of Computer and Communication Engineering, University of Science and Technology Beijing, Beijing, China
hnliuqian@163.com

Abstract. With the development of integrated module, FPGA chip becomes more and more popular. Except for some special application, FPGA devices need an effective mechanism to receive and send data. The general FPGA is suitable for the connection technology of PCI Express. We always use it as a communication scheme between PC and FPGA board. However, the shortcoming is that the PCI Express scheme is expensive. Theoretically, we propose a very effective communication structure, which with core of UDP/IP is a point to point structure. We found that it can establish stable communication connection between PC and FPGA through combining IPV4 with UDP protocol by hardware. Through a simple way to calculate the frame header and to check IPv4 (supposing every computing model based on FPGA), we use less resource to achieve the establishment of a communication connection between PC and FPGA.

Keywords: PGA · Gigabit Ethernet · UDP

1 Introduction

Recent years, the Field Programable Gate Array (FGAP) chips or universal custom chips are becoming more and more popular [1]. With high-speed processing capacity, FPGA is easy to implement in large-scale systems. Except for some special application, FPGA devices need an effective mechanism to receive and send data. To exploit the full potential of FPGA, the time waiting for I/O operation of it should be minimized.

Currently, the common use of connect technology for FPGA is PCI Express. However, there are several drawbacks when using PCI Express as the solution of communication between PC and FPGA. First, there must be dedicated driver for PCI Express and not all of the FPGA chips support PCI Express. Recently, Xilinx developed a design for PCI Express [2]. But it also include PC driver. Similar to this, Alter PCI Express solutions also need to pay for it.

To solve this problem, we consider the use of Ethernet-based solutions. Because the development of Gigabit Ethernet and related applications based on PC are already quite mature, and PC port to an Ethernet port only requires a small amount of code and common hardware modules. These years, with the upgrading of the processing capacity of FPGA, FPGA-based Gigabit Ethernet system can achieve efficient transmission. Therefore, there is a very broad application prospects and great potential

Y. Yuan et al. (Eds.): ISCTCS 2013, CCIS 426, pp. 290–296, 2014.
DOI: 10.1007/978-3-662-43908-1_37, © Springer-Verlag Berlin Heidelberg 2014

economic value on the study of FPGA-based Gigabit Ethernet data network technology.

We designed a UDP communications platform. The key to this platform is that all static fields are stored in table where we call it as LUT. This design requires user to manually configure the device to initialize the table. When FPGA send data, many fields of information can directly be searched in LUT. So it just need to deal with non-static fields.

2 Static and Other Field

Considering the sending of UDP package need to go through UDP and IP encapsulation and many of the fields can be set in advance, we define these fields are static fields. The other fields which require calculation based on user data are non-static fields.

We use Internet Protocol (IP) and User Datagram Protocol UDP [2, 3]. As the issue only considers the special circumstances of FPGA applications, we define the values of many fields in IP packets and UDP packets are fixed, which are stored in the LUT. We call these fields as static field. Except the total length, header checksum of IPv4 and the length of UDP are non-static fields, the others are static. For these no-static fields, we need external logic to calculate.

3 Algorithm of Checksum

The standard calculation method of the checksum is defined in RFC 791 [4]. The checksum of IP only covers the header, while the data are not considered. The checksum of UDP and TCP need to cover the data.

During the computation progress, the actual value of the checksum field is set to zero. Then, we calculate the 16-bit of the one's complement sum of all 16-bit words in the header. When it receives an IP datagram, the receiver performs the same calculation process. Because the calculation process of the receiver contains the value of checksum from the sender, the receiver calculates the result should be 1 if there is no error during the transmission. If it is not 1, the receiver will drop the datagram.

Figure 1 shows the Flow chart about algorithm of checksum.

4 Transmission Unit of UDP

We have already described the static field and non-static field. Static field stored in the RAM, it can be read directly. The value of length fields can be got by adder. While the value of checksum need to be got by the checksum model. We should note that the checksum of UDP is optional, and this field is not to be used. So the value is 0.

The flow chart of the transmission is illustrated in Figs. 2 and 3. The output data of UDP transmission unit is chosen by a multiplexer between LUT, adder and the user input data bus.

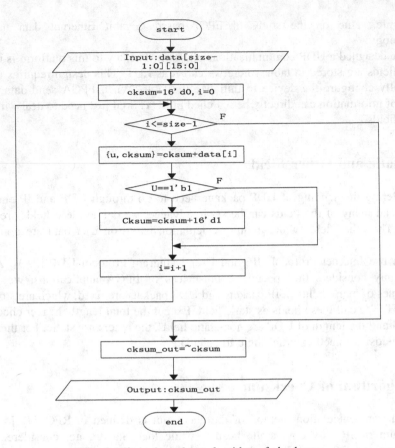

Fig. 1. Flow chart about algorithm of checksum

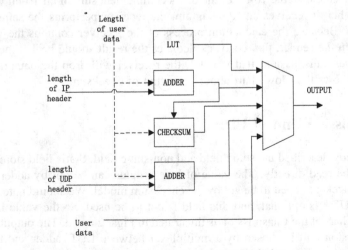

Fig. 2. Flow chart of the transmission

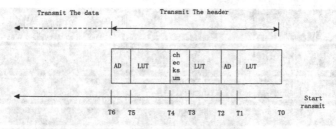

Fig. 3. Time of the transmit

As shown in Fig. 3, the system is starting to transmit a packet at T0 time. The static field header, which is stored in the LUT, is transmitted first during the time interval between T0 with T1. This progress requires 16 clock cycles. The Total Length IP and Length UDP fields are non-static fields. They are calculated by the respective adders. The transmission of LUT content stops at the 17th clock cycle, and the total Length is transmitted during the interval between T1 with T2, which is calculated by the adder. This progress requires 2 clock cycles. Then, the output is read from the LUT, this process lasts 6 clock cycles during the interval between T2 with T. When the protocol field has been transmitted, the progress of checksum will start between time T3 to T4. Then, the final several static fields are transmitted for 12 clock cycles between interval T4 with T5. After this interval, it comes to the UDP length during the interval between T5 with T6. When all static and no-static fields have been transmitted, we will start to send userdata.

5 Simulation Program

The simulation software environment is the ISE 14.2 suit [5, 6], which is developed by Xilinx. Hardware environment is the high-speed transceiver platform based on the Virtex-6 FPGA chip.

5.1 Simulation of Checksum

Figure 4 shows the simulation result of checksum.

In the Fig. 4, the data [15:0] is the input signal, and checksum out [15:0] is the output signal.

In the simulation, enter a set of data "4500 0031 89F5 0000 6E06 0000 DEB7 455D C0A8 00DC". We can see that, through the checksum module, the output data is DD38. This proves that checksum module can meet the design requirements.

5.2 Simulation of UDP

We defined the value of static fields as:
    Destination MAC Address: C8-9C-DC-F6-0D-48;
    Source MAC Address: FF- FF - FF - FF -...;

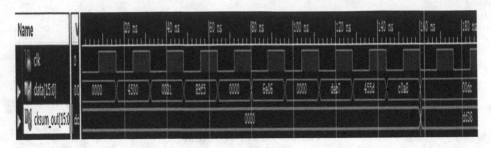

Fig. 4. Simulation result of checksum

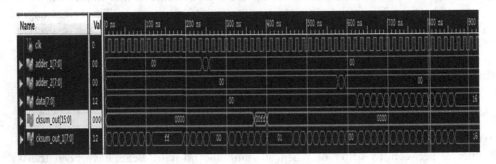

Fig. 5. Simulation result of UDP

Type: 00001000-00000000; Version and Header Length: 01000101; Service: 00000000;

Total Length range: 00000000-00100100 (20 + 8 + length of data);

Identification: 00000000-00000000; Flags and Fragment Offset: 0100000000000 00000;

Time To Live: 01000000; Protocol: 00010001; Header Checksum;

Source IP Address 1-1-1-2; Destination IP Address C0 (192)-A8(168)-8-1;

Source Port 13-C8(5064); Destination Port 13- C9(5065); Length 00000000-00010000; Checksum 00000000–00000000; User data.

Figure 5 shows the simulation result.

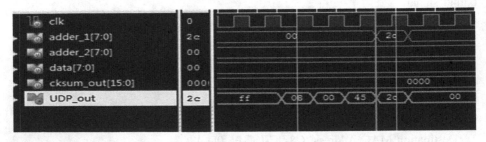

Fig. 6. Time of adder_1[7:0]

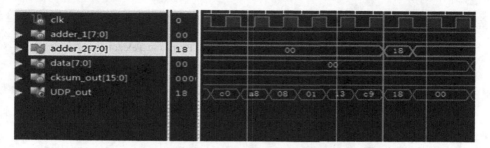

Fig. 7. Time of adder_1[7:0]

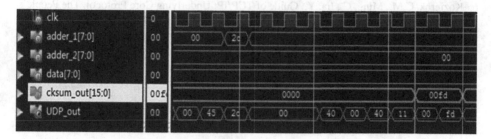

Fig. 8. Time of checksum

The yellow single is the final output data of UDP. The adder_1[7:0] and adder_2[7:0] are calculating the length IP and UDP. Enlargement Fig. 5 will get the next few chat. Figure 6 shows the time of adder_1[7:0]. Figure 7 shows the time of adder_2 [7:0]. Figure 8 shows the time of checksum.

From the simulation results, we can see the design meets the design requirements and we have achieved the sending of UDP.

6 Conclusion

This issue is designed for a particular system to achieve high-speed data transmission between the PC and FPGA based on Gigabit Ethernet. As a high-speed interface of PC and FPGA, it is important to design data transmission based on Gigabit Ethernet. We design a new architecture based on the Gigabit Ethernet for an efficient communication between a PC and a FPGA.

Acknowledgement. This research was supported by the National Natural Science Foundation of China (No. 61072039) and Special Fund for the Development of the Internet of things of the Ministry of Industry and Information Technology: Integrated Information Service Platform for Internet of Things of Hebei Logistics.

References

1. Chen, W.: Design of Altera FPGA/CPLD. The People's Posts and Telecommunications Press (Posts & Telecom Press), Beijing (2005). (EDA Pioneer Studios)
2. Xilinx: Bus Master DMA Performance Demonstration Reference Design for the Xilinx Endpoint PCI Express Solutions. http://www.xilinx.com/support/documentation/application ~ notes/xapp1052.pdf (accessed 03 February 2010)
3. IEEE Draft P802.3z/D3. Media Access Control (MAC) Parameters, Physical Layer, Repeater and Management Parameters for 1000 Mb/s operation, June 1997. http://standards.ieee.org/faqs/order.html
4. Virtex-6 FPGA Select IO Resources User Guide
5. Virtex-6 FPGA Embedded Tri-Mode Ethernet MAC User Guide
6. Kozierok, C.M., Ming, C., Jia, Y.: Guide of TCP/IP: Underlying Core Protocol. The People's Posts and Telecommunications Press (Posts & Telecom Press), Beijing (2008)
7. Postel, J.: Internet Protocol, RFC 791 (Standard), Internet Engineering Task Force, September 1981. (Updated by RFC 1349)

Research on Efficient Dynamic Cloud Storage Ciphertext Access Control

Ningning Song[✉], Zhen Mei, and Lin Yao

School of Computer and Communication Engineering,
University of Science and Technology Beijing, Beijing 100083, China
6221294@163.com

Abstract. Cloud storage, a new service system, springs up after the development of cloud computing. Along with the birth of cloud computing, massive data storage needs specialized cloud storage service provider to provide. Ciphertext traditional access control is achieved by controlling the ciphertext key management and distribution of keys for each file to be distributed to each user. However, in case of changing a file's access permissions, the calculation of data for the Lord's re-encryption computation is considerably large. Therefore, on the basis of attribute-based encryption and appropriate design of encrypted calculation, part of the calculation of re-encrypted data moves to the Cloud storage provider side without disclosing additional information design of appropriate encryption algorithm, so that the effective processing by the cloud could significantly improve the access time and improve the computational efficiency. The effectiveness of the plan has been verified through model experiment described at the end of the paper.

Keywords: Cloud storage · Attribute-based encryption · Ciphertext · Access control

1 Introduction

Along with the development of cloud computing, cloud storage came into being. The simple cloud-oriented access control data stored on the server side is realized under completely credible circumstances. The protective measures of uploading the plaintext data onto the cloud storage platform is thereby fully provided by the cloud storage service provider [1]. However, faced with a complex network environment and ever-changing commercial interests, it has been a question held by several users that whether cloud storage service providers are able to ensure the effectiveness of security mechanisms, or whether their commercial secrets are properly kept, or in another word, whether the provider is trustworthy. The ensuing text access control technology should be built on the circumstance that the server side is not trustworthy, which is an assumption in line with the psychology of the majority of the users. In this case, there is no need to worry about any unauthorized access. At present, several studies have been insofar done in the secret access control [2, 3]. In the initial ciphertext access control method, each data file owner uses separate keys to encrypt the data and distributes the files to the authorized users, or authorize the users to access the server to get the data key in the sever end after the users encrypt the public key on the

Y. Yuan et al. (Eds.): ISCTCS 2013, CCIS 426, pp. 297–303, 2014.
DOI: 10.1007/978-3-662-43908-1_38, © Springer-Verlag Berlin Heidelberg 2014

encrypted data. By doing so, if some change takes place to the user's authority, the required amount of computation will be substantial. For example, 1,000 files correspond to 1,000 authorized users; but when the access right is changed, the need for calculation formula 1,000 * 1,000 = 1,000,000 times to calculate the key and distribution. The amount of computation is too great. Therefore, the attribute-based encryption algorithm is proposed.

There have been many current ciphertext access controls for the studies conducted. Such methods can solve the problem of data confidentiality [4–9], but due to the fact that the acquisition of the key users of the data is fully controlled by the data owner, the complexity of right management will significantly increate based on the data volume and growth of sub, leading to the bottleneck in the owner end. So we designed a ciphertext for cloud storage access control system, through which part of the calculation was handled by the cloud side.

2 System Framework Design

While structuring the experimental platform for the entire cloud storage, we mainly simulated data owners' application of the main data file permissions, design and develop the system by means of today's popular Java language combined with the application of Web Design. Summary architecture design is shown in Fig. 1.

User client module is designed by the user in order to achieve ciphertext control. The user logs into the user files based on identity management module, in which user or file is assigned with different access control permissions. These permissions management processes are done in the background processing module with logic processing, including the uploaded file encryption, file access control structure generation, and so on. The main provider of cloud service providers end database and file storage, which also includes a portion of the data processing. In this module, the re-key encryption process is completed.

3 Algorithm Design

The ciphertext file encryption uses symmetric encryption algorithm, but for the key encryption algorithm, this paper uses an asymmetric algorithm. Through the transformation of the access control structure of CP-ABE, we designed an algorithm to meet the requirements which we called SCP-ABE. SCP-ABE is to achieve the re-encryption of the cloud base. In describing the SCP-ABE, we ought to make the following definition [1, 5].

Definition 1. Simple access control structure (SAS). If an access control structure is to meet the following three characteristics:

1. Containing only 'and' and 'or' relationships;
2. Being disjunctive;
3. The degree of each node 'and' most being 2.

This structure is called a simple access control structure.

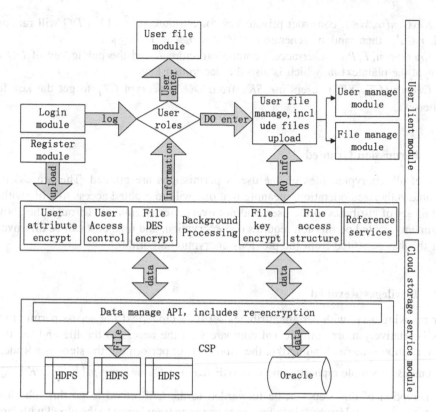

Fig. 1. Schematic framework

Definition 2. Simple access control structure secret sharing (SSS, SAS secret sharing). SAS is set to be the root node of shared values s. Starting from the root node s_i for each value of the non-leaf nodes i, top-down assignment is as follows:

If the correspondence i relationship is 'or': set s_i value of each child node i.

If the correspondence i relationship is 'and': take random number s', then set s' as the value of the left child node, while setting $s_i + s'$ as the value of the right child node. This secret sharing method node uses subtraction rather than addition secret sharing. By doing so, it is easier to achieve permission to withdraw.

Definition 3. Simple ciphertext policy attribute-based encryption (SCP-ABE, simple ciphertext-policy attribute-based encryption) algorithm: SCP-ABE includes the following four sub-functions.

Setup() is used to construct the associated space, including encryption using bilinear group, the corresponding bilinear mapping attribute space required for the system. Construct a bilinear group G_0, mind its generator is g, corresponding to the two-lane map $e : G_0 \times G_0 \to G_T$. And define the properties of space systems A, for each attribute $a_i \in A(1 \leq i \leq k)$, generate a random selection $x_i \in G_0(1 \leq i \leq k)$.

KeyGen(*w*, *MK*): construct private key for attribute set *w*. First *DO* will random pick $r \in Z_P^*$, then random generate $r_i \in Z_P^*$ for $a_i \in w(1 \leq i \leq k)$.

Encrypt(*m*, *T*, *PK*): user access control structure *T* and the public key of *DO* to encrypt the plaintext *m*, which is also the decryption key.

Decrypt(CT_T, SK_w): users use SK_w from *DO* to decrypt CT_T to get the key for ciphertext.

3.1 Permission Granted

First of all, encrypted files on the user's permissions are granted. The process has become authorized operation, meaning that one will be granted access to a file with a certain set of attributes to the user, and not every user is granted. Through the above argument, granted permission requires one encryption, and time cost can be improved, and this has benefited from the previous encryption algorithm.

3.2 Privileges Revoked

For revoking users with certain attributes set for a ciphertext file access permissions, this is relatively more complicated compare with the access to the file and the user authorization process. Finding that the time cost for performing the steps is not ideal, we can use a simple ciphertext policy ABE features $C'_{k'_f} = Encrypt\left(k'_f, T'_f, PK\right)$. The re-encryption of this step will be forwarded to the CSP cloud to go through cloud cluster processing. Hereby, since time cost has been transferred to the cloud with large computing power, the efficiency on the client side will be greatly optimized.

We can easily verify the above $C'_{k'_f} = Encrypt\left(k'_f, T'_f, PK\right)$, which further demonstrates that this method is able to achieve CSP cloud re-encryption process.

4 Experimental Analysis

After the design, part of the re-encryption work has been handled for the cloud to process, including part of the work authorization and revocation of operating authority to operate in the part. As described in the previous section, during the authorization process authorized users only need to add a new set of attributes corresponding key, regardless of the size and access control structure. Meanwhile, privilege revocation only requires the re-encryption done by the owners. Other operations, done by the cloud, are irrelevant to the file access control structure. All these will greatly remedy the time cost of the owner.

Here we will design experiments to validate the above analysis. Generally speaking, the number of properties, which are owned by individual users, are relatively limited, fixed, and the size of individual data file access control structures may vary with the complexity of the access rights of their growth [1, 6]. Without loss of generality, we can assume that the user has an average number of attributes to 5, and the data access control structures fluctuate in size from 0 to 50. For a single data file size, three kinds of typical situations, respectively 1 MB, 4 MB and 10 MB were tested. Here are our results. Firstly, we might look at the permissions granted to the performance. The comparison result of the data is listed in Table 1.

Table 1. Time table

Y	5	10	15	20	25	30	35	40
Local	99	98	100	102	98	96	89	120
Gen	220	342	450	576	613	725	829	1093

Y corresponding line indicates the access control data file size of the structure; the unit of the data is millisecond (ms) (Fig. 2).

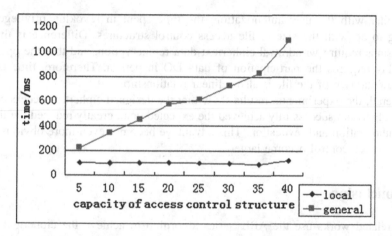

Fig. 2. An authorization files access control time and its relations with size of the structure

The figure displays the time spent on the user authorization cost comparison before and after the use of the designed system. Since the user authorization is only related to the key ciphertext without considering the size of the data file regardless of using the system designed in this paper, there is no need to take the size of the data file into account. In other words, the size of data file does not affect the user's authorization. For brevity, we take the general size of 1 MB for example. Through the figure we can see clearly that with the general ABE algorithm the time it takes for access control and data structure is almost a positive linear relationship when the user is authorized to operate. The greater the access control structure is, the longer time it takes to process authorization. However, such time is not basically and not affected on our system.

The following graph makes a comparison of the time required for users to revoke privileges. The experimental data is shown in Fig. 3.

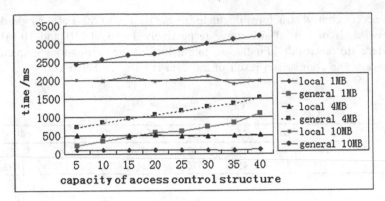

Fig. 3. The relations of one-time privilege revocation and the size of file access control structures

Similar with the user authorization, the time spent in revoking privileges has nothing to do with the size of file access control structures. Difference is that the permissions require withdrawal ciphertext data re-encryption, and that the operation inevitably requires the participation of data DO in person. Therefore, time cost to withdraw the size of the file is also a linear relationship.

Overall, the experimental results show that the designed ciphertext access control system algorithm successfully achieved the expected goal, greatly reduced the time of user authorization and revocation. This advantage becomes even more obvious when the file access control become larger.

5 Conclusion

Many related works use the ABE Series algorithm to achieve the ciphertext cloud storage access control. However, the ciphertext dynamic change requires permission to re-encrypt the data and the distribution of each user's key at the initial stage, causing serious efficiency problems in the era of big data. In line with the high cost of ABE re-encryption, this paper proposes a solution to transfer part of the re-encryption work to the cloud. Through the transformation of the access control structure and transfer of re-encryption work to the cloud, the data owners' management costs could be reduced. Experimental data shows that the scheme is, to some extent, really effective to achieve the established optimization goal. The efficiency of the optimized access control policy increases together with the complexity of control strategies. This is even more obvious along with the growing number of users.

Acknowledgement. This research was supported by the National Natural Science Foundation of China (No. 61072039) and Special Fund for the Development of the Internet of things of the Ministry of Industry and Information Technology: Integrated Information Service Platform for Internet of Things of Hebei Logistics.

References

1. Cheng, H., Zhang, M., Feng, D.: Achieving efficient dynamic cryptographic access control in cloud storage. J. China Inst. Commun. **32**(7), 125–132 (2011)
2. Goyal, V., Pandey, O., Sahai, A.: Attribute-based encryption for fine-grained access control of encrypted data. In: 13th ACM, pp. 89–98 (2010)
3. Bethencourt, J., Sahai, A., Water, B.: Ciphertext-policy attribute-based encryption. In: IEEE Symposium on Security and Privacy, SP'07, pp. 321–334 (2007)
4. Hong, C., Zhang, M., Feng, D.G.: AB-ACCS: a cryptographic access control scheme for cloud storage. J. Comput. Res. Dev. **47**, 259–265 (2010)
5. Lv, Z.Q., Zhang, M., Feng, D.: Cloud storage access control scheme ciphertext of computer science and exploration. Jisuanji Kexue yu Tansuo **5**(9), 835–844 (2011)
6. Sun, G.Z., Dong, Y., Li, Y.: CP-ABE based data access control for cloud storage. J. China Inst. Commun. **32**(7), 146–152 (2011)
7. Liu, F., Yang, M.: Ciphertext policy attribute based encryption scheme for cloud storage. Jisuanji Yingyong Yanjiu **29**(4), 1452–1456 (2012)
8. Yu, S., Wang, C., Ren, K.: Achieving secure, scalable, and fine-grained data access control in cloud computing. In: 2010 Proceedings IEEE INFOCOM, pp. 1–9 (2010)
9. Li, M., Yu, S., Ren, K., Lou, W.: Securing personal health records in cloud computing: patient-centric and fine-grained data access control in multi-owner settings. In: Jajodia, S., Zhou, J. (eds.) SecureComm 2010. LNICST, vol. 50, pp. 89–106. Springer, Heidelberg (2010)

Research on the Inverted Index
Based on Compression and Perception

Ningning Song[✉], Longqun Zou, and Yunluo Liu

School of Computer and Communication Engineering,
University of Science and Technology Beijing, Beijing 100083, China
6221294@163.com

Abstract. Ciphertext retrieval can meet security requirements, but the complex structure of index and retrieval has hindered it from being widely used. This article, taking both safety and efficiency into account, designs an inverted index structure on the basis of compressed sensing to meet the security requirements and full-text retrieval efficiency. Index structure, based on compressed sensing, will be able to effectively resist the statistical analysis attack, static analysis attacks and tracking attacks, so that the index files exist in the form of ciphertext, without decryption in case retrieval. While using chunked encoding compression and indexing sensing technology, the retrieval system could adapt to adjust the storing method and block form of index structure, which can greatly reduce its server requirements and improve the retrieval efficiency. Compressed sensing inverted index structure, based on compressed sensing, will secure a balance in both security and retrieval efficiency, and thus meet the needs of retrieval.

Keywords: Ciphertext retrieval · Security · Efficiency · Index structure

1 Introduction

With the rapid development of information technology, information leakage has turned to be a prominent problem. People are deeply concerned about their information security. At the same time, the full-text search, offering a very efficient mode of information retrieval, has facilitated people to get information. Today, how to meet the demands of full-text retrieval while ensuring the retrieval security has become a key point [1–3]. Now, the ciphertext retrieval is very popular and makes a host of innovations for ciphertext retrieval. In the 1990s, Ostrovsky and Goodrich proposed a scheme that not only ensured that the database administrator could not acquire the data files, but also enabled the ciphertext data to be stored in the database server. This scheme has made tremendous contribution to ciphertext storage and provided a reliable premise for ciphertext retrieval. On a practical stage however, Ostrovsky and Goodrich talked only about storage application, which meant the improvement of storage safety, failed to improve search pattern and efficiency.

Boneh proposed a scheme that was based on keyword and public key searches encryption. The key point of this scheme is public key system. Its feature is to put user identity information and the retrieval keyword together for storage and retrieval [5].

Y. Yuan et al. (Eds.): ISCTCS 2013, CCIS 426, pp. 304–310, 2014.
DOI: 10.1007/978-3-662-43908-1_39, © Springer-Verlag Berlin Heidelberg 2014

Due to this feature, although this method had improved the safety of the ciphertext retrieval, it limited the scope of application. Under the situation of large amount of data and multi-user retrieval, its retrieval efficiency will drop dramatically.

Another retrieval scheme was proposed by Song from California. Its feature is to use symmetric encryption algorithm to encrypt the plaintext. At the same time, its keywords will product random sequence and check sequence, exactly equal to the sum of the ciphertext message length [6]. This scheme has a strong ability to resist the statistical analysis, while it also contains a weakness that each match is done one by one. In this case, it would be difficult to apply in case of large amount of data.

Based on Boolean (Bloom) retrieval mode, Stanford En-Jin Goth proposed his mode by analyzing the text and then building index [7]. This mode could be retrieved when the ciphertext went through the security index. With Bloom searches, this mode had surely improved the safety and retrieval efficiency, but still lacked accuracy and scalability. There existed many obstacles in index maintenance, which was conducive to flexible information storage and retrieval.

At present, retrieval and data encryption ciphertext studies in both China and overseas countries are becoming more mature, but it has a long way to go in terms of full text retrieval [8, 9]. The core issue about Ciphertext retrieve is the safety and efficiency, and the core part of the issue is the ciphertext index file. Therefore, the core problem lays how to build efficient and secure ciphertext index file, so as to meet users' need for both security and efficiency.

2 Design

2.1 System Framework

The server receives a request from the client to handle its word. According to a searched word, the server divides the information. At this time, based on the index positioning, the server retrieves documents, obtains the corresponding result set and returns the results to the client. Later on, the client receives the result set, performs the decryption process, and then sends the required document identifier to the server. The client downloads the ciphertext document, and then the document is decrypted to obtain the plaintext (Fig. 1).

3 Program Implementation

3.1 Compression Index

In terms of the compression technology, we adopt the method of value compression to the logical record address pointer. We put the biggest memory address values as the base, and other value is obtained by subtracting the value into the index structure. Let $L = \{L_1, L_2, \ldots L_n\}$ denote the memory address set, and we set L_t as the biggest memory address value, then according to the definition above, the compression results is $L = \{(L_t - L_1), (L_t - L_2), \ldots, L_t, \ldots, (L_t - L_n)\}$.

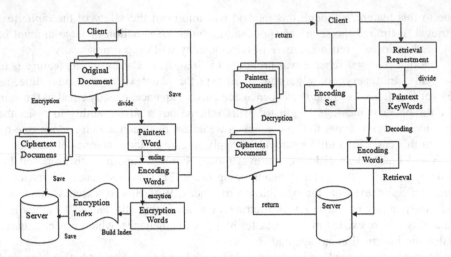

Fig. 1. Ciphertext store and retrieval process

For sure, the index structure also contains a lot of other information such as keywords, the frequency of the keywords in the document, the positions of the keywords in the document. Keyword is in the form of character type, so we can compress it through coding.

Let W denote keyword, let H_W denote hash code value and let = denote ciphertext index. The client encoding keywords, based on the hash value, go through the hash function to find the corresponding keywords list. So the denote hash code value is $H_W = hash(W)$, and information that is stored in the index structure entry is $K_W = E(hash(W))$.

3.2 Encryption Policy and Key Management Strategy

In terms of the encryption algorithm, we use the hardware encryption card and separate encryption and retrieval. The benefit of it lies that encryption algorithm can dynamically change according to the different encrypted content. Meanwhile, the change in algorithm will be more flexible, able to meet the demand of different encryption.

In the process of retrieval, users will enter the identity key to identification and feedback confirmation information after going through the server-side test. Only with the user identity could the user proceed to the next step of retrieval request, for the index file contains encryption granularity. Therefore in the process of retrieval, the keywords, with a retrieval document, will be sent to the server side synchronously. The server decrypts the corresponding index structure through the cipher text form of retrieval. The keywords determine the corresponding ciphertext document information collection. After finishing the cipher text document information collection, document collection with those lines of cipher will be returned to the client; the client then decrypt the cipher text document with the key and get the desired information.

3.3 Dynamic Perception

For index structure, we adopt multi-stage block. The server, while building the index, will determine block level according to the word segmentation information collected after original documents segment the words. Level 1 block for maximum frequency information, which is the most commonly used retrieval word set.

After the gate value perception partitioned, whether partitioned part shall be put into memory is also a dynamic decision. Whether the permanent memory of K value for gate valve, it is defined by the users themselves. When the result is less than the gate valve, a Boolean value is 'yes', that partition will be put into memory, otherwise will not be put into.

4   Performance Analysis

4.1   Build Index Performance

For constructing the ciphertext index, due to the encryption processing and the existence of the block model, the time cost in this process will be much more than that of constructing plaintext. By contrast with the same number of documents, the time performance for both ciphertext index and plaintext index is shown in the following figure (Fig. 2):

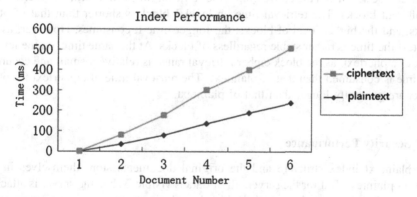

Fig. 2. Index performance

As can be seen from the above simulation, when the number of documents is 1000, 2000 to 6000, the time consumption of plaintext index grows slowly and shorter. On the other hand, for the ciphertext, as it needs to deal with encryption and sensory block processing, the time consumption grows quickly and becomes linear growth. On the basis of the above simulation, it is easy to see that the time consumption of plaintext is faster rather than ciphertext. The consumption of ciphertext index, compared with that of plaintext index, will grows bigger and bigger as the time goes by.

4.2   Retrieval Performance

In the process of retrieval, we need to encrypt the keywords of documents, and then locate the position of the block in the index structure through the client encoding. In the common block index words, since the ciphertext index adopts binary search, its retrieval processing takes relatively less time than that of plaintext index simply because the words to be retrieved are less. The process of retrieving public word will need to locate different blocks. On the other hand, for plaintext, no matter what search terms, it will be looked up in the same order, so its retrieval time will be stable. Specific retrieval performance is shown as follows (Fig. 3):

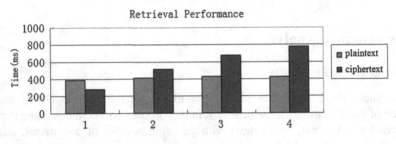

Fig. 3. Index performance

As can be seen from the above graph, the retrieval time differs while ciphertext sits on different blocks. The retrieval time on level 1 block is shorter than that of other blocks; and the higher level of blocks, the longer time it consumes. However, as for plaintext the time is rather stable regardless of blocks. At the same time, on the level 1 block of ciphertext, as the block cipher retrieval range is relatively small and accurate, less time is consumed than that of plaintext. The retrieval time of ciphertext for other blocks are generally longer than that of plaintext.

4.3   Security Performance

Both plaintext index structure and the original documents store themselves in the server as plaintext. But for the server, all of data is visible. When the server is attacked by statistical analysis, static analysis and track analysis, people can easily get access to key information. Even for statistical analysis attacking, making analysis of index structure can lead to key information in the server, so an attack on the entire server is not at all necessary. But for ciphertext retrieval, both index structure and original documents are stored in the server. The client retrieves the keywords on the coding process, at the time of statistical analysis on index structure. It will not be able to obtain keywords retrieval information, and cannot locate the key information of server document. The retrieval process will greatly improve the safety performance. By attacking the number and the number of hits to compare the safety of the retrieval process performance, the effect is as follows (Fig. 4):

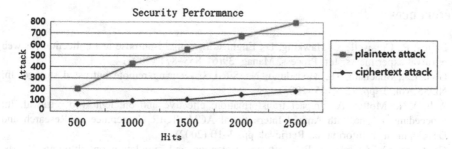

Fig. 4. Security performance

Above attacking performance includes a comprehensive effect of statistical analysis, static analysis and track attack analysis. Within the attack frequency between 500 and 2500, the ciphertext attack hits are obviously less than that of plaintext, and the growing speed is relatively slower. On the contrary, the plaintext attack hits are more than of ciphertext and the growing speed is faster. Therefore, on the same attack numbers, the safety performance of plaintext is definitely far less than that of the ciphertext.

Based on compression perception of ciphertext inverted index structure, due to the compression processing of the ciphertext index structure and dynamic perception of index blocks, the memory consumption of ciphertext is significantly less than that of plaintext. Although plaintext excels in time consumption, it is far weaker than ciphertext in face of outside attacks. Based on the analysis of the full text, we know that the index of the structure in this paper possesses a great deal of flexibility and has good safety performance. The retrieval efficiency can also satisfy the users' basic needs for retrieval.

5   Conclusion

With the development of information technology, people pay more and more for the frequent leakage of information. In the field of full-text retrieval, an urgent problem lies ahead: how to meet people's needs of information security as well as retrieval performance. As described in this paper, the ciphertext index structure, based on compression of perception, can compress the size of the index structure, dynamically load the index structure into memory and encrypt the index structure. It has important meaning for cipher full-text retrieval.

Acknowledgement. This research was supported by the Fundamental Research Funds for the Central Universities (FRF-TP-13-015A) and the Conjunction Project of Guangdong Province and Ministry of Education on integration of production, education and research (2012B091000052).

References

1. Bailey, P., Creswell, N., Hawking, D.: Engineering a multi-purpose test collection for web retrieval experiments. Inf. Process. Manag. **39**(6), 853–871 (2003)
2. Goh, E.J., Shacham, H., Modadugu, N.: SiRiUS: securing remote untrusted storage. In: NDSS, vol. 3, pp. 131–145 (2003)
3. Anh, V.N., Moffat, A.: Impact transformation: effective and efficient web retrieval. In: Proceedings of the 25th Annual International ACM SIGIR Conference on Research and Development in Information Retrieval, pp. 3–10 (2002)
4. Goldreich, O., Ostrovsky, R.: Software protection and simulation on oblivious RAMs. J. ACM (JACM) **43**(3), 431–473 (1996)
5. Boneh, D., Di Crescenzo, G., Ostrovsky, R., Persiano, G.: Public key encryption with keyword search. In: Cachin, C., Camenisch, J.L. (eds.) EUROCRYPT 2004. LNCS, vol. 3027, pp. 506–522. Springer, Heidelberg (2004)
6. Song, D.X., Wagner, D., Perrig, A.: Practical techniques for searches on encrypted data. In: 2000 IEEE Symposium on Security and Privacy, pp. 44–55 (2000)
7. Goh, E.J.: Secure indexs. Technical report 2003/216, Cryptology ePrint Archive. http://eprint.iacr.org
8. Boneh, D., Goh, E.-J., Nissim, K.: Evaluating 2-DNF formulas on ciphertexts. In: Kilian, J. (ed.) TCC 2005. LNCS, vol. 3378, pp. 325–341. Springer, Heidelberg (2005)
9. Huang, R., Gui, X., Yu, S., Zhuang, W.: Research on privacy-preserving cloud storage framework supporting ciphertext retrieval. In: 2011 International Conference Network Computing and Information Security (NCIS), vol. 1, pp. 93–97(2011)

Term Committee Based Event Identification and Dependency Discovery

Kuo Zhang[1]($\boxtimes$), Juanzi Li[2], and Gang Wu[2]

[1] Sogou Tech Development, Beijing, China
zhangkuo@sogou-inc.com
[2] Tsinghua University, Beijing, China
{Ljz,wug03}@keg.cs.tsinghua.edu.cn

Abstract. With the overwhelming volume of news stories created and stored electronically everyday, there is an increasing need for techniques to analyze and present news stories to the users in a more meaningful manner. Most previous research focus on organizing news set into flat collections (topics) of stories. However, a topic in news is more than a mere collection of stories: it is actually characterized by a definite structure of inter-related events. Unfortunately, it is very difficult to identify events and dependencies within a topic because stories about the same topic are usually very similar to each other irrespective of the events they belong to. This is because stories within a topic usually share some terms which are related to the topic other than a specific event. To deal with this problem, we propose two methods based on event key terms to identify events and discover event dependency accurately. For event identification, we first capture some tight term clusters as term committees of potential events, and then use them to find the core story sets of potential events. At last we assign all stories to an event. For event dependency discovery, we emphasize the terms closely related to a certain event. So similarity contributed by topic-popular terms can be decreased. The experimental results on two Linguistic Data Consortium (LDC) datasets show that both the proposed methods for event identification and event dependency discovery have significant improvement over previous methods.

Categories and Subject Descriptors: H.3.3 [**Information Systems**]: Information Search and Retrieval; H. 4.2 [**Information Systems Applications**]: Types of Systems – decision support.

General Terms: Algorithms, Experimentation

Keywords: Event identification · Event dependency discovery · Term committee

1 Introduction

Common people and news analysts alike are usually interested in learning new events and event evolvements (dependencies between events) that happen in the news. With the overwhelming volume of news stories created and stored electronically everyday

Y. Yuan et al. (Eds.): ISCTCS 2013, CCIS 426, pp. 311–327, 2014.
DOI: 10.1007/978-3-662-43908-1_40, © Springer-Verlag Berlin Heidelberg 2014

at many news agencies, there is an increasing need for an event analysis system which is able to detect new events and discover event dependencies accurately. Topic Detection and Tracking (TDT) program aims to develop techniques which can effectively organize, search and structure news-oriented text materials from a variety of newswire and broadcast media [1]. Traditional TDT tasks consider news topics as flat collections of news stories. However, a topic in news is more than a mere collection of stories: it is actually characterized by a definite structure of inter-related events [4]. Although news stories were not organized into related events in TDT evaluations, TDT indeed gave the definitions of news Topic and news Event. A Topic is defined as "a seminal event or activity, along with directly related events and activities" [2]. An Event is defined as "something (non-trivial) happening in a certain place at a certain time" [3]. For instance, when an oil tanker sinks in Atlantic Ocean, that is the seminal event triggers the topic. Other events in the topic may include salvaging efforts, environmental damage, the commercial impact and so on. Besides that, we will also model the dependencies between events (e.g., the seminal event and the event of environmental damage have causal dependency).

In [4], Nallapati et al. first presented the concepts of event identification and dependency discovery within news topics, and corresponding evaluation metrics and experimental corpus were also provided. In that paper, cosine formula is used to compute news story similarity, and at the same time they use the time difference between two stories to decay the similarity. Finally agglomerative clustering is employed to identify news events. However, within the same topic, even two stories describing different events may have a considerable portion of overlapping words. Therefore, the methods widely used in Topic Detection (like agglomerative clustering) can hardly achieve satisfying accuracy. In this paper, we propose a new method which attempts to find key term sets (term committee) of events at first, and then use the term committees to help find key story sets of events (each event corresponds to a story set), finally assign the rest of the news stories to the key story sets according to their similarity. We used the same experimental corpus as paper [4] for the sake of comparison, the experimental results show that our proposed event identification method improves significantly in accuracy.

For event dependency discovery, Nallapati et al. proposed five models, among which a model named *Best Similarity* performs the best. For an event *e*, The *Best Similarity* model considers the most similar event e_p that happened before *e* as the parent event of *e* when their similarity exceeds a preset threshold. In this model, the similarity of the two events is computed by averaging the similarities of all pairs of stories between them. As analyzed before, since only a small portion of key terms can represent an event properly, this model still cannot give satisfying results in event dependency discovery. Therefore, we propose a new event dependency discovery method, in which event key terms are emphasized in event similarity computing. The experimental results show that the proposed method performs better than all the previous methods.

The rest of the paper is organized as follows. We start off this paper by summarizing the previous work in Sect. 2. In Sect. 3, we give the definitions of the problems and some discussions. Section 4 describes our new methods on event identification and event dependency discovery. Section 5 gives our experimental data and evaluation metrics. We finally wrap up with the experimental results in Sect. 6, and the conclusions and future work in Sect. 7.

2 Related Work

In the traditional TDT tasks, such as Topic Detection and Topic Tracking, news topics are considered as flat collections of news stories [5, 6, 7]. In TDT-2003, a hierarchical structure of topic detection has been proposed and some useful attempts to adopt the new structure are made [8]. However, this work still did not explicitly model any evolving relations between events.

Li et al. believed that news stories are always aroused by events; therefore, they proposed a probabilistic model to incorporate both content and time information in a unified framework [9]. This model also gave new representations of both news articles and news events. Fung et al. identify burst features within a time window at the first step, then group the burst features and use them to determine the hot periods of the bursty events [10]. Paper [11] derives the concept terms of a story from statistical context analysis between sentences in the news story and stories in the concept database at first, and then uses a modified agglomerative clustering algorithm to identify events. Although these methods are called "event identification", their concept of "event" is more like the concept of topic in TDT, bigger than the concept of event in TDT. Consequently, none of them have considered the relations between "events" since the bigger "events" (topic in TDT) usually do not have explicit relations.

Juha suggested modeling news topics in terms of its evolving events, but no specific model to the problem was proposed [12]. Nallapati et al. explicitly gave the concepts of event identification and event dependency discovery within a news topic, including evaluation metrics and datasets. The paper uses time decay when calculating similarity of story pairs, and agglomerative clustering is employed to identify news events. They also proposed five models for event dependency discovery, among which a model named Best Similarity performs the best. For an event e, The Best Similarity model considers the most similar event ep that happened before e as the parent event of e when their similarity exceeds a preset threshold. However, the methods proposed in [4] still have considerable room for improvement in accuracy.

Another related work is a novel clustering algorithm named Clustering By Committee (CBC) [13]. It initially discovers a set of tight clusters, called committees, that are well scattered in the similarity space. The algorithm proceeds by assigning elements to their most similar committee. Our term committee based event identification algorithm is different from CBC significantly. The committee elements are terms (features) in our algorithm, while the committee elements are documents (samples) in CBC.

3 Problem Definitions and Analysis

We use the same definitions of event identification and event dependency discovery as paper [4].

Event Identification (EI): event identification detects events within a news topic. Let $\mathbf{D}=\{d_1, d_2,\ldots, d_n\}$ be the entire story set of a certain topic $\mathbf{T}$, where n is the number of stories in topic $\mathbf{T}$. Each news story d is represented by a 2-tuple (*text*, *time*), in which *text* is the document vector and *time* is the publication time. The results of event identification is a event set $\mathbf{E}=\{e_1, e_2, \ldots, e_m\}$, where m is the number of events in topic $\mathbf{T}$. Each event is a set of stories. The events have the following constrains:

i. $\forall i \quad e_i \subseteq \mathbf{D}, e_i \neq \phi$
ii. $\forall i,j \quad i \neq j \rightarrow e_i \cap e_j = \phi$
iii. $\forall d_i \quad \exists e_l \in \mathbf{E} \text{ s.t.} d_i \in e_l$

Event Dependency Discovery (EDD): event dependency discovery models the dependencies between events within a topic. The result of EDD is a set of directed edges $\psi = \{(e_i, e_j)\}$, which denote dependencies between events. For a pair of events e_i and e_j, if at least one of the two following conditions is satisfied, then $(e_i, e_j) \in \psi$, and we call event e_i a parent of event e_j, event e_j a child of event e_i:

i. when event e_i and event e_j have causal dependency, which means that event e_j is a consequence of event e_i. For instance, event e_i is "a bomb exploded in a business center", and event e_j is "the polices start investigating".
ii. when event e_i and event e_j have temporal ordering dependency, which means that event e_i happened before event e_j, and they are related. For instance, e_i is "Pope arrives in Cuba", and e_j is "Pope meets Castro".

EI and EDD are strongly related to Topic Detection and Tracking, but also different from it significantly. They are built beyond news topics, and model smaller clusters, i.e. events, as well as the dependencies between them. Because of the following problems, EI and EDD are more challenging than traditional TDT tasks:

i. The number of events in a topic is hard to determine.
ii. Stories of different events are usually too similar to each other within a topic. As shown in Table 1, *S-event* means the average cosine similarity of all pairs of stories in the same events; *D-event* means the average cosine similarity of all pairs of stories belonging to different stories. *S-event(T)* and *D-event(T)* are the similarity obtained by using time decay according to the difference between two story's publication time. The time decay method is defined as follows:

$$sim_D(d,d') = sim(d,d')e^{-\frac{\alpha|d.time-d'.time|}{T}} \tag{1}$$

where $d.time$ and $d'.time$ are the publication time of story d and story d' respectively, and T is the time difference between the earliest and the latest story in the given topic. α is the time decay factor and set to 1 here. We can see that, the difference between *S-event* and *D-event* is not significant in most topics, even when time decay is used in similarity calculation. In Table 2, we give the average story cosine similarities of all pairs of stories in the same topics and different topics. From the statistics, we can see that, stories in different topics tend to have very low similarities. Obviously, traditional agglomerative clustering based method for topic detection is not suitable for event identification within topics.

Table 1. Average story similarities in the same and different events for some topics in TDT2 corpus

TopicID	S-event	D-event	S-event(T)	D-event(T)
20001	0.068	0.048	0.051	0.036
20012	0.286	0.278	0.252	0.207
20022	0.454	0.421	0.37	0.315
20026	0.408	0.377	0.338	0.298
20032	0.442	0.421	0.4	0.332
20033	0.172	0.136	0.136	0.104
20041	0.432	0.354	0.426	0.168
20056	0.264	0.202	0.233	0.157
20070	0.315	0.215	0.245	0.164
20071	0.262	0.228	0.226	0.18
20077	0.351	0.267	0.321	0.202
20087	0.217	0.185	0.185	0.133
20096	0.222	0.189	0.199	0.132
Average	0.299	0.255	0.260	0.187

Table 2. Average story similarities in the same and different topics in TDT2 and TDT3 corpus

	S-topic	D-topic	Topic-number
TDT2	0.265	0.007	28
TDT3	0.272	0.010	25

iii. Without enough background knowledge, the dependency between events is hard to model and discovered automatically.

4   Term Committee Model

In this section, we give our proposed methods to the two parts of event modeling, i.e. event identification and event dependency discovery, in Subsects. 4.1 and 4.2 respectively.

4.1   Event Identification

For simplicity, it is assumed that all stories in the same topic are available at one time, rather than coming in a text stream. Traditional methods to event identification make use of terms (including common terms and named entities, e.g., person name and location name) and time difference to calculate story similarity, and employ agglomerative clustering or probabilistic model to identify events [7, 9]. However, as shown in Table 1, the average S-event value of the listed topics is 0.299, while the average *D-event* value of the listed topics is 0.255, which is as high as 85 % of *S-event*. Although it is a little better when time decay is used in similarity computing, *D-event(T)* is still as high as 72 % of *S-event(T)*. The reason of the fact is that, stories within a topic usually share some terms which are related to the topic other than a specific event. Usually, only two or three key terms in a story is strongly related to a specific event. Therefore, to deal with this problem, we propose a new event identification method based on term committee. A term committee here is defined as a set of words which are the key terms of the corresponding event. Term committees are captured at first and then used for later event identification steps.

The experiments in paper [4] showed that many on-topic stories share the same person names and location names irrespective of the event they belong to, so these features may be more useful in identifying topics rather than events. For instance, the event "Pope arrives in Cuba" and event "Pope celebrates masses, preaches in Cuba" share the same person and location. Hence we will not seek for special way for better use of named entities in this paper.

As shown in Fig. 1, the approach proposed in this paper consists of four phases. At the first phase, we preprocess the news stories and generate 2-tuple representation for each news story. At the second phase, for each term, we first use the stories containing the term to generate a story vector, each dimension of which is corresponding to a story. Then the story vector is used to compute similarity between terms and we discovery a set of tight term clusters (high intra-group similarity), called term committees, that are well scattered in the similarity space (low inter-group similarity). At the third phase, we capture the core story set for each event represented by a term committee. By core story set, we mean the set of stories those are near the space center of the event they belong to. At the last phase, the approach proceeds by assigning each of the news stories to their most similar core story set when their similarity exceeds a preset threshold, otherwise form a singleton event for the story. The details of this approach are given by subsequent subsections.

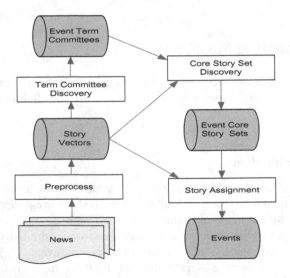

Fig. 1. Event identification procedure based on term committee

4.1.1   News Story Representation

Preprocessing is needed before generating story representation. For preprocessing, we tokenize words, recognize abbreviations, normalize abbreviations, add part-of-speech tags, remove stopwords included in the stop list used in InQuery [14], replace words with their stems using K-stem algorithm [15], and then generate word vector for each news story.

Thus, each story d is represented as follows:

$$d \rightarrow (\textbf{\textit{text}}, \textit{time}) \rightarrow (\{weight(d, w_1), weight(d, w_2), \ldots, weight(d, w_n)\}, \textit{time})$$

where $\textit{time}$ is the publication time of news story d, and n means the number of distinct terms in story d. And $weight(d, w)$ means the weight of term w in story d:

$$weight(d, w) = \frac{\log(tf(d, w) + 1) * \log((N + 1)/(df(w) + 0.5))}{\sum_{w' \in d} \log(tf(d, w') + 1) * \log((N + 1)/(df(w') + 0.5))} \tag{2}$$

where N means the total number of news stories, and $tf(d, w)$ means how many times term w occurs in news story d. And $df(w)$ is the number of stories containing term w.

We use cosine distance for the calculation of similarity between two stories. For two stories d and d', their similarity is defined as follows:

$$sim(d, d') = \frac{\sum_{w \in d, d'} weight(d, w) * weight(d', w)}{|d| \cdot |d'|} \tag{3}$$

Input: Term set $W = \{w \mid F(w) > 1\}$, threshold θ_1
Step 1:   Put all terms in W into a list of residues R.
Step 2:   Let C be a list of committees, and set $C = \Phi$.
Step 3:   Cluster the terms in R using average-link clustering.
For each term cluster c created in the clustering process
Compute the following score: $\log(|c|) \times avgsim(c)$, where $|c|$ is the number of terms in c and $avgsim(c)$ is the average pairwise similarity between terms in c.
Step 4:   If cluster c has the highest score, and c's similarity to each committee previously added to C is below the threshold θ_1, then add c to C.
Step 5:   Remove all the terms in c from residues R.
Remove all the terms in R whose similarity with c is above threshold θ_1.
Step 6:   If R is empty, then we are done and return C. Otherwise, go to step 3.
Output: A list of term committees C

Fig. 2. Term committee discovery algorithm

4.1.2   Term Committee Discovery

For each term w, we create a vector as follows:

$$F(w) = \{weight(d_1, w), weight(d_2, w), \ldots, weight(d_n, w)\}$$

where n is the number of stories in this topic. Each dimension is corresponding to a story, and the value is the weight of term w in the story.

The similarity of two terms w_i and w_j is defined as follows:

$$sim(w_i, w_j) = \frac{\sum\limits_{d \in D} weight(d, w_i) * weight(d, w_j)}{|F(w_i)| \cdot |F(w_j)|} \tag{4}$$

The details of term committee discovery algorithm are presented in Fig. 2. Because the number of terms which just appear in a single news story is very large, and these terms can not provide useful information for event identification, we just use the terms that appear in at least two stories as the input of this phase. θ_1 is a parameter that is tuned to the optimal value on training set. At step 1, we put all the input terms into a term set R. And then we initiate a term committee set C as an empty set in step 2. At step 3, we use agglomerative clustering algorithm to cluster the terms in R until all the terms belong to a single cluster, and we compute the score $\log(|c|) \times$ avg-sim(c) for each temporary cluster c created during the clustering procedure. The factor $\log(|c|)$ reflects a preference for bigger term sets, while the factor avgsim(c) reflects a preference for tighter term sets. Step 4 selects the cluster c with the highest score. If the similarity between cluster c and each previous term committee in C is smaller than threshold θ_1, then add c to C. Step 5 remove all the terms in c from residues R, and remove all the terms in R whose similarity with c is above threshold θ_1. Now if R is empty then return term committee set C as result, otherwise the algorithm jumps back to step 3.

4.1.3   Event Core Story Set Discovery

Although the central theme of an event can be summarized by a few key terms, some stories in an event may drift away a little from the central theme and do not have most of the key terms. So in this phase, we use term committee to discover the core story set for each event before identify event membership for all the stories. For each term committee c, we define the core story set D_c as follows:

$$D_c = \{d \mid |d \cap c| \geq \frac{1}{2}|c|\} \tag{5}$$

which means the core story set is composed of stories containing at least half of the terms in term committee c.

4.1.4   News Story Assignment

In this phase, we initiate a news story cluster for each core story set by adding its stories in the cluster. For each story d that is not included in any cluster, compute the similarity between d and all existing clusters. The similarity between a story and a cluster is defined as follows:

$$sim(d, c) = \sum_{d' \in c} sim_D(d, d') / |c| \qquad (6)$$

where $|c|$ means the number of stories in c, and $sim_D(d, d')$ is computed as formula (1). If all the similarities are below the threshold θ_2, then create a new cluster and put the story into it, otherwise put the story into the most similar cluster. θ_2 is another parameter tuned to the optimal value on training set.

4.2 Event Dependency Discovery

Modeling the dependencies between events is an extremely challenging problem. We believe that an accurate and robust EDD system needs various domain-knowledge and general understanding of how things operate in the world as background knowledge. However, as initial work, we will focus on how to make use of some features that are easy for computer to process.

In this subsection, we describe the method we considered for capturing event dependencies. In the rest of this subsection, we assume that we are given the event set **E** of each topic, and the event membership of all the stories, and we focus on modeling event dependency set ψ.

Paper [4] relies on surface-features such as time-ordering of news stories and event similarity to model the event dependencies. They use the average cosine similarities of all pairs of stories from two events to help determine whether there is dependency between the two events.

However, we find that the terms in an event can be classified into the following four classes:

i. Terms closely related to the whole topic. For instance, in the topic 20013 (about winter Olympic games in 1998) in TDT2 corpus, terms "Olympic" and "game" are closely related to the whole topic other than a specific event.
ii. Terms closely related to a specific event. For example, in the second event (about the Olympic game's opening) in topic 20013, "open" and "ceremony" are the terms closely related to this specific event.
iii. Terms closely related to a parent or child event. For example, there is a short piece of introduction of the third event (about Olympic game contest and results) in a story of the second event: "You'll see who won medals as soon as it happens. Watch the "CNN headline news" super ticker for complete Olympic results, starting tonight." The terms "medals" and "results" are only closely related to the third event, which is a child of the second event.
iv. Other terms, e.g., terms not closely related to any events and the topic, such as "see", "happen".

Apparently, terms of the first and fourth class can not provide useful information for event dependency discovery, since no matter whether there is dependency between two events, they may share the same terms of these two classes. Only the second and the third classes of terms can give hints about the dependency between events. Therefore, we propose a method which gives more weights to the second class of terms to increase similarity between parent and child events.

In a topic t, term weight in a story d of event e is modified as follows:

$$weight(d, w, e) = weight(d, w) * f(w, e) \qquad (7)$$

where

$$f(w, e) = \frac{df_e(w)/|e|}{df_t(w)/|t|} \qquad (8)$$

Where $df_e(w)$ is the number of stories containing term w in event e, and $df_t(w)$ is the number of stories containing term w in the whole topic t. $|e|$ and $|t|$ are the total number of stories in event e and topic t respectively.

The similarity between two events is computed by averaging the similarities of all pairs of stories from the two events e_1 and e_2:

$$AveSim(e_1, e_2) = \frac{\sum\limits_{d_i \in e_1} \sum\limits_{d_j \in e_2} sim_E(d_i, d_j)}{|e_1| \cdot |e_2|} \qquad (9)$$

where

$$sim_E(d_i, d_j) = \frac{\sum\limits_{w \in d_i, d_j} weight(d_i, w, e_1) * weight(d_j, w, e_2)}{|d_i| \cdot |d_j|} \qquad (10)$$

We use this modified event similarity calculation method on the best model proposed in paper [4]: *Best Similarity Model*.

To use time-ordering information, we define an event time function:

$$t_e: \mathbf{E} \rightarrow \{1, 2, \ldots, m\} \ s.t.$$

$$\forall e_i, e_j \in \mathbf{E} \ t_e(e_i) < t_e(e_j) \Leftrightarrow \min_{d \in e_i}(d.time) < \min_{d \in e_j}(d.time) \qquad (11)$$

where m is the number of events in $\mathbf{E}$.

In the *Best Similarity Model*, each event is assumed to have at most one parent event. The event dependency set is defined as follows:

$$\psi = \{(e_i, e_j) | AvgSim(e_i, e_j) > \lambda \cap$$
$$e_i = \arg \max_{e_k : t_e(e_k) < t_e(e_j)} AveSim(e_k, e_j)\} \qquad (12)$$

The model considers the event e_i as a parent of e_j, if and only if e_i is the most similar earlier event to e_j and the similarity exceeds a threshold λ.

5 Experimental Setup

5.1 Datasets

For the sake of comparison to experiments in paper [4], we use the same datasets and annotation results. The datasets include 28 topics selected from TDT2 corpus, and 25 topics selected from TDT3 corpus [16]. All the news stories are picked from CNN headline news since the stories from this source do not tend to digress or drift two far away from the central theme. It is believed that modeling such kind of stories will be a useful first step before dealing with more complex datasets. The datasets created a training set of 26 topics and a test set of 27 topics by merging the 28 topics from TDT2 and 25 from TDT3 and then splitting them randomly.

For each topic, annotation includes defining the event membership of all the stories and the dependencies between events. Table 3 shows some statistics for the training and test sets.

Table 3. Statistics of the training and testing data

Features	Training set	Testing set
Number of topics	26	27
Average number of stories/topic	28.69	26.74
Average story length	64.6	64.04
Average number of stories/event	5.65	6.22
Average number of events/topic	5.07	4.29
Average number of dependences/topic	3.07	2.92
Average number of dependences/event	0.61	0.68
Average number of days/topic	30.65	34.48

5.2 Evaluation Metric

Again, for the sake of comparison, we use the same evaluation metrics as paper [4]. For an automatically generated event model $M' = (E', \psi')$ and a true event model (annotated by human) $M = (E, \psi)$, we examine a pair of stories at a time and verify whether the generated model and the true model agree on their event membership and dependency. The related metrics and definitions are given in detail in the rest of this subsection:

- **Event pairs** $C(M)$: This set includes all the unordered pairs (d_i, d_j) of stories d_i and d_j that belong to the same event given a model M. Formally,

$$C(M) = \{(d_i, d_j) | d_i, d_j \in D \land \exists e \in E \text{ s.t.} (d_i \in e \land d_j \in e)\} \qquad (13)$$

- **Dependency pairs** $D(M)$: This set includes all the ordered pairs (d_i, d_j) of stories d_i and d_j such that there is a dependency from the event of d_i to the event of d_j in the model M. Formally,

$$D(M) = \{(d_i, d_j)|\exists(e_u, e_v) \in \psi \text{ s.t.} (d_i \in e_u \wedge d_j \in e_v)\} \tag{14}$$

- **Event Precision** *EP*: this is the probability that a pair of two randomly selected stories belongs to set $C(M)$ given that it belongs to $C(M')$.

$$EP = |C(M) \cap C(M')|/C(M') \tag{15}$$

- **Event Recall** *ER*: this is the probability that a pair of two randomly selected stories belongs to set $C(M')$ given that it belongs to $C(M)$.

$$ER = |C(M) \cap C(M')|/C(M) \tag{16}$$

- **Dependency Precision** *DP*: this is the probability that a pair of two randomly selected stories belongs to set $D(M)$ given that it belongs to $D(M')$.

$$DP = |D(M) \cap D(M')|/D(M') \tag{17}$$

- **Dependency Recall** *DR*: this is the probability that a pair of two randomly selected stories belongs to set $D(M')$ given that it belongs to $D(M)$.

$$DR = |D(M) \cap D(M')|/D(M) \tag{18}$$

And the well known F1-measure is used to combine the above measures:

$$EF = 2 \cdot EP \cdot ER/(EP + ER)$$

$$DF = 2 \cdot DP \cdot DR/(DP + DR)$$

$$JF = 2 \cdot EF \cdot DF/(EF + DF) \tag{19}$$

where EF and DF are the event and dependency F1-measures respectively and JF is the joint F1-measure used to measure the overall performance.

6   Experimental Results

Our experiments are composed of three parts: event identification, event dependency discovery and combined results. We compare our algorithms and previous algorithms in isolation and in association with other components. The following three subsections give the experimental results and related discussions for the three parts respectively.

6.1   Event Identification

For event identification, we implemented a system based on term committee and compare it to two previous systems:

SYSTEM-1: This system uses cosine distance as the similarity of stories, and employs agglomerative clustering based on average-link to identify events. This system is used as baseline system.

SYSTEM-2: This system is the same as SYSTEM-1, except that it uses formula (1) to adjust similarities according to time difference between news stories.

SYSTEM-3: This system is implemented based on the method proposed in this paper. It has four phases: story preprocessing, term committee discovery, core story set discovery and story assignment.

We tested our method on the test set with the parameter θ_1 and θ_2 fixed at their optimal values learned from training set. The results of three systems on training set and test set are shown in Tables 4 and 5 respectively. Each value in the tables is the average score over all topics. P-value that is marked by * means that it is a statistical significant improvement over the compared system (95 % confidence level, one tailed T-test). The *EF* result of our system on training set is 0.59 which is 0.13 higher than baseline system, and 0.06 higher than SYSTEM-2. On test set, our system's *EF* value is 0.10 higher than the baseline system and 0.06 higher than SYSTEM-2. On both the datasets, our system is statistically significant compared to SYSTEM-2 which performs the best in paper [4]. The results show that our method based on term committee can identify news events within a topic more accurately.

6.2   Dependency Discovery

For event dependency discovery, we implemented a system based on event key terms and compare it to three previous systems proposed in paper [4]:

SYSTEM-4: *Complete-Link model*. In this model it is assumed that there are dependencies between all pairs of events. The direction of dependency is determined by the time-ordering of the events. Formally,

$$\Psi = \{(e_i, e_j) | t_e(e_i) < t_e(e_j)\} \tag{20}$$

SYSTEM-5: *Nearest Parent Model*. In this model, it is assumed that each event can have at most one parent. And the set of dependencies is defined as follows:

$$\Psi = \{(e_i, e_j) \,|\, AvgSim(e_i, e_j) > \lambda \cap t_e(e_i) + 1 = t_e(e_j)\} \tag{21}$$

For each event e_j, only the nearest event happen before e_j is considered as a potential parent event candidate. The candidate is assigned as the parent only if the similarity between them exceeds the threshold λ. In this system, formula (3) is used to compute story similarity.

Table 4. Comparison of event identification algorithms (on training set)

System	EP	ER	EF	P-value
SYSTEM-1	0.39	0.67	0.46	–
SYSTEM-2	0.45	0.70	0.53	2.9e-4* (to SYSTEM-1)
SYSTEM-3	0.48	0.73	0.59	4.3e-3* (to SYSTEM-2)

Table 5. Comparison of event identification algorithms (on training set)

System	EP	ER	EF	P-value
SYSTEM-1	0.44	0.67	0.50	–
SYSTEM-2	0.48	0.70	0.54	1.4e-2* (to SYSTEM-1)
SYSTEM-3	0.52	0.75	0.60	1.1e-2* (to SYSTEM-2)

SYSTEM-6: This is the system implemented based on *Best Similarity Model*. In this system, formula (3) is used to compute story similarity.

SYSTEM-7:This system is implemented based on our method, which increases the weights of terms closely related to the event they belong to. In other words, formula (10) is used to compute story similarity.

At first, we obtain the best *DF* value by tuning the parameter λ on training set. And we test our method on the test set with the parameter λ fixed at the optimal value obtained from training. Tables 6 and 7 give the *DP*, *DR*, *DF* values averaged over all topics on training set and test set respectively. We can see that, on both training and test set, our system based on event key term reweighting performs better than all the previous systems. For experiments on training set, SYSTEM-6 performs worse than SYSTEM-5, while SYSTEM-7 achieves an improvement of 0.05 compared to SYS-TEM-5. According to observations on the experiment details, we find that this is because our new method can decrease the similarity between events with no dependency successfully. SYSTEM-7 is the same as SYSTEM-6 except that it gives more weight to key terms of events. So the fact SYSTEM-7 is statistical significant from SYSTEM-6 on both datasets indicates that our method of reweighting key terms is useful.

Table 6. Comparison of event dependency discovery algorithms (training set)

System	DP	DR	DF	P-value
SYSTEM-4	0.36	0.93	0.48	–
SYSTEM-5	0.55	0.62	0.56	0.04* (to SYSTEM-4)
SYSTEM-6	0.51	0.62	0.53	0.24 (to SYSTEM-4)
SYSTEM-7	0.58	0.66	0.61	8.5e-3* (to SYSTEM-6)

Table 7. Comparison of event dependency discovery algorithms (test set)

System	DP	DR	DF	P-value
SYSTEM-4	0.50	0.94	0.63	–
SYSTEM-5	0.61	0.60	0.60	– (to SYSTEM-4)
SYSTEM-6	0.71	0.74	0.72	0.04* (to SYSTEM-4)
SYSTEM-7	0.75	0.79	0.77	0.03* (to SYSTEM-6)

6.3   Combination Results

In the previous two subsections we have studied the event identification and dependency discovery algorithms in isolation. Now we combine the two components together to build the entire event model. The two baseline systems SYSTEM-1 and SYSTEM-4 are combined together as the baseline system here. We also tested the two methods we proposed in this paper SYSTEM-3 and SYSTEM-7 in association. Tables 9 and 10 are the results of four combined systems on training and test set respectively. The automatically generated event sets are used as input of event dependency discovery. All the parameters need to be retrained on the training set to optimize the new objective function JF, i.e., the joint F1-measure. From the results, we can see that: (1) although SYSTEM-1 is worse than SYSTEM-2 for event identification, and SYSTEM-4 is worse than SYSTEM-5 and SYSTEM-6 for dependency discovery, the combination of SYSTEM-1 and SYSTEM-4 performs better for the entire modeling surprisingly. This is because that the DR value of SYSTEM-4 is much higher than others, while all the system's DP values are as low as around 0.20. (2)

Table 8. Events and dependencies in topic 20013

Event No.	Event description	Father event
1	Preparation for olympics	–
2	Olympic games open	1
3	Olympic contests, results	2

Table 9. Combined results on the training set

System	EP	ER	EF	DP	DR	DF	JF	P-value
SYSTEM-1 +SYSTEM-4	0.58	0.31	0.38	0.20	0.67	0.30	0.33	–
SYSTEM-2 +SYSTEM-5	0.51	0.53	0.49	0.21	0.19	0.19	0.27	–
SYSTEM-2 +SYSTEM-6	0.45	0.70	0.53	0.21	0.33	0.23	0.32	–
SYSTEM-3 +SYSTEM-7	0.48	0.73	0.59	0.25	0.45	0.31	0.39	1.8e-3* (to SYSTEM-1 +SYSTEM-4)

Table 10. Combined results on the test set

System	EP	ER	EF	DP	DR	DF	JF	P-value
SYSTEM-1 +SYSTEM-4	0.66	0.27	0.36	0.30	0.72	0.43	0.39	–
SYSTEM-2 +SYSTEM-5	0.57	0.50	0.50	0.27	0.19	0.21	0.30	–
SYSTEM-2 +SYSTEM-6	0.48	0.70	0.54	0.31	0.27	0.26	0.35	–
SYSTEM-3 +SYSTEM-7	0.52	0.75	0.60	0.34	0.50	0.39	0.46	3.1e-3* (to SYSTEM-1 +SYSTEM-4)

After retraining, the *EF* value is a little lower when SYSTEM-2 is combined with SYSTEM-5 than combined with SYSTEM-6. We believe that this is because SYS-TEM-5 requires more precision on event identification to achieve good result. (3) The combination of the two methods we proposed performs better than all the previous systems. And on both data sets, it is statistically significant from the baseline system.

6.4   An example

To show how the proposed event identification method works, we give an example in this subsection. In TDT2 corpus, topic 20013 (about the 1998 Winter Olympics) has three events as shown in Table 8, and there are two dependencies between events (1, 2) and events (2, 3) respectively.

   Our event identification method uses the algorithm described in Fig. 2 to extracts three tight term committees from all the terms that appear in at least two stories:

   i.   torch, flame, leg
  ii.   open, ceremony
 iii.   gold, medal, hockey, team

   We can see that, these term committees can represent the three corresponding events very well. The topic-popular terms that broadly appear in this topic and are not strongly related to any specific event, like "Olympic" and "Nagano", are not included in any of the term committees. Then, stories can be assigned to proper events (with the help of term committees) without being disturbed by the topic-popular terms.

7   Conclusion

Most of the previous work, such as TDT, organizes news stories by topics which are flat collections of news stories. However, this paper aims to model events and their dependencies within a news topic. Due to the high similarity between stories of different events within the same topic (usually stories within a topic share lots of terms about the topic), we proposed an event identification method based on term com-mittee. We first capture some tight term clusters as term committees for potential events, and then use them to find the core story set of potential events. At last we assign all stories to an event. For event dependency discovery, we emphasize the terms closely related to a certain event. So similarity contributed by topic-popular terms can be decreased. The experimental results show that both the proposed methods for event identification and event dependency discovery have significant improvement over previous methods.

   In the future work, we plan to use news publication time to help find term com-mittees more accurately, since stories about the same event tend to be close to each other. We also want to test our methods on automatically generated topic story set, which may contain noisy stories that do not belong to the topic.

Acknowledgement. This work was supported by National High Technology Research and Development (863) Program (2011AA01A205). Any opinions, findings and conclusions or recommendations expressed in this material are the author(s) and do not necessarily reflect those of the sponsor. And I also want to thank Dr. Nallapati for his help and the valuable annotation results of the dataset.

References

1. http://www.nist.gov/speech/tests/tdt/index.htm
2. In: Topic Detection and Tracking. Event-based Information Organization. Kluwer Academic Publishers (2002)
3. Yang, Y., Carbonell, J., Brown, R., Pierce, T., Archibald, B.T., Liu, X.: Learning approaches for detecting and tracking news events. IEEE Intell. Syst. Spec. Issue Appl. Intell. Inf. Retr. **14**(4), 32–43 (1999)
4. Nallapati, R., Feng, A., Peng, F., Allan, J.: Event threading within news topics. In: CIKM'04, Washington, DC, USA, 8–13 Nov 2004, pp. 446–453 (2004)
5. Yang, Y. , Pierce, T., Carbonell, J.: A Study on retrospective and on-line event detection. In: Proceedings of SIGIR-98, Melbourne, Australia, pp. 28–36 (1998)
6. Papka, R., Allan, J.: On-line new event detection using single pass clustering TITLE2: Technical report UM-CS-1998-021 (1998)
7. Juha, M., Helena, A.M., Marko, S.: Simple semantics in topic detection and tracking. Inf. Retr. **7**(3–4), 347–368 (2004)
8. Allan, J., Feng, A., Bolivar, A.: Flexible intrinsic evaluation of hierarchical clustering for TDT. In: the Proceedings of the ACM Twelfth International Conference on Information and Knowledge Management, pp. 263–270 (2003)
9. Li, Z., Wang, B., Li, M., Ma, W.: A probabilistic model for retrospective news event detection. In: Proceedings of ACM SIGIR'05, pp. 61–81 (2005)
10. Fung, G., Yu, J., Yu, P., Lu, H.: Parameter free bursty events detection in text streams. In: Proceedings of the 31st VLDB Conference, Trondheim, Norway, pp. 181–192 (2005)
11. Lam, W., Meng, H., Wong, K., Yen, J.: Using contextual analysis for news event detection. Int. J. Intell. Syst. **16**(4), 525–546 (2001)
12. Juha, M.: Investigations on event evolution in TDT. In: Proceedings of HLT-NAACL 2003 Student Workshop, pp. 43–48 (2004)
13. Pantel, P., Lin, D.: Document clustering with committees. In: Proceedings of the 25th Annual International ACM SIGIR Conference, Tampere, Finland, pp. 199–206 (2002)
14. Callan, J.P., Croft, W.B., Harding, S.M.: The INQUERY retrieval system. In: Proceedings of DEXA-92, 3rd International Conference on Database and Expert Systems Applications, pp. 78–83 (1992)
15. Krovetz, R.: Viewing morphology as an inference process. In: Proceedings of ACM SIGIR93, pp. 61–81 (1993)
16. The linguistic data consortium. http://www.ldc.upenn.edu/

A Semantics Enabled Intelligent Semi-structured Document Processor

Kuo Zhang[1]([✉]), JuanZi Li[2], MingCai Hong[2], XueDong Yan[2], and Qiang Song[2]

[1] Beijing Sogou Technology Development Co, Ltd, Beijing, China
zhangkuo@sogou-inc.com
[2] Knowledge Engineering Lab, Department of Computer Science, Tsinghua University, Beijing, China
ljz@tsinghua.edu.cn,
{hmc,yanxd03,sq02}@mails.tsinghua.edu.cn

Abstract. Recent years, the amount of semi-structured documents available electrically has increased dramatically. Semi-structured documents usually are difficult to reuse due to the lack of explicit metadata. To enable integration and retrieval over semi-structured documents, the essential aspects in the documents should be described by metadata explicitly. The metadata could be assigned to documents and present part of their information content using various IE techniques. This paper also provides flexible user interaction mechanism to achieve better performance over less training sample documents. In semantic view extraction, by using similarity based rule induction, we have been able to improve the rule learning procedure. Experimental results show that our approach can significantly outperform most of the existing wrapper methods. We make use of the semantics that resides in document logical structure to help find relations between semantic entities. After semantic annotations of the documents, TIPSI allows those to be indexed with respect to the extracted text entities. To answer the query, TIPSI applies semantic restrictions over the entities in the KB.

1 Introduction

Recent years, the amount of semi-structured data available electrically has increased dramatically. Semi-structured data is data that is neither raw data, nor very strictly typed as in conventional database systems [1]. Semi-structured documents usually are difficult to reuse due to the lack of explicit metadata.

To enable integration and retrieval over semi-structured documents, the essential aspects in the documents should be described by explicit metadata. The metadata could be assigned to documents and present part of their information content using various IE techniques. This paper also provides flexible user interaction mechanism to achieve better performance over less training sample documents. And there are two interaction modes: specialist mode and end-user model.

Semi-structured documents are usually human readable. However, as the length of documents scales up dramatically, it is much harder for human to read the documents

Y. Yuan et al. (Eds.): ISCTCS 2013, CCIS 426, pp. 328–344, 2014.
DOI: 10.1007/978-3-662-43908-1_41, © Springer-Verlag Berlin Heidelberg 2014

and find valuable pieces. So we construct the document logical structure to help users read long documents.

And logical structure also can help semantics view extraction as we will see in the subsequent sections. We make use of the semantics that resides in document logical structure to help find relations between semantic entities. Contents in the same logical node are more likely to describe the same entity or have direct relations.

The intelligent processor of semi-structured information (TIPSI) is a concrete implementation of our approach. It is aimed to help users make use of large scale of semi-structured document corpus.

In the next section, we give the motivation of our work with an example. This paper presents first an innovative semi-structured document processor and its system architecture in the third section. In the fourth section, we give the method of document logical structure construction. Our semantic view extraction is presented in Sect. 5. The search on top of semantic view is outlined in Sect. 6. Section 7 contains the evaluation of IE technique used in our system. Some related works are given in Sect. 8. In the last section, we present our conclusion and our plan for future work.

2 Motivation

There are significant semi-structured documents, such as financial reports, project plans, and research papers, created in enterprise or academic work life. This kind of documents usually is organized in a logical structure and a document set usually has its own formal specification. For example, Shanghai stock exchange has thousands of financial reports for different companies. Even though the reports are not strictly restricted by a template like LaTex, they are required to contain the information needed, such as company contact information, the partners, and the profit .etc. We extract this kind of information including their relations, and describe them by a user defined metadata (XML Schema or Ontology). Then, we provide semantics enabled search for information that resides in the semi-structured documents. For example, Fig. 1 is a piece of a financial report.

Then, we construct the logical structure of the documents as follows (Fig. 2):

For each set of documents that has unified specification, user can define a schema to help create rules and extract semantic views. For instance, the following is a schema created for document in Fig. 1 (Fig. 3).

We can use some documents as training samples to induce extraction rules for each *literal* part in the schema. Then the rules can be applied to other documents to extract the text values. Figure 4 is the extracted results from document in Fig. 1.

Until now we know that there is a company named "Beijing SHENGLI" appears in this document. However, if users want to know the name of the company which has a partner named "Zhang JianPing", they still need to read the document by themselves. The reason is that the relationships between extracted text values are not recognized. So we use the logical structure to help construct the semantic relationships. Figure 5 is the final result:

一、 北京胜利公司简介
1、 公司法定中文名称：北京胜利电器股份有限公司
    公司法定英文名称：BEIJING SHENGLI APPLIANCES CO.，LTD.
2、 公司董事会秘书：张 阔
    联系地址：北京市海淀区建平路2号
    电话：(010)58357388
    电子信箱：sldsh@shengli.com
3、 公司注册及办公地址：北京市海淀区建平路2号
    公司邮政编码：200135
    公司国际互联网网址：http://www.shengli.com
    ......
9、 股东情况介绍
        股东名称   年末持股数量(股)   占总股本比例(%)
    9.1 北京电气总公司   211,981,080   47.28
    9.2 张建平   6,380,012   1.42
二、 西部电力公司简介
1、 公司法定中、英文名称
    公司法定中文名称：西部电力发展股份有限公司
    公司英文名称：WESTERN POWER DEVELOPMENT CO.，LTD
2、 公司董事会秘书：吴 刚
    联系地址：北京市朝阳区南滨河路1号
    电话：010-82332025
    电子信箱：xibu@sina.com
3、 公司注册地址：北京市经济技术开发区黄海西路4号
    公司办公地址：北京市朝阳区南滨河路1号
    邮政编码：100055
    公司国际互联网网址：http://www.xibudianli.com
    ......
9、 股东情况介绍
        股东名称   持股数   占股本比例(%)
    9.1 东部电力公司   155,810,340   34.00
    9.2 上海市电力公司   142,071,300   31.00
    9.3 虎威电力集团公司   45,368,280   9.90
    ......

Fig. 1. An example of a financial report

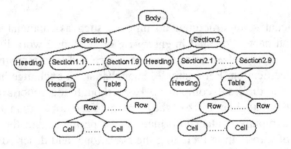

Fig. 2. Document logical structure. Heading is the title of the section. The two tables are unformatted table, they are constructed automatically in the logical structure construction process.

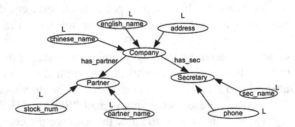

Fig. 3. User defined schema. L means the element is a *literal*.

公司中文名称: 北京胜利电器股份有限公司	董事会秘书姓名: 吴 刚	股东名称: 虎威电力集团公司
公司中文名称: 西部电力发展股份有限公司	董事会秘书电话: 010-82332025	股东持股数: 47.28%
公司英文名称: BEIJING SHENGLI APPLANCES CO.,LTD	董事会秘书电话: (010) 58357388	股东持股数: 1.42%
公司英文名称: WESTERN POWER DEVELOPMENT CO, LTD	股东名称: 张建平	股东持股数: 34.00%
公司地址: 北京市海淀区建平路2号	股东名称: 东部电力公司	股东持股数: 31.00%
公司地址: 北京市朝阳区南滨河路1号	股东名称: 上海市电力公司	股东持股数: 9.90%
董事会秘书姓名: 张 阆	股东名称: 北京电气总公司	

Fig. 4. Extracted text values.

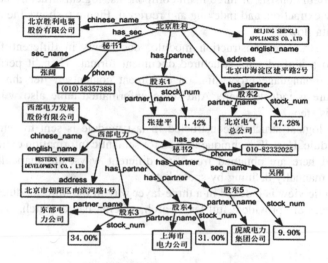

Fig. 5. Extracted semantic view with relationships.

Now we can provide flexible semantic search on top of the semantic view. For example, we can search for the web address for a company; we can search for partners who have more than 10 % stocks of "Beijing SHENGLI" company.

3 TIPSI System

3.1 System Introduction

TIPSI is aimed to help users make use of large scale semi-structured document corpus. TIPSI is aimed to help users make use of large scale semi-structured document corpus. To do this in a consistent fashion, it extracts information text from semi-structured documents based on user defined metadata according to the domain of documents. Semi-structured documents from a domain usually have a relative consistent format, for example, company annual reports from the ShangHai Stock Exchange usually have nine chapters and each chapter introduces a relative independent content.

In TIPSI, we formulize the problem of information content extraction as that of Logic View construction and Semantic View extraction. In Logic View construction, we try to convert documents in different formats (e.g. DOC format or HMTL format) into a unified format with logical structure. In Semantic View extraction, we, taking the logic views as input, perform the extraction by using rules, construct the semantic view, and output the final results. In TIPSI, we also aim to provide the function for navigating the logic views and for searching the semantic views.

3.2 System Architecture

The TIPSI system consists of three main components: logical structure construction, semantic view extraction, and indexing and retrieval. Figure 6 shows the architecture details and data flow.

In logical structure construction module, documents in different formats are converted into a unified semi-structured document format. Then, it performs some shallow natural language processing on document contents. After that, document logical structure is inducted here. And some unformatted table also will be reconstructed in this step.

Then, the logical structure constructed in last module is sent to semantic view extraction module. Here IE technique is used for semantic information extraction. And the rules used here are obtained from two different ways: automatically machine learning, and manually defining by specialists.

The semantic view is indexed in a three-layer way in the third module. And three kinds of services are provided: full text search, schema based search, schema based navigation.

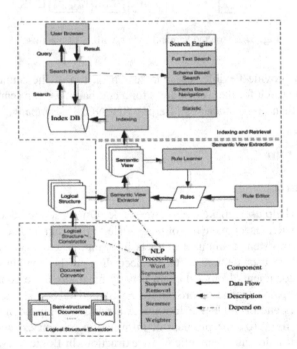

Fig. 6. The architecture of TIPSI system.

4 Logical Structure Construction

The definition of logical structure is given in [2] as follows:

Definition 1. *The logical structure of a document consists of a hierarchy of segments of the document, each of which corresponds to a visually distinguished, semantic component of the document.*

The automated discovery of logical structure in semi-structured documents is an important problem that recently has received a good deal of attention. It can enable navigation when browsing semi-structured documents. The document piece of interest can be found easier by readers with the help of document logical structure.

According to the definition, each document segment is a semantic component. A logical segment must both be distinguished by its layout, and has meaning as a semantic unit. Document components that appear in the same segment (or sub-segment) usually have a central issue (or sub-issue). Therefore, it can be helpful to semantic view extraction, especially for semantic relationship extraction.

A solution to logical structure construction is to create a hierarchy of components of the documents: sections, section-titles, paragraphs, tables, figures and lists.

At first, various types of the components are recognized. Tables, figures, and formula are recognized as leaf nodes in the logical structure tree. Then texts are classified into section-titles or text paragraphs. Text paragraphs and section-titles are also treated as leaf nodes in logical structure tree. Nevertheless, hierarchical sections are created according to the different features of the section-titles.

We use Naive Bayes classifier to recognize section-titles. Section-titles usually have some special content type and style type characters. The features listed in the following table are used to build the classifier:

Table 1. Features for section-title recognition

Features	Descriptions
Is-bold	Whether the text is bold
Is-italic	Whether the text is italic
Font-size	The font size of the text
Char-number	The number of the characters
Start-with-special-symbols	Whether the first token contains special symbols, such as ".",
Start-with-bracket	Whether the first token contains bracket symbol, such as "(",
Start-with-number	Whether the first token contains number symbols, such as "1", "II", "三(Chinese number)"

After the section-titles are recognized, we need to determine their logical level in the logical structure tree using their different features. For sake of easier explanation, we give the definition of brother section-titles:

Definition 2. *The brother section-titles are the highest section-titles under the same parent section-title. They have the same logical level. For example, title "3.1 System Introduction" and title "3.2 System Architecture" are brother section-titles.*

Due to the limited space, we do not give our logical structure construction algorithm in detail. Our algorithm is designed based on the following four observations:

i.   A set of brother section-titles should be started with one, such as the titles start with "1", "—"," i ", "4.1", and "A".
ii. If the first title t_1 of brother title set S_1 appears before the first title t_2 of another brother title set S_2, then title set S_1 has higher logical level than title set S_2.
iii. For two brother title set S_1 and S_2, four titles t_1, $t_2 \in S_1$, t_3, $t_4 \in S_2$, when t_2 appears between t_3 and t_4, it is not possible that t_3 appears between t_1 and t_2. That is, two brother title sets should not have title appear between titles of each other.
iv. Titles in the same brother title set have the same or similar values for the features listed in Table 1.

5 Semantic View Extraction

At the first step of semantic view extraction, the IE approach used in TIPSI system is based on rule induction. Then, logical structures are used to help extract the relationships between semantic text pieces from the first step. Extracting information from tables is also supported in TIPSI system.

5.1 Rules Based Information Extraction

We propose a tool, called iASA, which learns to automatically annotate web documents according to the metadata. iASA is based on the combination of information extraction (specifically, the Similarity-based Rule Learner—SRL) and machine learning techniques. Using linguistic knowledge and optimal dynamic window size, SRL produces annotation rules of better quality than comparable semantic annotation systems. Similarity-based learning efficiently reduces the search space by avoiding pseudo rule generalization. Due to the limited spaces, we just give a concise introduction to iASA in Sect. 5.1. More details can be found in [3].

Figure 7 shows the architecture of iASA. In Rule Learning, the input is annotated documents. We preprocess the annotated documents and construct the initial rule sets. We then use an empirical method to find the optimal window size for each slot in metadata. Next, we employ the similarity based rule induction on the initial rule set and obtain a set of annotation rules. After the pruning procedure, the output is the learned rule set. In Annotation, the input is un-annotated documents. We applied the learned rules to the un-annotated documents and annotate them according to the metadata. The metadata is defined to represent the annotated or un-annotated documents.

5.1.1 Related Definitions
In both Rule Learning and Annotator, the annotated and un-annotated documents are splitted into a sequence of tokens $\{t_0, t_1...,t_n\}$. Each token can be a word, a name entity or a gazetteer entry. Each token is associated with linguistic attributes.

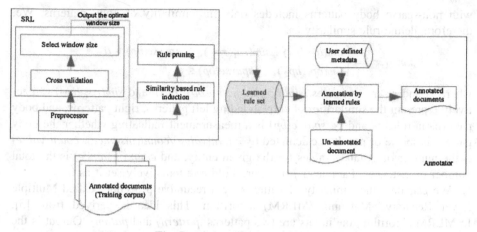

Fig. 7. The architecture of iASA

Specifically, linguistic attributes of word include: "kind", "orth", "type", "pos" and "name". A pattern is a sequence of tokens with length n (n could be zero). Formally, a pattern can be written as:

$$pattern = \{t_0, t_1, \cdots, t_n\}$$

where t_i is the i-th token in the pattern.

Each rule has an entity name and consists of three parts: (1) left pattern: it is used to match the text that immediately precedes the instance (w tokens to the left); (2) body pattern: it corresponds to the instance of an entity (tokens contained); (3) right pattern: it is used to match the text that immediately follows the instance (w tokens to the right).

5.1.2 Similarity Based Rule Learner

In rule induction, we first construct the initial rule set that contains the mostly specified rules from the training annotated documents. Then we use SRL to learn rule set to extract from un-annotated documents.

Rule similarity is the basic idea in SRL. SRL runs in an iterative mode. In each iteration, we always try to select the most similar pair of rules for generalization. Califf et al. adopt a random selection strategy for the rule selection [4]. The similarity based selection method seems more reasonable. There are two reasons for this: similarity based method is more efficient than random method by avoiding the pseudo generalization and learned rules by the random method may be not consistent.

We then need to define the similarity of a pair of rules. Typically, a rule can have three patterns. We can calculate the similarities of the three corresponding patterns and then sum them into an aggregate one. But soon, we found that there are mainly two kinds of rules: rules with sparse body patterns and rules with non-sparse body patterns.

Our proposal is that similarity of rules with sparse body patterns are calculated by the similarities of corresponding left patterns and right patterns, and similarity of rules with non-sparse body patterns includes only the similarity of body patterns. We, therefore, define rule similarity as:

$$sim(r_1,r_2) = \begin{cases} sim(lp_1,lp_2)+sim(rp_1,rp_2), & sparse(bp) > \mu \\ sim(bp_1,bp_2), & sparse(bp) \leq \mu \end{cases}$$

where r_1 and r_2 are two rules. $sim(bp_1,bp_2)$, $sim(bp_1, bp_2)$, and $sim(rp_1, rp_2)$ respectively represent the similarities of corresponding left patterns, right patterns, and body patterns in rules r_1 and r_2. $sparse(bp)$ is a measurement indicating whether the body pattern is sparse or not. It is calculated by $count(value)/count(instance)$. $count(value)$ is the number of instance values for the given entity, and $count(instance)$ is the total number of instances. Parameter μ is a threshold (we tentatively set it as 0.5).

We calculate the similarity of patterns by a recursive procedure called Multiple Layer Recursive Matching (MLRM) algorithm. This idea is derived from [5]. In MLRM algorithm, the inputs are two patterns: $pattern_1$ and $patten_2$. Output is the similarity score of the two patterns.

5.1.3 Optimal Dynamic Window Size Based Context

Analysis on our preliminary experimental results shows that different entities prefer to contexts with different window sizes. For example, in the task of annotating CMU Seminar announcements, with the increase of window size (tested from 2 to 8), the results (evaluated by F-measure) for entity *etime* becomes better; but for entity *stime*, the results becomes worse.

We perform the window size selection for each entity by using cross-validation, a typical approach for experimental selection [6]. Cross validation is a commonly used technique in machine learning to prevent bias. The main idea is based on the following assumption: if the rules learned from a subset of the training data produce accurate result, it is also likely that it will produce high accurate predications when trained on the entire dataset.

In this method, to determine w for each entity, we evaluate the performance on training corpus with contexts of different window sizes using cross-validation. Specifically, let T be the training corpus. The examples in T are first randomly divided into d equal parts T1, T2, ..., Td (we use $d = 10$ in our experiments). Next, for each part $Th_i \wedge$ [1,d], we try to learn the rules from the other (d-1) parts, then apply the learned rules to the examples in T_i. Finally, we select the window size that performs best for each entity. Section 7 will show the comparison of dynamic window size and fixed one.

5.1.4 User Interaction

In semantic view extraction, TIPSI provides two modes: general user mode and specialist mode. In general user mode, users can provide initial rules just by selecting text pieces for slots in metadata. Then the automated rule learner described above can generate new rules that are applicable for unseen documents.

In specialist mode, TIPSI provides GUI to help specialists modify rules. Specialists can modify the patterns, tokens and attributes of tokens by using the GUI shown in Fig. 8. The rules generated by iASA are usually comprehensible to specialists, so specialists can read and modify the rules to make it more effective. This is very important, especially when the amount of training samples is small.

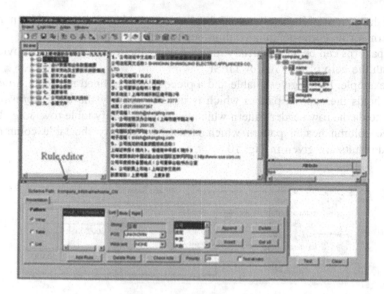

Fig. 8. The Rule Editor

When modifying the rule, we provide three additional functions: rule assistance, rule overlap check, and rule conflict check.

After rules are created, user can modify the rules. However, some rules cannot extract the original texts after modification. Rule Assistance is a feature that can be used to perform the check. If the revised rules cannot extract the original texts, Rule Assistance will prompt a confirm window to notify the user.

Two created rules may overlap with each other. If rule 1 covers rule 2, we say that rule 2 is a redundant rule. Overlap check can find the overlapping relationship between rules. The overlapping relationship includes: 'cover', 'is covered by', 'is the same as'.

More serious, two rules may conflict. For example, rule 1 is defined for company Chinese name, and rule 2 is defined for company English name. If the two rules are found overlapping to each other, we call that the two rules conflict. Because in this case, rule 1 may extract text that is company English name, or rule 2 may extract text that is company Chinese name.

5.2   Information Extraction from Tables

In semi-structured documents, some important information, such as experimental results, financial statistics, is usually displayed in tables. However, due to lack of surrounding text (left pattern and right pattern) for target text in a table cell, the approach proposed in the last section is not suitable for extracting information from tables. So we designed table rules to deal with this problem.

A table rule consists of two parts: patterns to locate table and patterns to locate the target cell. At first, the target table is identified by matching the pattern of its section title and the pattern of its caption. And then, a target table cell is located by matching the patterns of its corresponding column header cell and row header cell.

The patterns can be automatically induced using the training samples provided by users with the help of the GUI of TIPSI.

For example, Fig. 9 gives a table and a piece of user defined metadata. *sales_info* element holds the caption pattern which is used to identify the table. *software_dep* element holds the row header pattern which is used to identify table row. *sale* element holds the column header pattern which is used to identify the table column. The extracted results are given in Fig. 10.

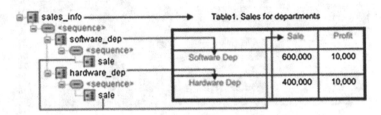

Fig. 9. A table extraction example

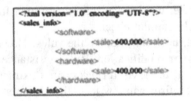

Fig. 10. Extracted result from table

5.3 Semantic Relationship Extraction

Currently, most of the annotation systems are designed only for web pages. However, semi-structured documents are different from web pages, because they usually do not contain hyperlinks, and authorized in strict logical structure. Therefore, we need a new algorithm that fits in the features in this kind of documents.

The existent semantic annotation systems mainly discover the relationships making use of web linkage or sentence structures. As a result, only relationships between pages or within a sentence can be extracted.

In this section, we propose an approach that exploits document logical structure to extract relationships. We first extract target text pieces with iASA. Then we construct the result structure using assumption: the closer two text values are in logical structure, the closer they are in the result structure. For example, company Chinese name 北京胜利电器股份有限公司 and English name "BEIJING SHENGLI APPLI-ANCES CO.,LTD." are both in logical structure 1.1. Company Chinese name 西部电力发展股份有限公司 and English name "WESTERN POWER DEVELOP-MENT CO., LTD" are both in logical structure 2.1. We can know that

北京胜利电器股份有限公司 and "BEIJING SHENGLI APPLIANCES CO.,LTD."
are for the same company.

6 Semantic Search

After semantic annotations of the semi-structured documents, TIPSI allows semantic
search based on user defined metadata. To enable efficient semantic search, TIPSI
make use of three-layer indexing structure which is shown in Fig. 11. Each term
corresponds to a list of metadata nodes, and each metadata node corresponds to a list
of documents containing this term in the metadata node. So if the search is confined in
a metadata node, only the documents that has query terms within the metadata node
will be considered. For example, if a user wants to search within metadata node N1
using terms "computer" and "science", only document D3 will be returned from
indexing. Even though D1 has both the two terms, it will not be returned because the
two terms appear in different metadata nodes (Fig. 12).

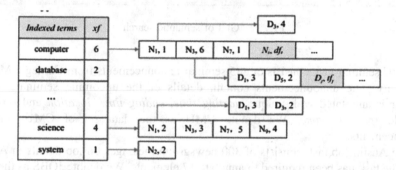

Fig. 11. Three-layer indexing structure

TIPSI provides three types of search:

i.   Full-text search. This type of search provides exactly the same function as
     traditional information retrieval.
ii. Semantic search. Users can use the metadata to help express the query more
     accurate. The following figure shows that how to search for companies that have
     "上海" appear in company Chinese name.
iii. Navigation. It provides navigation from entities to other related entities with the
     help of metadata.

7 IE Evaluation

Our experiments for iASA are performed on two standard tasks: the CMU seminar
announcements [7] and Austin job announcements [4][1].

---

[1] http://www.isi.edu/info-agents/RISE/repository.html

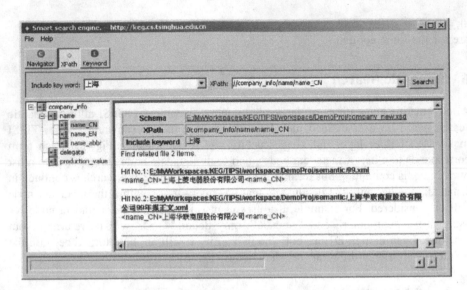

Fig. 12. GUI of semantic search

CMU seminar task consists of 485 seminar announcements from Carnegie Mellon University. The announcements contain details of the upcoming seminars. Each seminar is annotated with unique *starting time*, *ending time*, *location* and possible multiple *speaker name*. We denote CMU as the data set of CMU seminar announcements.

The Austin job task consists of 300 newsgroup messages on job details in Austin area. The task has been required to annotate 17 elements. We denote JOBS as the data set of Austin job announcements.

In experiments, we used a random 50:50 split of the two datasets and repeated 10 times. We used 50:50 because the results for BWI, RAPIER and LP^2, etc. [8] use the same splits for each system.

Table 2 shows the comparison between iASA and several algorithms on CMU. The columns respectively represent the Algorithm, F-score on entity *starting time*, *ending time*, *location*, *speaker name*, and average of these F-scores.

Table 2. Comparison of the seven methods on CMU (%)

Algorithm	Stime	Etime	Speaker	Location	Average
BWI	99.6	93.9	67.7	76.7	83.9
HMM	98.5	62.1	76.6	78.6	82.0
SRV	98.5	77.9	56.3	72.3	77.1
Rapier	93.4	96.2	53.0	72.7	77.3
Whisk	92.6	86.0	18.3	66.4	64.9
LP2	99.0	95.5	77.6	75.0	86.0
iASA	99.8	95.2	75.7	76.5	85.8

As shown in Table 2, we can see that iASA outperforms most of the other algorithms (averagely +2.26 % wrt BWI, +4.63 % wrt HMM, +11.28 % wrt SRV, +11.0 % wrt Rapier, +32.2 % wrt to Whisk), and is competitive with $(LP)^2$ (−0.2 %).

In JOBS, It requires to annotate the seventeen kinds of information related to computer job (some are unique and some are not). We used half of the corpus to train, and the rest to test the learned rules. Table 3 shows the experimental results. The columns respectively represent the entities that are required to annotate, three algorithms (Rapier, BWI, an $(LP)^2$), and iASA. We see averagely iASA significantly outperforms Rapier (by +19 %) and $(LP)^2$ (by +6.3 %).

Table 3. Comparison of the four methods on JOBS (%)

Entity	Rapier	(LP)2	iASA	Entity	Rapier	(LP)2	iASA
Id	97.5	**100.0**	**100.0**	Platform	72.5	**80.5**	82.4
Title	40.5	43.9	**89.1**	Application	69.3	**78.4**	73.8
Company	69.5	71.9	73.6	Area	42.4	**66.9**	55.3
Salary	67.4	62.8	**80.0**	Req-years-e	67.1	68.8	73.7
Recruiter	68.4	80.6	**91.3**	Des-years-e	87.5	**60.4**	66.7
State	90.2	84.7	**91.5**	Req-degree	81.5	**84.7**	65.9
City	90.4	93.0	**95.6**	Des-degree	72.2	**65.1**	80.0
Country	93.2	81.0	**96.6**	Post date	99.5	**99.5**	100.0
Language	80.6	**91.0**	83.2	Average	75.1	**84.1**	89.4

8   Related Work

8.1   Annotation Frameworks

There are a number of systems designed particularly for annotation, for example: Annotea [9], Ontobroker [10], OntoMat-Annotizer, SEAN [11], etc.

Annotea is a Web-based shared annotation system based on a general-purpose open resource description framework (RDF) infrastructure. In Annotea, the annotations are modeled as a class of metadata. Annotations are viewed as statements made by an author about a Web document.

Ontobroker facilitates manual annotation of HTML documents with semantic markups.

SEAN automatically discovers and labels concept instances in template-based, content-rich HTML documents according to an ontology. It combines structural and semantic analysis for annotation. SEAN focuses on well-organized documents, for example documents generated from databases.

8.2   (Semi-) Automated Annotation with Support from Information Extraction

Recently, efforts have been put into automating the annotation task by using machine learning methods. For example, S-CREAM [12], MnM [13] and Melita [14] are three systems exploiting IE algorithm LP2 to automate the procedure of annotation.

S-CREAM is a comprehensive framework for creating annotations, relational metadata in the semantic web, including tools for both manual and semi-automatic annotation of pages. It also comprises inference services, crawler, document management system, ontology guidance/fact browser, document editors/viewers, and a meta ontology.

MnM produces semantic markups with the support from IE algorithm. Besides LP2, it also integrates other IE components (Marmot, Badger, Crystal) from the University of Massachusetts at Amherst (UMass). It allows the semi-automatic population of ontology with metadata.

Melita is a tool for defining and developing automatic ontology-based annotation services that provides different views over the task. It provides manual and semiautomatic annotation, as well as a rule editor for IE experts to edit the annotation rules.

AeroDAML [15] is a tool which takes ontology as metadata and automatically produces a semantic annotation using NLP techniques. It supports only DAML language.

The KIM platform provides semantic annotation, indexing, retrieval services and infrastructure. It performs information extraction based on ontology and a massive knowledge base [16]. The information extraction process in KIM is based on the GATE platform. GATE, s pattern-matching grammars have been modified so as to handle entity class information and to allow generalization of the rules. But, GATE does not provide the ability to learn the annotation rules.

SCORE Enhancement Engine (SEE) supports heterogeneous contents, followed by an automatic classification with extraction of context relevant, domain-specific metadata. Extraction of semantic metadata includes not only the identification of the relevant entities, but also the relationships within the context of relevant ontology. It also presents an approach to automatic semantic annotation [17].

Li et al. propose to combine natural language understanding with learning to automatically generate annotations for specific domains [18]. They aim to learn the syntactic structures from the sentences.

SemTag aims to annotate very large number of pages with terms from a standard ontology in an automated fashion based on disambiguation annotation [19]. SemTag operates as a centralized application with access to the entire database and associated metadata. SemTag manipulates the text linking in web page to its correct resource by disambiguation technology.

Esperonto has an annotation service that helps content providers bridge the gap between the current Web and the Semantic Web. It uses wrapper technology and methodology to upgrade content to Semantic Web content [20, 21].

9   Conclusion

In this paper, we have investigated the problem of semantic annotation for semi-structured documents. We have proposed a tool, called TIPSI, which learns to automatically annotate documents according to metadata defined by users. By using document logical structure induction, we provide high readability for long documents and foundation for semantic view extraction. In semantic view extraction, by using similarity based rule induction, we have been able to improve the rule learning procedure. Experimental results show that our approach can significantly outperform most of the existing wrapper methods. After semantic annotations of the documents, TIPSI allows those to be indexed with respect to the extracted text entities. To answer the query, TIPSI applies semantic restrictions over the entities in the KB.

As the future work, we plan to use machine learning to help semantic relationship construction. Different metadata nodes usually have regular relative logical structure position and regular appearance order (e.g. company name always appears before company address). We also want provide more flexible SQL like search function which makes fully use of metadata.

Acknowledgement. Thanks to anonymous reviewers for their valuable comments. This work was supported by National High Technology Research and Development (863) Program (2011AA01A205).

References

1. Abiteboul, S.: Querying semi-structured data. In: Proceedings of the International Conference on Database Theory, Delphi, Greece, January 1997
2. Summers, K.: Toward a taxonomy of logical document structures. In: Electronic Publishing and the Information Superhighway: Proceedings of the Dartmouth Institute for Advanced Graduate Studies (DAGS), pp. 124–133 (1995)
3. Tang, J., Li, J., Lu, H., Liang, B., Huang, X., Wang, K.-H.: iASA: Learning to Annotate the Semantic Web. In: Spaccapietra, S. (ed.) Journal on Data Semantics IV. LNCS, vol. 3730, pp. 110–145. Springer, Heidelberg (2005)
4. Califf, M.E.: Relational learning techniques for natural language information extraction. Ph.D. thesis. University of Texas, Austin (1998)
5. Soo, V.W., Lee, C.Y., Li, C.-C., Chen, S.L., Chen, C.: Automated semantic annotation and retrieval based on sharable ontology and case-based learning techniques. In: Proceedings of the 2003 Joint Conference on Digital Libraries. IEEE (2003)
6. Schaffer, C.: Selecting a classification method by cross-validation. Mach. Learn. **13**(1), 135–143 (1993)
7. Freitag, D., Kushmerick, N.: Boosted wrapper induction. In: Proceedings of 17th National Conference on Artificial Intelligence (2000)
8. Lavelli, A., Califf, M., Ciravegna, F., Freitag, F., Giuliano, D., Kushmerick, C., Romano, N.: A critical survey of the methodology for IE evaluation. In: Proceedings of the 4th International Conference on Language Resources and Evaluation (2004)
9. Kahan, J., Koivunen, M.R.: Annotea: an open RDF infrastructure for shared web annotations. In: Proceedings of World Wide Web, pp. 623–632 (2001)
10. Fensel, D., Decker, S., Erdmann, M., Studer, R.: Ontobroker: or how to enable intelligent access to the WWW. In: Proceedings of 11th Banff Knowledge Acquisition for Knowledge-Based Systems Workshop, Banff, Canada (1998)
11. Mukherjee, S., Yang, G., Ramakrishnan, I.V.: Automatic annotation of content-rich HTML documents: structural and semantic analysis. In: Fensel, D., Sycara, K., Mylopoulos, J. (eds.) ISWC 2003. LNCS, vol. 2870, pp. 533–549. Springer, Heidelberg (2003)

12. Handschuh, S., Staab, S., Ciravegna, F.: S-CREAM – Semi-automatic CREAtion of metadata. In: Gómez-Pérez, A., Benjamins, V. (eds.) EKAW 2002. LNCS (LNAI), vol. 2473, pp. 358–372. Springer, Heidelberg (2002)
13. Vargas-Vera, M., Motta, E., Domingue, J., Lanzoni, M., Stutt, A., Ciravegna, F.: MnM: ontology driven semiautomatic and automatic support for semantic markup. In: Proceedings of the 13th International Conference on Knowledge Engineering and Management (EKAW 2002), Siguenza, Spain (2002)
14. Ciravegna, F., Dingli, A., Iria, J., Wilks, Y.: Multi-strategy definition of annotation services in Melita. In: ISWC'03 Workshop on Human Language Technology for the Semantic Web and Web Services, pp. 97–107 (2003)
15. Kogut, P., Holmes, W.: AeroDAML: applying information extraction to generate DAML annotations from web pages (2001)
16. Popov, B., Kiryakov, A., Manov, D., Kirilov, A., Ognyanoff, D., Goranov, M.: Towards semantic web information extraction. In: Proceedings of the ISWC'03 Workshop on Human Language Technology for the Semantic Web and Web Services, pp. 1–21 (2003)
17. Hammond, B., Sheth, A., Kochut, K.: Semantic enhancement engine: a modular document enhancement platform for semantic applications over heterogeneous content. In: Kashyap, V., Shklar, L. (eds.) Real World Semantic Web Applications. IOS Press, pp. 29–49, December 2002
18. Li, J., Yu, Y.: Learning to generate semantic annotation for domain specific sentences. In: Proceedings of the Knowledge Markup and Semantic Annotation Workshop in K-CAP 2001, Victoria, BC (2001)
19. Dill, S., Eiron, N., Gibson, D., Gruhl, D., Guha, R., Jhingran, A., Kanungo, T., McCurley, K.S., Rajagopalan, S., Tomkins, A., Tomlin, J.A., Zien, J.Y.: A case for automated large-scale semantic annotation. J. Web Semant. Sci., Serv. Agents World Wide Web 1, 115–132 (2003)
20. Buitelaar, P., Declerck, T.: Linguistic annotation for the semantic web. In: Annotation for the Semantic Web, Frontiers in Artificial Intelligence and Applications Series, Vol. 96. IOS Press (2003)
21. Handschuh, S., Staab, S.: Annotation for the Semantic Web. Frontiers in Artificial Intelligence and Applications, vol. 96. New IOS Publication (2003)

Introduction and Analysis of Simulators of MapReduce

Yuanquan Fan[✉], Wei Wei, Yan Gao, and Weiguo Wu

Department of Computer Science and Technology,
Xi'an Jiaotong University, Xi'an, China
{vcivc,wwtfs}@163.com, wgwu@mail.xjtu.edu.cn

Abstract. Recently MapReduce has emerged as a popular model for supporting modern data-intensive computing. Hadoop, Apache open source project, has implemented MapReduce, which becomes the most popular tools for many programmers due to its ability to process parallel programming. However, to control the resource allocations and power efficient among the jobs, working on simulate the MapReduce is still important. So, there are a large number of simulating tools available to simulate distributed environment. In this paper, we conclude some typical simulator on MapReduce and analysis their work flow and defect to help the programmer of MapReduce to model the real execution process of MapReduce job.

Keywords: MapReduce · Hadoop · Simulator · Power saving

1   Introduction

Currently, data-intensive computing is emerging as an available model of enabling fast time-to-solution for modern large-scale data-intensive applications, which has become a hotspot in the academic and industrial community. Cloud computing, which was coined in late of 2007, recently emerges as a hot topic due to its abilities to offer flexible dynamic IT infrastructures, QoS guaranteed computing environments and configurable software services. Google has designed and implemented the Google File System (GFS) [1] to meet the rapidly growing demands of Google's data processing needs. GFS is driven by key observation of data-intensive applications workloads and technological environment. At the same time, Google developed MapReduce, which is a programming model and an associated implementation for processing and generating large data sets. Hadoop, the open source clouding computing architecture, which developed by Apache, has implemented the MapReduce [2] and Google's GFS named Hadoop Distributed File system (HDFS) [3]. At this time, Hadoop become an interest of academic and commercial areas.

HDFS provides reliable storage and high throughout access to data. Hadoop implements a Rack-Aware-Based data block replication policy for the data that is stored on HDFS. For the default replication factor of three, it's replica placement policy is to put the first replica of the block on one node in the local rack, another one on a different node in the same rack, the third one on a node in some other rack, which is really important for fault tolerance and data availability. So HDFS is suitable for

Y. Yuan et al. (Eds.): ISCTCS 2013, CCIS 426, pp. 345–350, 2014.
DOI: 10.1007/978-3-662-43908-1_42, © Springer-Verlag Berlin Heidelberg 2014

applications that have huge data sets, especially the MapReduce programming framework for data-intensive computing. Based on above mentioned, it has widely used and become a popular storage application for cloud computing.

MapReduce, a cloud computing programming model, which takes a set of input data key/value pairs, and produce a set of output key/value pairs. The only thing the user of MapReduce to do is expressing the commutation as two functions: Map and Reduce. Map takes an input pair from HDFS and produces a set of output, named intermediate key/value pair, then the shuffle stage passes intermediate data to the Reduce function to deeply process. Reduce function accepts an intermediate key/value pair and merge together the values to form a possible result set of values. Finally, it writes these results to HDFS. In detail, the map task can be roughly divided into 4 phases: Initialize the task, read input data to buffer, parse input data as key/value pairs (map function), partitioned the map output and write them to sort-buffer. The reduce task fetches data from data from map to local memory buffer, after that merge data in the buffer, serialize and write it to temporal local files. It is important to understanding the processing of MapReduce.

Power-saving has become an important concept in data-intensive computing for every company. So, some companies begin to develop a simulator of MapReduce to reduce the cost of cluster. Actually, it is really a good idea to do it. This paper will introduce some popular simulators of MapReduce and catch up with some challenges of it.

2   Introduction of Simulators

We have performed some research on some typical simulators on MapReduce, such as Mumak, MRPerf, SimMR. We have found a lot of problems and challenges during the study. Now we will show it.

2.1   Mumak

The goal of Mumak [4] is to build a discrete event simulator conditions when a Hadoop MapReduce Scheduler performs on a large-scale specific workload. Mumak is composed of following entities: simulator client, simulator Job Tracker, simulator Task Tracker and the main part named simulated engine. The simulator Engine maintains an event-queue and manages all the events and entities in virtual time. It will fire the right handler when the relevant event occurs. The various event-types are HeartbeatEvent (an event which instructs a specific Task Tracker to send a heartbeat to the Job Tracker), TaskCompletionEvent (an event which denotes the completion (success/failure) of a specific map or reduce task which is sent to the Task Tracker), JobSubmissionEvent (an event which instructs the Job Client to submit a specific job to the Job Tracker). The simulator Job Tracker receives heartbeats from all simulator Task Trackers and it tracks the progress of the current jobs and merges together the schedule information from scheduler, then make the task-scheduling decisions. Figure 1 shows the architecture of Mumak.

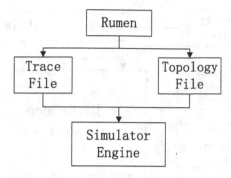

Fig. 1. Mumak design

Before the Mumak simulation, it needs trace file and topology file produced by Rumen [5]. The Rumen process job history logs to produce file describing detailed job trace information and the network topology as inferred from the host location and rackeIDs. Then Mumak uses data from real experiment to estimate completion time for map and reduce tasks.

But, Mumak can be used to enable easy debug and verify on Job Tracker/scheduler design by simulating Hadoop. Currently Mumak can only simulate base on the log information of a previously finished work. And the system settings, for example, number of nodes, the processing power of each node, cannot be changed. So it can only debug and verify on current setting. So, the situations it can simulate is quite limited. In conclusion, Mumak does not support for different number of nodes, cannot simulate the network traffic, disk traffic and the shuffle phase.

2.2 MRPerf

The goal of MRPerf [6] is to provide fine-grained simulation of MapReduce setups at sub-phase level. MRPerf has two simplifying assumptions: first of all, a node's resources are equally shared among task assigned concurrently to the node; secondly, it cannot simulate OS-level asynchronous prefetching, and it only overlaps I/O and computation across threads and processors.

MRPerf adopts packet-level simulation and its main job is to model the map and reduce tasks, manage their associated input and output data, make scheduling decisions and simulate disk and processor loads. To use the simulator, one has to provide four files: node specification, cluster topology, data layout and job description. The output information is a detailed phase-level execution trace, which provides job execution time, amount of data transferred and time-sorted of each phase of the task and so on. Figure 2 shows the design of MRPerf.

The Job Tracker is responsible for spawning map and reduce tasks, keeping a tab on when different phases complete, and producing the final results. Most of the Job Trackers' behaviors are simulated in response to receiving different messages from other nodes.

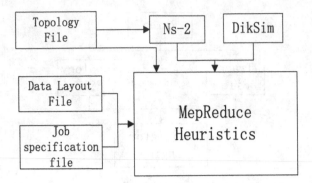

Fig. 2. MRPerf architecture

When the Job Tracker receive a message to start a map task form the queue of events, firstly instantiate a JVM for the task, then get the necessary data from local disk or remotely, thirdly performs the map sort and spill operation on the input data until all of it has been consumed, finally notify the Job Tracker a message indicating the completion of the map task. On receiving a message to start a reduce task, the Job Tracker get the data from all the map tasks, then it processes the intermediate data with application-specific reduce function. Finally, a message indicating the completion of reduce task is send to Job Tracker, and the process waits for its next assignment. Figure 3 show the control progress of Job Tracker.

But, currently MRPerf is limited to simulating a single storage device per node, supporting only one replica for each block of output data. It also cannot simulate the

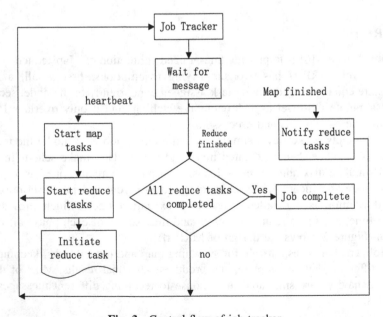

Fig. 3. Control flow of job tracker

speculative execution, which is an optimization method working well. The simulator cannot support advanced exceptions, such as a node running slower than others or partially failing.

2.3 SimMR

MRSim [8] is a simulator based on discrete event simulation, which is aimed to simulate data mining algorithms on Hadoop environment. It uses SimJava to accurately simulate interactions between different entities within cluster. MRSim use GridSim [9] as the basic tool to simulate the network topology and network traffic, but it simulate data splits locations and splits replications in local rack only, which is really a limitation. Before simulation, MRSim need two files: cluster topology file and job specification file. The former records the topology information by key/value pairs and the letter records some parameters of a MapReduce job, such as map slots, reduce slots and so on. So, it enables the user to estimate the best job configurations to get optimum performance for certain algorithms.

3 Conclusion and Future Work

In this paper, we introduce and analysis some popular simulators of MapReduce jobs. Mumak is designed to use data from real experiments to estimate completion time for map and reduce tasks with different scheduling algorithm, but currently Mumak is quite constrained. It can only perform simulations with the same job setting as the real job performed. If we want to know how long the work will run with a different setup, for example, a larger cluster, then the change in topology and the time to do shuffle and sort has to be considered. To achieve this, we may make modification to the Rumen logs in following approaches: add some random variables to simulate the situations, such as resource contentions, node failures and so on; we could analyze the simulator log result, encapsulate the program as a library and extract several APIs. After that, other Hadoop programs could invoke the API and return the result directly. MRPerf is a realistic phase-level simulator for widespread MapReduce framework, toward designing, provisioning, and fine-tuning Hadoop setups. But the only defect is that it cannot model speculative execution, the lower node and resource contention. SimMR can quickly replay production cluster workloads with different scenarios of interests, assess various what-if questions, and help avoiding error-prone decisions, but if it can simulate the jobs with much detail, the result will be much better.

Simulation of MapReduce job is really a hard job because the complexity of cluster environment. Most of the simulators are based on logs produced by expired jobs, using the logs to extract workloads and job traces information to simulate the same type jobs even the same jobs. The other important point is how to simulate the data block placement to improve the locality of map task with each data has three replicas. So, we really face a lot of challenges during the simulation of MapReduce jobs.

As mention above, most simulators of MapReduce work on the old MapReduce framework. But as the MR2/Yarn has emerged as a new framework which has a lot of changes comparing with MR1, it is important to consider the MR2/Yarn and develop a new simulator of MR2/Yarn.

Acknowledgement. This work is supported by the National High-Tech Research and Development Plan of China under Grant No. 2011AA01A204 and 2012AA01A306, National Key Technology R&D Program under grant No. 2011BAH04B03, National Natural Science Foundation of China under grant NO. 61202041, and the Fundamental Research Funds for the Central Universities under grant 08142007.

References

1. Ghemawat, S., Gobioff, H., Leung, S-T.: The Google file system. In: Proceedings of the 19th ACM SOSP, pp. 29–43, Dec 2003
2. Dean, J., Ghemawat, S.: MapReduce: simplified data processing on large clusters. In: Proceedings of the 6th USENIX Symposium on Operating Systems Design and Implementation (OSDI2004), pp. 137–150 (2004)
3. Apache Hadoop. http://hadoop.apache.org
4. Mumak.: Map-Reduce Simulator ASF JIRA. https://issues.apache.org/jira/browse/MAPREDUCE-728. Accessed 21 Apr 2010
5. Apache.: Rumen: a tool to extract job characterization data from jobtracker logs (2010). https://issues.apache.org/jira/browse/MAPREDUCE-751
6. Wang, G., Butt, A.R., Pandey, P., Gupta, K.: Using realistic simulation for performance analysis of MapReduce setups. In: Proceedings of the 1st ACM Workshop on Large-Scale System and Application Performance, Garching. ACM, Germany (2009), pp. 19–26
7. Verma, A., Cherkasova, L., Campbell, R.H.: PlayItAgain, SimMR!. In: Proceedings of the 2011 IEEE International Conference on Cluster Computing (Cluster'2011)
8. Hammoud, S., Li, M., Liu, Y., Alham, N., Liu, Z.: MRSim: a discrete event based MapReduce simulator. In: 2010 Seventh International Conference on Fuzzy Systems and Knowledge Discovery (FSKD), vol. 6 (2010)
9. GridSim.: Get GridSim: A grid simulation toolkit at SourceForge.net. http://sourceforge.net/projects/gridsim/. Accessed 21 Apr 2010
10. Howell, F., McNab, R.: SimJava: A Discrete Event Simulation Library for Java. Simulation Series, vol. 30, 1998
11. Wang, G., Butt, A., Pandey, P., Gupta, K.: A simulation approach to evaluating design decisions in MapReduce setups. In: International Symposium on Modelling, Analysis and Simulation of Computer and Telecommunication Systems (2009)

Level Set Method Based Image Segmentation
by Combining Local Information
with Global Information

Cong Yang[✉], Weiguo Wu, and Yuanqi Su

School of Electronic and Information Engineering, Xi'an Jiaotong University,
Xi'an, China
yccd425@163.com, wgwu@mail.xjtu.edu.cn

Abstract. A novel level set based image segmentation method is proposed in this paper. After analyzing advantages and drawbacks of SBGFRLS and LSD model, we propose a way to combine local information and global information through utilizing weighted energy generated by SBGFRLS model to reduce segmentation error and accelerate curve evolution. The total energy of proposed method comprises of local energy term, length term and weighted global energy term. In our experiments, two alternative values for the coefficient of global term are 0.1 or −0.1. Experiments on images with noise and intensity inhomogeneities show that the proposed method is effective and more accurate than both SBGFRLS model and LSD model.

Keywords: Image inhomogeneities · LSD · SBGFRLS · Global statistical information · Local statistical information

1 Introduction

Image segmentation is to partition the image plane into several areas corresponding to different objects from the background. Among existing segmentation methods, i.e., split and merge [1, 2], region growing [3, 4], feature based schemes [5–8] and so on, level set method [9–15] has been one of the most successful methods due to its desirable advantages over traditional methods, such as, sub-pixel accuracy and topology variability. Existing level set based segmentation methods can be divided into two main categories: the edge-based methods and the region-based methods.

Edge-based methods [9–12] adopt image gradient information to attract active contour toward desired boundaries. One of the most famous methods is the GAC [11, 12] model, which utilizes edge stopping function (ESF) and a balloon force term to control the motion of contour. Edge stopping function which is utilized to stop the evolution while the contour is on the object boundaries is constructed by using image gradient, and. And the balloon force term is introduced to shrink or expand the contour. But it is difficult to design the balloon force, if it is not well designed, the contour will either pass through the weak edge or may not pass through the narrow part of the object.

Region-based methods [13–15] use region statistical information to guide curve evolution. CV model which is based on Mumford-Shah segmentation technique [16]

Y. Yuan et al. (Eds.): ISCTCS 2013, CCIS 426, pp. 351–361, 2014.
DOI: 10.1007/978-3-662-43908-1_43, © Springer-Verlag Berlin Heidelberg 2014

is one of the most popular region-based models, it achieves good performances on images with intensities homogeneity and has been successfully applied in binary phase segmentation. However, it has some drawbacks, i.e. it often gives inaccurate segmentation results while segmenting images with great intensity inhomogeneities. To solve this problem, piecewise smooth model in [14] was proposed. However, in order to keep the level set function close to a signed distance function, these methods always need to re-initialize the level set function to a signed distance function periodically, this procedure is highly computational cost. Chunming Li proposed penalizing energy [17] to avoid re-initializing procedure.

In order to dealing with images with intensity inhomogeneities, local methods [18, 19] were proposed. Chunming Li et al. introduced a local binary fitting (LBF) [18] energy by a kernel function. And Li Wang proposed local Gaussian energy [19] Motivated by Chunming Li and Li Wang, Lingfeng Wang et al. proposed a novel model which adopts local signed difference energy (LSD) [20, 21] to drive contour evolution. Zhang et al. proposed SBGFRLS model [22] which shares the advantages of the CV and GAC models. They utilize a SPF function to substitute for ESF.

As SBGFRLS model is based on the assumption that the images are intensity homogeneity, thus making it hard to deal with images with intensity inhomogeneities, despite that it's very effective, and robustness to noise. LSD model often gets inaccurate results while the desired objects occupy locations near border of the images. In this paper, a method integrated SBGFRLS model and LSD model is proposed, experiments show that the proposed method is effective and more accurate than both SBGFRLS and LSD model.

The rest of this paper is organized as follows. In Sect. 2, a brief introduction of some popular models will be presented. Then we will describe the proposed segmentation methods and its implementation in details in Sects. 3 and 4. In Sect. 5 experiment results will be provided. Section 6 concludes the paper.

2 Previous Work

2.1 The SBGFRLS Model

Zhang introduces a SPF function instead of ESF in GAC model. Let $\Omega \in R^2$ be the image domain, $I : [0, a] \times [0, b] \rightarrow R^+$ be a given image, and $C(q) : [0, 1] \rightarrow R^2$ be a parameterized planar curve in Ω. Its energy functional and the corresponding level set formulation of GAC are given as follows:

$$E^{GAC}(C) = \int_0^1 g(|\nabla I(C(q))|)|C'(q)|dq \tag{1}$$

$$\frac{\partial \phi}{\partial t} = g|\nabla \phi|(div(\frac{\nabla \phi}{|\nabla \phi|}) + \alpha) + g \cdot \nabla \phi \tag{2}$$

Where α is the balloon force, g is the ESF defined as

$$g(|\nabla I|) = \frac{1}{1 + |\nabla G_\sigma * I|^2} \tag{3}$$

Where G_σ denotes the Gaussian kernel with standard deviation. And the level set formulation of SBGFRLS model can be written as

$$\frac{\partial \phi}{\partial t} = spf(I(x)) \cdot (div(\frac{\nabla \phi}{|\nabla \phi|}) + \alpha) + \nabla spf(I(x)) \cdot \nabla \phi \quad x \in \Omega \tag{4}$$

Where α is a balloon force, and $spf(I(x))$ is defined as

$$spf(I(x)) = \frac{I(x) - (c_1 + c_2)/2}{\max(|I(x) - (c_1 + c_2)/2)} \tag{5}$$

And c_1 and c_2 are solved as follows:

$$c_1(\phi) = \frac{\int_\Omega I(x) \cdot H_\varepsilon(\phi)dx}{\int_\Omega H_\varepsilon(\phi)dx} \tag{6}$$

$$c_2(\phi) = \frac{\int_\Omega I(x) \cdot (1 - H_\varepsilon(\phi))dx}{\int_\Omega (1 - H_\varepsilon(\phi))dx} \tag{7}$$

Where H is the Heaviside function, and is usually selected as

$$H_\varepsilon(x) = \frac{1}{2}(1 + \frac{2}{\pi}\arctan(\frac{x}{\varepsilon})) \tag{8}$$

The SPF function defined in Eq. (4) is constructed by using global statistical information. As SBGFRLS model has no convolution procedure, it's more efficient than both GAC and CV model. However, experiments show that the model doesn't achieve satisfactory performance on images with intensity inhomogeneities as shown in Sect. 5.

2.2   The LSD Model

Wang et al. proposed a novel LSD in [20], the total energy is defined as

$$E(\phi) = \int_\Omega W(x)E_{lsd}dx + \mu L(\phi) + \nu P(\phi) \tag{9}$$

Where $W(x)$ is the weight of the pixel at the location x, μ and ν are two positive weighting constants. It is utilized to control the evolution of the contour, and defined by as follows:

$$W(x) = \int_{\Omega_f} K_{\sigma,x}(y)dy \int_{\Omega_b} K_{\sigma,x}(y)dy \tag{10}$$

In Eq. (9), Ω_f and Ω_b stand for foreground and background of the image. $K_{\sigma,x}(x)$ is a Gaussian kernel function and chose as

$$K_{\sigma,x}(y) = \begin{cases} \frac{1}{c_k 2\pi\sigma^2}\exp^{\frac{-(||x-y||^2)}{\sigma^2}} & ||x-y|| \leq 2\sigma \\ 0 & ||x-y|| \geq 2\sigma \end{cases} \tag{11}$$

In Eq. (8) E_{lsd} is given by

$$E_{lsd}(x) = \frac{\int_{\Omega_b} K_{\sigma,x}(y)I(y)dy}{\int_{\Omega_b} K_{\sigma,x}(y)dy} - \frac{\int_{\Omega_f} K_{\sigma,x}(y)I(y)dy}{\int_{\Omega_f} K_{\sigma,x}(y)dy} \qquad (12)$$

From Eq. (11) we can see that E_{lsd} is generated by local statistical information, it utilizes the deference between the local foreground cluster and the local background cluster which can help holding global consistency as presented in [20]. However, the curve will stay near initial contour when the background is pure as shown in Sect. 5.

In Eq. (8), $L(\phi)$ is the contour length term which is the prior knowledge on the contour. And $P(\phi)$ proposed by Li [17] is the regularization term which serves to maintain the level set function as a signed distance function. Its definition is

$$L(\phi) = \int_\Omega |\nabla H(\phi(x))|dx \qquad (13)$$

$$P(\phi) = \int_\Omega \frac{1}{2}(|\nabla\phi(x)| - 1)^2 dx \qquad (14)$$

The level set formulation is

$$\frac{\partial\phi}{\partial t} = -\delta_\varepsilon(\phi)DF + \mu\delta_\varepsilon(\phi)div(\frac{\nabla\phi}{|\nabla\phi|}) + v(\nabla^2\phi - div(\frac{\nabla\phi}{|\nabla\phi|})) \qquad (15)$$

$$DF = \int_\Omega (K_{\sigma,x}(y)I(y) \int_\Omega K_{\sigma,x}(y)dy)dx$$
$$- \int_\Omega (K_{\sigma,x}(y) \int_\Omega I(y)K_{\sigma,x}(y)dy)dx \qquad (16)$$

Where $\delta_\varepsilon(x)$ is Dirac function, and it can be obtained by derivation of $H_\varepsilon(x)$.

$$\delta_\varepsilon(x) = \frac{1}{\pi} \cdot \frac{\varepsilon}{\varepsilon^2 + x^2} \qquad (17)$$

3   The Proposed Method

After analyzing advantages and drawbacks of SBGFRLS model and LSD model, we proposed a novel way to combine local information and global information, its total energy is defined as

$$E(\phi) = \int_\Omega W(x)E_{lsd}dx + \mu L(\phi) + \lambda \int_0^1 spf(|\nabla I(C(q))|)|C'(q)|dq \qquad (18)$$

Where $spf(x)$, $W(x)$ and E_{lsd} are given in Eqs. (5), (10) and (12). While E_{lsd} and has locality and $spf(x)$ has globality, the total energy comprises of local energy term, length term and weighted global energy term. The level set formulation of our method is

$$\frac{\partial \phi}{\partial t} = -\delta_\varepsilon(\phi)DF + \mu\delta_\varepsilon(\phi)div(\frac{\nabla\phi}{|\nabla\phi|}) + \nabla spf(I(x)) \cdot \nabla\phi$$
$$+ \lambda(spf(I(x)) \cdot (div(\frac{\nabla\phi}{|\nabla\phi|}) + \alpha)|\nabla\phi| \quad \cdot$$

(19)

The *DF* term is defined in Eq. (16).

The SBGFRLS model has global region segmentation property, it's hard to deal with images with intensity inhomogeneities. The LSD model gets inaccurate results near the edges of the image. Another drawback of LSD model is that the curve evolution process will be very slow while dealing with binary images. We utilize SBGFRLS model to reduce segmentation errors produced by LSD model, and accelerate the evolution. We also adopt $L(\phi)$ as the prior knowledge on the contour. Experiments show that the problems above are well solved by integrating SBGRFLS model and LSD model.

4 Implementation

As pointed out in [22] inspired by [23] and [24], we can use a Gaussian filtering to regularize the level set function to substitute for the curvature-based term $div(\nabla\phi/|\nabla\phi|)|\nabla\phi|$. As the function *spf* is derived from global statistical information, it has a larger capture range and capacity of anti-edge leakage [22]. So the $\nabla spf(I(x)) \cdot \nabla\phi$ term can also be removed. Hence the Eq. (19) can be simplified as

$$\frac{\partial \phi}{\partial t} = -\delta_\varepsilon(\phi)DF + \mu\delta_\varepsilon(\phi)div(\frac{\nabla\phi}{|\nabla\phi|}) + \lambda\alpha spf(I(x))|\nabla\phi| \quad (20)$$

In Eq. 20, we note that $\lambda\alpha$ is equal to a balloon force, here we mean to diminish the influence of SPF for stability and accuracy, we always set λ rather 0.1 or -0.1. In order to compared with SGBFRLS model, we set α the same in both methods, then we will see how does λ affect curve evolution in the proposed method.

5 Experiments

The proposed method has been tested on images from different modalities, and the model is implemented by Matlab2010a on a computer with Intel(R) i5-2400 CPU 3.10 GHZ, 8.0 G RAM and WIN7 operating system.

Our model is compared with three state-of-the-art methods, namely, CV, LSD, SBGFRLS, the parameters for the methods above are set as:

For CV model, the parameter μ is the same as ours, and the time-step Δt is set as a constant 0.5;

For LSD model, the parameters are set equal to ours, and $v = 1$. In order to achieve the best performance, we set μ a little different from ours for some images;

For SBGFRLS, the time-step Δt is set to 1.

In our experiments, the default settings of parameters are $\Delta t = 0.1$, $\mu = 0.002 * 255 * 255$, $\alpha = 35$, $\lambda = 0.1$, and $\sigma = 1$, μ is the same as [20]. In the following part, green rectangles stand for initial contour in the figures.

5.1 Comparison with Three State-of-the-Art Methods

Figure 1 shows comparisons of our method with some other models for synthetic image with hole, real image in which some desired boundaries are near edges, image with intensity inhomogeneities, and the weak boundaries blood vessel image. Table 1 shows the consuming time and iterations of each method.

There is a background region surrounded by the desired objects in the first image. As shown in Fig. 1, CV model and the proposed method achieve the best segmentation result. From the definition of E_{lsd} in Eq. 12, when the background is global pure and the initial contour is far away from foreground, we can easily get that E_{lsd} regions near the initial contour is zero as shown in Fig. 2, c1 stands for the intensity of background. However, the length term which leads to segmentation errors of LSD model will make the contour near initial contour stop driving to the boundaries.

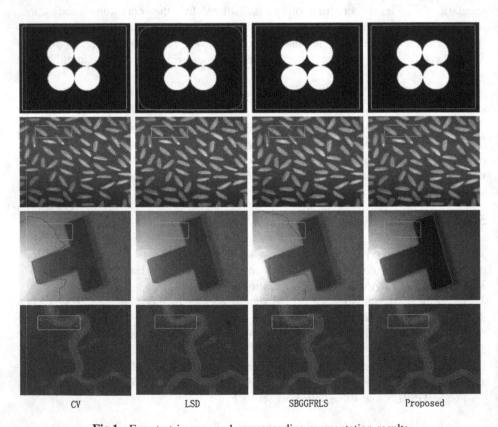

| CV | LSD | SBGGFRLS | Proposed |

Fig.1. Four test images and corresponding segmentation results

Table 1. Comparisons of consuming time and iterations

	First image		Second image		Third image		Fourth image	
	Time(s)	Iterations	Time(s)	Iterations	Time(s)	Iterations	Time(s)	Iterations
CV	17.4877	638	17.9713	1536	8.3617	931	5.1168	496
SBGFRLS	0.2652	40	0.0780	50	0.0312	24	0.0624	50
LSD	15.6781	700	0.1092	20	2.2464	440	0.2808	50
Proposed	1.9032	58	0.0936	15	0.3588	53	0.2340	30

Through experiments under this condition for LSD model, we found when μ is set as approximate to zero the effect is better improved.

The second image is one rice image corrupted by intensity inhomogeneity. In the test we found that the length term would affect the result at the locations near borders, so we set $\mu = 0$ for both LSD model and the proposed model, latter we will discuss how the length term influence the contour evolution. The LSD model segments all the objects out, but there are some errors at the location near top and bottom of the image.

The third image is a typical image with great intensity inhomogeneity. Figure 1 shows that CV model and SBGFRLS model do not work well with images of this type. The LSD and the proposed model achieve almost the same result. But Table 1 shows that both time consuming and iterations, our model are much less than the LSD model, that means our model is more efficiency while handling the case.

The fourth image is a medical image whose boundaries is quite weak, in this test, the parameter is a little different from the default, we set $\mu = 0.0027 * 255 * 255$, for SBGFRLS model, in order to achieve the best result, we adjusted α from 20 to 200, and σ from 1 to 3, the result in Fig. 1 is one of the satisfactory segmentation.

Table 1 shows the consuming time and iterations of each model. From it, we can easily get that the SBFFRLS model is the fastest model, and the proposed model is not only efficient but also accurate as shown in Fig. 1 and Table 1.

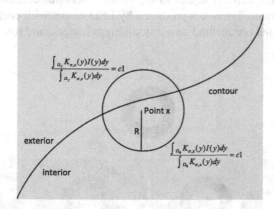

Fig. 2. The local signed difference energy is 0

5.2   Noise Sensitivity

The original image and four noise images with different noise level are shown in the Fig. 3. We utilize Gaussian function integrated in Matlab function library to add noise. And the corresponding truly noise level from left to right in the second line is 0.05*255*255, 0.10.05*255*255, 0.150.05*255*255, 0.2 0.05*255*255.

Segmentation results of each method are presented in Fig. 4. As demonstrated before, CV model gets not good enough results while dealing with noise image; and other three methods get approximate results while noise level is now. However SBGFRLS and LSD occur segmentation errors with increase of noise level. We can observe in Fig. 4, even the noise level approaches 0.2*255*255, the proposed method returns result which is highly approximated to the truly boundaries, that proves our method is more robustness to noise than the other three models. In our experiment, we noticed that when the noise level is higher than 0.5*255*255, our method will get segmentation errors, too.

5.3   Multiphase Segmentation

Figure 5 shows a synthetic image with three different intensity objects and segmentation results using the proposed method. The grey levels of three objects from top to down and left to right are as follows: 240, 116 and 26, the background is 6. And the parameters are as follows: $\Delta t = 0.1$, $\mu = 0.0005 * 255 * 255$, $\alpha = 20$, $\lambda = 0.1$, and $\sigma = 1$. However, the proposed method is the same to SBGFRLS and LSD model while dealing with images having higher intensity and lower intensity than background objects simultaneously.

5.4   Parameters Analysis

In this section we mainly focus on λ and μ. Figure 6 shows segmentation results with parameter λ which respectively equals to -0.1, -0.2, 0.1 and 0.2. SBGFRLS model is used to reduce segmentation errors produced by LSD model with coefficient λ. In our experiments, we tested our method on many different images, and found that when λ is

Fig. 3. Original image and noised images

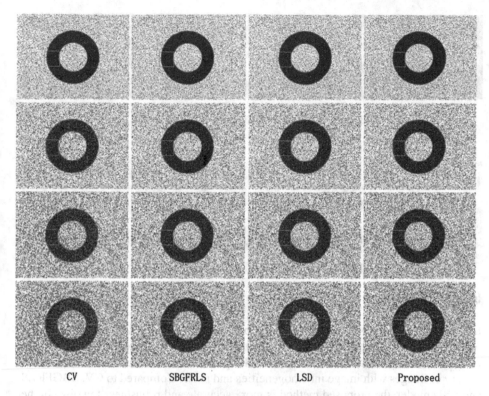

| CV | SBGFRLS | LSD | Proposed |

Fig. 4. Four noise images with different noise level and the corresponding results

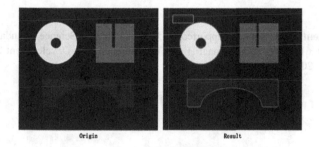

Origin   Result

Fig. 5. Multiphase segmentation result

assigned to −0.1 or 0.1, we got the best result, whether λ is assigned to plus or minus is depended on the energy produced by LSD and SBFGRLS model.

Figure 7 shows how the length term affects segmentation result, μ is assigned to 0 *255*255, 0.001*255, 0.003*255 and 0.005*255, and other coefficients are $\Delta t = 0.05$, $\alpha = 20$, $\lambda = 0.1$, and $\sigma = 1$. From Fig. 7, we conclusion that with increase of μ, the length term affects the contour at narrow parts of the desired objects, such as locations between the middle finger and the ring finger, While the length term is more weighted in total energy with increasing of μ, the contour will join together rather than passing through it at such locations.

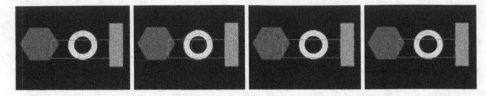

Fig. 6. Segmentation results with different λ

Fig. 7. The length term affects segmentation

6 Conclusions

In this paper, we propose a novel method by integrating SBGFRLS model and LSD model. The main contribution is that we utilize a weighted energy to reduce segmentation error produced by LSD model. The proposed method has been valued on a variety of images with image inhomogeneities and noise. Compared to CV, SBGFRLS and LSD model, the proposed method is more accurate and robustness to noise. In the future, we will propose a novel energy formulation including global and local energy involved.

Acknowledgement. This work is supported by National Natural Science Foundation of China under Grant NO. 61305051 and National High-Tech Research and Development Plan of China under Grant No. 2012AA01A306.

References

1. Ilea, D.E., Whelan, P.F.: Color image segmentation using a self-initializing EM algorithm. In: Proceedings of the 6th IASTED International Conference on Visualization, Imaging, and Image Processing (2006)
2. Chen, K.M., Chen, S.Y.: Color texture segmentation using feature distributions. Pattern Recogn. Lett. **23**(7), 755–771 (2002)
3. Pappas, T.N.: An adaptive clustering-algorithm for image segmentation. IEEE Trans. Sig. Process. **40**(4), 901–914 (1992)
4. Junqing, C., Pappas, T.N., Mojsilovic, A., Rogowitz, B.E.: Adaptive perceptual color-texture image segmentation. IEEE Trans. Image Process. **14**(10), 1524–1536 (2005)
5. Zoller, T., Hermes, L., Buhmann, J.M.: Combined color and texture segmentation by parametric distributional clustering. In: 16th International Conference on Pattern Recognition, Vol II, Proceedings (2002)

6. Ilea, D.E., Whelan, P.F.: CTex - An adaptive unsupervised segmentation algorithm based on color-texture coherence. IEEE Trans. Image Process. **17**(10), 1926–1939 (2008)

7. Kato, Z., Pong, T.-C.: A Markov random field image segmentation model for color textured images. Image Vis. Comput. **24**, 1103–1114 (2006)

8. Serrano, C., Acha, B.: Pattern analysis of dermoscopic images based on Markov random fields. Pattern Recogn. **42**(6), 1052–1057 (2009)

9. Kass, M., Witkin, A., Terzopoulos, D.: Snakes: active contour models. In: Proceedings of the 1st International Conference on Computer Vision (Cat. No.87CH2465-3) (1987)

10. Sundaramoorthi, G., Yezzi, A., Mennucci, A.C., Sapiro, G.: New possibilities with Sobolev active contours. Int. J. Comput. Vis. **84**(2), 113–129 (2009)

11. Caselles, V., Kimmel, R., Sapiro, G.: Geodesic active contours. Int. J. Comput. Vis. **22**(1), 61–79 (1997)

12. Paragios, N., Deriche, R.: Geodesic active regions and level set methods for supervised texture segmentation. Int. J. Comput. Vis. **46**(3), 223–247 (2002)

13. Chan, T.F., Vese, L.A.: Active contours without edges. IEEE Trans. Image Process. **10**(2), 266–277 (2001)

14. Vese, L.A., Chan, T.F.: A multiphase level set framework for image segmentation using the Mumford and Shah model. Int. J. Comput. Vis. **50**(3), 271–293 (2002)

15. Tsai, A., Yezzi, A., Willsky, A.S.: Curve evolution implementation of the Mumford-Shah functional for image segmentation, denoising, interpolation, and magnification. IEEE Trans. Image Process. **10**(8), 1169–1186 (2001)

16. Mumford, D., Shah, J.: Optimal approximations by piecewise smooth functions and associated variational-problems. Commun. Pure Appl. Math. **42**(5), 577–685 (1989)

17. Chunming, L., Chenyang, X., Changfeng, G., Fox, M.D.: Level set evolution without re-initialization: a new variational formulation. In: 2005 IEEE Computer Society Conference on Computer Vision and Pattern Recognition, Proceedings (2005)

18. Li, C.M., Kao, C.Y., Gore, J.C., Ding, Z.H.: Implicit active contours driven by local binary fitting energy, In: 2007 IEEE Conference on Computer Vision and Pattern Recognition, Vol. 1–8, 2007

19. Wang, L., He, L., Mishra, A., Li, C.M.: Active contours driven by local Gaussian distribution fitting energy. Sig. Process. **89**(12), 2435–2447 (2009)

20. Wang, L., Wu, H., Pan, C.: Region-based image segmentation with local signed difference energy. Pattern Recogn. Lett. **34**(6), 637–645 (2013)

21. Wang, Y., Wang, L.F., Xiang, S.M., Pan, C.H.: Level set evolution with locally linear classification for image segmentation. In: 2011 18th IEEE International Conference on Image Processing (2011)

22. Kaihua, Z., Lei, Z., Huihui, S., Wengang, Z.: Active contours with selective local or global segmentation: a new formulation and level set method. Image Vis. Comput. **28**(4), 668–676 (2010)

23. Shi, Y.G., Karl, W.C.: Real-time tracking using level sets. In: 2005 IEEE Computer Society Conference on Computer Vision and Pattern Recognition, Vol 2, Proceedings (2005)

24. Perona, P., Malik, J.: Scale-space and edge-detection using anisotropic diffusion. IEEE Trans. Pattern Anal. Mach. Intell. **12**(7), 629–639 (1990)

Trustworthiness in the Patient Centred Health Care System

Enjie Liu[(⊠)] and Xiaohua Feng

Department of Computer Science and Technology,
University of Bedfordshire, Bedfordshire, UK
enjie.liu@beds.ac.uk

Abstract. The trend of the future health care system is patient centred, and patients' involvement is a key to success. ICT will play an important role in enabling and helping patients or citizens to manage and communicate on the individual's health related issues. This includes private and confidential information. Trustworthiness is therefore one of the most vital aspects in such systems. This paper first presents the prototype structure of the health care system, and then discusses questions regarding the trustworthiness of the system.

1 Patient Centred Health Care

In the modern health care system, patients' involvement has increasingly showed its importance. This is especially true in the case of chronic diseases. According to [1], 'management of care for people with long-term conditions should be proactive, holistic, preventive and patient - centred'. National Health System (NHS) England's National Director for Patients and Information, Tim Kelsey also pointed out that the modern health service is to achieve authentic patient participation; patient care should 'engage, empower and hear patients and their carers throughout the whole system' [3].

In 2007, Diabetes UK and the Department of Health, used diabetes as an example, launched a pilot project, to encourage patients to articulate their needs, decide on priorities, agree goals, and jointly develop a plan for achieving these [2]. The patient centred health care system is described by [1] as 'house of care'. Personalised care planning is at the centre of the 'house'. This is a collaborative process designed to bring together the perspectives and expertise of both the individual and the professional(s) involved in providing care, offering tailored personal support to develop the confidence and competence needed for effective self-management [1]. From the ICT perspective, we need to provide platforms and services that inform patients of the necessary knowledge and information about their conditions and choices; and systems that allow patients to manage and share their health conditions and records; and a portal that collects patients' health related data.

2 Patient Empowered System Architecture

In order for the future health care to be engaging and empowering for patients, there are many services and systems that have been introduced. In this paper, a generic block diagram of the system is shown in Fig. 1.

Y. Yuan et al. (Eds.): ISCTCS 2013, CCIS 426, pp. 362–365, 2014.
DOI: 10.1007/978-3-662-43908-1_44, © Springer-Verlag Berlin Heidelberg 2014

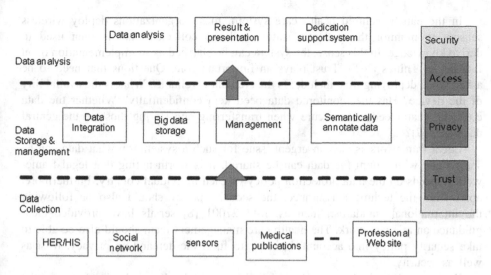

Fig. 1. Block diagram of patient empowered system architecture

In the data collection layer, data can be collected from various and heterogeneous sources. In the data storage and management layer, efficiently storing big data and semantically annotating large amount of data are technically challenging. In the data analysis layer, mining meaningful knowledge from large amount of heterogeneous data is challenging.

As can be imagined, the system includes multiple sources for data, which may be linked to the outside data systems, such as Electronic Health Record (HER) and Health Information System (HIS). On the other hand, patients can use this system to share private and in this case, health related information, with other patients or health professionals. Therefore, security is one of the main concerns. Access regulates different users' rights to the data stored. The privacy guards the information.

3 Trustworthiness for Patient Empowered System Architecture

Trust is one of the issues in security field [4]. When patients put their privacy into the centralised electronic database system, trust turns out to be an obvious issue. In terms of trust in cyber security, development has been carried out since the 20th century. There are several trust platform modules developed; such as on J3210, TSSOP28 and TSOP48 etc. applied on serials of architectures. More trust platform modules are under development.

For the future patient centred health care system, in order to receive data confidentially and with integrity and availability, a trust framework needs to be applied to evoke the users' trust and to allow them to make informed decisions on the trustworthiness of the system.

In the patient centred health care system, many organizations deploy wireless sensors to monitor the patient's status, and the collected data is then used to derive knowledge. In this sense, the system can be clarified as an implementation of an Internet of Things (IoT). Trust plays an important role. Questions that need to be asked when deploying trust include: Is the element is reliable? What is the availability of the device? Has the monitored data been kept confidentially? Whether the data could be guaranteed to be secure when transferring and storing those to the central databases [7]?

Legal framework is also an urgent issue for such a system, on what data can be shared and with whom the data can be shared. It is worth noting that legal frame-work depends on the data protection policy of each individual country. Furthermore, apart from the technical assurance, the security policy should also be following the international standards. Such as, ISO 27001 [8] serials have provided clear guidance on relevant work. The health care management team should also be able to take security policy into account, in order to fulfil the demand on privacy, trust as well as security.

With regards to the layers in the block diagram, in the data collection layer, for the interoperable devices that feed data into the system, approaches for privacy and data protection mechanisms need to be established for protecting the users' private data.

In the data storage and analysis layer, trust platform development is based on the theory of cryptography; deploying a combination of public key and private key infrastructure, to implement data security [5]. In addition, for large datasets, the data may be stored and processed in a cloud environment, and medical professional teams may be in multi-states, and discussion of treatment for a sophisticated case may deal with more states. Therefore it is needed to ensure that only the authorised parties can access data and the data is secured during the transmission. Apart from making sure secure communications and storage facilities are in place, an additional test of safety and data recovery is embedded in the proposed infrastructures [6].

Nevertheless, trust, privacy and security considerations may affect services occasionally. It is still outstanding to set up a proper threshold in between. For each individual circumstance, to emphasise an aspect is reasonable. Sometimes we have to make compromises to achieve a certain goal.

4   Conclusions

To make the future patient centred health care system works efficiently, a well defined trust system and policy should be in place. For a patient centred health care system, a patient's requirement should be a top priority. To achieve this, a better trade-off in service and trustworthiness is important. Satisfying one aspect may affect another. The strategy we suggest is to systematically take them both r into account, and find a good balance in between, in order to achieve an appropriate level of care in a patient's health system.

References

1. Coulter, A., Roberts, S., Dixon, A.: Delivering better services for people with long-term conditions – building the House of Care. King's Fund, Oct 2013
2. Diabetes UK.: 'Thanks for the Petunias': a guide to developing and commissioning non-traditional providers to support the self management of people with long term conditions. Diabetes UK, London (2011)
3. Kelsey, T.: Personalised care plans will give patients control of their own health (2013). http://www.england.nhs.uk/2013/09/25/tim-kelsey-2/
4. Anderson, R.: Security Engineering, 2nd edn. Wiley, New York (2008). ISBN: 0470068523
5. PA Consulting Group.: Trust in the age of information security. PA Consulting Group (2013)
6. Chin, S.-K., Older, S.: Access-Control, Security, and Trust: A Logical Approach. CRC Press, Boca Raton (2010)
7. Hochleitner, C., Tscheligi, M., et al.: Making Devices Trustworthy: Security and Trust Feedback in the Internet of Things. University of Salzburg, Austria (2012)
8. ISO.: 27001 Information/Data Security. ISO (2005)

Multidisciplinary Trust Conceptualization: A General Model for Customer Trust Building in e-Commerce

Manawa Anakpa[1(⊠)] and Yuyu Yuan[2]

[1] Centre Informatique et de Calcul (CIC), Université de Lomé, Lomé, Togo
anakpa@yahoo.fr

[2] School of Software Engineering, Key Laboratory of Trustworthy Distributed Computing and Services Beijing University of Posts and Telecommunications (BUPT), Beijing, China
yuanyuyu@bupt.edu.cn

Abstract. Without trust, life in our complex and interdependent societies would be a disaster. Therefore, numerous of studies have been conducted by several researchers across various disciplines such as psychology, sociology, and electronic-commerce. Despite its importance which garnered the attention of many researchers from numerous research fields, trust has no general definition, and its concept varies depending on the field of study, and even within a given field, trust has different meanings. This leads both practitioners and researchers into a total confusion.

In this paper, we first examine the antecedents variables of trust across the variety of definitions found in the literature, and based on a deeper analysis, we categorized all these variables into six groups according to their similarities found in the literature. After that, we propose a general model for building consumer's trust in electronic commerce. This conceptual model describes in high-level, constructs such as customer propensity to trust, Web-based trust, interpersonal trust, trusting intention and the related trust behavior of an e-consumer. It also suggests a construct of trusting beliefs in witnesses that we believe will affect e-consumer's final intention to trust or make any transactional decision with an unknown e-vendor.

Keywords: Trust · Trust concepts · Trust model · Trust antecedents

1 Introduction

The concept of trust has been widely studied and several articles on this concept can be found in various fields such as psychology, sociology, philosophy, economy, Electronic-commerce, and others. Despite its importance, trust has no general definition, and its concept varies depending on the field of study, and even in a given field, there is often a lack of agreement between researchers [1].

Building consumer trust is a strategic imperative for online vendors because trust strongly influences consumer intentions to transact with unfamiliar vendors via the web technology. Several trust models have been proposed for consumer's trust

Y. Yuan et al. (Eds.): ISCTCS 2013, CCIS 426, pp. 366–373, 2014.
DOI: 10.1007/978-3-662-43908-1_45, © Springer-Verlag Berlin Heidelberg 2014

decision making in online transactions but there is lack of agreement on factors that influenced trust. Therefore, each of the proposed models has its own shortcomings due to the limited number of variables considered by each researcher.

In this article, we believe that a general model that considers all factors of trust will build a successful and long-term transactional relationship between e-customer and e-vendor in e-commerce. We firstly make a wide search on trust in the literature. This first step allows us to build an important and large database on trust for multi-disciplinary interest. After that, we make a deep analysis of trust antecedent factors. From this analysis, we propose a general model of trust, applicable in online community mapping an overview of this often misunderstood concept and providing a better understanding of what is really the complex nature of trust.

2 Concept, Importance and Definition of Trust

Trust is a complex concept which involves a multitude of disciplines. Despite its complex nature, researchers from various disciplines do acknowledge the value of trust. Without trust, life in our interdependent societies would be a total disaster.

Our conceptual investigation begins by searching the meaning of trust in the multidisciplinary literature. Trust is not a feeling of warmth or affection but the conscious regulation of one's dependence on another [2]. Trust makes cooperative endeavors happen [3]. Other researchers stated that trust is a key to positive interpersonal relationships in various settings [4, 5]. During periods of uncertainty due to organizational crisis, trust becomes even more central and critical [6] and in situations of interdependence, trust helps reducing uncertainty [7].

Psychologists generally agreed that trust is an important and vital to personality development and social life building [8]. Sociologists are concerned with the position and role of trust in social systems. The interest in trust has grown significantly since the early eighties, from the early works done in [7]. Economics consider trust as an economic lubricant, reducing the cost of transactions between parties [9]. Trust is a social capital and social trust benefits the economy [10] and that a low level of trust inhibits economic growth. Trust has emerged as a central strategic asset for organizations [6, 11]. Practitioners acknowledge the importance of trust as much as do scholars.

In the electronic commerce field, trust concept shares similar characteristics to those of offline trust, but there are significant distinctions that are unique in an online environment. Bandura [12], and Solomon and Flores [13] defined trust objects to be moral agent that has intentionality and free will. In contrast, Nass et al., [14] have addressed this issue and as Marcella, [15] the Internet technology itself is an object of trust. The lack of trust stops consumers from transacting with web vendors [15, 16]. Lee and Turban [17] asserted that, trust is the willingness vulnerability, based on the expectation that the Internet merchant will behave in certain agreeable ways. Some Internet researchers focused on attributes of trust than its definition [18–20].

3 The Need of Suggestions

A deeper analysis of data listed in the above Sect. 2 shows that all the related concepts of trust can fall into six major concepts: benevolence, openness, predictability, competence, integrity, and other. We summarized all these variables and their components in the following Table 1.

Table 1. Main and second order associated concepts of trust

Main concepts	Definition	Second order concepts
Benevolence	"is the confidence that one's well-being, or something one cares about, will be protected and not harmed by the trusted party" [2, 3, 5, 6, 21]	Benevolence, caring, goodwill, goodness, responsive, good morality, loyalty, receptivity
Openness	"is the extent to which relevant information is not withheld; it is a process by which people make themselves vulnerable to others by sharing personal information" [6, 22]	Openness, shared personal information, transparency feedback linked to other sites
Competence	is one's willingness to be vulnerable based on the belief that the other party has enough ability or skill to fulfill his expectations properly	Competence, ability expertise dynamism performance
Integrity	is the consumer willingness to belief that the web vendor will act ethically, honestly, faithfully and credibly fashion to fulfill promises, and adhere to an accepted set of principles or standards	Integrity, ethical, honesty, faithfully, credibility, fulfill promises, respect of principles & standards, reliability, discreetness, congruence, consistency
Predictability	"means that one believes the other party's actions (good or bad) are consistent enough that one can forecast them in a given situation" [23]	Predictability, familiarity, past experience
Other	——— ———	Risk, reputation, culture, usefulness, auditing, third party seals, performance, security, privacy, assurance, Altruism, etc.

Table 1 shows, the six main concepts associated to trust and their associated second order concepts. It also gives some definitions found in the literature of the main concepts related to trust. Most of the classifications were intuitive, but based on the existing literature across all the disciplines.

4 The Proposed Model

Now that the nature of trust has been explained, and its related concepts have been given, we can look to integrate the construct further into electronic commerce field to offer additional insights into the nature of online trust, as the e-consumers' trust building in electronic commerce is our concern in this paper. From this mapping, a general model of trust types has been proposed as shown in Fig. 1 below.

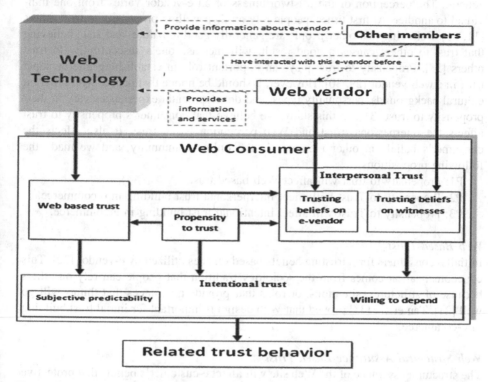

Fig. 1. General model for building customer trust in electronic commerce. *(The bold arrows indicate the direction of the influence relationship of trust between the entities and sub-entities.)*

From the model presented above (Fig. 1), one can observe that the e-consumer trust propensity affects the Web perception-based trust (technology-based trust), and also affects both trusting beliefs on e-vendor and trusting beliefs on witnesses (interpersonal-based trust), and finally, it affects the intentional trust, which will determine the final trust decision of the e-consumer (related trust behavior).

4.1   Entities Descriptions of the Conceptual Trust Model

Web Consumer
The web consumer characteristics are those factors that influence his propensity to trust. Shankar et al., [24] conceptualized that consumer's self-confidence, Internet savvy, past behavior, and Internet shopping experience affect trust. These factors can be associated with the cultural and interpersonal traits that influence the process of trusting to others. In addition, skills and experience in computers and Internet [25], openness and other factors affect e-consumer's disposition to trust [23, 26, 27].

Web Consumer Propensity to Trust

Propensity to trust is a tendency to believe in the positive attributes of others in general. The perception of the trustworthiness of an e-vendor varies from one individual to another. At first times, people rely on their willing propensity to trust others [11, 26]. Believing that other people are generally good in nature, and also, believing that trust to others causes a good result, will increase one's susceptibility to trust others [28]. Propensity to trust plays an important role in establishing interpersonal trust in a web-vendor [29, 30]. However, it should be notice that people with different cultural backgrounds, personality types, and developmental experiences vary in their propensity to trust [31]. In this study, we believe that consumer's propensity to trust affects the interpersonal trust and Web perception based trust. It also affects the consumer's beliefs in other members in the online community, and we made the following propositions:

P1: Propensity to trust will affect Web based trust.

P2: Propensity to Trust will affect interpersonal trust building in e-commerce.

P3: Propensity to Trust will affect intentional trust building in e-commerce.

Web Based Trust

Initially, consumers form trusting beliefs based on cues utilized by e-vendor [32]. This conceptualization comes from the sociology tradition that people can rely on others because of structures, situations, or roles that provide assurances that things will go well [21]. Tan et al., [33] proved that Web design is important for initial trust building in e-commerce.

Web Structural Assurance Based Trust

The structural assurance of the Web site will affect e-customer's beliefs that protective structures such as guarantees, legal recourse, and procedures are in place for successful transactions with unknown web-vendor [34]. Web-based trust is relevant when e-consumers mainly transact with new or unknown e-vendor [35]. We assume that the openness or link of the Website to other reputable sites will encourage customers to transact online. Using encryptions to protect users' personal information will bring them to trust the Website and purchase from it [20].

Interpersonal Trust

The interpersonal (person-to-person) trust is adopted in any of the various disciplines. In the electronic commerce, many researchers consider the web technology and the web-vendor to be one party. In this paper, we consider the website and the e-vendor completely separated. In this way we can look at interpersonal trust building with new perspectives such as witnesses (other members in the system who have at least one past experience with the given e-vendor) whose witness information or viewpoints will also count in the trustors' trust evaluation.

Web Vendor Attributes

The main attributes of an e-vendor are; benevolence, integrity, openness, competence, predictability. Doney and Cannon [36] have defined reputation as the degree to which customer tend to believe in the competent, honesty, and benevolence of the vendor.

Witness Information

Witness information and direct experience are used by researchers such as Huynh et al., [37] to evaluate trust or trustworthiness and reputation of services providers. While direct interaction experience is interested in the prior, witness information is interested in the collected information about past experiences of other e-customers who have interacted with the e-vendor. We believe that witness information will affect the initial trust of e-customer and therefore, determine whether or not an online transaction will occur.

Intentional Trust

Intentional trust of the e-customer contains his willingness vulnerability and subjective predictability to depend on an e-vendor [23]. We believe that one's propensity to trust, interpersonal trust and Web based trust will affect one's final intention to trust. Note that, the subjective predictability to depend on an e-vendor will increase with long-term experience between e-consumer and a given e-vendor.

Related Trust Behavior

In the offline world, consumers' behaviors are often affected by social cues such as color, music, lighting, store layout, and social media [38]. In online transactions the behavioral trust is determined by Web-based and interpersonal trusts that affect e-consumers intentional behavior. It is important to keep track on the online customers' related behaviors in order to improve services and e-vendor reputation and trustworthiness.

5 Conclusion and Future Work

This paper presents a broad overview on trust concept that can be found in the existing literature, across many disciplines. It theoretically discusses the highly complex and multi-dimensional nature of trust. Furthermore, this paper shows that there is a lack of agreement on trust concepts, definitions, and antecedent variables influencing trust relationships, across disciplines and even within a given discipline. To provide an adequate solution to the lack of trust between the actors in electronic commerce field, we collected all the related concepts influencing the formation of online trust and then, after a thorough analysis, we classified these factors into six categories (see Table 1 in Sect. 3), based on their similarities that we found in the most existing trust meanings in the literature. We've proposed a general model for building customers' trust in electronic commerce. Our proposed model, included witnesses influence on e-customer trust building in online transactions with unknown e-vendor. We've clarified by explaining how all the constructs of our model are related to each other in the online environment. With the consideration of the large range of factors affecting consumer trust in online transactions, a development of a new online trustworthy community based on our proposed model, will bring many customers to freely purchase or make any online transactional decisions with any unknown web-vendor.

We assume that, the best way to avoid these confusions is to construct a mathematical model that can clearly explain the trust concept with good outcomes and help to compute online trust in an efficient way. Thus, we wish to build a mathematical formalism for computing e-customers' trust behavior based on our proposed model in our future research works.

References

1. Lewicki, R.J., Bunker, B.B.: Trust in relationships: a model of development and decline. In: Bunker, B.B., Rubin, J.Z. (eds.) Conflict, Cooperation, and Justice: Essays Inspired by the Work of Morton Deutsch, pp. 133–173. Jossey-Bass, San Fransicso (1995)
2. Zand, D.E.: Trust and managerial problem solving. Adm. Sci. Q. **17**, 229–239 (1971)
3. Arrow, K.J.: The Limits of Organization. Norton, New York (1974)
4. Lewis, J.D., Weigert, A.: Trust as a social reality. Soc. Forces **63**(4), 967–985 (1985)
5. Gambetta, D.: Can we trust trust? In: Gambetta, D. (ed.) Trust: Making and Breaking Cooperative Relations, pp. 213–237. Blackwell, New York (1988)
6. Mishra, A.K.: Organizational responses to crisis: the centrality of trust. In: Kramer, R.M., Tyler, T.R. (eds.) Trust in Organizations: Frontiers of Theory and Research, pp. 261–287. Sage, Thousand Oaks (1996)
7. Luhmann, N.: Trust and Power. Wiley, New York (1979)
8. Rotter, J.B.: Interpersonal trust, trustworthiness, and gullibility. Am. Psychol. **35**(1), 1–7 (1980)
9. Morgan, R., Hunt, S.: The commitment-trust theory of relationship marketing. J. Mark. **58**(3), 20–38 (1994)
10. Zak, P.J., Knack, S.: Trust and growth. Econ. J. **111**, 295–321 (2001)
11. Mayer, R.C., Davis, J.H., Schoorman, F.D.: An integrative model of organizational trust. Acad. Manage. Rev. **20**(3), 709–734 (1995)
12. Albert, B.: Selective moral disengagement in the exercise of moral agency. J. Moral Educ. **31**(2), 101–119 (2002)
13. Solomon, R.C., Flores, F.: Building Trust in Business, Politics, Relationships, and Life. Oxford University Press, New York (2001)
14. Nass, C., Steuer, J., Tauber, E.R.: Computers are social actors. In: Proceedings of the Conference on Human Factors in Computing Systems CHI '94, pp. 72–78. ACM, New York (1994)
15. Marcella, A.J.: Establishing Trust in Vertical Markets. The Institute of Internal Auditors, Altamonte Springs (1999)
16. Jarvenpaa, S.L., Tractinsky, N., Vitale, M.: Consumer trust in an internet store. Inf. Technol. Manage. **1**(1–2), 45–71 (2000)
17. Lee, M.K.O., Turban, E.: A trust model for consumer internet shopping. Int. J. Electron. Commer. **6**(1), 75–91 (2001)
18. Benassi, P.: TRUSTe: an online privacy seal program. Commun. ACM **42**(2), 56–59 (1999)
19. Cranor, L.F.: Internet privacy. Commun. ACM **42**(2), 28–31 (1999)
20. Hoffman, D.L., Novak, T.P., Peralta, M.: Building consumer trust online. Commun. ACM **42**(4), 80–85 (1999)
21. Baier, A.: Trust and antitrust. Ethics **96**(2), 231–260 (1986)
22. Butler, J.K., Cantrell, R.S.: A behavioral decision theory approach to modeling dyadic trust in superiors and subordinates. Psychol. Rep. **55**, 81–105 (1984)
23. McKnight, D.H., Choudhury, V., Kacmar, C.: The impact of initial consumer trust on intentions to transact with a web site: a trust building model. J. Strateg. Inf. Syst. **11**, 297–323 (2002)

24. Shankar, V., Urban, G.L., Sultan, F.: Online Trust: a stakeholder perspective, concepts, implications, and future directions. J. Strate. Inf. Syst. **11**(3–4), 325–344 (2002)
25. Lai, K.W., Tong, W.L., Lai, C.F.: Trust factors influencing the adoption of internet-based interorganizational systems, Electron. Commer. Res. Appl. **10**, 85–93 (2011)
26. Harrison, M.D., Larry, C.L.: Initial trust formation in new organizational relationships. Acad. Manage. Rev. **23**(3), 473–490 (1998)
27. Jones, K., Leonard, N.K.: Trust in consumer-to-consumer electronic commerce. Inf. Manage. **45**, 88–95 (2008)
28. Teo, T.S.H., Liu, J.: Consumer trust in e-commerce in the United States, Singapore and China. Omega **35**, 22–38 (2007)
29. Gefen, D.: E-commerce: the role of familiarity and trust. Omega Int. J. Manage. Sci. **28**, 725–737 (2000)
30. McKnight, D., Chervany, N.: What trust means in e-commerce customer relationships: an interdisciplinary conceptual typology. Int. J. Electron. Commer. **6**(2), 35–59 (2002)
31. Hofstede, G.: Motivation, leadership, and organization: do American theories apply abroad? Org. Dyn. **9**(1), 42–63 (1980)
32. Urban, G.L., Sultan, F., Qualls, W.J.: Placing trust at the center of your internet strategy. MIT Sloan Manage. Rev. **42**(1), 39–48 (2000)
33. Tan, F.B., Tung, L.-L., Xu, Y.: Study of web-designers' criteria for effective business-to-consumer (B2C) websites using the repertory grid technique. J. Electron. Commer. Res. **10**(3), 155–177 (2009)
34. Shapiro, S.P.: The social control of impersonal trust. Am. J. Sociol. **93**(3), 623–658 (1987)
35. Pavlou, P.A., Gefen, D.: Building effective online marketplaces with institution-based trust. Inf. Syst. Res. **15**(1), 37–59 (2004)
36. Doney, P., Cannon, J.: An examination of the nature of trust in buyer-seller relationships. J. Mark. **61**, 35–51 (1997)
37. Huynh, T.D., Jennings, N.R., Shadbolt, N.R.: An integrated trust and reputation model for open multi-agent systems. Auton. Agent. Multi-Agent Syst. **13**(2), 119–154 (2006)
38. Bitner, M.: Servicescapes: the impact of physical surroundings on customers and employees. J. Mark. **56**, 57–71 (1992)

Concept of Service Trustworthiness Management System (STMS)

Miandrilala[1](✉) and YuYu Yuan[2]

[1] University of Antananarivo, Antananarivo, Madagascar
miandrilala9@yahoo.fr
[2] Beijing University of Posts and Telecommunications, Beijing, China
yuanyuyu@bupt.edu.cn

Abstract. There are a lot of services online and trust service is increasingly complex. People must take high risk online if they want to perform service. The high quality of service is not enough for the people to trust a provider online. For instance, one service can provide a high quality service, but use customer's information to hack his account bank. So we desire to establish a system to avoid that situation. Our key laboratory would like to give system where people can execute with low risk level service online. In the near future we believe to be able to realize the service trustworthiness management system (STMS). At the beginning; we use descriptive approach that means to determine the nature and characteristics of the components of the system and to establish associations between them.

Keywords: Trustworthiness · Trust · Concept · IT service · Provider

1 Introduction

Nowadays, internet services are more integrated in human's daily life so that the probability of trustworthiness of the provider is mandatory. Building trustworthy system to verify the trustworthiness became a new challenge for many computer science searchers. To establish that and reach this goal, Preliminary studies and researches must be undertaken. Making a concept of service trustworthiness management system is among first important step to consider. A key point of our system is to quantify service behavior trustworthiness. To measure service behavior trustworthiness, firstly we must build standard service behavior. Secondly, we should formalize service behavior, and after we should compare standard behavior and real behavior. That is our motivation and purpose for this research.

In this paper, our goal is to give a clear description of STMS. For that, first of all, we will define trust and trustworthiness and after that, we will talk about the standard of STMS, finally we survey each entities of service trustworthiness management system.

2 Definition of Trustworthiness and Trust

For more understanding of our concept it is necessary to define the trustworthiness and trust. Trustworthiness and trust have a close relationship.

Y. Yuan et al. (Eds.): ISCTCS 2013, CCIS 426, pp. 374–381, 2014.
DOI: 10.1007/978-3-662-43908-1_46, © Springer-Verlag Berlin Heidelberg 2014

Definition (1): According to [1], Trust is the willingness of a party to be vulnerable to the actions of another party based on the expectation that the other party will perform a particular action important to the Trustor, irrespective of the ability to monitor or control that other party.

Definition (2): Trustworthiness is the demonstrated ability of the trustee to perform a specified action while adhering to a set of stated principles (integrity) and acting in the best interest of the trustor (benevolence) [2].

3   The Standards of STMS

The standard is a document that contains all of our conventions. The standard takes an important place in our STMS because it is like our guideline and reference. Formalization of our standard has for goal that STMS can recognize the standard content. The machine cannot discern bad and good thing so STMS uses formalized standard to judge service behavior. Our family standard is composed in the top of level by all terminologies such as vocabulary and concepts and then in the next level by requirements for a service trustworthiness management system. And the lowest level concerns the general guidelines; it provides four standards such as the formal representation, monitoring and recommendation for measurement and finally recommendation for evaluation of service behavior trustworthiness.

4   Entities of Service Trustworthiness Management System

In our point of view, Service Trustworthiness Management System is composed by ten entities: Constructor, Maintainer, Trustor, Trustee, Collector, Trusted third party, Trusted Judge of Conflict, Controller, Service Platform and Trustor evaluator.

5   Constructor

Plan construction and then construct service platform, maintainer, controller, trusted judge of conflict, trusted third party, trustor evaluator and make a connection between each other. Brief, constructor build all entities need to be constructing in the system. Constructor must respect the requirement of service trustworthiness management system [2].

We have two categories of constructor:

- Conceptor: Builds a conceptual model of the system where describes and exhibit the structure, behavior and more views of a system (multiple views). "Conceptual modeling is the activity of formally describing some aspects of the physical and social world around us for the purposes of understanding and communication". [3]
- Implementor: Follow all instructions in the conceptual model of the system built by Conceptor. Realize, execute and perform it. Implementor must have ability to perform the conceptual model.

Conceptor and implementor are two complementary entities that work closely. In general, constructor works only during the construction of STMS but in our case we always need constructor within the STMS is to be implemented. Knowing that constructor has built the system so understanding clearly the STMS (Fig. 1).

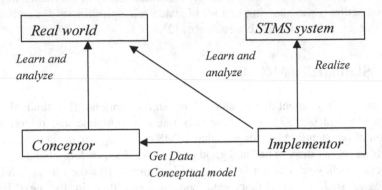

Fig. 1. ER model of constructor in STMS

5.1   Maintainer

Maintain STMS, any change in our system must be certified by our standard. In other words, any update must be respecting our standard. We have three categories of maintainer

- Entity to detect anomaly such as a bug.
- Entity to analyze for more accuracy of STMS.
- Entity to resolve the anomaly or improve the accuracy, for instance, this entity updates some modules, improve some algorithms.

In these entities, building software such as detection anomaly is useful and adequate for our system. Our proposal maintainer ER model is as in Fig. 2.

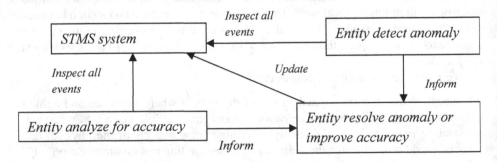

Fig. 2. ER model of maintainer in STMS

5.2   Trustor (User)

Trustor is the user who trusts our system. Lower risk will increase user willingness to trust [2]. User trust, interact and execute the service. According the trust definition, Trustor is willing to be vulnerable to the action of trustee (service provider). Therefore user does not need to control or monitor the service behaviors.

5.3   Controller User's Behavior

In our system, all of kinds of user (Hacker, liar, honest person…) can trust the service provider; therefore we need to control user's behaviors. In addition, User misbehavior affects trustworthiness value of service provider; for instance, user can give fake comments to the system. Lan Li et al. describe a conception of controller user's behavior [4]. For respect user decision; user need to certify the agreement to be controlled in our system. Conversely, our system declares with honor to keep user information, respect the user privacy and does not use it for doing something wrong. Also our system must explain the reason of control and where is the boundary of control.

5.4   Trusted Judge of Conflict

It resolves some conflicts between trustee and trustor. Judges and evaluates conflicts by referring to our standard and analyses its according past data of service behavior and user's behavior. According to M. Afzalur Rahim, the conflict is a situation or a type of behavior. It is also an interactive process manifested in incompatibility, disagreement or dissonance within or between social entities [5]. We describe the process of judgment of conflict like:

- Detecting conflict between trustee and trustor.
- Collect all information concerning the conflict such as trustworthiness of service.
- Search what is the reason of this conflict.
- Determine the level and type of conflict.
- Determine all conflict's damages to the trustor and the trustee.
- Analyze the existing information about conflict.
- Evaluate the result and give the solution.

5.5   Trustee (Service Provider)

Trustee will have its own probability of trustworthiness based on trusted third party evaluation. According the Definition (2), Trustworthiness of service provider change dynamically in terms of following factors: Ability, integrity and benevolence, all of those factors are independent to the trustor. In the papers we will consider another factor: "Reputation". References [6, 7] are focused on the relationship between trust and reputation. Reference [8] illustrated the relationship between reputation and trust like:

(1) "I trust you because of your good reputation."
(2) "I trust you despite your bad reputation."

In our STMS, we only consider that trust influence reputation not the opposite, we don't focus if reputation influence trust. If user trusts and then users execute the service that influences the reputation value and increase the trustworthiness value of service provider. In our point of view we consider four factors of trustworthiness of service provider: ability, integrity, benevolence and reputation.

5.6   Collector

This entity collects and stores information from all entities in STMS. In addition, this entity must collect intelligently such as detect if data is duplicate, etc. This entity is responsible for saving the information. We need this entity because we are going to handle a lot of data. We divide the collector in three categories:

- Basic collector: responsible of getting all data in our system.
- Filter: detect duplicate data, not useful dataset, incorrect information, etc. This category requires data mining and machine learning technology.
- Storage: classify the data such that it will easy to find and manage.

5.7   Trusted Third Party

Monitor measures and evaluates trustee dynamically, this entity is the most important one in our STMS system. In Trusted third party, we can describe distinct following sections: Trusted monitor, trusted measurer and trusted evaluator. Next, we explain these sections one by one.

Trusted monitor of STMS: is an entity that gives for you the possibility to see in real time all events and all data information in STMS. We can describe four categories of monitor.

Transaction Monitor : exhibits all transaction between these entities.

Process Monitor : exhibits all process in the STMS.

Data value Monitor: exhibits all data value in the STMS such as trustworthiness value of service behaviors.

Main Monitor: manages monitor section, responsible of blackbox task and detect a usual situation such as lower trustworthiness value service behavior.

Trusted measurer of STMS: is an entity that provides objective evidence of correct behavior or of possible misbehavior [2]. For measuring trustworthiness of service provider, there are a lot of methods to achieve it. The best way is to established trustworthiness formula of an service provider with the factors ability, integrity, benevolence, and reputation, notes $T[S](\alpha, \beta, \gamma, \varepsilon)$. Where S is an service provider; α is ability and belongs to $[-1, 1]$; β is integrity and belongs to $[-1, 1]$; γ is benevolence and belongs to $[-1, 1]$. ε is reputation and belongs to $[-1, 1]$ and Trustworthiness value $T[S] : (\alpha, \beta, \gamma, \varepsilon)$ is belong $[-1, 1]$. We suppose that value -1 is the lower value (bad), value 0 is the undetermined situation and value 1 is the best value for all factors and trustworthiness formula. Therefore we consider that

$$T[s](-1, -1, -1, -1) = -1$$
$$T[s](0, 0, 0, 0) = 0$$
$$T[s](1, 1, 1, 1) = 1$$

Trusted evaluator of STMS: is an entity that uses the result of trusted measurer of STMS, service behaviors and our standard to give the evaluation of trustworthiness of service behavior and user risk. Each atomic behavior can have influence to the trustworthiness factor. The main task for evaluating trustworthiness of service provider will be to describe all atomic behaviors and detect which factors are influenced by each atomic behavior (Fig. 3).

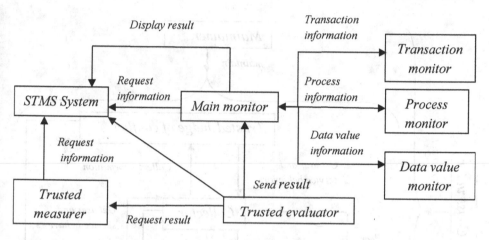

Fig. 3. ER model of trusted third party in STMS

6 Trustor Evaluator

This entity is due to evaluate the number of user who really trusts service provider. Sometimes, the user performs our system because of another reason such as price of service. Thanks to that entity we can know the efficacy of our system. To reach that, with high knowledge and concept of trust, we defined a list of user's behavior characterize a trustor behavior. In other words, we need to describe and formalize the user's behavior that trusts the service provider. We can give example for detecting if user really trusts our system. We agree that the following examples are not enough to satisfy our need but it gives us an overview of our idea:

– Verify the number of service providers visited by user in the web site until he has decided to choose one service provider. If users visits more than ten services, we can admit that user probably trust service.
– Verify how many times user consumes the service if the user executes the service more than three times in the same service provider, we can suppose that he trust the service provider. These three times can be describing: first time, user risks and test

service, second time user want to prove the trustworthy of service, third time user is sure that service is trustworthy.

- Consider user comments or feedbacks. Give feedback is better if it's optional in the service platform. A lot of feedback implies good probability

7 Service Platform (Web site)

This entity is the location where user and service provider interact. Trusted third party has a strong connection with Service platform. Service platform is a service access interface. It is also responsible for managing the information about services in the system such as name of service provider, details of service information, etc. (Fig. 4).

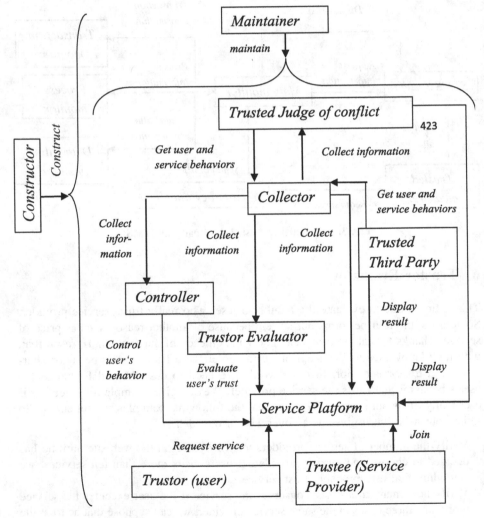

Fig. 4. Entity-relationship model of STMS

8   Conclusion

In conclusion, describing STMS system pushes us to see more clearly. We can know how many entities we need to have in STMS. We can continuous our research more deep and more details. For future work, answering to following questions is appropriate:

- How to implement trusted judge of conflict entity on using information technology?
- How to measure the trustworthiness service behaviors [8]?
- How to know that user trust a service provider?

One important domain for building our STMS is machine learning [9]. We need to focus on that for future work. And more, in real word, the communication takes a big place for improving trust between Trustor and Trustee. That is the same in new world of IT services. We believe that after few years, we can use adequate communication technology who response our needs in our system.

References

1. Mayer, R.C., Davis, J.H., Schoorman, F.D.: An integrative model of organizational trust. Acad. Manag. Rev. **20**, 709–734 (1995)
2. Bøegh, J., Yuan, Y.: Towards a standard for Service Behavior Trustworthiness Management. In: 2012 Second International Conference on Digital Information and Communication Technology and It's Applications (DICTAP), pp. 189–194 (2012)
3. Mylopoulos, J.: Conceptual modeling and Telos1. In: Loucopoulos, P., Zicari, R. (eds.) Conceptual Modeling, Databases, and Case: An Integrated View of Information Systems Development, pp. 49–68. Wiley, New York (1992)
4. Li, L., Zhang, S., Fan, L.: Behavior-aware role based trust management. In: 9th International Conference for Young Computer Scientists, ICYCS, pp. 1919–1924 (2008)
5. Afzalur Rahim, M.: Managing Conflict in Organizations, p.16. Transaction Publishers. ISBN 978-1-4128-1456-0. Retrieved 11 Oct 2012
6. Mui, L., Mohtashemi, M., Halberstadt, A.: A computational model of trust and reputation. In: Proceedings of the 35th Annual Hawaii International Conference on System Sciences, HICSS, pp. 2431–2439 (2002)
7. Alfred, I., Radu, L., Slavescu, R.: A model of trust and reputation in e -commerce based on multimodal logic. In: IEEE International Conference on Intelligent Computer Communication and Processing, ICCP, pp. 119–122 (2011)
8. Wu, X., Chen, Y.: Trustworthiness expectation of real-time Web services. In: 7th International Conference on Ubiquitous Intelligence & Computing and 7th International Conference on Autonomic & Trusted Computing (UIC/ATC), pp.292-298 (2010)
9. Poggio, T., Smale, S.: The mathematics of learning: dealing with data. Notices Am. Math. Soc. **50**, 537–544 (2003)

Android-Based Remote-Control with Real-Time Video Surveillance for Wi-Fi Robot

Changning Song[1,2(✉)]

[1] School of Software Engineering, Beijing University of Posts
and Telecommunications, Beijing, China
[2] Key Laboratory of Trustworthy Distributed Computing and Service (BUPT),
Ministry of Education, Beijing, China
scn1026@gmail.com

Abstract. This paper presents an Android-based wireless remote-control system for a wheeled mobile robot. A micro Wi-Fi controller board running OpenWrt Operating System was introduced to control the video streaming and communication between mobile robot and android device remotely through Socket Connections. A network camera is mounted on the Wi-Fi board through an USB interface to acquire images, which are displayed on the control device for the remote operator's operation. The RS232 serial port linking the Wi-Fi board to the robot and long run batteries are used to give them power supply without any cable connected. The designed Wi-Fi Robot can be remotely operated from anywhere inside the scope of wireless coverage as long as there is an android device that running the control system.

Keywords: Android · Remote · OpenWrt · Wi-Fi Robot · Video stream

1 Preface

In recent years, the applications of mobile robot have gradually become more diverse, which makes the robot closer to people's daily life. However, the increasingly complex control process and some special application which is called for high real-time requirement has presented challenges to the existing motion robot design pattern. In this paper, we present a Wi-Fi wireless control approach for a mobile robot. The performance bottlenecks of developing the intelligent robot focused on the following three aspects. The first contradiction is between the development cost and the hardware performance. We often use cost-effective hardware to reduce the cost. However, when the controls became more complex, precise increase gradually, the performance of the original hardware would be inadequate. Rebuild the robot will not only increase the cost of inputs, but also waste the robot's life cycles seriously. The next contradiction is between complexity of controls and the real-time performance. When the hardware performance is insufficient to complete the control of the higher complexity task, the system often sacrifices time to compensate the lack of hardware performance. The third contradiction is the growing demand for user experience nowadays. Operations of the remote control [1] app must be as simple as possible and the UI interfaces should be easy to learn, meanwhile, the reliability of the communication between the

Y. Yuan et al. (Eds.): ISCTCS 2013, CCIS 426, pp. 382–388, 2014.
DOI: 10.1007/978-3-662-43908-1_47, © Springer-Verlag Berlin Heidelberg 2014

remote control system and the mobile robot is becoming increasingly vital to which attention was not paid enough in the early years.

2 Overall Design

To settle the problems above, we proposed the OpenWrt based wireless control [2] system design scheme, which use the popular AR9331 processor architecture. The Atheros AR9331 is a highly integrated and cost-effective IEEE 802.11n 1×1 2.4 GHz SoC for wireless local area network AP and router platforms. The OpenWrt [3] is a Linux based excellent open-source operating system for embedded devices such as residential gateways and routers. We increase the efficiency of hardware resources by operating system task scheduling, use the embedded application software to make up for lack of hardware resources, which introduce a number of software tools directly to the mobile robot system to complete the complex intelligent control tasks and intelligent decision making tasks, so that we can exploit the maximum performance of hardware resources, ensure the stability of mobile robots with real-time while we make sure the control of complex tasks in the case of cost savings.

The overall structure of this system is shown as Fig. 1, the right side is an android device with remote control software inside, the left side is the Wi-Fi Robot consists of robot controller, wireless controller and a USB camera. The wireless controller is part of the Wi-Fi Robot which acts the most important role to communicate with the android device through Wi-Fi. Embedded mobile robot can be equipped with sensors based on actual demands, to achieve measuring distance, counting, automatic obstacle avoidance, data acquisition, pattern recognition and provide other functions. The wireless controller can also mount peripherals through the onboard USB interface to achieve more basic mechanical functions with the servo and transmit the collected data to the android device. In this paper, the embedded wireless controller equipped with a micro CCD camera used to implement video capture.

Figure 2 shows the hierarchical structure of wireless controller. The bottom layer is physical layer of hardware circuit. We choose the integrated circuit board with AR9331 Microcontroller to generate and manage wireless network, and use the extended interfaces, RS232 and USB, to connect mobile robot and video camera. Enhanced functionalities can be achieved by using a USB hub to mount some other related peripheral devices.

Fig. 1. Overall structure of Wi-Fi Robot

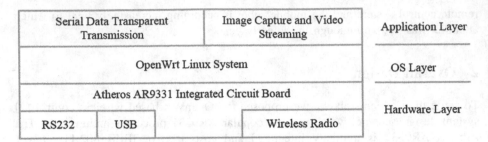

Serial Data Transparent Transmission	Image Capture and Video Streaming	Application Layer
OpenWrt Linux System		OS Layer
Atheros AR9331 Integrated Circuit Board		Hardware Layer
RS232	USB	Wireless Radio	

Fig. 2. Hierarchical structure of wireless controller

The layer above hardware circuit layer is the operating system layer. We use open-source OpenWrt [4] Linux to do the basic management of hardware resource which means it is possible to reduce cost of development to a great extent and gain higher performance. OpenWrt is described for embedded devices, it provides a fully customizable ability through the use of packages to suit any application.

The application layer is the upper layer of the operating system layer. Application software provides a large amount of enhancements to the system, such as transparent transmission for serial data and video capture and streaming. The former transmits control instructions from the android device through Socket connection to the mobile robot by serial port, meanwhile collects feedbacks from the mobile robot and sends them to the android device.

The wireless control board splits the wireless transmission work from mobile robot and is completely in charge of video processing. It can not only reduce the word load of the processor of the robot to improve the reliability and accuracy of motion control, but also make the system easy in configuration and maintenance with good scalability and integration.

3   Software Design

The whole software system of Wi-Fi Robot, shown on Fig. 3, is assembled by three parts: mobile robot's motion control program with motor driver, serial data forwarding program, video stream program and remote control application with UI on android.

The Packet Reader and Sender program is an application program running on an ARM development board, which mainly responsible for collection of the robot's status, sending the collected data to the user, receiving the instruction of the user, sending the motion related instructions to the motion control circuit.

The communication between mobile robot and android device is implemented by ser2net software. The ser2net [5] is a fully open-source proxy that provides a way on Linux system for a user to connect from a network connection, usually TCP connection, to a serial port. The program comes up normally as a daemon, opens the TCP ports specified in the configuration file, and waits for connections. Once a connection occurs, the program attempts to set up the connection and open the serial port.

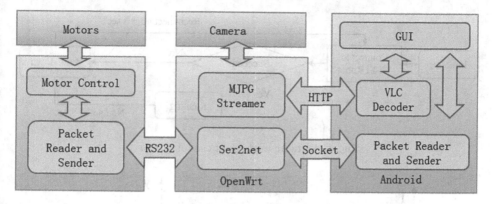

Fig. 3. Software modules of control system

The video capture and streaming is implemented by MJPG Streamer [6]. It is Simpler and faster than most streamers which make it ideal for the crucial real-time video purposes. In this System, the MJPG-streamer takes JPGs from a Linux-UVC [7] (USB Video Class) compatible webcam and streams them as M-JPEG via HTTP to remote control program. While receiving the M-JPEG stream, the client must decode the stream into JPGs and display them sequentially on the screen. To decode the stream we introduce the core library of VLC [8] for Android which is an Open-source cross-platform powerful multimedia player into the remote control program by JNI interface.

The remote control software is designed to support Multiple Operator Single Robot (MOSR) mode. MOSR allows several operators to be connected to the robot (to the embedded Socket server). However, only one operator can take a task of controlling the WIFI Robot, the other operators can only monitor at same time. If another user is already using the connection or serial port, the connection is refused with an error message. This design can avoid unnecessary interference from other terminal and ensure structural integrity of control instructions.

There are two type of connections between the Android and Wi-Fi-Robot: the video connection and the control connection. Each connection should be kept alive as soon as the initialization of Wi-Fi Robot is complete and the control software are ready to remote. For the convenience of the user's operation, we introduce the mechanism of auto-connection and auto-reconnection in case of any connection is broken caused by environmental or network error. A universal flow diagram is used to illustrate the design of the remote control software which is shown on Fig. 4.

The remote control GUI is designed [9] as Fig. 5, which divides the screen into two areas, the left area accept and identify the left hand gestures, the right area accept and identify the left hand gestures. Each area will display the respective joystick on the position of the first touch and change value along with finger move until release the touch. The right side of the screen is a two-axis joystick which control the speed and direction of the robot. The y axis control the speed of forward and backward while the x axis control the direction of turning left or right. The other side of the screen is a joystick with only one axis which control the pitch of the camera.

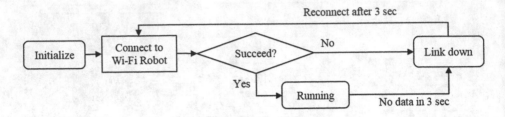

Fig. 4. Software modules of control system

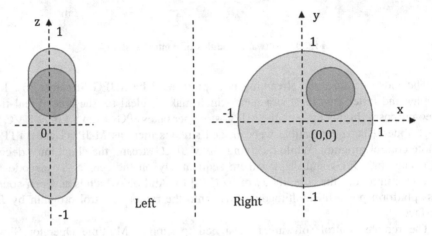

Fig. 5. Virtual joysticks on the screen of android device

Each axis that mentioned above will return a float factor value between −1 to 1 while the user touch and move on the joystick. The instructions corresponding to the axes are listed in Table 1.

4   System Tests

After the development of whole system is completed, we did an integration test for the whole system through a simple remote experiments. Figure 6 shows the graphical user interface of the android software. The average Video delay is 150 ms. Video frame rate is 10.62 fps–15.16 fps. The response time of remote control is 50 ms, the real-time performance of the whole system is within an acceptable range.

Table 1. Instructions corresponding to the axes

	>0	<0	|1|
x	Turn right	Turn left	Maximum direction
y	Forward	Backward	Maximum speed
z	Rise	Lower	Maximum pitching angle

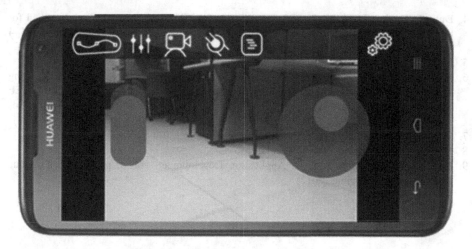

Fig. 6. Screenshot of GUI on android device

5 Conclusion

We designed and implemented a wireless remote control system with Real-Time Video Surveillance based on Android for Wi-Fi Robot in this paper. And we suggested a solution which ensures the reliable wireless communications. We connected a Wi-Fi multi-function board to the Mobile Robot, transfer instructions from user's gesture and receive running states with video stream to the screen. This can not only break the hardware performance bottlenecks of the Mobile Robot, but also increase the ability to scale. Eventually, we verify the feasibility of the final design through a simple remote experiments. According to the practical application, The Wi-Fi Robot can be extended to perform a task by a specified path, automatic obstacle avoidance, robot wireless localization and other fields of application in real life.

Acknowledgement. The authors are grateful to the anonymous reviewers for their insightful comments which have certainly improved this paper.

This research was supported by National 863 Program (No. 2011AA01A205), National 973 Program (No. 2011CB302702), P. R. China.

References

1. Hopp, C., Stoll, S., Konigorski, U.: Remote control design and implementation using the Internet. In: Proceedings of the 5th Biannual World Automation Congress, vol. 14, pp. 481–486 (2002)
2. Potgieter, J., Bright, G., Diegel, O., Tlale, S.: Internet control of a domestic robot using a wireless LAN. In: Proceedings of Australian Conference on Robotics and Automation, pp. 212–215, Auckland (2002)
3. Palazzi, C.E., Brunati, M., Roccetti, M.: An OpenWrt solution for future wireless homes. In: 2010 IEEE International Conference on Multimedia and Expo (ICME), pp. 1701–1706, July 2010

4. Dutt, S., Habibi, D.: A low cost Atheros System-on-Chip and OpenWrt based testbed for 802.11 WLAN research. In: TENCON 2012 - 2012 IEEE Region 10 Conference, pp. 1–4 (2012)
5. Ser2net Manual. http://manpages.ubuntu.com/manpages/hardy/man8/ser2net.8.html
6. Kim, J.-W., Choi, B.-D., Park, S.-H., Kim, K.-K., Ko, S.-J.: Remote control system using real-time MPEG-4 streaming technology for mobile robot. In: Proceedings of 2002 IEEE International Conference on Consumer Electronics, vol. 02CH37300, pp. 200–201, Los Angeles, CA, June 2002
7. Alan Cox. Video4 Linux Programming[EB/OL] (2000) [2011-01-20]
8. VLC Media Player. http://www.videolan.org/vlc/
9. Lee, W.-M.: Beginning Android Application Development, vol. 4, pp. 11–12. Tsinghua University Press, Beijing (2012)

Characterizing and Comparing User Location Preference in an Urban Mobile Network

Chengli Mei[✉], Min Zhang, Zhongang Qi, and Qi Bi

Technology Innovation Center, China Telecom, Beijing, China
{meichl, zhangmin, qizha, qibi}@ctbri.com.cn

Abstract. With fast increasing numbers of 3G mobile subscribers and accompanying growth in traffic, a deep understanding of user mobility and traffic usage patterns is vital for network resource allocation and optimization in order to maintain or even improve user experience. In this paper, we report results from a one-week network trace of an urban mobile network with over 200,000 users. We first propose several normalized metrics such as the ratio of active users (RAU) and its z-score (ZLP) either by time or by user group, which allow comparison of location preferences across different user groups. Next, we apply these metrics on an area of 50 km^2, composed of 358 lattices. The results show that the top ranked favorite lattices are located in the west and middle parts of this given area. The k-means clustering of lattices reveals their time sequence feature patterns. Furthermore, we specifically analyze users having different ARPU (Average Revenue Per User) levels. We quantify and compare the degrees of location preferences, and present them numerically and visually. These statistics would be utilized in various practical scenarios for enhancing user experience.

Keywords: Mobile network · User mobility · Location preference

1 Introduction

With the widespread use of smart phones and tablets, global mobile data traffic is predicted to increase 13-fold between 2012 and 2017 [1]. This rapid growth in mobile data and users requires network operators to transition to smart pipes by improving awareness capacity, optimizing resource utilization, and laying the groundwork for a smooth evolution to LTE in the future.

Understanding mobile users' location preference is one of the key issues for network traffic management; this includes identifying users' top ranked locations, characterizing time sequence feature patterns of location preferences, comparing location preference among different users, etc. To this end, one measurement study is conducted in an urban network, covering a metropolitan area by capturing overall data service records. After examining the trace integrity, we identified the number of users per cellular sector per hour. We then proposed several metrics based on the number of users to better evaluate their location preference. Our main findings are as follows:

- In general, the favorite places are mainly located in the west and center of the observation region.

Y. Yuan et al. (Eds.): ISCTCS 2013, CCIS 426, pp. 389–396, 2014.
DOI: 10.1007/978-3-662-43908-1_48, © Springer-Verlag Berlin Heidelberg 2014

- Our further clustering analysis reveals the different time sequence feature pat-terns of cellular sectors. It allows us to classify the small areas covered by cellular sectors into several groups: typical residential areas, office hot-spots, and so on.
- Moreover, we explored and quantized the degree of location preference per user group, which is visualized by fading colors. The comparison by ARPU infers the variety of favorite places. High-valued users like to visit the west more than the east, whose location preferences are to some extent opposite to the low-valued users.

From the network operator perspective, we consider that these quantized values and metrics would be utilized in our traffic control mechanisms, in order to enhance user experience with location-based personalization services. Moreover, these results would also help other applications and services to understand the location preference of crowds, particularly in regard to location-based mobile advertising, trade location evaluations, and so on.

The rest of the paper is organized as follows. Related analysis work is discussed in Sect. 2, followed by our measurement setup and the collection traces described in Sect. 3. In Sect. 4, we characterize and compare user location preference. Section 5 concludes this work.

2 Related Work

With the global fast-growing mobile traffic, there are plenty of studies focusing on characterizing mobile data traffic recently. References [2, 3] conducted small scale active measurements for characterizing user behavior; while some others [4] passive measured the 3G data network from network operator. For example, [2] profiled the diversity of users' activities by tracking 255 smart phones. References [3, 5] reported the mobile traffic offloading through Wi-Fi by over 400 smart phones. The traces obtained passively from network operator are generally large-scale. Using one flow-level trace at a national scale, Ref. [6] made its important step in filling the lack of usage behaviors knowledge of mobile applications, such as the spatial and temporal prevalence, locality, and correlation of applications. Based on a seven day 3G data trace of a large metropolitan area, Ref. [4] characterized the relationship between users' application interests and their mobility properties. In this paper, we conduct data traffic measurement over our own 3G network, and characterize location pref-erence via connecting user position and base station location along time.

3 Measurement and Datasets

The key components of the cellular CDMA2000 network are illustrated in Fig. 1. The AAA servers [7] provide Internet Protocol functionality to support the functions of authentication, authorization and accounting, by the support of RADIUS protocol (Remote Authentication Dial in User Service) [8]. And the PDSN is the connection point between the radio access and IP networks, managing sessions between the mobile provider's core IP network and the mobile station. Our capture point is just set

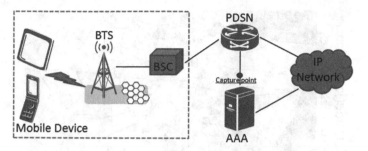

Fig. 1. CDMA2000 network architecture.

between the AAA and PDSN, in purpose of passively recording each data service session information: start time, end time, anonymized mobile device number, anonymized cell identification, connection type, bytes, active duration, connection duration, etc.

In this August, we conducted our measurement over a metropolitan area in eastern China. One typical urban area is chosen as observed object, covering 50 km², 358 cellular sectors and about 75,000 daily data users. Many commercial, institutional, recreational and residential buildings are located in this area. It has similar cellular scale to [9], and less than half users of its San Francisco Bay area traces.

4 Analysis of Location Preference

In this study, we focus on exploring the variety of location preference along time by different user groups. This urban area is separated into 358 lattices by voronoi diagram [10]. In Fig. 2, the different base stations are shown as gray dots, and the lattice enclosed by black lines marks the approximate reception area of each base station.

Before addressing our main work, we gave a quick glance at this urban area by calculating the amount of users per sector. After examining its cumulative distribution function (CDF) of user numbers, we learned the amount of users per cellular sector ranges from 7 to 9,000 whose median value is 1,228. Those heavy sectors (top 10 %) whose amount of users is triple the median value would be taken as the hot-spots naturally. Moreover, we marked them with black lattices in Fig. 2. It indicates that these favorite places (in black) are located in the west and middle part of this given area.

4.1 Definitions and Metrics

In order to explore the location preference and quantize the difference, several evaluation metrics are defined as follows:

- **active user (AU):** user who has data session connection during the observation time interval. We assume that a user occurs in one voronoi lattice while he has session connections under the corresponding cellular sector.
- **ratio of active user (RAU):** the percentage of active users. For cellular sector i, its RAU (denoted as R_s) in hour j is calculated as:

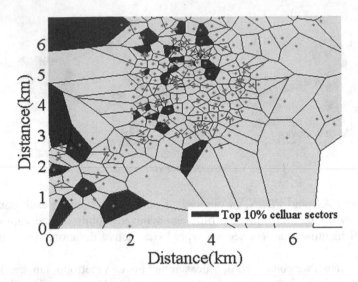

Fig. 2. The geographic location of the top 10 % cellular sectors.

$$R_s(i,j) = N_s(i,j)/\sum_i N_s(i,j) \tag{1}$$

where $N_s(i, j)$ is the number of active users in cellular sector i during the hour j. The higher RAU of cellular sector i means it has more active users, therefore we consider this place is more popular. For user group i, its number of active users occurring in cellular sector j is defined as $N_u(i, j)$, and then the RAU of user group i (denoted as R_u) in sector j would be given as:

$$R_u(i,j) = N_u(i,j)/\sum_i N_u(i,j) \tag{2}$$

– **z-score of location preference (ZLP):** to represent the degree of like/dislike for user group. The z-score of $R_u(i, j)$ for user group i is taken as (Eq. 3):

$$z(i,j) = (R_u(i,j) - \mu)/\sigma \tag{3}$$

where μ is the mean of $R_u(i, j)$ and σ is the standard deviation. Generally speaking, the absolute value of z-score represents the distance between the raw score and the mean popularity score in units of the standard deviation [11]. Here, we assume that the negative z-score ($R_u(i, j) < \mu$) indicates user group i dislike to visit place j and the positive one means the preference degree of place j for user group i.

4.2   Categorizing Lattices

Here, we study the location preference along time, by applying k-means algorithm. It successfully groups sectors into several patterns differing in their variations of active users' ratio by hours in one day. We utilize the clustering to distinguish cellular sectors, and then deploy the corresponding traffic control rules for each group.

Since the coverage area and users vary with the sectors, we normalize the ratio of active user for each sector by day. As defined in previous subsection, the ratio of active user in one day for cellular sector i is denoted as (Eq. 4):

$$\bar{R}_s^{(i)} = (R_s(i,1), R_s(i,2), \ldots, R_s(i,24))'$$ (4)

The normalized *RAU* for each sector, which is used as the feature in the clustering, is defined as (Eq. 5):

$$x^{(i)} = (x_1^{(i)}, x_2^{(i)}, \ldots, x_{24}^{(i)})$$ (5)

where $x_j^{(i)} = R_s(i,j)/(\frac{1}{24}\sum_{n=1}^{24} R_s(i,n)) - 1, j = 1, 2, \ldots, 24$.

Figure 3 shows the cluster results of the sectors. These four patterns, whose cluster centroids are marked as black lines, are described as follows:

- **Cluster 1.** The curves of the normalized RAU ascend during the morning (8AM–11AM), then level off or even decline a little during the afternoon. During the early evening, the curves ascend again and reach their peaks of the day. These sectors are located in the residential area or business district.
- **Cluster 2.** The curves of the normalized RAU descend during the daytime, while the declined proportions are small. They are located in the residential area.
- **Cluster 3.** The curves of the normalized RAU ascend a lot during the morning (7AM–10AM), then reach their peaks and level off during the noon and the afternoon (11AM–3PM), caused by people at work. During the late afternoon the curves descend. These sectors are always located in the office area.
- **Cluster 4.** The curves of the normalized RAU ascend during the daytime, while the increased proportions are small. They are located in office area of low activity.

In addition, we notice that the variations of proportions for each cluster are small, except the values of Cluster 3, which represents the cellular sectors in the office area of high activity, decrease a lot on Saturday and Sunday. Figure 4 shows the cluster maps of the sectors on Saturday and on Monday respectively, in order to visualize the

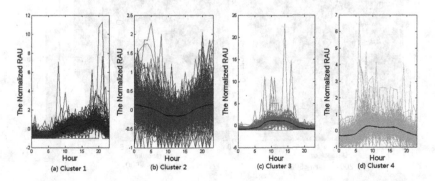

Fig. 3. The cluster results of the cellular sectors by the normalized RAU.

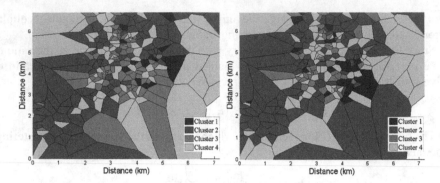

Fig. 4. The sector cluster visualization by RAU changes (left: Sat., right: Mon.).

geo locations of different sector patterns. On Monday, the increasing of the number of active users during the daytime is caused by people at work. Consequently, the lattices which belong to Cluster 3 increase in Fig. 4. The lattices which belong to Cluster 4 represent the office districts of low activity. These lattices decrease on Monday

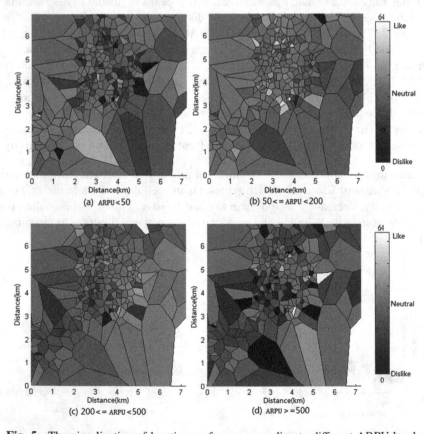

Fig. 5. The visualization of location preference according to different ARPU levels.

because the activity of these office districts becomes higher on workday. Moreover, we also verify that the lattices which belong to Cluster 1 and Cluster 2 on Saturday and turn to Cluster 3 on Monday are mainly located in the residential and business mixed districts based on Google map.

4.3 Comparison by Users

Here, we make our attempts at exploring the preference difference among user groups divided by monthly consumption. Figure 5 represents the location preference according to different ARPU levels of users. The percentages of users, from the left to the right, are 15.6 %, 67.5 %, 12.1 %, and 0.7 % respectively. The cluster results of the cellular sectors by the normalized RAU. These four sub-figures show the values of ZLP for the different groups.

We learned that:

- The majority users prefer to stay in the center of urban area, except ones in Fig. 5(a) whose ARPU less than 50.
- To these four groups, their top favorite places marked as lattices in light gray (close to white) are not overlapped.
- Compared to the east part, the west part is more welcomed by high-valued users to some extent. And we also noticed that the preferences are almost opposite between high-valued users Fig. 5(a) and low-valued users Fig. 5(d).

5 Conclusion

In this paper, we characterized location preference patterns of mobile data users in an urban cellular network. Our analysis not only reveals time sequence feature pat-terns of the sectors by clustering, but also explores the characterizations of location preference by different user groups. Based on the proposed metrics of location preference, the comparisons by visualization show their differences vividly. Both these analysis results and metrics would benefit network resource optimization and user experience enhancement, in purpose of providing differentiated services.

Acknowledgments. This work is supported by the National 973 Program of China (2012CB316005).

References

1. Cisco Visual Networking Index. Global mobile data traffic forecast update, 2012-2017. White paper (2013)
2. Falaki, M.H., Mahajan, R., Kandula S., et al.: Diversity in smartphone usage. In: Proceedings of MobiSys2010, San Francisco, USA (2010)
3. Fukuda, K., Nagami, K.: A measurement of mobile traffic offloading. In: Roughan, M., Chang, R. (eds.) PAM 2013. LNCS, vol. 7799, pp. 73–82. Springer, Heidelberg (2013)

4. Trestian, I., Ranjan, S., et al.: Measuring serendipity: connecting people, locations and interests in a mobile 3G network. In: Proceedings of IMC2009, Chicago, USA (2009)
5. Jin, Y., Duffield, N., Gerber, A., et al.: Characterizing data usage patterns in a large cellular network. In: Proceedings of Cell Net 2012, Helsinki, Finland (2012)
6. Xu, Q., Erman, J., Gerber, A., et al.: Identifying diverse usage of behaviors of smartphone apps. In: Proceedings of IMC2011, Berlin, Germany (2011)
7. Wikipedia. AAA Protocol. http://en.wikipedia.org/wiki/AAA_protocol
8. Wikipedia. RADIUS Protocol. http://en.wikipedia.org/wiki/RADIUS
9. Zhang H., Bolot, J.: Mining call and mobility data to improve paging efficiency in cellular networks. In: Proceedings of MobiCom2007, Montreal, Canada (2007)
10. Gonzalez, M., Hidalgo, C., Barabasi, A.: Understanding individual human mobility patterns. Nature **453**, 779–782 (2008)
11. Wikipedia: Standard score. http://en.wikipedia.org/wiki/Standard_score

Security Testing Approaches – For Research, Industry and Standardization

Axel Rennoch[✉], Ina Schieferdecker, and Jürgen Großmann

Fraunhofer FOKUS, Kaiserin-Augusta-Allee 31, 10589 Berlin, Germany
{axel.rennoch, ina.schieferdecker,
juergen.grossmann}@fokus.fraunhofer.de

Abstract. Recently, in the Security testing domain a lot of knowledge has been collected from a significant amount of research. The contribution provides an introduction to advanced security testing methods and techniques in the context of European research and standardization projects. This includes numerous guidelines and best practices that have been identified and are applied in the context of industrial case studies. In particular it addresses risk modeling, security test pattern, functional security tests as well as fuzz testing, as important contributions to systematic, automatized test approaches in research, industry and standardization.

Keywords: Model-based security testing · Risk analysis · Test automation · Fuzzing

1 Introduction

In our daily life people all over the world rely on systems and services provided via open communication interfaces. Today many of these access points are used to exchange information that need to be protected since that protect critical infrastructures or are private.

As pointed out by the Software Engineering Institute, US, 2009: "The security of a software-intensive system is directly related to the quality of its software". In particular, over 90 % of software security incidents are caused by attackers exploiting known software defects. DIAMONDS [2] addresses this increasing need for systematic security testing methods by developing techniques and tools that can efficiently be used to secure networked applications in different domains. The RASEN project [9] is a follow-up project that especially addresses security assessments of large scale networked systems through the combination of security risk assessment and security testing, taking into account the context in which the system is used, such as liability, legal and organizational issues as well as technical issues.

2 The DIAMONDS and RASEN Projects

In the DIAMONDS project 23 partners from six European countries have been worked together over two and a half years to build up an innovative approach for model-based security testing applicable in different industrial domains.

Y. Yuan et al. (Eds.): ISCTCS 2013, CCIS 426, pp. 397–406, 2014.
DOI: 10.1007/978-3-662-43908-1_49, © Springer-Verlag Berlin Heidelberg 2014

DIAMONDS introduced four main innovations in the field of security testing methods and technologies:

- Advanced model-based security testing methods that combine different techniques to obtain improved results applicable to multi-domain security.
- Development of autonomous testing techniques based on automatic monitoring techniques to improve resilience of dynamically evolving systems.
- Pre-standardization work on multi-domain security test methodologies and test patterns to offer interoperable security test techniques and tools.
- Open source platform for security test tool integration to provide a common platform, which provides the user a single user interface towards various test tools, as well as a single reporting interface to have concise report from the various tools.

The RASEN project is a follow-up project with partners from DIAMONDS and deals with the subject of risk-based security testing, especially with:

- Compositional approaches that allows for conducting risk assessments for smaller parts or aspects of a system and systematically compose these assessments to obtain a global risk picture.
- Techniques, tools and methods to derive security test cases from security risk assessment results and to verify and update of the security risk assessment based on security test results.
- Continuous security assessment in which the security assessment is performed iteratively in such a way that results from previous assessments can be reused, and the security risk assessment picture can be rapidly updated with respect to changes in the system and its environment.
- Assess the risks related to non-compliance to legal norms by developing methods for risk assessments, which specifically take into account legal aspects of relevance to security.

Both projects aim at building a pre-standard for model-based security testing targeting heterogeneous and distributed systems and services and represent the enabling technology necessary for the introduction of formal security testing in industry.

3   Methods and Tools

3.1   Test Process

From the testing perspective one of the major changes is the integration of risk identification, prioritization, test selection and result consideration for the used security models.

Risk-based security testing approaches help to optimize the overall test process. The result of the risk assessment, i.e. the identified vulnerabilities, threat scenarios and unwanted incidents, are used to guide the test identification and may complement requirements engineering results with systematic information concerning the threats and vulnerabilities of a system. A comprehensive risk assessment additionally introduces the notion of probabilities and consequences related to threat scenarios. These risk values can be additionally used to weight threat scenarios and thus help identifying which threat scenarios are more relevant and thus identifying the ones that need to be treated and tested more carefully. We have identified the following two extensions to traditional testing or security testing processes.

- Risk-based security test planning: The goal of risk-based security test planning is to systematically improve the testing process during the test-planning phase. Risk assessment is used to identify high-risk areas or features of the system under test (SUT) and thus determine and optimize the respective test effort that is needed to verify the related security functionality or address related vulnerabilities. Moreover, selected test strategies and techniques are identified that are dedicated the most critical sources of risk (e.g. potential vulnerabilities and threat scenarios).
- Risk-based security test selection: Finding an optimal set of security test cases requires an appropriate selection strategy. Such a strategy takes the available test budget into account and also provides, as far as possible, the necessary test coverage. In functional testing, coverage is often described by the coverage of requirements or the coverage of model elements such as states, transitions or decisions. In risk-based testing coverage can be described in terms of the identified risks, their probabilities and consequences. Risk-based security test selection criteria can be used to control the selection or the selected generation of test cases. The criteria are designed by taking the risks as well as their probabilities and consequence values to set priorities for the test selections, test case generation as well as for the order of test execution.

Figure 1 is derived from ISO 29119 [8] and illustrates the extension of the traditional security testing process with risk assessment activities. The test planning (step 1) is the activity of developing the test plan. Depending on where in the project this process is implemented this may be a project test plan or a test plan for a specific phase, such as a system test plan, or a test plan for a specific type of testing (such as a performance test plan).

In step 2 risk assessment refers to the process of using risk assessment to support the test planning and test technique identification. The activity of test design and implementation (step 3) is the process of deriving the test cases and test procedures. Step 4 covers the test environment set-up and maintenance process and is the process of establishing and maintaining the environment in which tests are executed. In the context of step 5, risk assessment refers to the process of using risk assessment to prioritize the test cases which should be executed.

The test execution (step 6) is the process of running the test procedure resulting from the test design and implementation process on the test environment established by the test environment set-up and maintenance process. The test execution process may need to be performed a number of times as all the available test procedures may not be executed in a single iteration. This step is related to the activity of prioritizing and selecting tests to be executed. The selection criteria may e.g. be based on a risk assessment. The activity may also involve mutation/fuzzing of concrete executable test cases.

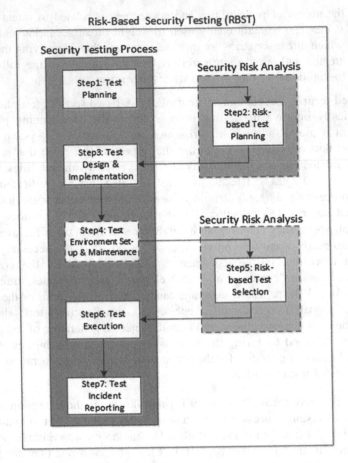

Fig. 1. The generic process for risk-based security testing.

The test incident reporting (step 7) is the process of managing the test incidents. This process will be entered as a result of the identification of test failures, instances where something unusual or unexpected occurred during test execution, or when a retest passes. In test-based risk assessment, the incident reporting activity may involve an assessment of how the test results impact the risk picture and change the risk model.

3.2 Tools

Previous project results have shown that methods and tools used for model-based testing need to be combined, may depend on the industrial domains and have to be integrated in the productive environment of the customers (see e.g. D-MINT [5]). From this perspective it is not a surprise that we are facing a similar situation in the context of security testing.

Following the introduction of the generic model-based security process described above it is obvious that different procedure steps may require different tools. The DIAMONDS industrial case studies have used tools from both, the developments by project partners and existing tools from third parties. The following twelve tools have been created or extended by project partners during the project lifetime [3]. Even that some tools have multiple functions they may be assigned to three main different tool groups: modelling, active and passive testing.

Test Modelling and Generation Tools

- CORAS (Sintef) is a risk modelling tool with a graphical editor. It is based on a model-driven risk analysis method.
- FUZZINO (FhG Fokus): Fuzzino is a test data generator for fuzz testing. With fuzzing, it is possible to find security-related weaknesses in your code. It's about injecting invalid or unexpected input data to a system under test. That way, security-relevant vulnerabilities may be detected when malicious data is processed instead of rejected.
- CertifyIt (Smartesting): Model-based security testing from behavioral models and test purposes is an extension of functional model-based testing (MBT): The model for test generation captures the expected behaviour of the system under test (SUT). This model is dedicated for automated generation of security tests, and generally formalizes the security functions of the SUT but also the possible stimuli of an attacker as well as the expected answer of the SUT. The test purposes are test selection criteria that define the way to generate tests from the test generation model.
- RISKTest (FhG Fokus): is a tracing tool especially designed for security testing. It enables traceability between security testing artefacts, e.g. identified risk elements, system objects and test data. The traceability allows interaction and combination of different security engineering and testing tools and is the basis for determining coverage and completeness metrics like risk coverage.

Test Execution Tools

- Defensics (Codenomicon) uses behavioral models to alter the behavior to generate millions and millions of nearly-valid messages that systematically anomalies some parts of the information exchange to test the target system for robustness.
- TTworkbench (TestingTech) supports the entire lifecycle of TTCN-3 based tests with textual and graphical editors, a TTCN-3 to Java compiler, and a test execution management environment composed of graphical tracing, debugging and reporting facilities for centralized and distributed test components.
- KameleonFuzz (INT) automatically detects Type-1 and Type-2 Cross Site Scripting (XSS) in Web Application.
- TRICK tester is a platform used for penetration (intrusion) testing. It contains all the main software tools to test web applications and network systems like Web Servers.

Test Analysis and Monitoring Tools

- MMT (montimage) is a monitoring solution that combines: data capture; filtering and storage; events extraction and statistics collection; and, traffic analysis and reporting.
- LiSTT (INT) performs intra- and inter-procedural dataflow analysis on the binary code. The produced result is the set of vulnerable paths that have been detected with respect to an input source.
- TestSym-P (Telecom sudParis) aims at passively testing an Implementation under test (IUT) to verify if it respects the protocol requirements represented as IOSTS property.
- Malwasm (itrust) helps reverse engineers understand what a binary does, it can identify static and dynamic malware analysis.

Based on this toolset the following approach is proposed for the application of model-based security testing:

- Model, identify risks and navigate to learn about vulnerabilities in your system.
- Combine and (re)use selected DIAMONDS models, methods, techniques and tools to test and monitor countermeasures, verify security risks and discover vulnerabilities.
- Evaluate your models and risks and repeat the application of DIAMONDS model-based security testing approaches to enjoy a more secure system and life with your assets.

Figure 2 illustrate the co-operation of a set of four tools, two from DIAMONDS and two from other sources, which have been combined to build a model-based security testing platform: Risks models have been built with CORAS, ProR manages

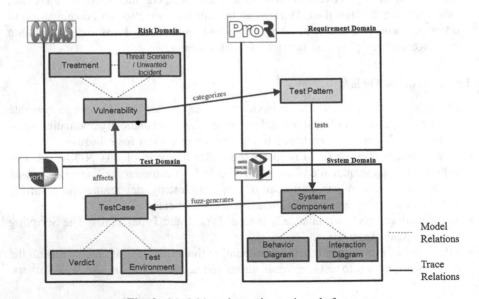

Fig. 2. Model-based security testing platform

the requirements, the UML tool introduces the use/test cases, and TTworkbench has been applied for test execution with TTCN-3 [6]. A detailed presentation of all DIAMONDS tools is available in [3].

4 Industrial Case Studies

The major focus of our work has been the industrial case studies in the following domains: Radio protocols, automotive, smart cards, telecommunication, banking and industrial automation.

One of the DIAMONDS case studies from the banking domain consists of a banknote processing system that counts and sorts banknotes depending on their currency, denomination, condition and authenticity. Banknote processing machines are used in central, large and medium banks and also in CITs (cash in transport) and other organizations that handle large amounts of banknotes. These machines are usually configured to work in a network as shown in Fig. 3. Currency processors, reconciliation stations, vault management systems and control centers are connected on a network either on a LAN or WAN.

Configuration and monitoring information is exchanged between the currency processor and the control center. The type of information exchanged requires a high degree of security.

The focus of security tests is on the currency processor and the reconciliation station. The currency processor as well as the reconciliation station was provided as virtual machines for VMware Workstation where external interfaces are replaced by simulation and were supplemented with snapshots. That allows creating a consistent state of the SUT before executing a test case and is necessary for batch execution of test cases. The test bed at Fraunhofer FOKUS consists of the two virtual machines, one for the currency processor and another for the reconciliation station. Windows 7-based host system runs the virtual machines. The main focus of security tests will be the components inside the virtual machines. The available interfaces are the Message Router (.Net Remoting implementation) over LAN, as well as keyboard, USB and other peripherals through the hardware abstraction layer of the virtual machine. There is a database running inside the virtual machine.

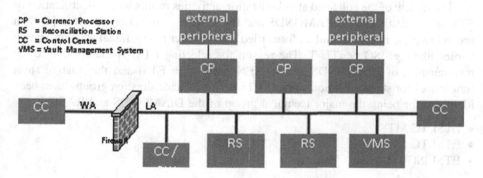

CP = Currency Processor
RS = Reconciliation Station
CC = Control Centre
VMS = Vault Management System

Fig. 3. Banknote counting machine.

The underlying threats were used as starting point for the risk analysis. A risk analysis following the CORAS approach [1] was performed and the potential vulnerabilities as well as the consequences of the threats were analyzed. CORAS provides several kinds of diagrams for different phases of the analysis. As a result of the risk analysis, several vulnerabilities were considered that should be tested whether they actually exists within the system under test (SUT). In order to generate appropriate tests for these vulnerabilities, security test patterns provide a suitable way to select test generation techniques or test procedures.

In order to test for the abovementioned vulnerabilities identified during risk analysis, both well established and new developed methods were applied to the system. Data fuzzing approaches for SQL injection were applied by a new developed fuzz testing extension for TTCN-3. Data fuzzing sends a large number of invalid values to the system under test at certain points within a test case.

Based on the risk models, 30 behavioral fuzz test cases were executed on the SUT regarding an authentication bypass. By executing these test cases, the risk of an authentication bypass using behavioral means was covered by applying behavioral fuzzing. The developed behavioral fuzzing approach extends existing functional test cases towards tests of security aspects. Therefore, the applied fuzzing approaches can take advantage of the effort made for functional testing of the SUT and do not require development of new test cases for security testing.

For further case studies reports please refer to ETSI TR 101 582 [7].

5 Standardization

One of the most important standardization bodies for IT security is the International Organization for Standardization (ISO). Its subcommittee SC27 is responsible for IT security techniques. This work also covers methods and techniques for security evaluation in the context of the common criteria (CCRA). The international ITU Telecommunication Standardization Sector concentrates on international standards for the telecom domain. Several documents have been identified in the context of security. Furthermore the European Telecommunication standardization institute (ETSI) has several technical committees (TC) and industrial specification groups (ISG) that are working for security techniques.

The review of the collected standardization activities results in the identification of ETSI as the first focus of DIAMONDS and RASEN standardization activities [4]. In a second step the results should be forwarded also to other international standardization bodies like e.g. ISO or ITU-T. The reason for selecting ETSI is mainly due to the memberships of DIAMONDS and RASEN partners in ETSI and the relative short timeframes for standardization work at ETSI. Three standardization groups have been identified for being the major technical group of the DIAMONDS and RASEN:

- ETSI TC MTS
- ETSI TC INT
- ETSI ISG ISI

The new ETSI TC MTS special interest group for security aspects has been working on security in three directions: modelling/specification (of system risks etc.), (paper-based) risk analysis, and testing that includes scanning (libs) on known attacks, functional/traditional testing, and negative testing to discover unknown vulnerabilities, configuration mistakes (using e.g. fuzzing, penetration). The work in TC INT has been concluded in the technical report: IMS/NGN Security Testing and Robustness Benchmark.

The work in ISG ISI will propose a way to produce security events and to test the effectiveness of existing detection means. Scenario catalogues will give inspiration for test/monitoring objectives and allow faster implementation. Examples of frequent security test pattern will be used to illustrate some powerful means and methods of event testing. The definition and use of a test (pattern) catalogue for test implementation allows: introduction of dedicated sets, reasonable efforts, and comparison of results.

Figure 4 illustrates our approach from project work package results to international standardization bodies.

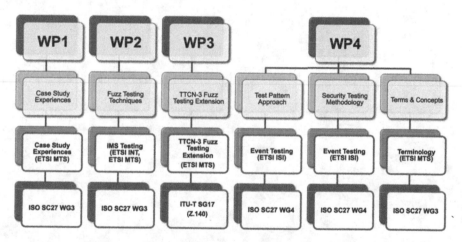

Fig. 4. Contributions from DIAMONDS work packages

6 Outlook

During the project lifetime several presentations and exhibition have been performed. The project approach and results have been accepted as a valuable contribution to the improvement to security testing. It has been proposed to initiate a community for advanced security testing tools. From the project viewpoint we like to remind security testing experts: Do IT with models.

We thank our colleagues from FOKUS and the other DIAMONDS and RASEN partners for the great work and cooperation in the project, as well as the ITEA and national authorities and the European Union's Seventh Framework Program (FP7/ 2007-2013) under grant agreement no 316853 for their support.

References

1. CORAS. Risk analysis method and tool. http://coras.sourceforge.net/
2. DIAMONDS project. http://www.itea2-diamonds.org
3. DIAMONDS deliverable D5.WP3: Final Security Testing Tools (May 2013)
4. DIAMONDS contributions to Standards Organizations. Project restricted deliverable (May 2013)
5. D-MINT   project.   http://www.fokus.fraunhofer.de/en/sqc/projekte/projekt_archiv/2009/ D-MINT/index.html
6. ETSI ES 201 873: Testing and Test Control Notation, version 3 (TTCN-3), http://www. ttcn-3.org
7. ETSI TR 101 582: Methods for Testing and Specification (MTS); Security Testing; Case Study Experiences
8. International Standards Organization. ISO 29119 Software and system engineering - Software Testing-Part 2: Test process (draft) (2012)
9. RASEN project. http://www.rasenproject.eu/

Author Index